SEATTLE 1900–1920

From Boomtown, Urban Turbulence,
to Restoration

RICHARD C. BERNER

Charles Press
Seattle, Washington

ISBN: 0-9629889-0-1

Library of Congress Catalog Card Number: 91-74159

Published by Charles Press
3616 East Cherry Street
Seattle, WA 98122

This book is printed on pH neutral, acid-free paper.

Contents

List of Photographs

Abbreviations Used

P-I	*Seattle Post-Intellingencer*
PNQ	*Pacific Northwest Quarterly*
PSP&L	Puget Sound Power & Light
PSTP&L	Puget Sound Traction, Power, & Light
RMN	*Railway & Marine News*
SEC	Seattle Electric Company
Times	*Seattle Times*
TC	*Town Crier*
UR	*Seattle Union Record*

Acknowledgments

Acknowledgments are due to many. It is obvious from the sources cited that the collections at the University of Washington Libraries provided the main body of source materials used. Special thanks is due to Karyl Winn, Head of the University Archives and Manuscripts Division, for providing me with a carrel, which began to feel like a home away from home, and to her two principal assistants, Janet Ness and Jo Lewis, for their unflagging retrieval of collections from on-site and from more remote storage on and off campus.

Glenda Pearson, Head of the Newspapers and Microform Section and her assistant, Terry Kato, provided exceptional services, not least of which was constant trouble-shooting of archaic and/or defective equipment, but also interest and encouragement along the way. When poor microcopy proved resistant to deciphering, she also substituted the original hard-copy when it was available. (Unfortunately, the originals of the *Times*, *Post-Intellingencer*, and *Star* have all been prematurely destroyed years ago.) Both the *Union-Record* and the *Argus*, fortunately, have survived administrative onslaught.

The Special Collections Division houses principally the printed collection of regional sources, scrapbooks, photographs, and maps. Carla Rickerson, Susan Cunningham, and Richard Engeman were particularly helpful, generously allowing use of the hard-copies of some weeklies and monthlies that had been poorly microfilmed. Identifying selected photographs was provided by Engeman.

Many courtesies also were extended by the staff of the Government Publications Division: Eleanor Chase, Andrew Johnson, and David Maack, in particular. Help in getting materials not in the Libraries' holdings has already been provided for the second volume, and though it was not required for this first volume, it has been comforting to know that it would be cheerfully provided, as it was for my book on archival history, by Ruth Kirk and her assistant Anna McCausland, of the Interlibrary Borrowing Section. Guela Johnson, Head of the School of Social Work Library, provided background on African American churches.

Outside of the University of Washington Libraries, critical assistance was provided by the History Department staff of the Seattle Public Library in giving access to the minute books of the Chamber of Commerce and Commercial Club. City Archivist, Scott Cline, in bringing the first-ever controls over the previously neglected City records, lent his skills and advice in locating relevant source materials. Fortunately for the City of Seattle the City Council has seen fit to support this newly created position over mayoral opposition; administrators, as well as researchers are becoming a constituency for maintaining this position as a permanent arm of City administration. Rick Caldwell, thinly supported Librarian of the Museum of History and Industry, provided access to the records and scrapbooks of the Ladies' Musical Club, and to the rich photographic collection of which the Museum is justly proud. Dave Freeh, Photographer for City Light, lent his valuable help in selecting photographs from that department's photographic archive. Eleanor Toews, as Archivist of the Seattle Public Schools, provided easy access to that body's records. Thanks is due also to the *Seattle Times* for its permission to reproduce the photograph depicting the Potlatch Riot of July 18, 1913. The Washington State Historical Society is also to be thanked for granting permission to reproduce the Mosquito Fleet photograph from its Asahel Curtis Collection.

Special gratitude is due the Puget Sound Power and Light Company for permission to quote from its records. Its sense of historical perspective is to be applauded; the company is not like it was in the early years of this century, though, even then it was a more humane institution than its counterparts elsewhere in the country. Appreciation is due also to the Chamber of Commerce of Greater Seattle for permission quote from its Minute Books in the Seattle Public Library. To the University of Washington Press gratitude is expressed for permission to reproduce maps and charts appearing in Calvin Schmid's *Social Trends in Seattle.*

I feel particularly indebted to Jane Sanders, whose book, *Cold War on Campus: Academic Freedom at the University of Washington, 1946-64* (University of Washington Press) is one I have long admired. Dr. Sanders volunteered her services, and was the first to read the manuscript in its earlier life; her sharp, detailed critique guided me throughout the course of revising that draft: syntax, organization, content, punctuation, and tense consistency come foremost to mind. Professor Donald T. Williams, Jr. came to my aid with the loan of a copy of his unpublished biography of Henry Suzzallo, a copy of which is in the University Archives. Homer T. Bone's biographer, Terry Slatten, brought to my attention and lent me a copy of E. V. Minich's affidavit in the Bone papers at the University of Puget Sound; this item filled in some blanks left by other sources.

Special thanks is due Murray Morgan and Professor Carlos A. Schwantes for their critical reading of the manuscript.

Dedication

This history is dedicated to the memory of my mother
and father, who started their family in the teens,
while working first in Everett, then in Seattle, she as a
waitress (she later established a local reputation as a
fine restaurant cook), he as a machinist.

Preface

In serving first as the original head of the Manuscripts Section of the University of Washington Libraries, from 1958 to 1967, then as Head of the University Archives and Manuscripts Division from 1967 until my retirement on December 31, 1983, I had the enriching experience of building the archival program and holdings from modest beginnings made by some predecessor librarians operating with little administrative support, to one of national reputation. Making this process especially rewarding was the opportunity of working closely with Professor Robert E. Burke (and also before his untimely death at the hands of a murderous driver, Professor Charles M. Gates). Having apprenticed as a graduate student under his administration, when Burke was Curator of Manuscripts of the Bancroft Library, I found him readily at hand for advice on the development of the collection at the University of Washington, each of us having joined up at the university at almost the same time in 1957. Professor Burke had expected to bolster the largely unsupported efforts of Professor Gates and Reference Librarian J. Ronald Todd in collection development, and to assist Professor Gates in the editorship of *Pacific Northwest Quarterly*.

These two History Department faculty planned to inspire graduate studies on the region's history; but they first needed a collection to underpin such advanced studies in the form of master's theses and doctoral dissertations. As will be apparent from the author's use of these graduate studies—as well as the collection itself—they succeeded admirably. After Professor Gates's death Burke assumed primary responsibility for this graduate program, and for the editorship of *Pacific Northwest Quarterly*.

These graduate studies, plus those segments of the city's history that Murray Morgan chose to deal with in his *Skid Road*;

which Roger Sales selected for emphasis in his *Seattle: Past to Present*; and Robert Friedheim, in his *Seattle General Strike*, have provided the author with an intermittent trail to tread. My objective has been to use their respective works where they are most useful, but also to integrate them into the historical continuum by additional research in archival and newspaper sources. For the state as a whole, Robert Saltvig's unpublished dissertation on the "Progressive Movement" has done this in large part; it has served the author better than any other study.

Returning to *Pacific Northwest Quarterly*: Vernon Carstensen joined the faculty to fill the void left by Professor Gates, including the conduct of graduate studies, primarily in nineteenth-century regional history, as well as backing up Burke as "Adjunct Editor" and *PNQ*'s distinguished Associate Editor, Emily Johnson. *Pacific Northwest Quarterly* provided an outlet for publishing the results of these graduate studies, thereby benefiting a broader public that might in turn be induced to read the larger monograph upon which any article was based. The listing of articles appearing in *Pacific Northwest Quarterly* should impress the reader—and university administrators—of the critical importance of that and other scholarly journals as essential means of communicating the results of scholarly research. Even that of a limited regional scope has wider significance, since the cities and towns of the Pacific Northwest states are really parts of the national scene. Local is not "yokel". Not everything of importance takes place in Washington, D.C. The regions and sub-regions, indeed, interact with national policies, shaping them, as well as being affected by them. This volume and the ones to follow amply demonstrate this interactive process.

Extended biographical descriptions are deliberately slighted in order to confine the narrative within reasonable bounds. The context in which people are mentioned is intended to convey whatever personality characteristic emerges in that setting. Beside the biographies and autobiographies specifically cited, good biographical descriptions of most of the key figures can be found in Murray Morgan's *Skid Road*, Roger Sales's *Seattle Past to Present*, Neal Hines's *Denny's Knoll*, Robert Friedheim's *Seattle General Strike*, Norman Clark's *Dry Years*, and Clarence Bagley's *History of Seattle*. Omitted entirely is any reference to the literature produced by Seattle's citizens; that is for someone else to do.

Richard C. Berner
Seattle, Washington

Metropolitan Seattle in 1908

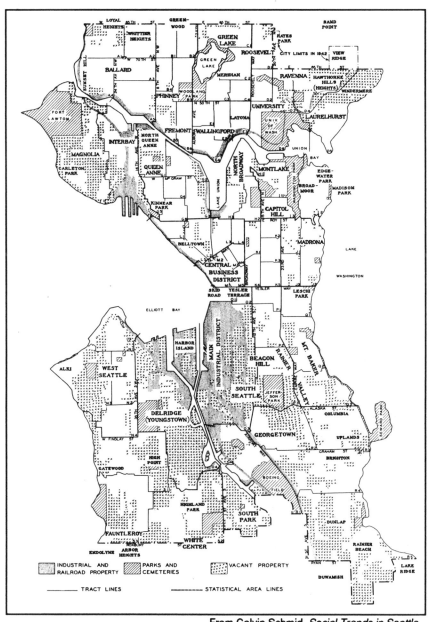

From Calvin Schmid, *Social Trends in Seattle*

Base Map Showing Major Land Use Patterns, Census Tracts and Names of Districts, Seattle, 1942

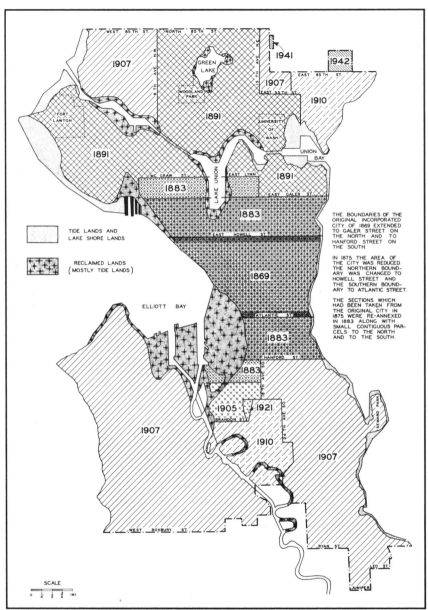

From Calvin Schmid, *Social Trends in Seattle*

Territorial Growth, Seattle, 1869 to 1942

Part I

The Institutional Setting

1

An Overview, 1900-1920

The period of history discussed in *Seattle, 1900-1920: From Boom-Town, Urban Turbulence, to Restoration* traces the immediate origins of the city's twentieth century institutions from the 1890s through the immediate aftermath of World War I.

The book's first section provides an institutional setting in which political dynamics, industrial relations, the public ownership movement, reform campaigns, and civil liberties fights were conducted against forces trying to maintain the status quo.

Beginning with the interplay between business and politics, the city's economy is then described in some detail, much evidence presented being taken from sources either previously not used or not substantially explored. Population characteristics are then outlined, followed by discussions of the public school system, the University of Washington, and the part these institutions played in the social uplifting of the period.

The opening section concludes with a survey of the city's popular entertainment scene, its more structured art and musical institutions, and with a description of physical and geographic amenities, such as parks, playgrounds, and the boulevard system.

With the above outline in place, the dynamic interplay of the public ownership movement, industrial relations, and campaigns for political and moral reform are traced in a chronological context. The public ownership movement, for instance, is shown to have been a coalition of aspiring local recruits from business and professional classes, organized labor, and women's organizations who joined together to fight the absentee-owned corporations that dominated Seattle's utilities and waterfront.

In their struggle, proponents of publicly owned electric utilities, found themselves confronting the National Electric Light Association's nationwide campaign to thwart local control, or "home rule," by transferring the authority to regulate franchises and rates to state public service commissions which they were confident of controlling. The resolution of these issues extend beyond the period covered in this volume. It was not until the 1920s, after the Grange District Power Bill Initiative and a ruling by the State Supreme Court, that municipally owned utilities were able to undercut the National Electric Light Association's strategy by selling surplus power to distributors outside their corporate jurisdictions.

As to control of Seattle's waterfront, even the Chamber of Commerce allied itself temporarily against railroad domination, seeking legislation that authorized the establishment of port districts under municipal control. But just as quickly, the Chamber resumed its efforts to re-establish private control through a subsidy scheme that became a potential source of scandal. The Bogue Plan for comprehensive city development got lost in this political maneuvering, but the Port of Seattle emerged from the controversy as a viable entity.

Sale to the city of Stone and Webster Management Corporation's traction system (a street railway operated by its subsidiary, Puget Sound Traction, Power and Light) appeared to be timely, if not "divine," intervention for Stone and Webster and an almost satanic calamity for the city. The railway sale bailed out the company, but debt obligations incurred by Seattle became part of a Stone and Webster strategy to take over Seattle's lighting department—"City Light." This issue would dominate city politics throughout the 1920s. But a knowledge of events that transpired in these earlier decades is essential for understanding what followed.

Industrial relations in the first decades of the twentieth century were characterized by a resurgent trade unionism and employer militancy in the form of an open-shop movement. Pro- and anti-union forces clashed throughout the period, and although confrontations were less brutal than in the East and Midwest, the same basic elements were involved: the use of labor spies, infiltration of union leadership, routine use of strikebreakers, dependence by management on friendly courts to grant injunctions, and support of businesses by the local constabulary.

But in all cases, Pacific-Northwest employers were less successful than their counterparts elsewhere in the nation in combatting unionism. Politically alert union leadership formed successful alliances with state farmer groups (Joint Legislative Committee), the Federation of Women's Clubs, the clergy, and occasionally with state and local professional and business groups.

Among early cooperative efforts undertaken by labor, professional organizations, and business groups was the Municipal League, formed in 1910. Along with the Federation of Women's Clubs, the Central Labor Council, and neighborhood improvement groups, the Municipal League emerged as a strong backer of the above-mentioned municipal ownership movement.

Civil liberties issues were threaded throughout by attempts of reform organizations to alter Seattle's status quo. Every time a group or class achieved an economic advance, an increase in political effectiveness, or a new cultural attainment, it meant a broadening of its civil liberties—essentially giving its members more control over their daily lives. Until World War I, substantial gains were made in a number of areas, but as with reform in general, civil liberties were substantially eroded by the federal government's wartime activity. In the wake of Russia's Bolshevik Revolution in 1917 and communist uprisings elsewhere, Seattle's open-shop employers were caught up in a wave of hysteria that swept the nation. Decrying all forms of dissidence, they took full advantage of the ill-considered General Strike of February 1919.

Throughout this period and on into the 1920s, the thorny issue of the open town policy versus that of a closed one persisted. At the center of this struggle was the police department's relationship with operators of saloons, illegal gambling interests, and businessmen promoting prostitution.

Attempts were made to confine prostitution in particular to a "deadline" district south of Yesler Way where several saloons and theaters provided assignation "boxes" for lusting guests. But, too often, operators promoted prostitution across the deadline toward uptown, in some cases invading residential neighborhoods. Since these illegal practices were fairly common knowledge, they could not have continued without police protection. Consequently, they made good newspaper copy and inspired grand jury investigations; corruption associated with prostitution even lead to the murder of the young Chief of Police William Meredith by John Considine, a theater magnate and vice operator.

When state-wide prohibition took effect in 1916, bootlegging was added to the list of practices requiring police protection to survive. Seldom were bootleggers driven from the city; never were their activities brought under control.

To understand Seattle politics in the early twentieth century it is also important to examine the role played by the city's newspapers. All were partisan; often they were vicious when stating editorial positions, attacking their enemies with foul language that bordered on libel.

The most reliable of the bunch was the *Argus,* an outspoken independent Republican weekly controlled by Harry Chadwick, an editor whose strong suit was political satire. Since Republicans dominated early twentieth century Washington politics, most political controversy of the time occurred within their party. Rarely was there an issue on which Chadwick did not flay the *Post-Intelligencer's* owner, ex-Senator John L. Wilson, for being responsible to the railroad interests, or for so dividing King County's Republican Party that the county had neither a congressman nor a senator to represent it. In contrast, he argued that Tacoma had both: Senator Addison Foster and Congressman Frank Cushman. Tacoma and Pierce County consequently benefited often at Seattle's expense in Chadwick's opinion.

Chadwick's other weekly target was Alden J. Blethen, a man whose irrepressible flamboyance was easily confused with demagoguery. Coming to the city in 1896 from Minneapolis, where he had owned two failed newspapers, he purchased the *Seattle Times.* In Chadwick's view, Blethen would have made the paper a Republican voice if Wilson had not preempted that role. Consequently, the *Times* became fiercely Democratic at times, less than enthusiastic in its support of Democratic positions at others. But generally it opposed anything advocated by the *P-I.* Gradually Blethen slipped over to the Republican side, supporting most Republicans in the 1904 city election and all but one in 1906—the one exception being mayoral candidate, William Hickman Moore, a Democrat.

Both Wilson and Blethen opposed municipal ownership and trade unions. Both also advocated an open town policy; Blethen was even part owner of a hotel—the Morrison—which was a known gambling spot above the deadline. The *Argus's* Chadwick, favored municipal ownership as a means for opposing the franchise monopolies over electric power and the street railway established by Stone and Webster's subsidiary, the Seattle Electric Company. He also attacked the Great Northern Railroad for the methods it used to gain control over waterfront and adjacent lands, and for its role in trying to restrict entry of other transcontinentals into the city. Chadwick believed these absentee interests controlled the City Council and he produced evidence to back up his claims in almost every issue.

Since common laborers, as well as the city's burgeoning middle classes, appeared helpless before the corporate political clout arrayed before them, Chadwick also favored the trade union movement that was gaining momentum at the time. He spoke favorably of the newly established labor weekly, the *Union Record*, but he barely tolerated the *Seattle Star*, which the Scripps chain started up as a self-proclaimed voice of labor.

On other issues Chadwick's views were less "enlightened." He was virulently anti-Japanese and anti-Black. On the latter issue, however, he drew the line at the kind of racism he witnessed at a popular carnival-booth act of the time—"the nigger and egg," in which a Black male stuck his head through an opening in some canvas sheeting and was then pelted with rotten eggs. Chadwick demanded that this vulgarity be banned in future carnivals.

As to woman suffrage, Chadwick opposed it as affording no escape from political corruption; in his opinion, a woman's place was in the home anyway. Even though he did not rise above contemporary social postures on these issues, Chadwick's editorial comments do provide insightful views into the city's political and cultural institutions. More accurately than any other Seattle newspaper of the early twentieth century, his *Argus* enunciated the frustrations of professional and business classes, as well as those expressed by "responsible" trade unionists in their attempts to extract economic benefits from the city's established elites. These business and working-class activists were impatient with the wonder-working of trickle-down economics and with a political system that protected those at the top from "interlopers' " demands. So was Chadwick.

2

Seattle's Political Economy, 1900-1910

Seattle and the Twentieth Century

Seattle's dramatic rise to prominence in the early twentieth century was not foretold before the 1890s. Founded in 1853, the modest village grew gradually to become an active town by the time of its great fire in 1889. Trading in the Puget Sound basin, servicing its own community and the adjacent hinterland is what shaped the city's economy and provided opportunities for Seattle merchants to gain commercial experience. Manufacturing, in its contemporary sense, was alien to Seattle at the time.

In the course of being rebuilt after the 1889 conflagration, the city's facilities took on a modern look as the community set about establishing its own water supply, paving the way for a municipally owned source for electrical power in the process. A beginning was also made toward leveling hills that impeded the town's commercial development.

However, two events in the 1890s propelled Seattle into the future. First was the extension of the Great Northern Railroad into the city in 1893. The railroad gave the community a transcontinental connection that would enable it to compete with its Puget Sound rival, Tacoma (which had been the Northern Pacific terminus since 1883). Once in Seattle, James J. Hill of the Great Northern fought continuously to keep his transcontinental rivals out of the city.

Special Collections Division, University of Washington Libraries

Figure 1: *S.S. Portland* arriving with its "ton of gold," July 15, 1897.

Hill's local strategist was Thomas Burke, a railroad man himself, but also a lawyer who probably wielded more political power in the city-to-be than any other. In Washington, railroad interests dominated the legislature as they did in other states along the northern tier. It was in these august bodies that politics blended with economics, effectively protecting advantages given to the railroads' absentee owners.

The second crucial event to affect Seattle's destiny at the end of the nineteenth century was the 1897 discovery of gold in Alaska's Klondike. Coming on the heels of the 1893-1896 depression, the Klondike gold rush became a kind of platform from which Seattle took its great leap forward.

After the gold rush, with the city bursting at its seams as it prepared to monopolize the Alaska trade, mechanisms for maintaining law and order broke down. Political leaders hesitated to exercise their public responsibility. The police department, when not directly in league with the "vice lords," simply found itself outnumbered. The "open" versus "closed" town issue became the moral yeast that served as leaven for much subsequent political action. When combined with economic and social grievances voiced by the city's newcomers, this "moral" issue consolidated opposition to established downtown elites. It is within this broad framework that Seattle's early twentieth century political economy should be seen.

James J. Hill and the Great Northern

Before James J. Hill's Great Northern Railroad provided Seattle with its first transcontinental transportation connection in 1893, the city's economy rested almost entirely on coastal maritime trade in the Puget Sound basin, along the British Columbia coast, and into the fjords and harbors of southeastern Alaska. Logs, lumber, coal, livestock, and food products were traded. At the time, Seattle did not have an industrial economy based on manufacturing; the few finished goods produced in the city were, in fact, consumed locally.

After the first of the transcontinental railroad lines (ultimately there would be four) reached Seattle, lumber and salmon were shipped in large quantities to the nation's interior markets and as far east as New York. Trade with the Orient expanded apace. Commerce with Japan more than doubled between 1895 and 1896, and then almost tripled the next year, attaining a value of $8,052,857 by 1899. Altogether, Seattle's commerce experienced an eight-fold expansion between 1895 and the beginning of the twentieth century.

While railroad entrepreneurs hoped to develop the Oriental trade, thus enhancing the potential value of their newly constructed rail links with the East, local waterfront interests in Seattle were able to take advantage of the 1897 Klondike gold rush, making the city the main jumping-off place for north-bound gold seekers in the process.

Railroad development in the Pacific Northwest of the 1890s seemed both to threaten and promote Seattle's economic development simultaneously. This ambiguity was clear at the time to Seattleites who resented the Northern Pacific's choice of Tacoma as a western rail terminus. On the other hand, citizens applauded when they learned that James J. Hill decided to run his Great Northern tracks to the shores of Seattle's Elliott Bay.

But such expressions of civic gratitude proved to be short lived. For when Hill gained temporary control of the rival Northern Pacific in 1902, he effectively eliminated rail competition in the State of Washington. He and the other major railroad entrepreneur in the region, Edward Henry Harriman, went so far as to divide up the Pacific Northwest: Harriman's Union Pacific would not enter Washington; Hill's railroads would not go into Oregon. The Hill-Harriman understanding insured that high freight rates would continue to be levied against products produced in the Pacific Northwest, thus making them less competitive in Midwestern and Eastern markets.

Problems caused by Hill's virtual monopoly over rail traffic north of the Columbia led the Pacific Coast Lumber Manufacturers' Association to file suit with the Interstate Commerce Commission in 1907 charging restraint of trade. The action reflected a perennial enmity with which customers, not only in Washington, but also those in Idaho, Montana, and in the upper Midwest regarded Hill's business practices. Great Northern executives, however, were unfazed.

Virtually all railroads pressured municipalities and state governments to grant special franchises designed to exclude competition. In many states, the companies bought influence within the major political parties and were able, thus, to control legislative action. In Washington, railroads had the greatest leverage within the Republican Party. And except for a conservative, Populist interlude that lasted from 1896 to 1901, Republicans dominated state government.

As a result, the Great Northern and Northern Pacific successfully thwarted attempts to regulate railroad activity time and again. Among their early successes was a campaign to stall the creation of a state railroad commission until lobbyists were confident that the body would be sympathetic to their corporate interests. In Seattle, the Great Northern wielded a "whip hand" over any competitor who might charge lower wharfage rates. Having acquired tideland and waterfront property by way of city-granted franchises and outright purchase, the Hill interests were able to establish "tie-in contracts" with shippers and warehouse owners as a condition for sale of these properties. Exercise of this power became so blatantly obstructive that business leaders temporarily joined in opposition to railroad domination of the waterfront once they caught scent of profits that the Panama Canal might generate after being completed.

By the end of the 1890s, many citizens believed that railroads would ultimately control the destiny of Seattle and the other cities along the shores of Puget Sound. Tacoma had its own cargo lumber mills, shipping coastwise and throughout the Pacific Rim. The Northern Pacific Railroad, chiefly through its special contract with the St. Paul and Tacoma Lumber Company, gained rail access to Midwestern markets. Other big mill companies in the Puget Sound basin being owned by San Francisco firms, shipped directly from their own harbors: Port Blakely, Port Gamble, Seabeck, Port Madison, and Port Ludlow. Seattle had no cargo mills, and not until 1893 did it finally gain its rail connection. Then the mammoth Port Blakely mill on Bainbridge Island began shipping an increasing proportion of its lumber to the Midwest through facilities along the shores of Elliott Bay.[1]

Reginald H. Thomson and Civic Development

During these crucial years at the beginning of the twentieth century, Reginald H. Thomson, city engineer from 1892 to 1911, laid out a strategy for Seattle's future urban development. If we are to believe Thomson's roseate self-appraisal, without his guiding hand and firm integrity, the city would have become the plaything of dominant economic interests: the railroads, the private utilities, and the shipping firms. In his view, there were elements of city and regional development that could not be left unfettered in the hands of private enterprise.

In laying out a blueprint, Thomson had, in fact, expanded on plans outlined by his predecessor, City Engineer Frederick H. Whitworth, who believed that the Cedar River watershed was a key to Seattle's development. Pure, clean water for drinking, for flushing sewage, and for hydroelectric power was absolutely basic, and it must be under municipal control to assure its permanence. When recounting his earlier efforts for the benefit of Welford Beaton in 1914, Thomson sketched out his grand scheme to make over Seattle as a modern city. He declared that it had been essential to connect the downtown district with outlying areas: with the Lake Union basin and Interbay/Ballard to the north, with the Rainier and White River valleys to the south (the White joined with the Green River to form the Duwamish, flowing into Elliott Bay).

> To open and keep open lines of easy communication between the center of the city, and these territories became a ruling passion with me....One of the greatest difficulties was to prevent the erection of permanent structures in the way of extensions.

As an example of his civic spirit, Thomson pointed to the time when the City Council, over his protest, granted a franchise to the Great Northern that would have blocked First Avenue South and closed streets leading south between First and Fifth avenues. James J. Hill, who had come to respect Thomson, asked the reasons for his opposition. When the city engineer explained his position, Hill agreed and withdrew the proposal, apparently choosing a suggested tunnel route instead. Furthermore, Hill, according to Thomson, "brought the other roads into line."

Filling out Thomson's grand strategy, Westlake Avenue was constructed to connect the city center with the Lake Union basin; Dearborn Avenue to connect with Rainier Valley; and Magnolia Way was laid out to connect with Interbay and Ballard, across Salmon Bay.[1]

Argus editor, Harry Chadwick, disagreed with Thomson's self-portrayal. Chadwick found Thomson subservient to the Hill interests, seeing the city engineer as instrumental in:

1. assuring that the City Council granted franchises to the Great Northern in exchange for unfulfilled promises to build a suitable depot;

2. giving Hill tunnel rights through the city without specifying where the tunnel was to be routed;

3. executing Hill's plan to combat the Northern Pacific's efforts to enter the city.

Chadwick also believed that Thomson backed Hill's program by opposing the Northern Pacific's efforts to gain access to its own docks that required crossing the Great Northern's waterfront tracks. In return for these concessions, the only thing Seattle obtained from the Great Northern was a promise to build a depot in 1900. Simultaneously, Thomson thwarted the Northern Pacific's application to erect a similar structure after that railroad finally completed a direct route to Seattle. The city engineer's position complemented nicely the motives of James J. Hill, who wanted his Great Northern to monopolize Seattle's Oriental trade. Further supporting Chadwick's assertion that Thomson functioned as a pawn of railroad interests was the fact that, by the time the Union Station was finally completed in 1906, the NP and GN had been awarded additional grants of land by the City Council merely for making a series promises to construct a depot at some time in the future.

Adding to Chadwick's frustration over the city engineer's activities, as well as to the consternation of businessmen who wanted open access to the waterfront, many Great Northern practices appeared to deter commerce. At times, freight cars became almost insuperable obstacles, sitting in long lines on Great Northern's Railroad Avenue tracks for hours at a time. Further, railroad employees tended to disregard established safety precautions designed to protect both vehicle and pedestrian traffic.[2]

Chadwick complained about Thomson's actions in other areas, as well. In particular, the *Argus* editor was opposed to the way the city engineer managed the massive regrade of Seattle's hills that was undertaken in the late 1890s. He was angered by the way contractors tore up city streets, by the prolonged abandonment of work while citizens suffered through summers of dust and dirt, and by the muck and mud through which pedestrians had to slog during the rainy season. A contractors' combine was suspected of being at the bottom of this mess; and Thomson was found guilty, at least in Chadwick's eyes, for not writing time-limit and penalty clauses into contracts for the regrade.[3]

Thomas Burke, Spokesman for James J. Hill

In the many battles waged over Seattle's turn-of-the-century economic and commercial development, James J. Hill's interests were represented mainly by Thomas Burke, an attorney and one-time judge who settled in the city in 1875. Burke had formed a law partnership with John J. McGilvra soon after his arrival, and then married McGilvra's daughter, Caroline, to boot. Burke was a railroad enthusiast himself, and had once promoted his own enterprise, the Seattle, Lake Shore, and Eastern, a line described as starting ". . . from so many places and reaching anywhere."[1]

Before the Great Fire of 1889, however, two rival railroad companies had franchises to the land along the meander of Seattle's shoreline (the so-called "Ram's Horn"), thereby blocking access to the waterfront by Burke's road, which owned a thirty-foot-wide strip upland from the Ram's Horn. But lawyer Burke was not easily defeated by adversity. In 1887, he negotiated a transfer of title to the city for the land beyond the Ram's Horn; he then secured deeds to this upland property. Although the Great Fire destroyed buildings on the Ram's Horn, title to the land remained intact. But the city, in regrading streets in the area, shifted rights of way to its property beyond the meander line, naming a street on the new land Railroad Avenue. Shortly, Burke transferred most of his Railroad Avenue right of way to the Great Northern. Then, while Ram's Horn owners were litigating their own disputed rights of way, the City Council gave a franchise for a sixty-foot-wide strip of Railroad Avenue to Hill's Great Northern subsidiary, the Seattle and Montana Railroad. Agitation over this grant spanned the next decade. Hill's was a simple strategy; he wanted to block access to the waterfront by other railroads. And it was Burke who convinced both the City Council and the Chamber of Commerce that these actions should be accepted.

Although the Great Northern gave Seattle its first direct transcontinental connection in 1893, it exacted a price for what they

Special Collections Division, University of Washington Libraries

Figure 2: Railroad Avenue from Washington Street—"endangering pedestrians' life and limb," ca. 1905-1906.

had done. Serving as the Great Northern's western counsel, Burke, consistently insured that whenever economic gain might accrue to the city, that it should also coincide with Hill's interests. By 1910, the Great Northern, the Northern Pacific, and a third organization, the Pacific Coast Company, effectively controlled almost the entire length of Seattle's active waterfront. Consequently, the railroads came to own a large number of the docks, wharfs, and warehouses, as well as the transport agencies operating up and down the Pacific Coast and in Puget Sound. How this state of affairs came about is of interest, for it sheds light on political alignments of the period.

The Fight for the Waterfront

As originally written, the Washington's constitution specifically prohibited private control of tidelands. But prior to the state's 1889 constitutional convention, private parties had already begun to build on tideland. Because these activities were clearly illegal, they led to a series of conflicting claims that had to be adjudicated. Concern over how delegates to the state constitutional convention would respond, actually set off a tidelands rush in Seattle. To resolve the problem, constitutional framers established a harbor lines commission to draw shoreline boundaries and to specify tidelands that were to be designated as municipal property. The five commissioners began hearings in 1890.

Seattle Lighting Department photo archive

Figure 3: Downtown regrading in progress, as viewed from 3rd Avenue North and Columbia Street, February 1907.

Burke hinted at the start of these proceedings that the Great Northern might not terminate its line at Seattle if rulings mandating public-tideland ownership were permitted to stand. But when the commission's first report, issued in October, declared shoreline to a width of 600 feet to be public property, Burke and the railroads counterattacked by filing a prohibition writ in superior court to enjoin the commission from filing its maps. Judge Lichtenberg, who owed his appointment to Burke, compliantly issued the requested injunction. However, the Washington Supreme Court reversed Lichtenberg's ruling on July 5, 1891.

Burke then appealed to a federal court, where Judge Cornelius Hanford (who also owed his appointment to Burke) ruled in favor of Great Northern interests without even hearing the state attorney general's rebuttal. In turn, Hanford was overruled by the district court. Burke next appealed to the United States Supreme Court, intending to delay Harbor Lines Commission action until the commissioners' terms expired. He succeeded, thus forcing the state legislature to appoint a new group of commissioners who were more hospitable to railroad views. The new commissioners redrew the harbor line, initially allowing a 300-foot strip to be devoted to public use. Two years later, Burke acquired that small strip for the Great Northern, thereby giving Hill virtual control of Seattle's waterfront.[1]

Reshaping the Waterfront

Before the 1890s, a number of civic leaders, including Arthur Denny, Governor John H. McGraw, Judge Burke, Burke's father-in-law John Jay McGilvra, along with several real estate speculators and settlers north of Shilshole Bay, expected to have a canal dug from Lake Washington to Shilshole. Burke and his allies believed that such a waterway would be important to the development of a steel industry they hoped to establish near Kirkland. At the time, Seattle, like Portland and many other cities, aspired to become the "Pittsburgh of the West." The canal would also provide a route to float raw timber from east of Lake Washington into Puget Sound; it would also mean that coal would no longer have to be barged, and then portaged, from east of the lake to Elliott Bay.

In 1893 this plan was unexpectedly sidetracked when former Territorial Governor Eugene Semple got a bill through the legislature that allowed private companies to construct public waterways across state-owned property and to charge liens on reclaimed tidelands that were sold to finance the work.

It was not apparent at the time of its passage, but this legislation threatened the Shilshole canal project—Governor McGraw, one of Burke's colleagues, had even signed the bill. This oversight became apparent when Semple filed his plans with the State Land Commission for a competing Lake Washington canal scheme. He intended to build his canal at the south end of Seattle, from Elliott Bay through Beacon Hill to Lake Washington, by sluicing part of the hill facing the bay onto the tide flats. In the process, Semple planned to dredge channels east and west of a huge man-made island, Harbor Island; both waterways would lead into the Duwamish River, which would be dredged to accommodate ocean-going ships.

Semple then lined up financial backers for this south canal project, obtained the blessing of the Chamber of Commerce, and after a mass meeting of four thousand headed by the mayor, he raised more than the required $500,000 to subsidize the project. A writer for the *Post-Intelligencer* declared the event "one of the great epochs in the history of Seattle."

Work on Semple's grandiose scheme began on July 29, 1895. By May 1896 nearly one hundred acres of tide flats had been filled and sales for the newly created waterfront were keeping pace with the earth-moving activity.

Enter Judge Burke and the Great Northern Railroad. Fearful that Semple would succeed in getting federal funds for his undertaking at the expense of the north-canal route, Burke, through his client, challenged the constitutionality of Semple's 1893 law by filing an injunction. This legal action brought south-canal construction to a halt for eighteen months while the Washington Supreme Court decided the issue.

Although the court declared the law to be constitutional in December 1898, the delay caused serious financial difficulties for Semple. In the process, the former governor lost the major backing of his St. Louis nephews, Edgar and Henry Ames (though Edgar would later reap immense profits in shipbuilding at Harbor Island during World War I).

Semple reorganized and, over Burke's heated protest, obtained a four-year extension on his state contract. The Great Northern lawyer became especially upset after the new State Land Commissioner, Robert Bridges, a politician of socialist reputation, denied him a hearing. Burke then exercised other options.

As western counsel for the Great Northern he was able to secure an injunction that prevented the filling of any more railroad property west of Hanford Street. Then, after failing to get the legislature to pass a bill terminating the south canal project, and with Semple reeling from delays caused by litigation, Burke negotiated a settlement that ended the injunction in May 1901.

Despite the fact that Semple's firm could, once again, take up work filling the tide flats, selling the recovered land, and digging through Beacon Hill, the 1901 settlement proved only to be a smoke screen for Burke's true intentions. In the interim caused by the litigation, he and other north-canal proponents were able to gather enough financial support to begin work on a ten-foot-deep channel between Shilshole and Salmon bays and to induce the Chamber of Commerce to endorse a plan to lower Lake Washington's water level.

These tactics finally committed the city to Burke's north canal. At the same time, the protracted south canal project began to wear the public's patience thin. Symptomatic of the prevailing attitude was a statement made by one of Semple's early supporters, former assistant city engineer, George Cotterill: "Stop knifing this community . . . attend to your business of filling in the tide flats." To complicate matters further, officials found that unexpectedly large quantities of city water were being used for the Beacon Hill sluicing at what were soon regarded suspiciously as cheap rates. The scent of corruption was in the air and Beacon Hill clay was not easily dislodged. Under fire for fiscal extravagance at public expense, Semple also knew that if the north-canal promoters were successful in lowering the level of Lake Washington, the south canal project would be doomed to failure.

Semple's position became even more difficult when, in January 1902, the Chamber of Commerce sent Erastus Brainerd to Washington, D. C., to lobby for north canal appropriations. Semple followed to join in the hearings; then Burke decided that he, too, needed to be in the nation's capital. And it was Burke who carried the day, testifying falsely to a congressional committee that the Washington Supreme Court had declared the law authorizing the south canal to be unconstitutional. Although congress granted only a token appropriation of $160,000 to underwrite Burke's north-canal project, these funds became seed money for completing the ten-foot-deep trench that doomed Semple's enterprise.

After returning from Washington, D. C., Burke closed in for the kill. Seeing Semple's dwindling resources, he wrote to the Great Northern's general manager, John F. Stevens, in September 1902 stating that he could purchase Semple's company for only $6,000. This action, he declared, would give:

> . . . us all their appliances, [and] enable us to proceed with filling depot grounds at our pleasure, and cheaper than in any other way. It would, moreover, prevent the disordering of the waterway across the tide lands on the South of our terminal grounds. . .and this at a cost to the three railway companies that would be a bagatelle in comparison with the advantages to be gained. . .

Stevens spoke to Hill immediately and then telegraphed Burke: "Close at once for control Seattle Lake Washington waterway [sic] per your message ninth." Semple was at the end of his tether; the demise of his Beacon Hill project was a foregone conclusion.

Unfortunately for the former territorial governor, he was unaware of how he was being set up. On the surface, his actions appeared to stymie the north-canal forces; workers had, after all, nearly completed his East Waterway and had begun construction on the West Waterway in August 1903. However, the demand for reclaimed tide flats outstripped the financial resources Semple had available to create them. He now had to pledge future revenue to secure badly needed credit, an action that forced him to reorganize his company. In the process, he surrendered much of his stock and ultimately lost control, as well. New management stopped work on the south canal and concentrated its efforts on filling in the tide flats. Railroads then refused to sign contracts with Semple's firm, the Seattle and Lake Washington Waterway Company, and began filling their own lands. The former governor's demise was underscored by a subsequent grand jury investigation into his water contract and by the city's issuance in May 1904 of a cessation order for work on the south canal.

Still, Semple's project was not a complete disaster. The filled-in area became Seattle's industrial heartland and the railroads reaped revenue from servicing the grain elevators, flour mills, steel plants, coal docks, tool-making and machinery plants, shipyards, and satellite operations that located there in the first two decades of the century. If this were not enough, Great Northern and Northern Pacific executives could also take satisfaction in the profits they made on land received in return for successive promises to build a union depot. In the end, Semple's south-canal enterprise failed because the railroads were able to place such vast resources at Thomas Burke's disposal when he set out to destroy the project. But Semple's tenacity must have amazed even the Great Northern's western counsel, accustomed as he was to having his way.[1]

3

The Economy, 1900-1914

An Overview

By 1914, Seattle's pattern of economic growth had been well established by events of the previous two decades. The most significant changes taking place during the next four years occurred in the city's shipbuilding industry and in those metal trades serving it. Several new facilities opened after World War I broke out in Europe and operations at Seattle's one large steel yard expanded dramatically. After the Allied victory in November 1918, shipbuilding experienced a predictable slump as the government cancelled contracts on a massive scale. Simultaneously, what started as a local shipyard labor action grew into the nation's first citywide general strike. Seattle's immediate postwar economy languished as a depression enveloped the country.[1]

During these years Seattle's pattern for business and industrial development differed radically from those of its three main West Coast rivals: Tacoma, Portland, and San Francisco. San Francisco's supremacy had been established earlier, in the mid-nineteenth century, after the California gold discoveries of 1848. Tacoma and Portland received economic head starts when transcontinental railroads linked them to Inland Empire and Midwest markets a decade before the Great Northern provided Seattle with a means to enter the competition.

Tacoma had its own cargo mills; San Francisco lumber firms owned similar facilities in Puget Sound. Few lumber or shingle mills located in Seattle, although that situation changed when Ballard was annexed in 1907; after that time, the city could boast that it controlled twelve percent of Washington's shingle production.

Few major manufacturing enterprises could be found in early twentieth-century Seattle; it was a commercial city with a hinterland expanding into the Puget Sound basin and extending northward to Victoria and Vancouver, British Columbia, and to Alaska.

When Erastus Brainerd, the Chamber of Commerce lobbyist in Washington, D. C., got the government to establish an assay office in the city in 1898, the facility gave Seattle a significant advantage, insuring a virtual monopoly of the northern trade. Successful gold-seekers cashed in their precious metal at the assay office, and then spent their earnings in the city and its environs. This steady flow of new-found gold into the economy stimulated the growth of vice and the rackets, as well as numerous outfitting establishments. When this influx of Klondike gold declined, Seattle's northern ties worked to promote the city's domination of Alaska's salmon fishery. As a result, Seattle became the nation's leading canned salmon exporter. Production figures for 1919 show the city's relative predominance of the Alaska fishery on the Pacific Coast. Of the 8,023,437 cases of canned salmon packed that year, 4,592,201 contained fish that originated in Alaskan waters. Of significance in reinforcing Seattle's position in this scenario, Puget Sound yielded the second largest pack, amounting to 1,295,626 cases.

The Spanish-American War in 1898 and the subsequent Philippines Insurrection also contributed to Seattle's commercial development. An initial stimulus came when the United States Army established Fort Lawton as a port of embarkation for troops bound for the conflict. But of more lasting value were the successfully negotiated United States Army transport contracts to supply the occupying army in the Philippines. The first transport ship to sail in this trade was the bark, *Marion Chilcott*, laden with lumber and hay. Nine months later, in May 1900, the Chamber of Commerce reported that nine steamships had sailed to the Philippines; all had been specially fitted in Seattle shipyards.

The Philippine trade remained steady for nearly a decade, carrying oats and hay for the Army's horses, flour and groceries for the troops. Homeward-bound ships carried hemp from the colony, stimulating the development of cordage manufacturing on Seattle's waterfront. The economic significance of this commerce was, however, to be valued less in dollars, than as a means of helping to establish the city as San Francisco's rival in the Far Eastern trade.

Waterfront improvements soon followed the expansion of the Oriental trade. The Chamber of Commerce, in its minutes of December 31, 1901, boasted that in the past two years, "Instead of the old irregular line of wharfs and bunkers, there is now a complete chain of piers constructed along similar lines and in general conformity with each other. . . . They represent a period of greatest development of the city."

Eighteen piers and warehouses were built in 1900, mainly by the Pacific Coast Company and the Northern Pacific Railroad. The Pacific Coast Company, which controlled the Green River coal fields in the southern part of King County, hauled coal to market on its Columbia and Puget Sound Railroad. The NP hauled coal in from its own mines at Roslyn and Cle Elum, Washington, tagging coal cars onto Seattle-bound freights already laden with manufactured goods from the Midwest and East.

Commodities imported by the Northern Pacific were consumed, in part, in the Puget Sound basin; what remained, was exported to Alaska, the Orient, or to British Columbia. Rail shipments of lumber and salmon were the main domestic products leaving Seattle for the Midwest and East. Imports of tea, raw silk, curios, camphor, matting, and braid from the Orient also were transshipped in Seattle. This trade amounted to $6,625,964 in 1904— before the market for raw silk boomed after 1905.

At the time, the Chamber of Commerce attached special significance to Pacific Packing and Navigation Company's new fish terminal. Chamber members believed that this facility would "practically remove the seat of the salmon trade to this city." Pacific Packing and Navigation controlled most of the Alaska, Oregon, and Washington canneries, according to the Chamber. The pack distribution for 1901 shows the Puget Sound fishery's significance: the Alaska pack was 2,022,704 cases; Puget Sound's was 1,410,444; British Columbia's, 1,350,790; the Columbia River's, 240,600 cases. Altogether, fifty-seven launches, 1,025 other craft, and about 5,000 men worked the fisheries out of Seattle.

Seattle's well-established hinterland trade enabled the city to respond quickly to fortune-seekers' demands when the gold rush occurred in 1897. To serve this newly expanded market, city merchants simply enlarged current operations. According to economic historian, A. N. McDonald, Seattle became the regional jobbing and trading center at this time. The Chamber of Commerce, in its December 1901 minutes, rated groceries as the most important of the city's wholesale trade commodities. Dry goods and clothing were next in significance, followed by meat packing (a number of eastern packing firms had established branches and agencies in the city). Hardware and machinery completed the list of major

Washington State Historical Society, Asahel Curtis Collection

Figure 4: Mosquito fleet dock at Pier 3, with some of fleet in action, 1912.

commodities involved in the hinterland trade. Since these were the same kinds of goods required by those participating in the Alaska gold rush, merchants were well prepared to fill the demand when it arose.

John Rosene, head of the Northwest Commercial Company, commenting on the early Alaska trade for the *Railway and Marine News* in 1914, credited the Pacific Coast Steamship Company with "bringing order out of chaos" by pressing its best ships into the Alaska service. Other companies, such as the Pacific Clipper Line, the Alaska Steamship Company, and Frank Waterhouse followed Pacific Coast Steamship's lead. Rosene claimed that, after 1905, Seattle interests owned ninety percent of the vessels involved, reversing an earlier situation. He saw his own purchase of the Northern Pacific's three ships in 1904 as a key factor in bringing about the change.

Closer to home, a "Mosquito Fleet" distributed commodities to Seattle's regional markets. The Chamber attributed "commercial greatness" to this flotilla of seventy small steamers that hustled products to 350 ports on the Sound—towns, villages, logging camps, and mill towns. This trade, along with the long-established cargo and lumber traffic helped prepare the city for its role as an international commercial port.

Small, local railroads complemented waterborne commerce. As mentioned above, coal, the city's second leading export, was carried by the Columbia and Puget Sound Railroad from the Green River fields; the surplus above local consumption was shipped mainly to California. The Seattle, Lake Shore & Eastern Railroad came around the north end of Lake Washington and headed to other coal fields near Issaquah, a few miles east of Seattle; this road also had a northern spur that passed through Snohomish and Arlington, pointing toward Vancouver.

Farmers on the east side of Lake Washington were connected to the Seattle market when a ferry run between Madison Park and Kirkland began operations in 1890. By the turn of the century, passenger boats shuttled between Madison Park and Bothell, a few miles north of Kirkland. Additional ferry routes were established soon after the Port Commission began functioning after 1911: to Bellevue and Mercer Island on Lake Washington and to Vashon Island southwest of the city on Puget Sound. The Seattle Electric Company even carried produce on its streetcars from farmers on the other side of the lake to the city's commission merchants.

The Port of Seattle's municipal dock provided farmers in the Puget Sound basin with ready access to the Pike Place Public Market after 1912; the dock was only a couple of blocks downhill, but on a five percent gradient.

In some ways, this unpretentious transportation network looked as if it had been actually planned; but it had only an inner logic that made it appear that way—locked out of more remote markets, Seattle merchants discovered that revenue received from the locale was just as good as that to be earned elsewhere.

In addition to the commodities already mentioned, McDonald listed other homely items that were exchanged. Imported from the hinterland, in addition to coal, were: lumber, beef, poultry, grain, fish, and vegetables. Exported were: processed foods, rubber boots, nails, beer, rope, donkey engines, plows, shovels, saws, and fish nets.

Once the Great Northern reached Seattle in 1893 the city's lumber and shingle exports increased, despite the devastating four-year nationwide depression that began in that year.

In its December 1901 minutes, the Chamber of Commerce noted that the Oriental trade had nearly doubled when the Nippon Yushen Kaisha Line and Hamburg's Kosmos Line expanded service, the new China Mutual was established, and the Globe Navigation Company began operating between Seattle and Honolulu. Parallel with this growth in international shipping was the addition of vessels to the coastal trade. Although crude, the Port Warden's statistics for 1901 provide a general picture of this commerce, showing a base from which expansion continued throughout the period:

> Foreign imports $10,590,511 (of which more than
>   ninety-five percent were merchandise)
> Foreign exports $20,519,982 (of which almost $18 million
>   were merchandise)
> Coastwise imports $13,323,345 ($12 million in merchan-
>   dise)
> Coastwise exports $15,854,346 ($13,745,450 in merchan-
>   dise; $1,410,807 in coal)
> Honolulu $ 312,592

Manufacturing: 1899 to 1909

It was in the context of its hinterland commerce that Seattle's manufacturing developed at the turn of the twentieth century. As with trade, this sector of the city's economy was determined by the nature of nearby raw materials. The 1900 United States census statistics point to the importance of lumber and timber products by identifying fourteen such Seattle establishments that employed 1,008 wage earners. But carpentry—utilizing local mill products—employed 1,372 workers, more than any other manufacturing sector. Together, lumbering and carpentry added $2,695,778 and $3,669,606 respectively to the expanding city economy. By comparison, the next largest sector (eight slaughter houses and meat-packing plants) added $3,072,195 to the economy. Considering the threefold population growth between 1900 and 1910, with attendant demands for housing, warehouse space, office buildings, and retail stores, mill workers and carpenters were kept fully employed during the decade.

Further illustrating the localized basis of manufacturing were the thirty-three businesses employing 585 "masonry, brick, and stone" workers. These trades added a value of $2,148,713 to the economy. Ranking just below carpentry and mill work was bridge construction, which employed 801 men. For the most part, these enterprises all used wood products—like shipbuilding, which was not listed as a line item. When all of these figures are combined, businesses employing construction workers dominated Seattle's fledgling manufacturing sector.

Foundries developed markets for their products locally, as well as in the Alaska trade. In 1900, there were thirty-four foundries employing 425 persons who added value of $1,296,929. These products would remain prominent in the city's manufactures. So too, flour and grist mills, of which there were only six in 1899, employed just seventy-three wage earners. This line also would become a mainstay of the city's exports by 1910 as wheat became regularly routed to Seattle, largely at Portland's expense. Fish canning—of Puget Sound fish—flourished at this time; seven firms seasonally employed 255 workers, adding a commercial value of $1,037,174. The local roots of manufacturing plants and of the markets for their products seemed clear at the turn of the century.

Like most other segments of the economy, shipbuilding (consisting almost entirely of wooden boats, barges, and river craft) received a big boost from the gold rush. Shipbuilding, in turn, stimulated other manufacturing: boilermaking, machinery work, tool making, and other specialties necessary to outfit and power the vessels. The Moran Brothers firm was the largest of the shipbuilding operations at the end of the nineteenth century. Its evolution is illustrative. After the great fire, the firm rebuilt its plant. In 1895, Moran Brothers received its first federal government contract, the construction of a steam plant at the Charlestown Navy Yard near Bremerton.

The gold rush brought a demand for machinery and boats (before the fire Robert Moran was heavily into marine machinery invention and production). According to Clarence Bagley, "the Seattle iron industry obtained its first real taste of outside business" at this time, and shipbuilding accounted for much of the trade.

Moran Brothers proceeded to build an entire fleet of twelve shallow-draft boats for the Yukon trade. Robert Moran, himself, skippered the lead boat; eleven completed the voyage, and all aboard the twelfth were rescued. Seattle's first steel and iron vessel was built by them in 1898, a torpedo boat for the Spanish American War. With confidence whetted by this venture, the firm bid for construction of the battleship USS Nebraska, after building a dry dock to accommodate large craft. The Navy Department would not accept the bid unless it was reduced by $100,000. Robert Moran returned to the city, talked to other business leaders; together they started a subscription campaign to raise this amount; in the end, they raised $135,000 and won the contract. Construction on the ship began in 1902 and was completed in October 1904 amidst great city-wide celebration. Moran Brothers was sold to Eastern capitalists in 1906; in 1912 it became the Seattle Construction and Dry Dock Company.

Bagley estimated that about 1,900 men were employed in about a dozen yards in 1900. By 1914 there were twenty-six shipbuilding firms in the city, employing an average of 198 employees. The number would increase by only two in 1919, but the average number of workers employed by each reached 2,430 by that time.

In terms of products made and consumed within the region printing and publishing should not be overlooked; forty establishments employed 270 persons.

Manufacturing growth in Seattle from 1899 through 1914 is registered in the number of businesses engaged. In 1899 there were but 352; by 1904 there were 467; and 1909 saw more than a doubling of the 1899 figure to 751. By 1914 there were 1,014 manufacturing firms. This growth is reflected in terms of wage earners employed; these figures were:

1899	7,780
1904	7,532
1909	14,014 (according to the 1910 census; but 12,429 according to the 1920 census recapitulation)
1914	11,523 (according to the 1920 census recapitulation)

In general, the expansion was not remarkable growth when population growth is considered in relation to that of manufacturing. The basic character of manufacturing had not changed significantly; it still looked mainly to the region for its markets. But as with the Oriental commerce, trade with California, Alaska, British Columbia and the local market expanded as well after 1908.

Apart from shipbuilding, the six major manufacturing fields that dominated Seattle's industry were: lumber/timber, foundry/ machine shops, furniture, bread/bakery, flour mills, and printing/publishing, wooden shipbuilding, and slaughterhouses. A listing of the number of firms and the average number of their employees for 1909, 1914, and 1919 give some idea of their scale. But only a small proportion of the city's population was employed in manufacturing—before 1910 the average was about six percent. McDonald concludes that "resource-based industries were the backbone of Seattle's industrial activities throughout the period from 1880-1910." Although lumber manufacturing was the chief industry, Seattle's twenty-seven mills in 1907 were relatively small; only two employed more than one hundred men; and the average work force was fifty-three. By way of contrast, Tacoma's twenty-one mills had an average milling production of 80,000 board feet a day, compared to Seattle's 47,000 feet. But Seattle's mills were keyed to the local market, requiring construction lumber and finished products.

	Firms			Average No. of Employees		
	1909	1914	1919	1909	1914	1919
Lumber/timber	65	55	52	3,268	2,337	2,669
Fndry/mach.	71	82	203	1,230	1,004	3,195
Furniture	17	24	27	166	100	214
Brd/bkry	78	132	117	295	534	788
Flour mills	7	10	11	155	279	559
Printg/pub	133	214	193	1,042	1,057	1,053
Shipbuilding	NA	26	198	NA	198	1,430
Slaughtering & meat packing	4	3	4	325	482	503

The average number of employees in manufacturing overall was: 11,523 for 1909; 12,429 in 1914. and 40,843 in 1919.

Relative to the state as whole, of the 3,360 manufacturing establishments in the state in 1901, 953 of them were in Seattle, 381 in Tacoma. Capital invested was $52,649,760 for the state, $10,131,651 for Seattle, and $8,146,691 for Tacoma. Product value was $86,779,072 for the state, $26,373,497 for Seattle, and $12,029,497 for Tacoma. Relative to their respective populations Tacoma had more manufacturing than Seattle. The Chamber of Commerce estimated that between 13,000 and 16,000 wage earners were employed in manufacturing in Seattle in 1901. The chamber drew special attention to the increasing capacity of the city's flour mills in response to the external trade: 101,110 barrels in 1897; 422,474 barrels in 1900; and 474,848 barrels in 1901.

By 1916, Seattle would become the leading port on the Pacific Coast in terms of dollar value of its exports and imports. But, unlike other port cities Seattle accomplished this feat in the absence of a major industrial base. By then the city's economy had become a mixed one, the result of the municipal ownership movement, which provided a key that unlocked the door to economic opportunity and political power for the fresh recruits to the middle classes.

As these citizens gained a foothold, they found allies among the ranks of organized labor, the clergy, and women's groups. In almost every case the already established interests thwarted their ambitions. The municipal ownership movement altered existing power relationships and broadened the base for participation in the democratic process—at least until the war changed all this. The war marked the beginning of the restoration in a large sense, as we shall see.[1]

The Port in Operation

When the *Railway and Marine News* (*RMN*) began publication in 1904, its editors observed that most of Seattle's waterfront improvements had been made since 1900, as the economy revived under the special stimulus of the Klondike gold rush. The editors reported, "In general terms it may be stated that the wharfs and warehouses of Seattle are owned and controlled by the three great transportation companies, the Great Northern Railroad Company, the Northern Pacific Railway Company, and the Pacific Coast Company." The latter operated exclusively in the coastal trade.[1]

The Great Northern began its Oriental trade in 1896 by contracting with the Nippon Yusen Kaisha line to carry the cargo. Hill had carefully sought some means to balance his eastbound and westbound rail traffic, and found it in exports of cotton, grain, and rails to Japan, a trade that steadily expanded. Writing for *RMN* in November 1905, Hill despaired of competing with German and Belgian manufacturers because "Our labor costs are too high". On the other hand, he found the wages of Japanese workers too low, "from 10 to 25 cents a day," for them to comprise a potential market. Herein lay a critical dilemma. Characteristically, Hill wanted advantages to flow exclusively his way by paying the lowest wages possible. Essentially other employers pursued ends identical to Hill's, joining together under the leadership of employer associations and the National Association of Manufacturers in mounting open shop movements. By keeping domestic wages depressed through militant anti-union practices, they suppressed the purchasing power workers needed to buy goods and fuel the economy. In other words, Hill and the open shoppers wanted it both ways.

Hill noted that the Northern Pacific had begun the Puget Sound's Oriental trade in the early 1890s by purchasing obsolescent ships from the Canadian Pacific when that company modernized its fleet. But, being a land-grant railroad and the largest landowner in the state, it routinely sold off forested land in exchange for traffic; and it continued operating its collieries at Roslyn and Cle Elum after bowing out of ocean shipping.

Geographically, on the waterfront, the Great Northern concentrated its facilities at the northern end of Elliott Bay in Smith's Cove; the Northern Pacific in the middle section between Pike and Washington streets; and the Pacific Coast Company, south of Washington Street. Independent wharfs were scattered among these facilities, catering to the Alaskan commerce and that in the Puget Sound Basin. Also scattered among these marine operations were shipyards, boiler works, and miscellaneous metal working and cordage plants. Both the NP and the PCC had coal bunkers on the waterfront as well; the latter, having just replaced its old one that had been operated by the original company since the 1880s (the Oregon Improvement Company).

As the downtown hills were leveled, and the dirt and rocks were sluiced and conveyed onto the tide flats, the promise of future trade with the Orient was being fulfilled as well. Betokening the end of the depression, the first ship of the Nippon Yusen Kaisha line arrived in Elliott Bay in 1896. Most of its cargo would be transshipped on the Great Northern to the east. This set the pattern for the Oriental trade: tea, silk goods, raw silk, curios, camphor, and soy oil would be the main imports; lumber, flour, raw cotton, machinery, and heavy hardware the major exports. Their respective proportions varied from year to year, but raw silk became the predominant import by 1904; and, by 1909, it constituted more than $14 million of the total $21,274,893 in commodities brought in from the Orient (Japan and China).

Because of silk's fragile nature, special handling was provided at the Great Northern's Smith's Cove, expediting it to Hoboken, New Jersey, within three days of receipt. Shipment by water took two weeks, even when special fast silk freighters were used.

Records of rail transshipments were kept for 1903 and 1904, but not for later years. Their significance is clear, though, because facilities had to be built and operated for the purpose, thereby providing the city an important source of capital.

In 1903 goods worth $6,625,964 were transshipped, including:

tea	$2,055,333
silk	1,243,297
curios	1,029,850
matting	1,056,394
braid	279,281

In 1904 the figures show a sharp decline because of the Russo-Japanese War; the figures total $1,440,315. They include:

tea	$438,332
matting	314,674
curios	255,603

Steamship companies began offering service to Seattle as early as the 1890s; the Nippon Yusen Kaisha started regular service beginning in 1896, the China Mutual Steam Navigation company in

1900; Kosmos (Hamburg) 1901; the Great Northern Steamship Line, 1905, and was noted for having the "largest cargo carriers afloat" (the *Minnesota* and the *Dakota*, sailing to Yokohama, Shanghai, Hong Kong, and Manila) Chargeurs Reunis Line (French) 1906; Osaka Shosen Kaisha, 1909; and the Matson Navigation Line to Honolulu, 1909. Others were steadily added to the list after 1909. By 1920, about thirty steamship lines sailed regularly to Seattle. Star status was granted the Great Northern's *Minnesota*; it ran to and from the Orient from 1905 to 1915 when it was sold to the Atlantic run once the 1915 Seamen's Act took effect and Chinese crews ostensibly could no longer be used. Hill's *Dakota* ran aground and stayed there.

A general overview of the port's commerce from 1901 to 1914, before World War I had a significant impact, shows Seattle's steady, but irregular, commercial expansion. (Figures are in thousands of dollars).

	Imports		Exports	
	Domestic	**Foreign**	**Domestic**	**Foreign**
1901	$13,323	$10,590	$15,854	$20,520
1903	23,245	20,340	32,172	12,895
1904	27,511	5,832	33,557	8,797
1905	31,125	11,297	40,228	31,700
1909	32,304	28,802	53,304	12,669
1912	36,554	25,666	38,000	21,205
1913	38,382	25,898	39,933	19,917
1914	49,175	40,165	48,748	16,512

It is clear that domestic trade steadily improved, particularly on the import side. And although domestic exports declined in 1912 and 1913 from a 1909 high, it showed unmistakable growth. Foreign trade was clearly more volatile; as World War I got underway this pattern would become even more apparent. A look at 1916 and 1917, alone, illustrates the war's distorting effect. (Figures are in thousands of dollars).

	Imports		Exports	
	Domestic	**Foreign**	**Domestic**	**Foreign**
1916	$98,220	$161,330	$56,764	$96,116
1917	109,097	268,895	69,543	152,056

Appendix One provides a comparison of commodity profiles associated with specific trading partners and is helpful pointing to the shift in trade that occurred before the World War I. The years chosen are 1903 and 1914; 1903, because its statistics are clearly delineated for comparison purposes. Statistics are from the annual reports of the port warden.[2]

4

City Politics, 1900-1904

The winter of 1900 witnessed a Seattle election featuring what would soon become known as the open town issue. Judge Thomas J. Humes headed the Republican ticket, running for reelection as mayor. His popular reception at the Armory in early February demoralized opponents in his own party who tried to contest his nomination. Humes had first become mayor in 1898 when his predecessor, William D. Wood, caught gold fever and fled to the Klondike. Wood, himself, had been appointed by the City Council after recently elected Republican Mayor Frank Black resigned. Black quit after discovering that the party had made campaign promises he could not keep. Humes had no such qualms and willingly fulfilled Republican pledges by opening Seattle to accommodate gold seekers and those who planned to live off them.

Many were the opportunities to benefit from an open town and from the inevitable disjointing of law and order that appeared with the waves of new immigrants: those just passing through, the camp followers, and those who planned to stay. Local Republicans, having reaped benefits during his first term, understood what Humes's reelection would mean. Harry Chadwick, more wishful than candid, found in him a professional and businessmen's candidate who had earned the electoral spot by merely seeming to control vice and crime. Chadwick's judgment was, however, colored by a deep aversion to the Democratic Party in general and "moral" reformers in particular.[1]

Chadwick also feared the election of Will H. Parry, a would-

33

be "dark horse" candidate backed by the *P-I*'s John L. Wilson. Parry, Chadwick believed, would solidify Hill's influence in Seattle. As noted in chapter two, these interests had already been established by Thomas Burke beginning in 1890. Shortly thereafter, Parry, who had been city comptroller from 1894 to 1900, dominated the City Council as Burke's man. With Burke firmly in command, he took the opportunity to acquire another newspaper to advance the Hill cause. (In 1890 Burke and Daniel Gilman had edited the short-lived *Seattle Telegraph* to counter the *P-I*; Hill advanced $20,000 for the venture.) The new opportunity presented itself when John Wilson, having just been "dis-elected" as Washington's senator, wanted to buy the *P-I*; Wilson appealed to James J. Hill, who immediately lent him the necessary $400,000. The railroad magnate now controlled Wilson.[2]

Assistant City Engineer George F. Cotterill headed the 1900 opposition Populist-Democrat fusion ticket; he stood little chance against the Republicans. Cotterill had laid out the city's bicycle paths along the wooded shores of Lake Washington and elsewhere, but he was also a prohibitionist. Somehow, this combination of virtues seemed curiously ill-suited to the time.

When Humes won in a landslide, Chadwick saw the victory as one confirming a "clean and honest businessmen's administration." He predicted that, under Humes, "gambling houses will be permitted to run, and subject to restrictions, saloons must be properly conducted, and the social evil will be restricted to certain sections and kept in as good control as possible."[3]

But the halo Chadwick bestowed on Humes came crashing down around the mayor's ears before the month of March ended. Police Chief Reed made no moves to combat a current crime wave; in fact, his department had become demoralized. Outlawed slot machines reappeared in the same old saloons; liquor sales to minors increased. Gaining a conviction on charges relating to any of these matters proved "almost impossible." The center of these operations was in a Humes stronghold, the First Ward.

Complicating the political scenario was Humes's plan to use the Seattle mayoral office as a stepping stone to the Washington governorship in the November 1900 election. To do so, however, the mayor first had to control the King County Republican convention. As a result, Chadwick accused Humes of "using every department of the city government over which he had control to this end." Fellow Republicans suspected that, as governor, Humes would pave the way for the legislature's election of Walla Walla's Levi Ankeny to the U. S. Senate, thereby depriving King County and Seattle of its voice in the nation's capital. In the end, Humes lost out and was forced to turn his attention back to the city's mounting problems. In the ensuing statewide campaign, Humes refused to support Wilson's candidate, State Senator and owner of Seattle's Washington Iron Works, J. H. Frink. This action alienated Wilson, thereby setting the stage for what followed.[4]

Indicative of Chief Reed's tolerance policy—a policy pursued with Humes's backing—was the chief's refusal to investigate race-track gambling at the Madison Park "Coursing Club" (coursing is a sport in which dogs are trained to chase game by sight instead of by smell). Reed went so far as to insist that a special ordinance be passed giving him authority to do so! Speaking for the "legitimate" businesses, Harry Chadwick asked that the tenderloin be restricted because the saloons, in association with all the other vices—gambling and the social evil in particular—were "ballooning" rents as they gravitated uptown.[5]

After the November 1900 general election, the City Council, now under fire from the *P-I* for its tolerance attitude, finally passed a resolution, by a five to five vote, to investigate vice conditions. The problem Seattle faced was readily apparent: "Thieves and pick-pockets, burglars, toughs, thugs, etc., abound everywhere. Gambling houses are connected by staircases with saloons. . . Boys are often seen in saloons and gambling houses." Reed was forced to resign and one of Humes's "strongest" campaign workers, William L. Meredith, replaced him and began enforcing the law with alacrity, targeting the operations of John Considine (Meredith had worked earlier on the city's police force where he had encountered Considine). He had even quit the force and left Seattle for Spokane with Considine during the depths of the depression that followed the Panic of 1893, a time when a closed town policy was in effect. Meredith returned to Seattle in 1899 and rejoined the police department as a detective. Later, Considine accused him of a double-cross and Meredith was demoted to a desk job. Consequently, when Meredith became chief of police a showdown was in the works.

Unfortunately for Meredith, he found himself trapped in the political crossfire within the Republican Party. The feud broke out after the *P-I*'s Wilson turned against Humes when the latter refused to support Wilson's gubernatorial candidate at the King County party convention. The *P-I* also attacked Meredith for his enforcement policy, thereby siding with Considine, who was also preparing his own counterattack. (Considine controlled a decisive bloc of votes in the Fourth Ward.)[6]

Before the Council's investigating committee, Considine admitted to having given bribes to the police in return for their allowing his saloons to be used as hangouts for "thugs and thieves." Throughout the hearings, the *P-I* suppressed Meredith's testimony against Considine, hammering hard on the young chief, seeking to get at Humes through him. The *Times*, in the spirit of the age, took the opposite tack, concentrating on testimony damaging to Considine. Finally, on June 21, the Council committee reported its findings to Mayor Humes, recommending that Meredith (and a detective named Charles Wappenstein) be dismissed for accepting bribes and providing police protection. Humes obliged. Soon, events took an ugly turn.[7]

A vengeful Meredith acquired a sawed-off shotgun and other armament. But before he could use them against his intended target, he received a note from Considine. Considine demanded that Meredith apologize in public for libelously accusing him of impregnating female contortionist Mamie Jenkins. Considine pointed out that the doctor attending the young woman had provided an affidavit attesting that the malady she suffered was really a rupture, not a pregnancy.

Meredith became even more inflamed. On June 25 he stalked Considine, waiting for him at the Yesler and Occidental cable-car crossing. Seeing the Considine brothers enter the Guy Drugstore on First Avenue, Meredith took after them, delivering a poorly aimed shotgun blast at John, who called to brother Tom for help. Within ninety seconds the feud ended: Meredith was dead, shot through the heart after Tom Considine had fractured his skull. John, suffering from a buckshot wound, was immediately arrested and charged with premeditated murder. The *Argus* claimed in July that other newspapers were joining it in laying blame for these events on the *P-I*. Chadwick had no doubt that Meredith had been murdered since he had been shot after being beaten senseless: Meredith was, the *Argus* editor declared, "hounded into his grave by as low a gang of political tricksters and cowards as ever polluted . . . any city in the world." The *Tacoma Ledger* agreed. At Considine's November trial, the jury accepted the defense's argument of "continuous struggle," and acquitted him. The *P-I* gloried in the defeat of Mayor Humes; Blethen sarcastically alleged it might now be open season on police chiefs.[8]

A decade later, when Burton J. Hendrick covered the 1911 mayoral recall campaign for *McClure's Magazine*, he noted that the restricted district had originated under Humes, and:

> Thus there arose in Seattle a small coterie of tenderloin capitalists—men who cultivated vice intensively and organized it in a way to wring from it the largest profits . . . [which,

according to a recent report of the Federal Immigration Commission, made] Seattle . . . one of the headquarters of the white slave trade.[9]

Humes had paved the way.

Following Meredith's death, the mayor appointed John L. Sullivan as the new chief. In the meantime, Considine steadily moved his box-houses above the deadline without police opposition; at the Lake Washington park resorts (Madison, Leschi, and Madrona) liquor continued to be sold illegally—the City Council refused Chadwick's advice to bring the practice under control through licensing.

That Humes's administration found favor for continuing these policies was underscored when Republicans nominated him to serve a third term. Even the high-toned *Argus* endorsed him, if for no other reason than his election would mean "defeat of the corrupt railroad ring who have attempted to dictate in their interests the politics of the city and the state." This barb was aimed at the *P-I's* John L. Wilson who opposed the *Argus's* favorite for United States senator, Harold Preston, who, in turn, wanted to bring the railroads under regulatory control. When Humes was reelected, Chadwick delighted in the symbolic defeat of Wilson and the railroad lobby; meanwhile Humes continued his open town policy unabated.[10]

By 1903, the City Council even issued saloon licenses above the deadline to Pike Street applicants. Next came the boxes to accommodate the inescapable social evil and the inevitable police protection. A subsequent grand jury investigation turned up enough evidence to implicate the mayor, as well as Police Chief Sullivan, but it was the latter who was forced out. When the prosecuting attorney was asked why he did not indict Sullivan, he contended that since Humes had been exonerated he could not sustain charges against the mayor's subordinate. Sullivan's successor, Chief Delaney, while doing relatively well, was advised to look uptown where "dens of vice [are being used] as recruiting stations for the [criminal and vicious] classes from the lower part of town."[11]

An inevitable backlash occurred in the wake of the grand jury investigation, leading to the election of the strait-laced Richard A. Ballinger in 1904. Ballinger promised to close the "blind pigs" in the parks. This promise overcame Harry Chadwick's reservations about the candidate's backing "by certain railroad interests"—the "saloon interests" had gone too far for the *Argus* editor's taste.[12]

5

Early Municipal
Ownership Movement

Public Power Forces Coalesce

Seattle's rapid diversification and growth after 1890 were of sufficient scale in and of themselves to cause serious social and political dislocation; but, it is important to remember that the years around the turn of the century were characterized by national upheaval, as well. Most significant among events of the time was the catastrophic depression that gripped the nation from 1893 to 1896. During those lean years Seattle lost nearly half of its residents to migration, only to see its population soar after the 1897 gold rush.

There were, however, myriad other forces beyond the city's limits that shaped Seattle's future. Modern corporations, for example, began to take shape after the American Civil War; they quickly developed techniques to mobilize capital efficiently and on a hitherto unimagined scale. Economic power became concentrated in these large business enterprises and in the trusts that managed them. Monopolies were generated that formed symbiotic alliances with political machines at all levels of government. "Muckrakers" (an epithet fastened on them by Theodore Roosevelt) like Lincoln Steffens, Ida Tarbell, and Burton J. Hendrick investigated these questionable practices and prominently exposed the corruption they uncovered.

Much ammunition for reform came from the Muckrakers' investigations. In the Pacific Northwest, as in the northern tier of states west of the Great Lakes (particularly in Wisconsin) opposition was aroused against state government control by the railroad lobby and the lumber barons. At the municipal level, in Seattle, franchises granted by the City Council to railroads and utility corporations came under suspicion—inspired in part by the weekly exposes by the *Argus*'s Harry Chadwick. The bitter partisanship of the city's three dailies also added kindling to his fire.

The manner in which utilities franchises were acquired and managed illustrates the complex financial arrangements of the time. Almost invariably the utilities became appendages of holding companies. Within these larger organizations, non-operating companies could issue stocks based on the earning capacity of only one or two operating companies. This practice became known as "pyramiding."

Stone and Webster Management Corporation of Boston, Massachusetts, presided over just such an operation. It owned and managed several transportation and electrical utilities in western Washington on the basis of franchises obtained from the various municipalities they served. The parent corporation made money by charging subsidiaries for engineering and financial services rendered; electrical rates were, of course, set exclusively by Stone and Webster. As a result, the corporation continually faced charges of corrupting city councils to gain monopolies, of failing to comply with franchise terms, and of excluding competition. In addition, charges for electrical rates and service by Stone and Webster's subsidiary, the Seattle Electric Company, were a constant source of customer complaints.

Reformers, including those in Seattle, soon concluded that, if stricter city-council regulation was beyond possibility because of Stone and Webster's political influence, then public ownership of utilities might provide a better answer.

The *Argus* played a leading role in supporting these actions; the paper was joined by the *Star*. *Argus* editor Harry Chadwick, subsequently accused both the *Times* and *P-I* of being "tied, body and soul" to "certain corporations," that wanted to eliminate the municipal power plant from competition with the company.

When a Populist governor and legislature finally came to power in Washington in 1896, little of their reformist platform was passed into law. They were unable to create a state railroad commission even though such action occupied the highest place on the Populist agenda. As the effects of the 1893-1896 depression diminished, voters became disillusioned with Populism. In the next election, Republicans regained control of the state legislature and were able to frustrate Governor John Rogers's feeble efforts to establish a railroad commission. Concurrent with the Republican resurgence, Seattle and the state experienced a return to general prosperity to which the Klondike gold rush added a special tonic. But such a sudden spurt of economic growth only accentuated the need to do something about the plight of the city's utilities.

In other words, Seattle's reform antecedents are to be found in events occurring in the decade following the Great Fire of 1889. Within a year of that event, civic leaders were trying to locate a reliable water source, first buying the facilities of a supplier, the Spring Hill Water Company, which pumped water from, then-pristine, Lake Washington to a Beacon Hill reservoir. Not content with this lake-water resource, City Engineer Benezette Williams had a survey run south of the city to Swan Lake on the Cedar River. While public officials appeared to pay little attention to Williams's survey data, E. H. Ammidown representing a group of Boston banks used information gleaned from the investigation to file a homestead claim above the city's proposed intake in 1893. Using information taken from the survey, the banks planned to run a pipeline from the Cedar River to the city limits at Hanford Street; on the basis of this scheme they planned to negotiate a contract for the sale of waters to the Seattle Power Company. Accordingly, they made an offer to the city in 1895.

For a time, the banks' plan seemed to be the only way for Seattle to acquire Cedar River water during the 1893-1896 depression. But then the Supreme Court ruled, three to two, in a Spokane case (*Winston vs Spokane*, 1895) that a city could issue bonds based on liens against revenue from water projects, and that general funds could be exempted from potential levies to pay off investors. This decision prompted the Seattle City Council to draw up and pass a new water ordinance, only to see it vetoed by the mayor. The issue was next submitted to the electorate in the form of $1.25 million bond issue. On December 10, 1895, voters approved it, 2,656 to 1,665, with "substantial and prominent citizens" opposing the action either because they had invested in the company or because they objected to public ownership. But then Seattle faced the dilemma of how to sell its water bonds in a depressed economy, particularly on the basis of a shaky three-to-two, supreme court decision. Matters were complicated further by the fact that bankers in general were opposed to municipal ownership schemes.

To strengthen the marketability of its bonds, the council sent a committee to meet with the 1897 Washington Legislature. These lobbyists were successful in getting a bill passed authorizing the issuance of revenue bonds. Fortuitously, success in Olympia was followed by the discovery of gold in Alaska and by the subsequent flow of revenue into the city's coffers; Seattle was now on its way to controlling its own water supply. But this control had yet to pass through a succession of ordeals, the first of which involved the city in a struggle between Snoqualmie Falls Power Company (SFPC) and the Union Electric Company (successor to the Seattle Power Company) for a monopoly of the city's electric power.

The Snoqualmie Falls Power Company had applied for an electrical franchise as early as 1898, expecting to be given the same generous terms as its competitor, Union Electric. (Union Electric's terms included no rate regulations and no payments to the city). Instead, the Snoqualmie Falls Power franchise required payments, prohibited rate discrimination among customers in the same service category, and prevented the company from raising existing rates on its own. This council action caused the *Times* and the *Argus* both to raise the specter of discrimination. Charles Baker, head of the SFPC, went further, charging that a "conspiracy" existed among Union, General Electric, and Stone and Webster to force an agreement with Union Electric, once Baker found that franchise terms inhibited his sale of securities. (In subsequent testimony before a 1903 grand jury Baker's son recalled that council members had solicited bribes from his father, "promising [also] to betray those who had been in the habit of bribing them.")

Although Union Electric essentially had a monopoly, the company needed its rival's hydro source to supplement the coal-fired steam facility for which its Renton mines were operated.

When Seattle Power Company sold its land above the city's planned intake after the 1895 bond issue election, the company purchased land upstream at Cedar Lake; this property was then sold to the Washington Power and Transmission Company, headed by S. Z. Mitchell and W. J. Grambs. Washington Power engineers were Charles Stone and Edwin Webster—*the* Stone and *the* Webster affiliated with Boston banking interests.

Baker and the Snoqualamie Falls Power Company tried to thwart this move by enjoining Seattle from contracting with the WPTC. But the City Council took offence, threatening to cancel the SFPC franchise. As this part of the struggle came to a head in August 1899, City Engineer Thomson recommended that Seattle should acquire Cedar Lake; a resolution was passed, followed by an ordinance on January 31, 1900, forcing the WPTC to sell its lands to the city. Baker, while seeming to win out, nevertheless contracted with the Union Electric Company for the sale of its power, thereby giving the latter a de facto monopoly over the

Seattle's electricity business. By the end of 1900 Union Electric changed its name to the Seattle Electric Company. The street railways were a part of the transaction.

The city's street railways presented Seattle with a special dilemma, but one that was eventually solved by consolidation of existing lines. One compelling reason for Seattle's street railway predicament lay in the random pattern of suburban development. When owners of real estate subdivided properties to sell lots, they needed to guarantee access to downtown. To make good on their promises, they induced some interested individual or company to build a streetcar line. But all too often these lines would sink into receivership when outlying population densities necessary to provide ridership and profitability did not come up to muster.

More than a dozen of these independent lines operated under city granted franchises in the 1890s. And during the depression of the mid-1890s, most of them were compelled to use maintenance capital to operate. This practice led to further deterioration of what were already poorly constructed trolley systems.

Into the picture stepped Jacob Furth, applying in April 1899 for a forty-year franchise to consolidate four such streetcar lines. Furth's backers were none other than Stone and Webster, this time representing two Eastern banking firms, Lee, Higginson and Company and Kidder, Peabody and Company. In addition, Stone and Webster held General Electric securities issued earlier to pay for equipment purchased by the companies in question. On May 12, 1899, escrow deeds were signed for the original four companies and two others, the Madison Street Cable Railway and the Seattle Traction Company. On March 9, 1900, a blanket forty year franchise was granted to Furth and his partner J. D. Lowman. The agreement covered approximately twenty-two routes, many of which only fed trunk lines; one problem here lay in the fact that, under franchise terms, no free transfers from one line to another were to be given.

A citizens' Committee of 100 tried unsuccessfully to block the agreement; members went so far as to have the University of Washington's J. Allen Smith argue their case before the City Council. Smith was sufficiently persuasive to get the council to shorten the life of the franchise to thirty-five years, to require free transfers, and to allow a twenty-five percent reduction in ticket purchase prices in lots of 100 or more. Further inhibitions were placed on the franchise by requiring that the council regulate fares and that minimum wage scales for employees be established (but wages would remain notoriously low). The new firm acceded to these demands and was incorporated as the Seattle Electric Company under Furth, Thomas Burke, Maurice McMicken, and three other prominent citizens.

As to the quality of service under the new arrangement, if there were improvements, *Argus* writers did not recognize them. The paper regularly ridiculed the SEC, and pointed to the City Council's probable collusion with the company. Chadwick claimed in January 1902: "The whole system is rotten to the core. . . . [It needs] complete revision." Overcrowding, erratic service, accidents, open cars even in winter still characterized operations. "This is not what the Seattle Electric Company promised when they were given their present franchise," Chadwick declared. Pussyfooting by the council in enforcing franchise terms was then charged; accusations of special privilege were raised later, when the council granted the company an exclusive franchise over the Westlake route in 1905.

The outcry against this action from north-end organizations was so loud and strenuous that a common-user clause was finally inserted into the agreement. Still, charges of favoritism were raised again in 1905 when well-known developer, James A. Moore, applied for a streetcar franchise; the resulting document was so loaded with conditions and clauses that operating the proposed line would have resulted in serious financial loss.

By 1902, it appeared that Stone and Webster had all but achieved its monopoly of Seattle's electrical business. However, this situation would last only until the city developed its own hydroelectric generating capacity, first on the Cedar River and later on the Skagit River. The municipal ownership struggle that accompanied these activities continued throughout this early period. But events in Seattle were, however, a part of a larger, nationwide process that tended in the same direction.[1]

The Electrical Industry Presses for State Regulation

The National Electric Light Association (NELA) was the electrical industry's trade association. As such, it aimed to set industry wide policy by consensus where possible and to serve as the industry's principal political lobbyist. NELA leaders, foremost of whom was Chicago utilities magnate, Samuel Insull, viewed the municipal ownership movement as an anathema. He succeeded, during the first decade of the century, in convincing a majority of the organization's members that state regulation was preferable to local control. Douglas Anderson, in his *Regulatory Politics and Electric Utilities*, convincingly documents the NELA campaign for state regulation as the best way of opposing "home rule." Insull saw the need to eliminate competition if utilities were to attract capital at low interest rates. State regulation would, he believed, offer exclusive franchise protection at a small price. The price came in the form of public regulation; the great benefit was that regulation would not be centered in localities served by the utilities in question.

Insull began his campaign within the NELA as early as 1898, but soon encountered strenuous opposition from those who equated regulation with confiscation. By 1904 he managed to form the Committee on Municipal Ownership within the larger organization; this body became the Committee on Public Policy in 1906; the reformed committee's object came to be the formulation of a doctrine that advocated public regulation as the only alternative to public ownership. Douglas Anderson considers a 1907 Committee on Public Policy report to contain NELA's basic philosophy regarding government regulation. The document stated:

> Municipal ownership is demanded largely because of the absence of proper regulation and control. Public regulation and control, if efficient, removes the necessity or excuse for municipal ownership. . . . If public regulation shall fail to establish a good understanding between the corporations operating public utilities and the customers of those corporations, we shall inevitably have a revival of the cry for municipal ownership. . . . The practical question is not whether there is to be such regulation and control as it is what the nature and form of them are to be.

As to the nature and form of control, the Subcommittee on Regulation and Control said, "That if state commissions be constituted, they should be appointed in that manner which will give them the greatest freedom from local and political influences. . . ."

The National Civic Federation, which included many industry representatives, as well as key labor figures and professionals, conducted parallel investigations on private and public utilities. Professor John R. Commons of the University of Wisconsin, was one such member. And when Governor Robert La Follette asked him to draft a bill for establishing a state regulatory commission in 1907, Commons incorporated most of the federation's recommendations into the Wisconsin bill. When his bill became law, it then served as model legislation for other states. In 1911 Washington became the twelfth state to enact a law regulating electrical utilities. Like most of the other states, Washington already had a railroad commission; therefore it simply enlarged that body's mandate to encompass all utilities and changed its name accordingly.

While promoting state regulatory commissions as a means to

counter the municipal ownership movement, NELA and its members also continued to use direct economic action to promote their cause. In a July 6, 1908, letter to James J. Hill's state political chief (the notorious J. D. Farrell, who was then in Chicago), R. H. Thomson, indicated his suspicion of such activity. He complained about the trouble Seattle was having in trying to sell its bonds: "... we have met with practically one response: 'this is not the class of bonds which well established bond houses care to handle.'" Seeing no good reason for this situation in the face of the excellent security the city offered, Thomson asked Farrell to inquire with Chicago brokers Harris and Halsey as to the real reasons behind these rejections. Thomson suspected a municipal bond boycott and sought to challenge brokers on this score.[1]

Seattle: Microcosm in the Macrocosm

Agitation grew in Seattle for the generation of electric power from the Cedar River after that facility had been completed in 1901. Added impetus came in March of that year when the City Council refused a Snoqualmie Power Company franchise to transmit power to the city. The *Argus* laid blame for that action on Councilman Thomas Navin, since he had a coal contract with the Seattle Electric Company. Even the Chamber of Commerce claimed that a city-owned plant could provide cheaper power and light than the Seattle Electric Company.

Businessmen generally resented what they saw as the monopolistic exactions of a "Boston syndicate." Indicative of the business community's hostility to the franchise was the formation of the Seattle Manufacturers Association (SMA) in 1900 to promote local industry and to combat labor unions. (One of the association's leaders was future City Councilman Oliver Erickson. At this time, Erickson began pressing for lower utility rates, an activity that would later characterize his distinguished career on the council.) The Seattle Manufacturers Association contended that the city should compete with the absentee corporation to drive down rates and to improve and extend services.

This same sentiment among businessmen and professionals, who were at the time excluded from Seattle's entrenched elite, led to the formation of the Municipal Ownership League, a coalition that had as its goal the breaking of the electrical franchise monopoly. In the city election of 1902 the league finally was able to get a proposition on the ballot authorizing construction of a generating plant at Cedar Falls. The *Argus* claimed, "No more important question is to come before the people ... than that of a municipal lighting plant." Chadwick accused both the *P-I* and *Times* of "allowing it to go by default"—the former opposed it outright. As to the Republican Party, the *Argus* carried a reminder in a front page box, in which article five of the party's platform favored such a plant. The proposition won overwhelmingly by 6,697 votes.[1]

Then, in August 1902, the City Council granted a franchise to the SEC to place its downtown wires underground before the city could do likewise. Chadwick saw company influence in this action. For his part, R. H. Thomson was accused of delaying tactics on dam construction. Chadwick had good reasons for his suspicions: by December, Thomson's preliminary surveys had not yet been completed and no indication was given that electricity would be distributed for more than street lighting. Further, Thomson's decision to market bonds locally was seen to be just another form of procrastination. If, in Chadwick's mind, these actions were not sufficient to show the city engineer to be "hand in glove" with the Seattle Electric Company, he found added proof in August 1903. In that month, when funds were finally available for construction, Thomson awarded the contract for generating equipment to the highest bidder, General Electric—a company linked financially to the SEC. The lowest bidder, a Seattle firm that had been manufacturing similar machinery for some years, was rejected out of hand because Thomson claimed to be unfamiliar with the business. Notwithstanding these problems, Seattle City Light began transmitting power for street illumination on January 10, 1905.[2]

But these moves against the municipal ownership of electrical power in Seattle were merely the beginning of an ongoing battle that City Light would face in the coming decades. Almost immediately, in August 1905, the *Argus* claimed the *Times* had joined the *P-I* in opposing municipal ownership: "[They were] tied, body and soul" to "certain corporations" which were trying to get the mayor and City Council to have the lighting department sell street lighting and that for public buildings below cost in order to force the department to charge higher residential rates to compensate for the loss. By June 1906 the *Times* argued that the "city will soon be selling at a loss"—variations on this theme were played like a tattoo in the years ahead. Despite this opposition, though, public ownership approval was registered in successive bond issues for expanding the Cedar River power project in 1906, 1908, and 1910.

While Seattle proper offered discomfiting resistance to the Seattle Electric Company's advances in 1904, two outlying communities that would soon be part of the city took the opposite approach. To the north, Ballard residents were disgusted with the independent Ballard Electric Company. The city engineer invited the SEC to apply for a "reasonable" franchise. Company officials forewarned the Engineer that the Seattle Electric Company ". . . had no money available to pay anybody for their vote or influence" (referring to the City Council). He was also told the SEC ". . . would accept no franchise that was loaded up with restrictions and conditions. . . ."

To the south, along the Duwamish River, South Park wanted a railway extension so badly that Seattle Electric Company officials ". . . got their promise that if we apply for a franchise they would not load it up with restrictions, would give us anything we asked, and would make the time limit [for construction] . . . two years." The difference between Seattle and its two neighbors lay in the fact that the bigger city threatened to take over the private company; Ballard and South Park were not in positions to consider such an undertaking.

City Light already had forced the Seattle Electric Company to reduce rates drastically. The mere threat of City competition caused the SEC to drop rates in October 1904 from twenty cents per kilowatt hour to twelve. Residential rates were set at eight cents per kilowatt hour and would remain fairly stable until 1911. Customers also were steadily lost to the city: 197 from October through December 1906; 233 for the period from January through May 1907.

Voters, disgusted with the seeming indifference to their needs, eagerly approved a 1904 bond issue, apparently agreeing that a city-operated utility would at least establish a yardstick for service and efficiency to goad the Stone and Webster operators. But the years ahead would be troubled ones until the Skagit site was acquired in 1918 despite bitter opposition and Stone and Webster chicanery.

By 1910, street lighting, instead of being a source of embarrassment, became a source of civic pride—"the best lighted city in the United States." City Light had gained more customers than the Seattle Electric, although distribution favored the latter because of its concentration in the business areas of the city; the company also retained sixty-five to seventy-five per cent of the power customers. However, of real and symbolic importance to residential consumers were rate reductions forced by City Light competition.

6

Industrial Relations

Early Labor Activism

Home rule was not the only issue Seattleites fought over during the early years of the twentieth century. Yet it can be seen, in many ways, as the framework in which entrenched downtown interests consistently structured their opposition to municipal ownership and other movements for change and reform. In contrast, municipal ownership proponents found support, not only among exasperated businessmen and frustrated residents of neighborhoods that lacked basic services, but also among the ranks of organized labor.

During the 1890s, labor union activism in Seattle grew apace with political activism. As with advocates for municipal ownership, labor organizers and other liberal or radical political activists confronted the corporate power structure that had become entrenched nationally and regionally after the American Civil War.

By the end of the century, business leaders found they could take advantage of provisions contained in the Sherman Anti-Trust Act of 1890 to guard against union organizing. Their efforts were aided by compliant court systems that ruled consistently against labor by enjoining unions from picketing during strikes; strikes themselves were often found to be illegal restraints of commerce. Executives felt threatened nevertheless; many saw union activity as a first step toward social revolution. As capitalists, they simply could not accept the notion that a politically active working class was a legitimate expression of countervailing economic power in a pluralistic society.

Despite these formidable obstacles—corporate, economic, and political power, an unsympathetic judiciary, and an appropriately riveted ideology—unions continued to exist. In good times, when workers were typically in short supply, unions thrived. But these organizations were threatened whenever there was a labor surplus.

The depression following the Panic of 1893 further discouraged labor's organizing activity in the Pacific Northwest. In fact, the American Federation of Labor did not penetrate the labor movement in Washington until after 1900 because most workers in the region were unskilled and were clearly not of interest to the craft-oriented Eastern organization.

During these years before the AFL arrived in the region, the Western Central Labor Union (WCLU) had been formed in 1888 from remnants of the Knights of Labor and several small miners' unions. Like the AFL, the WCLU was craft-oriented, decrying both industrial unionism and political activism. By 1900, proponents of regional craft organizations predominated over factions that advocated political partisanship and industry wide unions.

The WCLU did not, however, completely eschew politics. When, for example, the 1897 Populist platform was not enacted by Washington's legislature, the union joined with other organizations to form a lobbying group called the State Labor Congress. Three years later, in 1900, the WCLU established its own weekly newspaper, the *Union Record*. These actions so alarmed a number of Seattle-area employers that they formed the Seattle Metal Trades Association to counter the apparent worker threat. It was clear from these and other actions that employers wanted to protect their prerogatives for dealing with employees as individuals; they did not want to deal with them as members of a group. Such a policy was the nearest businessmen could come to maintaining absolute authority in the workplace under the U. S. Constitution.

A statement made by State Labor Commissioner William Blackman at a 1903 Chamber of Commerce gathering to commemorate Seattle's founding illustrates the general sentiment that city business leaders had toward unionism at the time. Blackman, who later mediated a longshoremen's strike, declared:

> "... now all the trades are organized and a large percentage of working men and women are within the ranks. Today Seattle has about seventy-five different labor organizations, with a membership of between six and seven thousand. . . . The workers, through their organizations, advocate fair wages for a day's work, they advocate shortening the hours of labor so that they may improve their minds in keeping with the

progress of the age. They are striving in turn to save from their earnings something for a home. Statistics gathered by the State Labor Bureau show that two-sixths of the wage earners own their own homes. This being the condition, such citizens must be given credit for being a factor in the community. The workers are taking an interest in legislation. . . . They are interested in passing good laws for the upbuilding of our government and the preservation of the home. They have learned that the strike and the boycott are fast growing to be a thing of the past. . . ."

That the chamber sought a spokesman known to be sympathetic with labor shows how indulgent they were of the worker activities at this early date. It would not be long, however, before Seattle's chamber would become as dedicated a foe of organized labor as the newly founded National Association of Manufacturers, which made the open shop its top priority.

And as for paying workers enough for saving to buy homes or for shortening hours enough to allow time for self-education, individual employers might consider such policies, but only at the risk of losing out in the marketplace. As it was, encouraging organized labor to influence legislation was not in line with even the most advanced thought of the Chamber.

The sharp resurgence of union-organizing activity in the early twentieth century seemed to threaten the Seattle business community's new-found prosperity. Seeking a broader base to counter these perceived threats, the recently established Seattle Manufacturers' Association invited the Chamber of Commerce to join the association's Citizens Alliance. The chamber wavered, offering instead, a resolution at its August 8, 1901, meeting calling for the creation of a sixty member "congress": thirty members representing the "labor union" and thirty from "associations employing labor." The proposal was tabled and the chamber remained neutral; it did not want to endorse the open shop principle as had been requested by the association.

Adding to employers' fears at the time was the formation of the Socialist Party of Washington (SPW) in 1900. In the view of labor historian Jonathan Dembo, the SPW's philosophy and program appealed to new immigrants, individuals who fled governmental repression in eastern and southern Europe only to be confronted by a seemingly hostile American government that appeared to be a political extension of the employers.

Conversely, the AFL was not interested in the new immigrants because they favored forms of unionism that would embrace them, industry wide. Few could gain entry to an AFL craft, given that organization's fixation on job protection for its members and its disinterest in organizing unskilled workers.

Indicative of the tension within labor's ranks was the action taken by the State Labor Congress in 1902 to form the Washington State Federation of Labor (WSFL); this move effectively isolated industrial unionists. Comparable factionalism also occurred in the Socialist Party where the radical "Reds" stood opposed to the more conservative "Yellows."

While the SPW endured its internal ideological struggles, the WSFL allied itself with the Grange, middle-class reformers, and often with the Washington State Federation of Women's Clubs. This coalition worked together to have several pieces of reform legislation passed in 1903—in particular a child labor law, an eight-hour day statute for employees on public projects, and an initiative law. This WSFL alliance with the Grange was unique; but to the Grange's conservative leadership it was disquieting, so much so that it caused an ongoing dispute between the state and national organizations throughout the period.[1]

These unsettling labor successes inspired Jacob Furth, president of Stone and Webster's Seattle Electric Company, to form another Citizens' Alliance in 1904, this time to "oppose the spread of the union shop, boycotts, and picketing"—as though the courts were not already providing adequate protection—and to counter labor's growing legislative threat. Moran Brothers Shipyard and several other companies pledged money to the effort. The first target was to lift the union boycott of an eating establishment, the Bismarck Cafe, in November 1904; then the alliance set about influencing the 1905 legislative session. At the level of actual company operations, strategies and suitable tactics were also set in motion to combat unionism.

At the Seattle Electric Company, for instance, infiltration of union leadership and the use of "inside" men as informers played a role. (It would be safe to assume that other large employers used similar tactics. All joined the Employers' Association of Washington when it was formed in 1912.) A "diary" entry for April 14, 1904, (presumably written by SEC manager H. F. Grant for Stone and Webster officials in Boston) records: "Saw Scott of Trainmen's Union No. 1." the entry describes how Scott complained of the pressure he was under for not taking in new union members. To these grumblings the diarist responded: "I told him not to worry about this as the course he was pursuing was to my mind the only proper one at this time. He had a nucleus of an organization and immediately on trouble showing up it would be a very easy matter to get to work and forestall it." These and other practices, including bribery and subversion, continued throughout the period. In the case of the jitney drivers, the company gained control and subsequently destroyed this union after an officer in their employment was elected to a leadership position.[2]

Solicitous city officials also helped the business community's cause. At one point, Mayor Richard Ballinger (future Commissioner of the General Land Office and Secretary of Interior) invited Seattle Electric Company representatives to his office and told them:

> ... that he wished to create an emergency force which could be called upon in time of strikes, riots, or other disturbances ... his idea being that the time to stop disturbances of that kind is at the inception.... We had a very pleasant discussion of these conditions and suggested improvements and also regarding new regulations which are to be put in force. The mayor expressed himself willing to appoint as special policemen without pay such men as I might recommend among our employees, who would serve in that capacity on and about the premises of the company, but he would wish these men to be passed upon by Chief Delaney before licensing. I agreed that this was right.[3]

For perspective, it should be noted that in 1900 only two percent of Seattle's labor force had joined a union, and those workers who had were of a conservative bent, seeking job protection once they had achieved a satisfactory pay scale and decent working conditions. Not until 1910 would union membership reach three percent. Nonetheless, business leaders girded for a showdown.

To enhance its effectiveness at organizing workers and to combat employer opposition, the Western Central Labor Union reorganized in 1905, becoming the Central Labor Council of Seattle and Vicinity (SCLC). Its constitution provided for the creation of industrially organized trade section committees, stopping short of authorizing industrial unions. Sections were established for building, metal, maritime, printing, amusement, brewery (later renamed provisions trades after prohibition was established in the state in 1916), and miscellaneous trades.

Throughout this period, the SCLC supported industrial unionism, vainly trying to compel its acceptance by the leadership of the American Federation of Labor. The most militant advocate for this course of action (and also a stern prohibitionist) was James A. Duncan, a machinist and secretary of the SCLC. As a result, the SCLC proved a constant source of embarrassment to Washington State Federation of Labor leadership whenever it dealt with the

AFL. Nonetheless, SCLC leadership remained conservative and drawn from the crafts where older immigrants were still dominant. There were, however, exceptions, such as Socialists Hulet Wells and *Union Record* editor Harry Ault.

When evaluating union activity in the early twentieth century it is important to note that, before 1916, statewide unemployment averaged about five percent. This constituted a labor pool that employers could count on when cutting wages and combatting unionization. Coupled with this general unemployment was a surge to the ranks of the unemployed that occurred regularly each winter in Pacific Northwest cities when logging camps and fish canneries closed and when harvest ended; in Seattle this number ranged between 10,000 and 15,000 workers before 1916.[4]

Labor Legislation: A Common Ground Found

That the State of Washington assumed national leadership in enacting and enforcing labor legislation was due to a conjunction of some special circumstances. For example, relatively few women and children were employed in manufacturing in the state; between the years 1899 to 1909 children constituted less than one percent of the manufacturing labor force; women made up about four percent of the total, compared to a national average of about twenty percent. Consequently, child and female labor laws received broad support among employer groups, in particular the conservative Seattle Civic Federation.

Another factor contributing to the enactment of this reform legislation was the high accident rate in the state's timber and mining industries. These accidents led to expensive litigation during the course of which the state supreme court justified the use of police power (over due process) in forcing the employers to assume liability.

The Washington Supreme Court at the time was composed of a majority that had been appointed by Populist Governor John Rogers (1896-1901) and his successor Henry McBride (1901-1904); it approved all labor legislation passed between 1901 and 1920. And since employers could not rely on the courts to relieve them of liability, the only parties benefiting from litigation seemed to be lawyers and liability insurance companies, which charged ever-higher rates.

While the Washington State Federation of Labor led the fight for legislation to protect workers, it was joined by other reform groups. Loosely to begin with, they worked together as the Joint Legislative Committee (JLC), from 1907 to 1919—the core of this organization was the labor federation itself, the Grange, and the Farmers Union; usually these groups gained support from the State Federation of Women's Clubs and the Seattle Ministerial Federation. In a number of instances employer groups also joined with them.

Much emphasis must be given to the fact that Seattle (and Washington as a whole) had drawn together a fresh middle class that had not yet developed a stake in sustaining the inequalities and iniquities that existed in the older cities of the nation's East and Midwest. As it advanced its own welfare and moral values, this middle class leaned toward to a more humane vision of society that gave support to a whole range of civic improvements. That members of this social stratum were active voters must not be overlooked; in the end, they proved to be the backbone of Seattle's municipal ownership movement.

In 1901, the Seattle Manufacturers' Association joined with the Western Central Labor Union to force the passage of a ten-hour-day law for women, which was upheld by the state supreme court in the *State vs Buchanan* decision (1902). This success was duplicated in the passage of a factory inspection law in 1903, and then a child labor law. The former resulted in the reduction of accidents caused by defective and unguarded machinery. Nonetheless, litigation increased, mainly in the lumber industry. In a series of "factory act" cases the Washington Supreme Court showed where it stood, beginning with *Hall vs West & Slade Mill Company*. In this case the court decided that employers were liable for industrial accidents when they did not install safeguards to prevent injury. The decision caused such a flood of litigation that the Washington Bar Association established a committee to reform the liability law.

During these years accident-case deliberation consumed about fifty percent of the supreme court's time, despite the fact that only an estimated one injured worker in eleven sued. And despite the fact that workers rarely won these cases, employers had to pay insurance rates that climbed from forty-five cents per $100 payroll in 1905 to $1.50 in 1910. Of the amount paid in premiums, sixty percent went for "administrative costs"; on the other side, lawyers took three-fourths of the award money granted to injured parties. This situation spawned widespread support for the Workmen's Compensation Act of 1911.

Adding to the growth of public sentiment favoring the 1911 act was State Labor Bureau head Charles Hubbard's unwillingness to enforce existing laws. Whereas the first two bureau heads, W. P. C. Adams (1897-1901) and William Blackman (1902-1904) had vigorously applied the statutes, this practice ceased when Albert Mead became governor in 1904; he appointed Hubbard, who held office until 1913. To meet the rising tide of criticism, Governor Marion Hay (1908-1912) appointed Blanche Mason as Assistant Labor Commissioner in 1909 to enforce existing regulations that applied to women and children. By 1911 the chief executive was pressured to remove her from office because of the energy she devoted to this mission.[1]

7

The Framework of
Life in the City

Introduction

At the turn of the century, Seattle was a bustling, thoroughly disorganized town of nearly 100,000—if people merely passing through the city on their way to Alaska were counted. Reputedly there were more saloons downtown than there were retail stores. There was neither housing nor hotel space to accommodate newcomers—neither those preferring to stay nor newcomers. The transient population included, not only those headed for Alaska, but also those who migrated from logging camps and fishing grounds to the city annually between November and March. Many of these temporary residents fitted nicely into Seattle politics, being paid by downtown ward bosses to register and vote according to instructions. This ward system would be replaced by the present, at-large electoral system; the campaign for this reform coincided with the grant of woman suffrage in 1910, a vote they first exercised in the 1911 election, contributing decisively to the recall of Mayor Hiram Gill.[1]

Ground-level transportation was mainly by foot, bicycle, streetcar, or horse-drawn carriage. The primary means of commercial transportation was the horse-drawn wagon. Given Seattle's hilly terrain, it was a form of teamstering that was brutal on drivers and animals alike.

These same hills, while serving as ideal view sites on which to construct residential neighborhoods, inhibited industrial devel-

Special Collections Division, University of Washington Libraries

Figure 5: At top of "Profanity Hill" is the County Courthouse, now occupied by Harborview Medical Center. To its right is shown the City Light plant and Administrative Building. City Hall is in center—the building above and slightly to right of the "Bohemian Beer" sign. Ca. 1906-07.

opment and handicapped the construction of warehouses, office buildings, department stores, and other retail establishments. The University of Washington's ten-acre tract, just a few blocks north of the business district and City Hall, resembled a cow pasture before 1910. It should be noted that, if the city was to accommodate commercial and industrial expansion, something had to be done.

The first decade of the new century was devoted to levelling those major downtown impediments. City Hall was but a ramshackle frame building bordering the "Deadline" to the south. The Deadline was an area where vice and the rackets were concentrated and protected. Uptown from there were to be found the established business and professional buildings, along with hotels, residences, and even schools (most of which survived until 1940). (See Appendix, Age of Dwellings.) Constant dislocation of street transportation was made even worse by the seemingly endless regrading of hills. Some streets were worked over two or three times, while others needing attention were neglected.

Seattle's premiere residential neighborhood was understandably First Hill. But when an area abutting John J. McGilvra's Madi-

Museum of History and Industry

Figure 6: Looking north on 2nd Avenue. Bon Marche on left occupied the block of 1419-1435 2nd Avenue. Moore Theater at far end of street is still in use. Ca. 1910.

son Park property was put on the market in 1900, James A. Moore's Investment Company bought it, then quickly improved it as a large residential area. In 1901, Moore acquired much of Capitol Hill, which the *Argus* touted as the last of the "high-grade resident properties to be platted." High-grade, indeed. No residence costing less than $3,000 would be permitted there—a high value in those days. But no sooner had he put in the sidewalks and asphalt paving than the Seattle Electric Company demolished them in order to lay down street railway tracks.

As to popular entertainment, by 1902, Harry Chadwick could claim that "Seattle is a good theatrical town." Streetcar lines ran to the three Lake Washington parks at the end of Madison Street, at Madrona Park, and from the steep cable car drop at 31st Avenue and Yesler Way to Leschi Amusement Park. That such spots were enormously popular is understandable. Given the limitations imposed by ground transportation, recreation necessarily had to be close at hand, particularly in view of the normal six-day work week.

The Sunday closing of saloons midway through the decade did not sit well with those seeking respite, so "blind pigs" in the

Museum of History and Industry

Figure 7: Pike Place Market, ca. 1910.

various parks flourished, fulfilling a popular demand. Pressure to close these recreational outlets led the *Argus* to plead in 1900 for the establishment of a "summer resort" at Alki Point (at that time reachable only by ferry across Elliott Bay).

The spectacle of uprooted people with money to spend, idling away their time as they passed through the city, the dramatic growth of a permanent population, these things and the city's reputation for loose law enforcement, proved irresistible lures to gamblers, salooners, thugs, pickpockets, thieves, pimps, and prostitutes. They followed the pack to Seattle and found easy pickings there. Gambling was rampant in the saloons, cigar stores, at the Meadows racetrack, at amusement parks, and in the various incorporated clubs where laws against boxing were easily evaded by subterfuge. Prostitution was entangled, not only with the saloon business, but with theater operations, and thievery of the customers. The uncertainty about the way in which it should be controlled, provided many irresistible opportunities for unscrupulous police officials to set up protection rackets.

Added to the widespread police corruption was the basic problem of police organization and administration. There were no precinct stations from which officers could be dispatched in force.

Horse patrolmen in residential neighborhoods were hardly threats to be reckoned with for seasoned burglars; and sending out reinforcements from downtown via streetcar could only have provided comic relief to all but the victims of such crimes. Police stations at Ballard, Georgetown, and other annexed areas of the city did become precinct stations. But within the core area of Seattle and in the newly located suburbs there were none. In fact, people in these locales had to fight continuously for police protection, as well as streetcar, electric, water, and sewage service.

Seattle's Population

Seattle grew from a town with a population of 80,671 in 1900 to become a major city of 237,000 in 1910 and 315,312 in 1920. One way to measure this growth is to compare the city's population increases with those occurring in the Puget Sound ports of Tacoma, about thirty miles to the south, and Everett, thirty miles to the north. Tacoma's 1900 population of 37,714 more than doubled to 83,743 in 1910 and expanded to 96,965 by 1920. Everett had a mere 7,838 residents in 1900; this number rose to 24,814 in 1910 and crept up to 27,644 by 1920.

In terms of a general overview, native-born whites made up about seventy-five percent of Seattle's population throughout this entire period; most migrated to the city from elsewhere in the state. Minnesota, followed by Illinois, Wisconsin, Iowa, and Michigan contributed the largest proportion of the city's population from outside Washington. Of these immigrants, fifty to sixty percent were between the ages of fifteen and forty-five—in the prime of their productive lives. By 1910, an increasing proportion of the populace began to arrive from the Pacific Coast and Mountain states.

In 1910 Seattle ranked twenty-fifth among major cities in the United States in terms of deriving its population from within its own state (16.1 percent); 53.8 percent of the city's people came from other states; and 28.4 percent migrated from foreign countries. By 1920 these percentages were 22.9 percent, 49.7 percent, and 25.7 percent, respectively. (See appendix two for population charts).[1]

Annexation of adjoining urban areas proved to be a major contributor to Seattle's population growth during the period from 1900 to 1910. The construction of street railways to Green Lake, Madison and Madrona parks, and to Queen Anne and Beacon hills, made these areas attractive to members of the city's existing elite, to fresh recruits from the East, and to senior white-collar workers who sought to escape the dense, city core. Real estate promoters and developers eagerly responded to the pressure for residential expansion and proved to be a constant irritant to privately owned utilities because of demands they and their clients generated for more and better service. Frustrations encountered in securing these services lay at the heart of the public ownership movement.

Sex ratios within the city's population reveal a preponderance of males over females during the period from 1890 and 1910, although there was a gradual decline in the percentage of males in the community. While there were 166 males for every 100 females in 1890, by 1910 the ratio fell to 136 to 100. In the twenty to forty age bracket the proportion was 2 to 1 in 1890; it fell to 1.5 to 1 by 1910.

Seattle's total foreign-born population was about 14,000 in 1890, about 22,000 in 1900, and 67,000 in 1910. Of the 156,523 people added to the city's population between 1900 and 1910, 54,851 were born outside the United States. From 1910 to 1920 the number of foreign-born increased to about 80,000. Like native-born residents, these immigrants were in the prime of life.

The fact that the majority of Seattle's foreign-born residents migrated originally from English-speaking countries, or from northern or western Europe, facilitated their assimilation into city life. Most came from Canada; next in number were those from Norway/Sweden, followed by immigrants from England and Scotland. Migration from Ireland remained steady throughout the period; that from Denmark increased from about 620 in 1900 to about 1,900 in 1910. The number of Italian immigrants living in Seattle between 1890 and 1910, about 150 and 3,500 respectively, grew more rapidly than that of any other European ethnic group.

The non-white population in Seattle (including native-born African Americans, Native Americans, and foreign-born Asians) was only 1.8 percent in 1890, and 4.8 percent in 1900, 1910, and 1920. Numerically, Native Americans counted by census-takers constituted the smallest group: only twenty-two in 1900, twenty-four in 1910, and 106 in 1920. Persons of Japanese descent were the most numerous non-white group in 1900 (2,990), while African Americans ranked second, with 406 residents; the number of Seattle's Blacks grew to 2,296 by 1910 and 2,894 by 1920. The tally of residents born in China rose to about 720 in 1910, after declining precipitously in the wake of the anti-Chinese movement and riots of 1885-1886. Residents of Japanese ancestry continued to predominate among the city's non-whites, numbering 6,127 in 1910, and 7,874 by 1920.

The poorest of Seattle's new arrivals settled in the central city, in and around Yesler Way. But once their countrymen established enclaves elsewhere, subsequent newcomers tended to bypass the downtown area and gravitate to these more outlying locales. This pattern held true for Scandinavians in Ballard (a community not annexed to Seattle until 1907).

Ballard became home to Norwegians and Swedes who found work there to which they had been accustomed in their homelands: woodworking and fishing. The other concentration of Scandinavians lay in Seattle's downtown sections where transient laborers and those who worked outside the city in logging camps, mill towns, canneries, in agriculture, and in the maritime trades could find cheap apartment houses and hotels.

Throughout this era of Seattle's expansion and growth, transient, single males and poorly paid blue-collar workers of many nationalities continued to occupy the seedy hotels and rooming and boarding houses, and to frequent the cheap restaurants and entertainments around and south of Yesler Way. This area became the heart of the city's vice district, being sustained in part by the meager earnings of its residents.

A large number of the inexpensive hotels and associated businesses were Japanese-owned, though some were operated by Chinese. Not all of these enterprises were legal; consequently, their owners were particularly vulnerable to "the shakedown" by Seattle police officers, some of whom coveted "skid road" beats to the point of paying superiors for these choice assignments.

While white owners of illicit operations also paid for police protection from arrest and prosecution, Asian and Black businessmen engaged in similar ventures were more readily victimized because of underlying racial attitudes of the day. This peculiar form of racial bias became accentuated as Seattle's central area filled up and whites who could afford to do so, moved out.

The movement outward from the city's core area helped to create new neighborhoods that proved attractive to newcomers. Some of these districts lay outside the city limits, becoming small but mature communities by the time they were annexed. At such times, residents demanded the same kind and quality of services—particularly utilties—that the more populous central city received. Before 1900, many areas north of Lake Union, including Green Lake, Wallingford and the future University District (extending to 85th Street), had been annexed. Residents from these communities would form the North End Federated Clubs as a political constituency favoring municipal ownership of utilities.

To the south, South Park—an area of truck gardens—became

a part of the city in 1905, followed in 1907 and 1910 by West Seattle, Columbia City, and Georgetown. To the north, Ballard, Ravenna, and Laurelhurst were added in 1907. The boundaries created by these additions would remain almost constant until after World War II.

The communities themselves were relatively mature at the time of their annexation. Ballard, for instance, was known as a "city of smoke stacks," having sprouted a number around the Stimson Lumber Mill and near Salmon Bay. By 1910, Ballard's ethnicity had become so pronounced that it became popularly known as "Swedetown," despite the fact that more Norwegians than Swedes lived there. When annexed, Ballard contributed about 17,000 people to the city's numbers. In 1905, the Chamber of Commerce estimated that Rainier Valley and Columbia City each had about 7,000 residents, South Park and Georgetown each had almost 4,000, and West Seattle had about 1,500.

During this expansion, Seattle's population became differentiated along occupational lines in a manner similar to patterns found in other American cities. The upper classes congregated on hilltops, beginning with First Hill (above downtown), then Queen Anne and Capitol hills, Interlaken, the ridge above Lake Washington, and later, Magnolia. Proceeding down from these broad crests, one encountered middle-class homes, then the residences of skilled blue-collar workers.

Skilled and clerical workers moved away from downtown as the city's core became a magnet for unskilled and transient labor. The upper stratum of organized labor and the lower middle class tended to congregate in the city's valleys and flatlands: Montlake, Wallingford, Rainier Valley, and Ballard are examples. By 1910, this geographical-topographical dispersion along occupational lines became relatively stable. There were, however, execptions to these settlement patterns based on class and wealth.

Seattle's earliest Chinese immigrants originally had been enticed from their homeland in Guangdong Province to work on the railroads and as farm laborers. Another ethnic concentration were the Japanese, many of whom had been imported by the Great Northern as construction workers; they were attracted to the general area near the rail terminus, just south of Yesler Way, where the Chinese also had found a partial haven from discrimination—"Chinatown" (after World War II, the International District). Those Japanese workers who migrated from the Sound's mill towns also were attracted to this area, gradually creating a "Japantown." As pointed out above, transient whites, particularly Scandinavians, also found in this area the cheaper lodgings, food, and cultural amenities that they could afford—they also provided the fodder for labor radicalism. Other notable exceptions to ethnic dispersion were Jews, Italians, and Black Americans. Because a significant measure of a society's civility lies in its treatment of newcomers an examination of these specific groups is merited.

Chinese in the City

The anti-Chinese movement that climaxed in the Northwest during the fall of 1885 and winter of 1886 resulted in the decimation of the city's Chinese population. The murder of Chinese hop pickers in Issaquah, which went unprosecuted, and much violence outside Seattle and Tacoma, inspired their flight to these cities for protection. Instead of a safe haven, they encountered mob violence that festered among the large numbers of unemployed whites. This activity was encouraged by members of the Knights of Labor, who turned on the Chinese as scapegoats. (Chinese numbers in King County more than doubled in the 1870-1880 decade from 2,120 to 4,429; and in Seattle from thirty-three in 1870 to 246 by 1880). Their Seattle numbers, never large, grew officially from 359 in 1890 to 438 by 1900, then doubling by 1910, reaching 924, slowly climbing to 1,351 in 1920. However, there was an unmeasured, "floating" population among them, who were hired as seasonal laborers, under contract, to work in fish and fruit canneries, as farm laborers, in the coal mines, and on the railroads (on which most originally worked before completion of the Northern Pacific in 1883, returning to the city between jobs.)[1]

Lew G. Kay, writing as a University of Washington student in 1909, noted that: "Many large business blocks are owned by some of the pioneer Chinese merchants who were shrewd enough to realize the future value of Seattle real estate." Being protected from the rioters of February 1886, these investments became the economic base of the city's Chinese community, centered around Washington and Main streets, between Second and Sixth avenues— the city's "Chinatown." The *Argus* admiringly drew attention to the opening of the Pekin Restaurant in 1909, it being "operated by a syndicate of wealthy Chinese."

This area became the nucleus, as well, for subsequent Asian immigrants, and a temporary home, often, for fresh Scandinavian immigrants and transient whites. Here were found Chinese foodstuffs and groceries, restaurants, import houses, antique and curio shops, hotels, laundries, tailor shops, among which tongs operated vice rackets, lotteries, and gambling, usually under some kind of police protection, but for a price. In a real sense, the Chinese served—though their social organization was unique—as role models for those Asians who later migrated to the area to try their luck at acceptance. This was inherently so because later Asian migrants took the place of Chinese as laborers after passage of the Chinese exclusion acts in the 1880s.[2]

One of these Chinese "pioneers" was a true sojourner, Chin Gee Hee. As a contract laborer he had worked in a wide array of jobs since 1875, from which he accumulated funds sufficient to enable him to invest in a store—the Wa Chong Store—and later the Quong Tuck Company (which was still operating in 1929). After the Seattle Fire of 1889 Chin Gee Hee was the first to build a new permanent building, the Canton Building. In 1905 he returned to China to become a railroad builder himself, perhaps inspired by his friend, Thomas Burke, whose many commercial ties led Chin to purchase most of his supplies from Seattle firms. Upon completion of his first railroad in 1917 the Seattle Chamber of Commerce, thus gratified, named him an honorary member.[3]

Chinese congregated in metropolitan areas once the demand for their labor on the railroads and mines diminished, and they sought the greater civil protection afforded in cities. They looked for "soft spots" in the labor force and business where they would escape discrimination; some gradually acquired enough money to invest in small-scale enterprises that did not seriously compete with those of the dominant population (laundries, produce stands, restaurants, curio shops). During the period covered here, Rose Hum Lee's depiction of the general setting seems applicable to the Seattle scene: "When the Chinatown is new and its members are primarily foreign-language speaking, they patronize the local shops and demand special goods and services, with the result that there are more carrying imported goods: food, religious appurtenances, clothing, herbs and delicacies. A merchant operating such an enterprise is fairly self-sufficient and important; he may be the contact-man between the larger society and the local non-English speaking residents."[4]

The social organization of Seattle's Chinese population probably followed the pattern established elsewhere in the United States, taking its bearing from that in San Francisco, which was the entry point for practically all Chinese immigrants. San Francisco, besides having the largest Chinese population, also was the site of the Six Companies, to which all disputes could be appealed from around the country; decisions made there were final. At the local level—as in Seattle—if families and clans from China (most came from eight of the ninety districts in Guangdong Province) were too small to serve effectively as an immigrant aid society, an association would be formed to carry out these functions. (One such association in Seattle was the Chong Wa Benevolent Association). In effect, associations functioned as the community support apparatus for the legitimate businesses, and in providing social and cultural services for the Chinese population at large. Tongs were another matter. According to Rose Hum Lee, "Tongs are synonymous with racketeering, white slave traffic, narcotics, gambling, . . . extortion, intimidation, [and] destruction of property." Later, they cloaked their activities under the guise of "Merchants Associations" or clubs, using secret rituals. The two sets of organization coexisted.[5]

Due to the linkage of police protection, vice, and gambling operations during the period covered, it is well to outline how the tongs carried on their business. Ivan Light has provided a useful description: "Chinatown vice resorts operated under the authorization of rival syndicates of Chinese criminals. The major tongs had branches in every American Chinatown. Each tong operated its own whore-houses, gambling joints, and opium dens—or it sold protection to Chinese specializing in these illegal services. The tongs also claimed territory in which each insisted upon a monopoly. . . ." Tong "wars" grew from these circumstances, the last one occurring during 1924-1927, which was "fought in every major Chinatown," including the one in Seattle.[6]

Coloring most aspects of Chinatown life was the combination of an extraordinarily high ratio of males to females, which declined only gradually; and a high median age. The combination discouraged family life, though some did develop. These sex ratios, though improving over time, strongly suggest the limited opportunity for family life to become the basis of Chinese American culture, as was the norm for the dominant population, and as it was in China itself. And, given the ghetto conditions in which the family—as the primary social unit—was compelled to develop, a second major obstacle thereby had to be surmounted. Only those who could migrate out of the ghetto stood much of a chance at true acculturation.[7]

Seattle's Japanese Community

Japanese immigrants to Seattle played a role in the city's development far out of proportion to their number. In the first decade of the century, most Japanese residents were working-class males who intended to return to Japan; they had this in common with single men from other immigrant groups. Few families made the trip from Japan to Seattle in these early years, though the signing of the Gentlemen's Agreement in 1907 altered this situation. In addition to railroad workers, there were other Japanese who were drawn by jobs in the area's lumber mills, particularly at Bainbridge Island's Port Blakely facility, a few short miles from Elliott Bay.

Some early migrants opened small shops, restaurants, cheap hotels, and other businesses catering to the needs of poorer, working-class whites, but also to Japanese workers employed in nearby mills and logging camps. The latter came to the district known as "Japantown" where these businesses were concentrated for rest and recreation.[1]

New arrivals directly from Japan differed from those who came to Seattle by way of California, according to Kazuo Ito, author of *Issei*. Ito suggests that immigrants who came directly to the community tended to be more intellectual; a number ultimately became members of the Japanese Diet and had distinguished political careers after returning to Japan. In Seattle's Japantown, residents formed themselves into associations for almost every purpose. The ensuing discussions, debate, and the inevitable schisms spawned by these organizations nurtured political life in the community. Forums were held regularly at Nihonkan (Japanese Hall) at which speakers addressed a broad range of subjects. The big issues were centered on politics; socialism was a frequent topic. Community newspapers sustained the ferment.

The umbrella organization for all of this activity was the Japanese Association of North America; and not surprisingly it split for a short time, from 1910 to 1912. The two camps allied with either the Tobo Company or the Furuya Company, two firms that competed in supplying railroad workers and in the import business. What brought the factions together again was a growing anti-Japanese sentiment in the white community.[2]

A recent study by Yuzo Murayama on the economic history of emigration from Japan puts to rest a mistaken assumption that Japanese immigrants always accepted wages that were lower than the scale prevailing among whites. Murayama shows how early wage differentials based on race tended to disappear by about 1910. Job mobility began to occur on the basis of market factors insofar as employment in the sawmills was concerned. Employers found they had to compete for workers with other industries, as well as with other mill operations.[3]

Among the 3,000-plus railroad workers in the state in 1908, about 600 were Japanese. Initially, railroad contractors played a key role in supplying immigrant workers. In Seattle, Ototaka Yamaoka's and Tetsuo Takahashi's Oriental Trading Company fulfilled this function most of the time for the Great Northern.

In 1904, when the Northern Pacific was about to renew its arrangement with a contractor for a lower wage scale, company officials colluded with the Great Northern to avoid the prospect of the two companies competing with one another. Great Northern executives would not, however, accept the NP's suggested wage scale: "There is so much demand for these men on work other than on railroads that the men we employ have got to take the market rate. The Oriental Trading Company will undoubtedly name any [rate] in the contract that we ask them to; but I can see no use in naming a rate that we know in advance cannot be adhered to." Murayama concludes that the beneficiaries of this kind competition were the Japanese workers.[4]

The resulting pattern, Murayama reports, was the investment by these wage earners in businesses in Japantown and in farms in the surrounding countryside. In the various sub-regions of this rural area they formed farmer associations through which they cooperated in all aspects of planting, cultivating, and marketing of produce. Their crops reached markets in the Midwest, as well as those in the Puget Sound basin. After President Theodore Roosevelt's executive order on March 14, 1907 (followed by the Gentlemen's Agreement of February 1908), slowed if not halted the supply of laborers coming from Hawaii, the region experienced a chronic shortage of unskilled Japanese labor. Broadly, these were the dynamic elements active among the Japanese in Seattle.[5]

In his study of Seattle's Japanese population, Shotaro Frank Miyamoto observed that the character of the Japanese community changed after 1908 to a "settling in" phase, typified by a trend to "ghettoization." One vital feature of this development was the creation of a number of "small shop" complexes. Illustrative of this tendency are statistics contained in a 1917 survey by the Ministerial Federation. Of the approximately 5,800 Japanese in the city, eighty-five worked for one of the three daily newspapers, thirteen were employed in one of three banks, twenty-seven were physicians, seventeen were involved in religious work, eighty-five worked in notion stores, thirty-three were interpreters, thirty-five were druggists; there were twenty-one midwives, twenty-eight photographers, twenty-eight employed in shoe repair shops, 100 tailors, 150 laundry workers, 250 worked in hotels, fifty-one in pool halls, fifty-six in barber shops, 142 in American food restaurants, 170 in Japanese food restaurants, 221 in grocery stores, thirty-eight in tobacco and fruit stands, fifty in clothing establishments (old and new), eighty-six in combined laundry, bath, and barber shops, nineteen in flower stands, and seventeen in the jewelry business; 2,000 men and 700 women were employed as laborers.[6]

Besides a growing "solidarity" among outlying Japanese farmers with those involved in ghetto business enterprises, Japanese laborers formed their own unions. Although these organizations were ostracized by the American Federation of Labor, their membership refused to become strikebreakers during the 1916 longshoremen's strike. Locally they gained recognition by being admitted through their own segregated local unions as non-voting members of the Central Labor Council.[7]

Japanese businessmen also were joiners. Few, however, were admitted to the Seattle Chamber of Commerce, so they formed a Japanese Chamber of Commerce, as well as a Japanese Hotel Owners Association. One of their number who did make it into the Seattle chamber was Masajiro Furuya, to whom the *Town Crier* paid special tribute in July 1914. He had migrated to the city in 1889, had become a millionaire, had become a source of capital for many Japanese businessmen, had "done much to dilute the prejudice against the Japanese," had founded night schools for his employees, and had helped them get college educations (thirty-five were at the University of Washington)—the list continued.

By the end of the period, Japanese began to settle on nearby Beacon Hill and in the Broadway High School district (the school was at Broadway and Pine Street). These areas were better-suited to raising families; and for the Japanese, this was particularly important because their children were by birth United States citizens and were, thus, able to own land, a privilege denied to the immigrants. At the center of the movement toward community solidarity was the Japanese Association of North America. Organized in 1900, it eased the path toward adaptation by performing the typical functions of an immigrant aid society.[8]

Despite these attempts to become assimilated into city life, a steady undercurrent of anti-Japanese sentiment continued to exist in Seattle. A sampling from pages of the *Argus* is indicative of racial attitudes adopted by many white Seattleites. In 1900 editor Harry Chadwick wrote: "The Japs are a menace to the Pacific Coast—as much as were the Chinese in their palmiest days." In 1903 Chadwick opposed admittance of Japanese into the "overcrowded" public schools; their parents pay no taxes, so their children get a "free education." Chadwick was appalled by the marriage of a "white girl" to a "Japanese house servant"; he proclaimed against miscegenation "red, black, or yellow." And he looked forward to the opening of the Panama Canal because Europeans would then be able to migrate directly to the Pacific Coast, supplanting the demand for Oriental labor.[9]

Seattle's Jewish Community

Like the Japanese, Jews played a more significant role in Seattle's civic life than their mere numbers would indicate.[1] But, unlike the Japanese, Jews were able to merge more readily into the community at large. A significant number were in some kind of business, and some even joined the business elite. Particularly notable was Jacob Furth, president of the Puget Sound National Bank, and an executive in a number of other financial institutions. He arrived in the city in 1882 from Colusa, California, after migrating there from Bohemia. With the backing of friends in Colusa he established a bank at Snohomish that started him off in the region. He helped Stone and Webster interests form the Seattle Electric Company in 1900, becoming its president.[1]

Other successful Jewish merchants included members of the Schwabacher mercantile family (Bailey Gatzert and Nathan Eckstein, as well as others in the main Schwabacher line) and the Schoenfeld mercantile family (which founded the city's largest furniture store). These wealthier Jews were politically conservative and were readily assimilated into the downtown elite. At the other end of the social spectrum, however, many Jewish workers were radicals or labor organizers, most notably, they were trade union activists like Ida Levi, the Pass brothers, and Philip Pearl.

The earliest source of Jewish migration to the Pacific Northwest was Germany; this also was true of Jewish migration elsewhere in the United States. These immigrants were relatively well-educated and had middle class values and expectations. With little capital, usually saved from money earned working in one of the trades, they tended to enter businesses requiring little investment: tailoring, clothing and dry goods, bakeries, a variety of retailing lines, wholesaling, and jobbing. The Schwabacher firm, for instance, starting in the early 1870s in the hardware and grocery business; it even provided local banking services to satisfy the currency needs of some firms at a time when financial services in the area were underdeveloped.

The 1893-1896 depression proved a difficult time for Seattle's Jewish community. As a testimonial, the city's first Synagogue building had to be sold in 1896 to satisfy creditors. However, factionalism contributed to the synagogue's sale, as well. But as times improved, one of the factions established Temple de Hirsch in 1899; and to assure that it too would not become factionalized, its organizers stated clearly that the temple "embraced the most advanced Reform thought of the day."

The first Sephardic Jews arrived in Seattle in 1903; there were two, in fact: Solomon Calvo and Jacob Policar, hailing from the Turkish island of Marmara. Rabbi Genss welcomed them into his congregation and gave Policar a job in his grocery and butcher shop. Calvo peddled fish; later, Policar sold produce—all occupations in which technical skills and literacy were unnecessary (this was true of all new immigrants). As letters from these first arrivals reached the homeland, other Jews from Marmara and the city of Tekirdag (to the north of Marmara on Turkey's European mainland) soon followed. From the Island of Rhodes came Nessim Alhadeff in 1904; he became a fish peddler also. Within a short time Solomon Calvo founded the Waterfront Fish Company, while Alhadeff established the Palace Fish Company, an establishment with the motto: "If it swims we have it."

Other Jews from Turkey now began to arrive in Seattle. Opportunities in the fishing industry and allied lines afforded them a chance to employ their Mediterranean skills in the Puget Sound basin. Their numbers grew slowly, however: seventeen men and one woman by 1906; about forty families, embracing about 600 persons by 1910 (out of a total Jewish population of about 4,500). It has been estimated that about eighty-five percent of this total lived in the Yesler Way-Cherry Street area east of 12th Avenue. By 1917 these Sephardic Jews numbered about 1,500, compared to the 8,500 Ashkenazim.

With limited resources and much less education than their German predecessors, and despite Rabbi Genss's friendly intercession, the Sephardim first had to convince the Ashkenazim that they also were Jews, despite differences in language and in the conduct of their religious services. Once they succeeded in this they were allowed to pray in the Ashkenazic Synagogue established by the German Jews, having borrowed their Rabbi already. Not until 1908 did the Sephardim have enough money to become independent; at that point, they rented a house. But by 1910 the Sephardic Jews decided that they also should separate into two groups. Those from Turkey formed the Sephardic Bikur Holim, while the Rhodes contingent established Ezra Bessaroth. In hand-me-down fashion, the former bought the old synagogue of the more affluent Ashkenazic Bikur Cholim at 13th and Washington Street when the latter built a new synagogue at 17th and Yesler Way. In 1907 the Reform congregation departed from the center of Jewish concentration, building its new Temple de Hirsch about six blocks to the north at 15th and East Union.

Fleeing pogroms in Russia and Poland, Jews also began arriving in large numbers from those countries by 1906. Unlike their Ashkenazic predecessors, they came with little or no education, and they were even poorer than the Sephardim from Turkey. In order to help these desperate newcomers, the Council of Jewish Women rented the lower part of a house on 12th and Washington Street in April 1906, calling it Settlement House (the present-day Neighborhood House is its descendant). It opened with a religious school and a sewing school; the latter enrolled thirty girls initially, 142 by 1912. By 1907, Settlement House moved to a flat on 11th Avenue, and then got the Seattle Public Library to establish a reading room (where English was taught). And since most immigrant dwellings had no bathing facilities, free baths were installed—the first public bath in Seattle. After an additional move, Settlement House finally acquired its own building in 1914, at 14th and Main; The structure's designer was B. Marcus Priteca, soon to become the architect for the Pantages Theater chain. Indicative of the desire for learning, Settlement House offered its Evening School twice a week, where ten teachers taught sixty-three men and women in 1912.

The influx of Jews escaping Russian and Polish persecution disturbed the equilibrium of some, if we can judge from the editorial comment of the *Argus's* Chadwick. Referring to Rabbi Hirsch's opposition to Russian Jews migrating to the United States, he wrote: "America has all the Jews just at present that she can assimilate—more, in fact. . . . The Russian Jews are, as a whole, far below the standard of this country. . . . They it is [*sic*] who work in the sweat shops at wages that enslaves [*sic*] free American citizens." Chadwick generally gave fulsome praise to established Jews, singling out Jacob Furth in particular. Although Chadwick consistently heaped biting criticism on Seattle Electric Company, almost anything he said that was good about the firm usually involved Furth.

Reflecting the general social concerns of many Jews was the establishment of a free dispensary by the Ladies' Hebrew Benevolent Association at the Arcade Building near First and University Street (the Association was itself established in 1903). In addition to the donated medical service, an attached clinical laboratory gave aid to the "deserving poor."

Seattle's Italians

Like Chinese, Jewish, and Japanese immigrants, Italians also tended to congregate in particular sections of the city. By 1910 there were 3,454 Italians in Seattle. They were almost uniformly poor and uneducated, usually of rural background, or with experience in mining and in work as common laborers. Many must have been attracted to coal mining in the Green River, Renton, and Newcastle fields. Some worked in the Roslyn-Cle Elum mines. As coal mining declined, many miners probably migrated to Seattle and Tacoma, and to the Puyallup-White-Duwamish valley between the two metropolises. In Seattle, Italians settled mainly in the Colman School-Rainier Valley area, and in smaller groupings in

South Park, Georgetown, Youngstown (where a new steel mill had been set up) and around Collins Playfield near the center of the Jewish population. Others established themselves near the south end of Lake Union where a number were employed by a garbage collection firm before 1910 (after 1910 the city took over garbage collection, resulting in a dispersion of this small colony).[1]

Ellen Roe, a graduate student in sociology at the University of Washington, studied the Italian population in 1915. She estimated that about eighty percent of the men were common laborers in unsteady employment; they supplemented their food supply by gardening at their home sites or on leased land. Between 200 and 300 men leased farm land, and about eighty sold their produce at the public market, or by peddling it from house-to-house. Roe reported that competition between Italian and Japanese farmers was "severe." Because seventy-five percent of the stalls at the Pike Place Market were operated by the Japanese, friction between the groups led to discriminatory legislation against the Japanese in 1921.

Among the entire Italian population in 1915, Roe recorded one lawyer, two medical doctors, a few wholesalers and importers, and some market-stall operators among the business and professional classes. Coming to the assistance of this impoverished ethnic group was Father Carmello of Our Lady of Mt. Virgin Catholic Church located near the Colman School; his efforts were abetted after 1910 by the newly established Deaconess Settlement.

Seattle's Black Community

Blacks tended to congregate in two separated sections of Seattle. The more transient residents lived in rented rooms in and around Chinatown, near the railroad stations, and extending up Jackson Street. Like other residents at the lower end of the socio-economic scale, they were attracted to these mixed racial sub-communities by low-rent housing, cheap apartments, and inexpensive hotels.[1]

The other concentration of Blacks was "cross town" in a radius south of Madison Street (restrictive covenants obstructed their settlement north of Madison). Being the most prestigious Black residential area, the Madison Street community was the one toward which the more upwardly mobile Blacks gravitated. Permanent settlers with their families, churches, and small businesses came to this area. The community had its origins in 1882 when Black pioneer, William Gross (sometimes written "Grose,"), bought twelve acres of land from Henry Yesler for $1,000; the land lay between 24th and 27th avenues and between Howell and Olive streets.

Before coming to Seattle, Gross had been a steward on the *Constitution,* a boat shuttling between Olympia and Tacoma in the late 1850s; he settled in Seattle about 1858, establishing a combination hotel-restaurant called "Our House." Shipbuilder Robert Moran proudly claimed to have been staked by Gross when he arrived penniless in Seattle.

After making his land purchase, Gross gave a few lots to friends and sold the rest. This area remained the nucleus of permanent Black settlement until after World War II.

Just as synagogues served as Jewish social centers, churches performed a comparable function among the Black population. Mount Zion Baptist Church (established in 1894) was the first "identifiable center" according to Joseph Sylvester Jackson, first director of the Seattle Urban League. The church's first structure was located at 3rd Avenue and University Street; the congregation later moved to 8th Avenue near Pike Street and finally to its present location at 19th and Madison Street. Although there were a number of smaller denominations that had churches within the city's Black community, the second African American cultural "center" was the First African Methodist Episcopal Church located originally at 5th Avenue and Pike Street.

By 1900 there were only 406 Blacks in the city; 2,514 statewide. Most were brought into the area as strikebreakers. The first arrivals worked in the coal in the Northern Pacific Railroad's Roslyn-Cle Elum mines in 1888. They were followed by another group who worked in the Franklin (in the Green River fields) and Newcastle mines of the Oregon Improvement Company in 1891. Many of these workers brought their families during and after the strikes; some remained to work alongside the white miners, reportedly amidst much social friction.

Black newspaper publisher Horace Cayton estimated in 1896 that 300 Blacks worked in each of the mines at Roslyn, Franklin, and Newcastle. Since Cayton migrated from Mississippi where Blacks were denied the franchise, he was interested in seeing Pacific Northwest Blacks exercise their right to vote. He counted "about eight hundred colored voters in King County ... most of them ... in Seattle, Franklin, and Newcastle." An undetermined number of these miners undoubtedly migrated to cities along the Pacific Coast and around Puget Sound. Some are also known to have homesteaded in Kittitas and Yakima Counties.

One Black Seattleite, I. Israel Walker, acted as an agent for two Yakima Valley irrigation companies when he brought Black homesteaders from his native North Carolina, and others from area coal fields. Most of these migrants were recruited by James Shepperson; he previously hired Black strikebreakers to work in Pennsylvania, Illinois, and Iowa. When the strikes occurred in Washington, mine owners turned to him.

By 1910 there were 2,296 Blacks in Seattle, 6,058 in the state; by 1920 there were 2,894 in the city and 6,883 statewide. Despite their small numbers their presence somehow aroused prejudice among whites. When, for example, a member of the Washington State Federation of Women's Clubs proposed that the color line be stricken from organizational bylaws in 1901, a "lively debate" preceded the ban's reaffirmation. And, although the Marine Cooks and Stewards Association did not establish a color line when it was formed in 1901, not more than two Blacks were founding members. The International Longshoremen's Association barred Blacks outright, a piece of discrimination that backfired—Blacks were subsequently used as strikebreakers during the disastrous 1916 longshoremen's strike-lockout.

Only one passenger ship line would employ Blacks; the Alaska Steamship Company employed them as cooks and scullerymen. During World War I, Blacks found jobs in local shipyards and in the federal civil service; but returning white servicemen often replaced them in these positions. Because the waitresses union barred Blacks from membership, those jobs were lost, in general to white women. As time passed, Black women who worked as domestics also found themselves being displaced, first by Swedish, then Japanese women.

While blatant social discrimination against Blacks was not apparent in Seattle before 1910, the potential for it lay near the surface. Even though the Black minstrel show, remained among the most popular forms of theatrical entertainment, Alexander Pantages refused first-floor seating to Blacks. In the *Argus*, Chadwick complained about putting Black prizefighters in the same ring as whites—never mind that this was the heyday of legendary black fighters like Jack Johnson and Sam Langford.

Some Blacks, like Horace R. Cayton, rose to social prominence, but not without experiencing prejudice. Cayton began publishing the only Black-owned newspaper in the state in 1894, the *Seattle Republican*. His associate and bride, Susie Revels, was the daughter of the first Black United States Senator, Hiram Revels, who Cayton met at Alcorn College in Mississippi (Revels was president of the institution at the time).

Cayton's *Seattle Republican* was a political paper and he was a staunch Republican of the Taft variety, not a Roosevelt supporter.

Harry Chadwick charged the Black editor with being under the influence of the *P-I's* John L. Wilson. Cayton was active in the party, being a delegate to state nominating conventions, serving on the state central committee, and as secretary of the King County Republican Club. He earned patronage for his newspaper, printing court notices, and getting some major advertisers—but not many overall. Biographical sketches of Republicans abound in the paper, along with sharp political commentary. To serve as role models, Cayton proudly published accounts of the lives of Black pioneers in the region and stories about the successful careers of contemporary Blacks. The *Republican* also included news of racial discrimination, violence, and lynchings in the South; this kind of news probably did not appeal to white readers.

As time passed, subscriptions fell off; Cayton had to sell his beautiful home near Volunteer Park. In 1913 the newspaper ceased publication. Just before its shutdown, Cayton purchased an apartment house at 22nd and Jackson Street, calling it the "Caytonian Court," and renting "2 and 3 room apartments at $10 and $15 a month."

More blatant forms of discrimination against Blacks began to appear during World War I; they were denied service in cafes, theaters, and other public places. In 1917, Cayton himself was refused service in a restaurant that he normally patronized. When the former editor filed a suit in court, the case was dismissed.

The Caytons were considered uppity by many members of the Black community, partly because of their social pretentions— which the former editor and his wife undoubtedly recognized as marks of racial equality that he sought for all Blacks. Only when they lost their economic underpinnings and suffered rejection did the Caytons rejoin the larger Black community and share in its prescribed second-class status.

The Pike Place Market and Ethnicity

Seattle's Pike Place Market (made into a "Historical District" in 1971) was a special microcosm for observing the social and ethnic tensions that existed in Seattle's working community.[1]

The Market, as it is called, was established in 1907 because of the combined frustration of the city's consumers (who were tired of paying high prices) and local growers (who wanted to cut out profits made by commission merchants). Commission merchants imported produce from California and, thus, shut out White-Puyallup river valley and Vashon and Bainbridge island produce growers (who were mostly Japanese and Italian). The merchants were also accused of destroying surplus produce to create short-ages that would sustain higher prices.

It was in this context that City Councilman Thomas Revelle got a proclamation passed for a "Market Day," August 17, 1907. Commission men and hucksters tried to sabotage the event by threatening farmers and by trying to get civil authorities to over-ride the proclamation.

But despite harassment, the day was such a success that it led to a breaking of the Western Avenue commission merchants' mo-nopoly. By week's end, seventy farm wagons showed up. With high expectations for the future, two men who had made money in the gold rush, John and Frank Goodwin, erected a market build-ing; it opened for business on November 30, 1907. One-hundred-and-twenty farmers lined up at stalls to sell mainly produce, poul-try, and eggs. About seventy to eighty percent of the stalls were operated by Japanese, and the rest, mainly by Italians.

In 1917 Frank Goodwin, who had guided the market from its inception, turned management over to his brother, Arthur. A few years later, in 1925 (after passage of the 1924 Immigration Act that restricted Japanese immigration) Goodwin and Joe Desimone bought out the "old" market and established Pike Place Markets, Incorporated, a "victory" of Italian interests over those of the Japa-nese.

Education in the City

Public education in Seattle was broadly supported through-out the period from 1900 to 1920. Given the unprecedented influx of new people who were in the prime of life and who brought with them high expectations, such support is not surprising. The historian of the Seattle Public Schools for the period, Bryce E. Nelson, regards the system as being "exemplary" when compared to those in the rest of the nation. Seattle's school superintendent for the years 1901 to 1922 was Frank B. Cooper; he had an oppor-tunity to build the system as the city itself grew. This was in contrast with his counterparts elsewhere who had to contend with established populations, politcal machines, and social instituions. "In Seattle, school supporters elected civic-minded progressives to the Board, the Board retained Cooper for twenty-one years, and until the 1920s taxpayers approved substantial school bond issues as part of the investment necessary to make Seattle a desirable place to live." This investment was reflected in an extensive school construction program, the retention of high-quality faculty in a context of general academic freedom, an inventive/responsive curriculum, the presence of social services, and a high rate of high school attendance.[1]

The number of Seattle's schools grew along with the city's burgeoning population, from twenty-six in 1902 to seventy by 1912. By another measure, teacher/pupil ratios steadily improved: In 1902 teachers tried to teach forty-six pupils at one time; by 1912 the number had been reduced to thirty-two. Teacher salaries increased, despite the fiscal conservatism of many Board members who represented the downtown business establishment. Seattle teachers earned an average of $793 annually in 1902, $1,126 by 1912.

Public schools fulfilled needs for members of the incoming middle class as they sought to establish families in friendly neighborhoods, each with its own elementary school, garnished with a park or playground. Labor's "upper class" must be included in this middle-class category. Together, these upwardly mobile groups worked to gain access to economic and social amenities that were being denied them by powerful downtown interests whose watchdogs on the School Board guarded against "unnecessary" expenditures.

School Board members during the period shared a common social outlook. Thirteen were drawn from the business community, the rest came from the professional class. All could afford the expense of time lost from their occupations; none were from the working class, although one, Judge Richard Winsor, was a Socialist. One member, the journalist and child welfare advocate Anna Louise Strong would be recalled for her defense of Louise Olivereau, an anti-war protestor who was convicted of sedition in 1917. Strong was the only woman elected during this period. The Seattle School Board dealt almost exclusively with business matters and building construction, leaving the curriculum and related issues to academic and administrative professionals.

Scientific management practices came in vogue during the first decade of the twentieth century; along with them, statistical measurement of efficiency, student time spent in each class, student achievement, and school operations cost-benefit analysis. Superintendent Cooper went along with these modifications and used them to advantage even though they led away from the humane atmosphere for learning and teaching for which he aimed.

Recognizing the relationship between good health and learning, he initiated a free and reduced-price milk program for students that protected the anonymity of recipients. He had to defend this program from attack on legal and fiscal grounds during his tenure.

The quality of Seattle's teachers and principals remained high during the Cooper era. Teachers' tenure tended to be long—unless they were women who married. Married male teachers seem not to have been affected by the presumed moral degradation that afflicted married females in the classroom. In general, there seems to have been a fear that married women teachers would have their loyalties divided between family and school.

Notwithstanding, most grammar school teachers were women, half of whom ranged in age from twenty-six to thirty years when hired, and about one-third of them taught for more than twenty-seven years. Few men were attracted to grammar school teaching because the pay was less than that for high school teachers. Women teachers had to overcome preferential hiring practices that favored and encouraged the hiring of men. The board's operating principle was "no male candidate of acceptable rating is denied." Consequently, males predominated among the high school teaching ranks. Despite these barriers, about four times as many women as men applied for teaching jobs in 1910-1911.

Women high school teachers continued to be paid less than their male counterparts until 1919, when the board was required to equalize their pay as the result of a piece of state "equal pay for equal work" legislation. Grammar school teachers, however, continued to be paid less, on an average, than high school teachers, although the gap was narrowed from $500 to $300 by 1919.

Early twentieth-century teachers lived in a kind of paradox. On the one hand, they were held in high esteem; they were expected to possess exemplary morals—drinking or smoking in public were grounds for administrative disciplinary action. On the other hand, they received low wages and were only grudgingly given sick leave—and that was at half pay. The Seattle School Board also refused to allow teachers to work during vacations, summers included. Cooper fought unsuccessfully to change this proscription. But when two teachers refused to remove protest notes from their contracts in 1919, they were fired by the board. These working conditions persisted in the face of adequate funds to support pay raises because the board could count on high turnover rates to deal with resignations and dismissals. Its attitude was that pay raises were usually "inexpedient."

The board's haughtiness toward teachers, while reflecting conventional business attitudes about labor in general, was not shared by Superintendent Cooper. Curriculum matters, for example, were decided through the work and cooperation of teachers and principals. Here, he allowed for trial periods to see if new policies would, in fact, work. School administrations in most cities did not follow this form of participatory management. Cooper believed that teachers "best understand the problems involved." The improved morale engendered by these progressive practices compensated somewhat for the School Board's mean-spirited personnel policies. Because Cooper's philosophy and approach became nationally known, he continued to attract top-rated teachers from elsewhere, according to Nelson.

School attendance became compulsory for children between ages eight and fifteen as a result of state legislation enacted in 1903. Cooper developed policies that aimed at making school a learning an enriching experience and not a retention pond for keeping children out of the adult work force. With this his motive, he steered the curriculum away from regimentation and toward flexibility, away from vocational training and toward a broadening of life expectations, away from stereotyped textbook learning and toward options for teachers and students. Fortunately, the board gave him a relatively free hand in these matters, so experimentation in Seattle's schools was a rule rather than an exception. A high place was assigned to music, art, physical education, manual training, and domestic science; but the focus in each of these cultural subjects was on achieving a life-enriching competence rather than establishing life-goals. All of this reflects a drift away from the traditional common course of study and toward differentiated tracks, none of which was prematurely confining. Some principals contended that Cooper's expanded idea of curriculum retained many students who might otherwise have joined the adult work force after school.

Given Cooper's sensitivity, it should not be surprising to note that he started special classes for children who were physically handicapped or who had behavior problems. Night school seems to have begun partly in response to a letter from a "working boy." The first classes were held in June 1902 at Central School; then the program gradually expanded to five other schools by 1906-1907. By 1907 he also introduced an evening high school class with a full set of courses from which to choose.

Cooper introduced manual training at all levels, at least partly in response to pressure from the Federation of Women's Clubs. Classes were provided for the deaf, blind, stammerers, slow learners, and those who were retarded. He even assigned a teacher to the Children's Orthopedic Hospital.

Auxiliary teachers were used to provide special tutoring that enabled students who had fallen behind to keep pace with their classmates. This auxiliary teacher system was "unlike that of any other city." Unfortunately, these programs became prime targets for elimination during the 1920s; programs like them would not be restored until the 1960s.

The Board tightly controlled expenditures, and although many grammar schools were built during the period (there were sixty-four in 1914) to keep pace with population growth, they were made to last. Most were constructed of brick, because that material was preferred by residents of middle-class neighborhoods—most neighborhoods were that in nature and in aspiration.

Community groups made use of these schools, a function that Cooper promoted so that "discussion of social and political issues [there, makes the schoolhouse] the seat of influence for the maintenance and perpetuation of free institutions." He drew strong support from the Municipal League on this issue when the Board was finally persuaded to withdraw its opposition in 1911.

While integrating grammar schools with their respective neighborhoods, Cooper kept outsiders out: solicitors for fund drives, seekers after student volunteers, or those who would divert teacher attention from classes in progress. When the nation entered the World War I in 1917, these policies were put to the test by super-patriots and political conservatives; the onset of hostilities marked the beginning of the end for the city's socially responsive tradition.

Unlike their counterparts in Eastern and Midwestern cities, Seattle's student population was ethnically integrated in neighborhoods that were themselves ethnically mixed. But non-white groups were practically invisible: between 1910 and 1921 the number of Japanese students enrolled rose from 287 to 1,035, Blacks from 208 to 308, and Chinese from eighty to 257. Among high school graduates in 1920-1921 there were 113 Japanese, forty-six Blacks, and thirty-eight Chinese; these minorities were concentrated in Broadway and Franklin high schools (the two other high schools—Lincoln and Queen Anne—were located in exclusively white areas).

In general, the Seattle School Board accepted a decentralized administrative policy. But in doing so, it descended to concerning itself with petty detail at times. In 1911, for instance, the board ordered telephones removed from schools because of monthly high rates. This action required that administrators communicate with one another by postcard and messenger. One result was more autonomy for individual schools than the Board might otherwise have allowed. By 1920 the board had the phones reinstated.

Coincident with the ascendancy of political and social conservatism that paralleled America's entry into World War I, Cooper's socially sensitive program was curtailed after he was forced into retirement in 1922. There were, however, some last ditch fights, primarily with ultranationalists whose egos remained inflated by America's victory in the war. In the end, the fiscal conservatives won out during a tax reduction program that was triggered by a postwar recession.

The University of Washington

When the University of Washington moved from its original location in downtown Seattle to the shore of Lake Washington near Union Bay in 1894, it really was on the periphery of the city. The new grounds were covered by virgin timber and other rain forest vegetation. It was four miles from the central city, and transportation between the campus and downtown by the Seattle Electric Company's streetcar line quickly earned a bad reputation. The trip was hair-raising at times, even when breakdowns did not occur.[1]

When Franklin P. Graves became president in 1898 he aimed to upgrade the school's curriculum to accreditable college standards and to lend support to the general improvement of public education. To accomplish the first goal he began recruiting faculty members with doctoral degrees.

However, J. Allen Smith was a Ph.D. he inherited; Smith would attract national attention to the university for his revisionist study of the United States Constitution and for his teaching and publications in the field of municipal government. He became a source of controversy as the intellectual leader of the municipal ownership movement, and as a supporter of worker unionization.

Graves added three more faculty members with doctoral degrees to the faculty: Horace Byers (chemistry), Thomas F. Kane (Latin), and Frederick M. Padelford (English). In his four years as president, Graves also added four new buildings, including two dormitories, a science building and a powerhouse. The student body was less than 200 in 1898; by the time Graves resigned under pressure from the regents, it numbered more than 600. The University of Washington was not yet integrated with city development, but it was finally beginning to resemble a traditional institution of higher learning.

At the same time that newspapers were applauding Graves for his achievements in 1902, Latin professor Thomas Kane was appointed acting president, then president. Graves's legacy was: six schools (College of Liberal Arts, Graduate School, Law School, College of Engineering, School of Mines, and School of Pharmacy), elimination of the preparatory school, and a substantial increase of faculty numbers.

Building on Graves's program, Kane, in recognition of the university's proximity to Puget Sound, established a marine biology laboratory, by appointing student/instructor Trevor Kincaid as site selector (Kincaid had already established pre-eminence in his knowledge of the region's natural history). Friday Harbor was chosen as the location and, in 1904, Kincaid and Dr. Theodore C.

Frye conducted the first summer course there. In 1904-1905 Kane also responded to another of the region's industrial needs by establishing a timber testing station. These innovations pointed toward integration of the University of Washington with the region's economy.

Additional faculty were hired accordingly, sixteen in 1903-1904. But low salaries led to inevitable desertions to better paying positions elsewhere. Enrollment increased to 706 in 1903-1904; these figures included thirty-five graduate students. Kane tried to improve salaries in order to hold good faculty, but the regents were lukewarm and the legislature resistant. And although more instructional and laboratory space was clearly needed, the legislature refused to authorize construction funds, even after the Regents pared their "wish-list" to only one building. Until the university occupied the buildings left behind after the 1909 Alaska-Yukon-Pacific Exposition, laboratory space was inadequate and classrooms overflowed. But despite unsatisfactory facilities, student enrollment jumped to 1,035 in 1905-1906 and thirty new faculty were hired (just how many replaced departing faculty is not known).

The year 1905-1906 marked a further integration of the university with the larger community when the high school accreditation program begun by Graves was upgraded. The new College of Education under Dean Frederick Bolton took the lead in this effort, with Kane and his faculty paying visits to schools across the state. This program was required as a substitute for the former preparatory school of the university—if high school curriculum and performance were not upgraded then admission standards of the university would have to be lowered if it were to continue on its growth curve.

After the University of Washington's grounds were chosen in 1906 as the site of the Alaska Yukon-Pacific Exposition, Kane pressed for the introduction of a forestry course, to be directed by personnel of the Timber Testing Laboratory in association with a professor of forestry. Approval followed; and the School of Forestry was founded a year later.

President Kane's ambitions for the university were fueled by the promise that three of the Alaska Yukon-Pacific Exposition buildings would be contributed to the school. A School of Journalism was established in 1907; a domestic science course was introduced in 1908-1909; and Kane tried to get the regents to approve an Oriental languages and literature course to prepare citizens for closer ties with the Orient as commerce expanded in that direction.

The University of Washington benefited more than the city

from the Alaska Yukon-Pacific Exposition. Given the Washington Legislature's resistance to granting construction funds, the choice of the university grounds as the exposition site presented the school with a golden opportunity, and it took full advantage. The administration began to realize, however, that three new buildings would not satisfy the growth needs of the institution. So other structures on the campus came under consideration—aesthetic disharmony receded as a factor in architectural consideration, giving way to a simmering sense of desperation and opportunism among the administrators in search of space. Before scheduled demolition of Alaska Yukon-Pacific Exposition structures could get underway, they requested that twenty be retained, despite their relatively flimsy construction as "temporary" buildings. The request was granted. An additional bonus of having the exposition on campus was the fact that much land had been cleared; this was an enormous undertaking that the university could not otherwise have afforded.

The exposition also drew the favorable attention of local citizenry as nothing else had done before. However, when the regents, in November 1909, approved a Seattle Electric Company request to build a trestle over the university property on Union Bay to connect with the burgeoning Laurelhurst community, students and faculty protested vigorously. During the ensuing year, 9,000 citizens signed petitions against the trestle project, and Kane joined with the Alumni Association in opposition. When the City Council met in March 1911 it endorsed the Regent's action of November 1909, but amended the act by routing the trestle to bypass the bay on its northern border along 45th Street.

Tension between President Kane and the Regents continued to mount; then student protests accumulated in 1911. Kane's reputation got tarnished by them: a majority of male students opposed a military drill act that the 1911 legislature passed; students in general were becoming fascinated by politics under the inspiration of J. Allen Smith and Teresa McMahon. Students had already been active in the recall of Seattle's Mayor Hiram Gill in 1911. Then, in the spring of that year both students and faculty enthusiastically greeted Theodore Roosevelt to the dismay of many of the regents and downtown interests. President Taft was, however, hosted by President Kane on his November 1911 visit; and Gifford Pinchot followed Taft just as the "Ballinger-Pinchot controversy" began to disappear after it had split the Republican Party.

Such interest in serious matters on the part of the university community disturbed the Board of Regents. Consequently, at their December 1911 meeting they passed a resolution barring political speakers who were not members of the student body from speaking on campus. They also voted to accept a gift of chimes from former regent Alden Blethen. The chimes gift brought forth only a single public dissent, this by student Glenn Hoover in the *University of Washington Daily*. The chimes gift would become an issue, later, in connection with Blethen's involvement in the Harbor Island scheme.

Under pressure from President Kane and the students, the Board of Regents tried in February 1912 to clarify its interpretation of the political speaker rule by declaring that, if one candidate for office were invited to speak on campus, all opponents must also be invited. Kane, speaking in April before the prestigious Monday Club, came out in favor of academic freedom by advocating student exposure to a variety of viewpoints as part of their education. But as the 1912 presidential campaign began heating up in the spring, Kane decided to ban all political speakers from campus. Then he quickly rescinded this action when students protested, and referred the matter to the Regents, who reaffirmed his earlier "gag rule."

Now the chimes issue fused with student excitement over the November 1912 general election. Ceremonies for dedicating the chimes were to be held on October 22. But a week before the event, the university's Stevens Debating Club decided that accepting the gift would place the school under obligation to the donor. Stuart Rice and Charles McKinley prepared a letter signed by fifty students, which *Daily* editor Andrew Eldred agreed to publish on dedication day. Kane ordered its suppression and suspended publication of the *Daily*. Simultaneously, he suspended Editor Eldred for refusing to obey. Students then published the protest letter in pamphlet form and distributed copies to guests exiting the ceremony. The fat was in the fire.

Kane turned the matter over to the Faculty Disciplinary Committee, which merely reprimanded the students, placing them on probation. The controversy also spilled over into city politics where support for the students was generated. For example, the Executive Board of the Washington Branch of the National Congress of Mothers and Parents Teachers Association sent a letter to the regents (with copies to outgoing governor Hays and to governor-elect Ernest Lister), questioning the moral condition of the donor, fearing that he would place the university in his debt. The organization congratulated student protesters for showing "fine discrimination" in objecting to acceptance of the chimes.

When the Board of Regents finally met to decide the issue it deadlocked and the matter slowly subsided, but not without causing Blethen to reconsider his former support for President Kane. In the opinion of Kane's biographer, Georgia Kumor, the chimes controversy was really sparked by Kane's gag rule; but the general distaste students had for Blethen, and he for them, contributed to the dispute. In the end, Kane became the victim.

By now, however, the University of Washington's destiny became bound with Seattle's future; the city had, in fact, grown up around the campus. But the issue of academic freedom raised in 1911-1912 would remain unresolved; its existence would always be under fire.

Popular Entertainment: Theater Life

Before the depression of 1893-1896 Seattle could boast a large number of theaters that included box houses (saloons with theaters attached), as well as stock companies for legitimate theater, variety, and vaudeville. When the depression hit, most of these enterprises closed down, and their owners (men like John Cort, John Considine, John Cordray, and George Beede) left for greener pastures. Cort, for instance, established a circuit of theaters along the Northern Pacific Railroad route, but ended up losing them. Those Seattle theater operations that survived the financial crisis were done away with by reform legislation enacted in the mid 1890s. Cort and Considine returned on the heels of the Klondike gold rush, and many independent theaters sprang up at that time, only to go out of business almost immediately.[1]

Only the legitimate theaters—Seattle Theater and the Third Avenue Theater—survived to greet the theater revivalists and the new arrivals after the mid 1890s. Keeping them alive was a contract they held with New York booking agents Klaw and Erlinger (K and E). But K and E rarely sent their better shows on the road, thereby convincing the Seattle Theater owners that they should offer more stock fare as a choice.

Upon returning to Seattle and obtaining a building permit, Cort proclaimed he would bring respectable vaudeville to the city for family entertainment. But his Palm Garden became a box house in the business district when he stopped construction once the structure's basement was finished—suggesting this was his intention all along (boxes, closed and open ones, usually were in saloon and theater basements). Protests followed, but Cort survived the fracas because of political control he exercised in the ward. Later, with fresh financing, he completed the Palm Garden, changing its name to the Grand Opera House—the city's "finest." It offered legitimate theater and vaudeville. The Grand lasted until a fire burned it to the ground in January 1917. The *Town Crier* claimed it was only one of many such structures "inviting disaster." When regrading forced the closure of the Third Avenue in 1907 Cort also became manager of the Moore Theater at Second and Stewart opposite James A. Moore's classy New Washington Hotel. There he offered his best shows, relegating secondary ones to the Grand.

Cort next decided to combat K and E by buying up the leases of theaters along the Northern Pacific route, forcing the syndicate to book through his newly formed Northwest Theatrical Association. He became their northwest representative in the process. After a dispute with K and E in 1910 he formed a rival national organization, the National Theater Owners' Association, which controlled about 1,200 one-night-stand theaters.

Mark Klaw responded by coming to the Northwest for the first time in September 1910 to line up theaters for the "syndicate" in competition with Cort. Klaw contracted with the Metropolitan Building Company for presenting shows at the Metropolitan Theater, then under construction for K and E. Cort ended his battle quickly, satisfied that in Seattle he would continue to manage the Moore, the Seattle Theater, and the Grand Opera House. At this point, K and E agreed to run its shows through the Cort houses.

John Considine was another of the returnees brought back by the gold rush. Considine had cooled his heels in Spokane for three years, where he managed the People's Theatre. In 1897 he left eastern Washington for boom-town Seattle when the Spokane City Council passed an ordinance barring employment of women in box-house theaters. His return corresponded with changes in attitudes on the part of city officials who, once again, acquiesced to open town policies. As noted above, Considine soon found his business ventures under attack from onetime subordinate, William Meredith, Seattle's new police chief. The grudge match that followed led to Meredith's murder. Considine's trial and subsequent acquittal in November 1901 opened the city to him. In Murray Morgan's words: "In a few months time Considine crossed the Line [separating the restricted district from the respectable one] and established himself as one of Seattle's most successful businessmen."

Launched in this uptown direction, Considine took half-interest in Seattle's first moving picture house, Edison's Unique Theater, with Considine introducing variety acts of his People's Theater in-between nickelodeon fare.Eugene Elliott credits him with having established the first popularly priced vaudeville chain in the world: ten- and twenty cent admissions at his People's Theater and others in his Northwest chain. In 1904 Considine joined with two other investors to build the Orpheum as part of an expansion program. He also booked his acts into several smaller theaters as well. Hoping to expand outside the region, he joined with New York Tammany Hall leader, Timothy Sullivan in 1906. With Sullivan's financing, Considine added a house in Butte, the Lyceum in San Francisco, and the Grand in Tacoma. Altogether, the two men accumulated twenty-one houses in the Pacific Northwest, affiliated with twenty more in California, and booked heavily in the Midwest. The Star and Orpheum became his two Seattle theaters. (His "Orpheum" was not, however, part of the Orpheum Circuit).

The Orpheum played five performances, each of one-hour's duration; while the classier Star gave three performances of eight acts each. Then, in 1907 Considine leased the block-long Coliseum from Martin Beck, agent of the Orpheum Circuit. Having completed the arrangement, he tore down the original Orpheum and reassigned that name to the Coliseum. Out of these expansion efforts Considine formed the Northwest Orpheum Circuit to allow rotation of shows from San Francisco to Minneapolis. The chain had become the first transcontinental, popularly priced vaudeville service in the United States, according to Elliott. In 1914, with Sullivan's death, reorganization occurred, with Considine selling all but his Northwest Orpheum chain.

Alexander Pantages was a newcomer to the Seattle theater scene in the twentieth century; he would, however, soon rival Considine's supremacy. Born in Greece, Alexander Pantages made his grubstake in Alaska by introducing entertainment to the saloons. In 1902 he set up the Crystal Theater on Seattle's Second Avenue, hiring practically no one, performing nearly every function himself, all for ten cents a customer. Abbreviated vaudeville was the fare, with fast-flying moving pictures mixed in. Success at the Crystal led to another Pantages venture, this one called the "Pantages" and located at Second and Seneca. He followed with a third in 1906, named after his wife Lois. The Lois was a stock theater that ran continuously to December 18, 1910. Next, he began expanding along the Pacific Coast.

Murray Morgan colorfully describes the Considine-Pantages rivalry; it was intense. When one or the other announced an act, the other would either try to steal the performers, or hire a better version of the advertised offering. When Considine expanded nationwide in 1906, Pantages bought out a six-theater chain that had lost its main house in the San Francisco fire. Since performers at the time sought long-term employment, the circuits competed on this basis as well. In the case of Considine-Sullivan, they could provide seventy weeks of continuous work; Pantages, sixty weeks. But Morgan gives the nod to Pantages for "better booking procedures" in Seattle and nationally. Pantages would personally review acts before booking; he knew what would sell, whether performed by famous actors or by unknowns.

When Considine sold out in 1914 and the deal fizzled in 1915, his insurance company foreclosed on the mortgages. Pantages then picked up the parts of the circuit he wanted. By 1920 his was the strongest theater organization in the country.

In many ways, 1910 marked a high point in the city's theater life. The *Town Crier* had listing for the Alhambra where Russell and Drew brought in stock shows with an emphasis on melodrama; Considine's "new" Orpheum, where he hoped to display the best vaudeville in the country; the Majestic, the Star, and Pantages's two theaters. The Dream Theater advertised itself as "the real motion picture show and home of the pipe organ." At the time, vaudeville still predominated. Moving pictures often were inserted between acts, but there were few motion picture houses. Russell and Drew sponsored the Baker stock players at the Alhambra where they put on the popular *Uncle Tom's Cabin* in the fall. This show was followed by the *Girl of the Golden West*, which the *Town Crier* proclaimed "the greatest triumph that has ever been witnessed in three generations of theatricals." The Lois resumed its "high class dramatic stock" in January 1911.

Not all theaters had box houses; certainly not the Moore. Above all, not the Metropolitan Theater in the University of Washington's downtown tract. In keeping with his goal of making the area an elite downtown section, John F. Douglas, manager of the Metropolitan Building Company, leased a piece of land to K and E in September 1910. The location, between Fourth and Fifth avenues on University Street, became the site of Metropolitan Theater. Its design was allegedly modelled on the Doge's Palace in Venice; its construction of expensive marble, terra cotta, and brick was a cut above any other Seattle theater. It was a kind of jewel in a ring of elegantly designed "permanent" office buildings that Douglas had completed between 1909 and 1911. The *P-I* viewed it as the "new center of Seattle." By 1925 it would become half-surrounded by the Olympic Hotel, also touted as the city's "finest."

An economic downturn in 1912 found Seattle's major theaters closed for much of the year. Cort moved to New York to crown his career. During his last decade in Seattle, he had played a key role in introducing vaudeville—at the expense of variety, which practically disappeared. The Seattle Theater became the leading vaudeville house at the time, and fell to his control when its owner, and short-lived partner, J. P. Howe, sold out to Cort in

1905. (Howe had introduced vaudeville of the Orpheum Circuit to the city in 1902.) Eugene Elliott also credits Cort with having introduced burlesque to the city along the way.

That Seattle entrepreneurs played such a vital role in regional and national theater development surely indicates the presence of a cultural vitality and urbanity in the city that is rarely appreciated. Elliott claims that, by the middle of the first decade of the century, Seattle was, if only for a time, second only to New York "as the most important theatrical center in the United States."

Popular Entertainment: Music and the Arts

Families and individuals who migrated from the East and Midwest brought much of their cultural baggage along with them. Women—usually the wives of well-to-do businessmen—often had received musical training before their arrival in the area. Twenty such women musicians gathered in early 1891 at the home of Mrs. George Bacon to form the Ladies' Musical Club. Their purpose was to "stimulate the development of musical activity in Seattle." They were fortunate to have in their midst a Franz Liszt student, German-born and trained, Martha Blanka Churchill. She was named music director, a position she held until her death in 1894.

The organization's first concert was given in March 1891, with members performing songs and short piano pieces. Group members claimed that theirs was the first organization of its kind on the Pacific Coast. By the turn of the century the Ladies' Musical Club had three categories of membership: active, associate, and student; all active members had to be musicians who had passed a club audition, after which they performed at monthly concerts.

By 1905, the club had grown to include ninety-five active and 217 associate members, including men; these numbers increased to 150 and 266 respectively by 1916; and to 158 and 360 by 1921. While the organization was never large, it nevertheless provided a solid core of classical music enthusiasts bent on uplifting the entertainment tastes of a community that really was a theater town.

By 1895, the Ladies' Musical Club gave monthly concerts of the kind noted above. Probably few large works were performed in their entirety at these events. Hoping to elevate the city's musical tastes, Rosa Gottstein (who would remain as executive secretary and music director until 1939) suggested in 1900 that the club sponsor what would become the Artists' Concert Series. In its first season the program featured Teresa Carreno, reputedly the greatest woman pianist of the time. When the Chicago Symphony performed during the 1901-1902 season, club women earned enough money to make it a part of their permanent program. The largess also forced the club to incorporate in 1902. Each year thereafter, Rosa Gottstein would go East, allegedly with at least $20,000 in contributions, and sign up artists.

By 1916 the club had sponsored seventy artists' recitals at a cost of $105,000 and had a surplus of $21,000, thereby assuring the program's continuance. In addition, the women continued to give monthly concerts. This pattern of activity has continued to the present.

The quality of artists in the Ladies' Musical Club series was of the first rank. A sampling of programs from that time confirms this: the well-known Spiering Quartet, performed the Schumann opus 46, number 2 and the Haydn opus 76, number 1 in 1903; after them, *prima donna* Zelie De Lussan gave a song concert. The baritone Emilio Gorgorza appeared regularly; Mischa Elman, Ferrucio Busoni, Jan Kubelik, John McCormack, Tetrazzini, Nellie Melba, Eugen Ysaye, the Flonzaley Quartet, the New York Philharmonic, Jascha Heifitz, Rudolph Ganz, Ernestine Schumann-Heink, Geraldine Farrar, Josef Hofmann, and Amelita Galli-Curci, all appeared at least once in the series. Fritz Kreisler and Harold Bauer presented a program in 1908 that might have been the outstanding performance of the era: Beethoven's *Kreutzer Sonata*, the Brahms *Paganini Variations*, Schubert's *Moments Musicaux*, and Schumann's *Fantasiestucke*!

The calendar for early 1917—as the city prepared for war— attests to the music scene's vitality: the Ladies' Musical Club presented Julia Culp at the Moore; the Seattle Symphony played at the Hippodrome; the Ballet Russe at the Moore; and the Musical Arts Society gave a concert—all in January. Subsequently, the Seattle Symphony appeared monthly, the Flonzaley Quartet performed; the New York Philharmonic with Efram Zimbalist, appeared at the Metropolitan and the Boston National Grand Opera Company at the Moore. Vaudeville even attained real class in May when Ruth St. Denis, her husband, and the "Denishawn Dancers" were held over for one week.

The Ladies' Musical Club, while a prime mover in this activity, was not the only organization to promote classical music. There were also the Seattle Musical Arts societies (there were two in 1917), a Schubert Society, and the Seattle Choral Symphony among others.

In 1903, Seattle musicians, under the direction of Harry West, organized themselves into an all male symphony, giving their first concert on December 29 at the Arcade Building auditorium. By 1905, audiences had grown so large that concerts were moved to the Grand Opera House. Until 1907 the group remained one composed of music-loving amateurs. Then the *Times* reported "open warfare" in musical circles, when a group of leading society women, who had become disgruntled with Choral Symphony Society leadership, formed the Seattle Symphony Orchestral Association.

Failing to spirit away the Choral Symphony's concert master, they hired Michael Kegrize, a professional conductor of wide experience. They gave their first concert, with Ladies' Music Club member Louise Van Ogle as soloist, in November at the Grand.

Kegrize was succeeded as conductor by Henry K. Hadley in 1909, and it was Hadley who conducted the symphony at the Alaska-Yukon-Pacific Exposition. The Moore Theater became the symphony's regular concert hall. In 1911, an offer from San Francisco proved too attractive for Hadley to resist; so he left to conduct that orchestra. His successor as conductor was John Spargur.

While Spargur's concerts tended to be more modest, he chose to expand symphony activity by giving programs for children beginning in 1912. Classical music appreciation was clearly spreading, not only laterally throughout the community but downward to the young, as well.

Responding in part to the Seattle Symphony's need for trained musicians, music teachers, at their association's 1917 convention, decided to press the state superintendent of education office to grant education credit for music courses given in cities of the first class, trying thus to fill the need of musicians for the symphony orchestra. Like other cities outside New York and Boston, Seattle was forced to develop its own musicians if it were to sustain a year-around diet of classical music.[1]

The war years were lean ones for the symphony; consequently the Symphony Society was financially reorganized by business leader James D. Hoge in 1919 after a funding campaign brought in $100,000. This infusion enabled Spargur to enlarge the orchestra to eighty-five members and to begin concerts at the new Masonic Temple near Broadway and Pine.[2]

In November 1914 Nellie Cornish returned to Seattle and to her friends after abandoning a frustrating career as a classical pianist and teacher in California. Cornish was dedicated to teaching, but in a novel way: she employed the "Fletcher Method," of Montessori origin, which she learned in Boston in 1904. In addition, she incorporated Calvin Brainerd Cady's music education ideas. She became familiar with Cady's theories in 1911 while teaching music teachers in Los Angeles. Cady, as "Aunt Nellie" relates in her autobiography, looked on music as a means of "furnishing opportunity for the development of logic, discrimination, and critical judgment." This approach appealed to a student's individuality, which in turn aided in developing a firm grasp of theory. Students were allowed to proceed at their own pace, not according to a regimen. Despite recent disappointments, she was inspired to teach; more significantly she wanted to start a school. In 1914, she left friends in Salt Lake City, and headed for Seattle, stopping in Oakland along the way to learn all she could about organizing a school from Cora Jenkins, who ran a successful one there.

With the help of banker friends in Seattle she rented the second floor in the Boothe Building at Broadway and Pine. A friend and piano teacher, Martha Sackett, loyally joined her, bringing her twenty-five pupils along. Two other friends were added to the faculty. Originally her intent was to teach children about all the arts, but to emphasize music. By the end of the first season eighty-five students had enrolled, and a violinist had been added to the faculty. The year 1915 began with 100 enrollees. Next, she added a normal school for teachers and the number of faculty members grew, though in a serendipitous fashion.[3]

Whenever a talented artist appeared on the scene, or whenever Cornish heard of a nearby talented instructor she fancied, she tried and usually succeeded in recruiting them. Wanting to add a course in eurhythmics, she found someone who had studied under its originator, Emile Jaques-Dalcroze. A French visitor, Lucien Perrot, became the school's French teacher, thus beginning a language department. An acclaimed artist in the city, John Butler, was added to teach painting—earlier he had given classes for the Seattle Fine Arts Society at its downtown gallery in the Metropolitan Building Company tract.

Voice teachers were added; then dance was introduced under direction of European-trained Mary Ann Wells. The high point of her program at this early stage was the hiring of Cady in 1916—the school became the incarnation of his educational ideas, after all. He soon became its associate director.

The Cornish School's immediate success, and burgeoning growth testified to the need that existed in the city for such a program. At the time, the bulk of its students must have come from the well-to-do and upper classes. The *Post-Intelligencer* correspondent on the arts commented in 1917, that the school "has among its patrons some of the leading families of the Northwest and has enrolled in its short existence over 600 pupils [making it the largest music school west of Chicago]." These Seattleites undoubtedly wanted their children to develop a taste for the arts beyond what the public schools could offer. The *Town Crier*, which prided itself on being exceptional in every way, gave ample space

to the school as it moved from success to success. The humble
Nellie Cornish, with her devotion to teaching and her demonstrated organizational ability was an ideal subject. Charles D.
Stimson stated the case well in 1919, when she told Nellie Cornish
"It strikes me that any citizen of Seattle who has made as good as
you have is a citizen we can't afford to lose." At that time, the
school was in crisis due to the onset of the post-World War I
depression. Her board of trustees came to the rescue by forming
the Cornish Realty Company as a means of getting funds to build
an appropriate school facility.

Cornish School trustees formed a kind of who's who of
Seattle's aristocracy—most were married to musically and artisti-
cally inclined wives. Among their number were Horace C. Henry,
whose art collection would form the original core of the Henry
Gallery; lumberman Thomas D. Stimson, who was also president
of the Metropolitan Building Company; Frederick K. Struve, Mrs.
C. D. Stimson, Agnes H. Anderson, Mrs. David E. Skinner, shipbuilder Edgar Ames, and Alton W. Leonard of Stone and Webster.
That funding was found should come as no surprise. Construction
began on the new building in early 1921.

A letter written by the secretary of the Seattle Fine Arts Society in September 1914 contains a description of the Seattle art
scene:

> Only just recently has any light been shown on the situa-
> tion. We have been a very flourishing little group, now 350 in
> number. . . . The art producers have been the back-bone of the
> organization with the added group of art patrons. [And a
> would-be art organization, the Washington State Art Associa-
> tion a rival group that has raised $40,000 to $50,000 that has
> gone only to "professional exploiters. They have gotten money
> from several "moneyed men" in Seattle trying to launch an
> Art Gallery scheme. But they have practically folded.] Now
> the SEATTLE FINE ARTS ASSOCIATION has a subscription
> campaign to raise $20,000 for a tract of land. A building fund
> will be required. We've had several good exhibitions [from
> the American Water Color Society, American Federation of
> Arts, and one from MacBeth's.]

Using the above letter as a kind of window on the early twentieth-century Seattle art scene it is possible next to fill in some of
the detail. The Seattle Fine Arts Society started up in March 1908
by sponsoring lectures by knowledgeable city residents, and visitors. The emphasis of these presentations seems to have been on
Oriental art and on American prints. (Imogen Cunningham, however, lectured on the "Art of Photography.")

The overall purpose of the Seattle Fine Arts Society was to foster local art and art appreciation. Although exhibitions were essential to their program, Pacific Coast cities were remote from established art organizations and galleries. Thus, they were forced to join together with groups in other cities to form a circuit and to share the costs of traveling exhibitions.

The West Coast's remoteness in 1916 can be underscored by the fact that Chicago was considered "West" in 1916, when the American Federation of Art (AFA) held its sixth annual convention there. The AFA, in 1912, asked where the SFAS planned to hold its exhibits, exclaiming that it hopes to "make circuits" to the Pacific Coast, "providing some one on the coast would undertake general arrangements." Other coast cities had also contacted the American Federation of Art about exhibits. Diffusion of the fine arts was clearly going to have to be more dependent on resources that lay outside the region than was the case with popular entertainment and classical music.

Not that there were no local artists. There were; but many traveled to Europe and elsewhere for further training and to pursue their careers. Thus, Helen Ross praised the Society of Seattle Artists (which later merged with the Seattle Fine Arts Society) for the quality of its Ninth Annual Exhibit in November 1913. She thought it the "best ever" because of the greater variety lent by paintings of "Eastern and foreign scenes by local artists studying abroad." She preferred these works over purely local scenes that were primarily landscapes. As examples, she cited Miss J. S.. Woodruff, Miss Electa Armour, Kathleen Houlahan, Mrs. Florence Curtis Cone, Lillian A. Pettingill, John Butler, and Maud J. Kerns. There were, however, other artists. Roy Partridge was, by 1917, "the most widely known." He married Imogen Cunningham, who apprenticed under Edward S. Curtis at his photography shop; together, Curtis and Cunningham helped to establish photography as an art form.

The Seattle Fine Arts Society joined the American Federation of Art in December 1912 and prepared to receive about fifteen paintings for exhibit at a cost of $500. The exhibit committee hoped to share the show and the cost with San Francisco. Items in the exhibit were actually offered for sale, with the Seattle Fine Arts Society receiving a ten percent commission. This practice had become established for traveling exhibits at the time.

As to the Seattle Fine Arts Society's rival, Washington State Art Association, it seems to have been largely a paper organization, although one of its members, Charles Platt, contributed a weekly column to the *Town Crier* on the national art scene, sometimes spiced with local commentary. In 1911 the Washington State Art Association claimed 1,900 paid members, including 600 life members from Seattle and 100 from Alaska. It had accumulated a building fund of $253,615 which organization officials planned to spend for an auditorium and gallery at the former Providence Hospital site on Fifth and Madison.

However, their scheme floundered in 1911 when it became tangled with the so-called Bogue Plan campaign. At that time, voters opposed a bond issue for acquiring the site because of the success pro-Bogue forces had in convincing the public that it would jeopardize the integrity of the Bogue Plan. The association existed without a facility until 1917, when it coalesced with the Seattle Fine Arts Society. The Washington State Art Association's days were numbered when the *Town Crier* offered to and became the "official organ" of the Seattle Fine Arts Society in September 1914.

The Seattle Fine Arts Society, after absorbing the Society of Seattle Artists, finally acquired regular exhibit rooms, where classes were also given by John Butler. These facilities were on the fourth floor of the Baillargeon Building. Twenty-five canvases from the MacBeth Gallery were the first to be exhibited: admission was free, the catalog cost ten cents. Monthly exhibitions followed.

In 1914 the new University of Washington Fine Arts Department discovered that few students could draw. To address this problem they induced the state teachers convention in Tacoma to pass a resolution requiring drawing as a prerequisite for all laboratory courses, introducing the subject into the curriculum generally, and requesting the state superintendent to appoint a state art supervisor.

As to the progress of the Seattle Fine Arts Society, its increasing popularity led it successively from leasing some small rooms in the Boston Block, to larger rooms in the Baillargeon Building, then to a new building at Third and Spring. Now, Society president, Charles Gould, asked University president Henry Suzzallo, to intervene with John F. Douglas, whose Metropolitan Building Company was developing the university's downtown tract; Gould wanted a fine arts gallery built on the tract. Suzzallo's persuasive powers must have worked because one week later, in February 1916, the university's Extension Division director wrote about subletting space in the "future" fine arts building and thereby help centralize the city's art institutions.

The final merger of the SFAS and the Washington State Art Association in January 1917 must have been part of the arrangement: collector and patron, Horace C. Henry, donated $500 to defray expenses, and lumberman R. D. Merrill was asked to contribute; these men previously supported the Washington State Art Association.

Douglas, in the meantime, agreed to have a building specially designed for Seattle Fine Arts Society use at Fourth Avenue and University Street. It was occupied in April 1917.

Linked with this new facility was the establishment of the School of Fine Arts, under the directorship of landscape painter, Paul Gustin. In trying to meet its goal of having the new structure serve as a general arts center, Douglas consented to allowing the Seattle Fine Arts Society sub-let rooms for compatible uses as well. That booster of sophisticated culture, the *Town Crier*, expressed genuine pride at the "increased interest being taken by people at large in the upbuilding of the city."

Undeterred by America's entry into World War I, in April 1917, the society continued to grow, claiming a membership of about 300 by mid-1919, and pointing with pride to its fostering of the "art spirit" throughout the Pacific Northwest by its monthly lectures, exhibitions, and "general cooperation with other organizations whose aims and interests run parallel to ours." By September 1920 the society was attracting viewers of its exhibits on the order of 3,000 to 6,000 per month. Like area musicians had done previously, Seattle artists had, by 1920 begun to cultivate their own talents, laboring to create an infrastructure for exhibiting their work at the same time. Within two more decades a distinctive "Northwest School" would spring forth from these modest beginnings.[4]

Outdoor Recreation: The Beginning of Organized Mountaineering and Conservation Movement

Much to the disgust of local professional sports promoters, whose livelihood is dependent on spectators in search of sedentary forms of recreation, Seattle traditionally has had a disappointingly high number of outdoor enthusiasts in its population. Boating, water sports, skiing, and mountaineering in all its various forms (from urban walks and trail hiking to rock climbing) have engaged large numbers of the city's residents since the first decades of the twentieth century.

Water sports were popular because of the easy access to Lake Washington, Green Lake, Lake Sammamish, and a score of smaller, outlying bodies of water. Two saltwater beaches (Alki at West Seattle and Golden Gardens at Ballard) also were popular. Boating, beyond rowing and canoeing, was affordable only to the wealthier classes.

But the organized sport of mountaineering attracted people from all walks of life, though leadership roles in this young pastime were assumed by professional people who tended toward "organization" by the very nature of their daily routines.[1]

Taking inspiration from Portland's Mazamas, the "Mountaineers," organized after "seven or eight" Seattleites accompanied the group from the south on a 1906 outing and climb of Mount Baker. This tiny cadre proceeded to enlist 150 men and women as charter members of the Seattle Mountaineers in 1906.

Starting with local walks and picnics to which boats, trains, and street cars could transport participants, the Mountaineers went on to plan the first of what would become annual summer outings of three weeks' duration. Mount Olympus was chosen as a destination in 1907, Mount Baker in 1908, Mount Rainier in 1909. It must be remembered that, at the time, access to the periphery of these peaks was normally by train. Expeditions then traveled by various means over rough, unsurfaced roads to the heads of primitive trails, or to places from which trails could be cut. Among the women summiteers, at least some abandoned their hampering skirts for trousers. Pack trains had to be organized. Food caches frequently had to be installed; then expedition members had to worry about whether or not bears, cougars, or rodents would beat the party to the supplies.

The 1908 Mount Baker outing required packing in through thirty miles of trailless terrain; thirty-nine party members reached the summit. Sixty-two members of the 1909 Mount Rainier outing climbed that summit—unroped, using only alpenstocks, and having no sense of the hazards that a slip on hardened snow or ice surfaces presented.

The year 1910 saw the Mountaineers approach 10,000-foot Glacier Peak from Buck Creek Pass, which meant the party had to drop down about three thousand feet to cross the fiercely grinding Suiattle River. Then they proceeded up the mountain proper. Fifty-seven reached its summit, including the first woman to climb the peak.

The 1911 outing was a long one. The group traveled by pack train to Mount Adams and the Goat Rocks by way of Longmire Springs near the base of Mount Rainier's south flank. Fifty-two of the party made it to the top.

The Mountaineers were, once again, on Mount Rainier in 1912, this time cutting a trail to the alpine meadow at Summerland. From there, they climbed to the summit via Emmons Glacier.

To enable people living in Everett and Tacoma to participate more directly in their activities and to expand membership, the

Mountaineers established branches: Everett in 1911 with forty-eight members, and Tacoma in 1912 with fifteen. Next, the organization leased Forest Service property about forty-five miles distant from Seattle, at Snoqualmie Pass to serve as a year-around operational base in the mountains. Members built a lodge there in 1914. To get to the location, Mountaineers had to travel over Snoqualmie Pass which was, at the time, a slightly improved wagon road.

At Mount Rainier, members began participating in winter sports soon after the peak achieved national park status. They spent five days at newly-built Paradise Inn in the winter of 1916, capping a snowshoeing and pack trip from the railhead at Ashford, six miles outside the park boundary.

Cross-country skiing started during the winter of 1915-1916, followed in 1917 with the opening of Paradise Valley to winter sports. Commercial photographer and mountaineering promoter, Asahel Curtis, initiated a guide service that year in order to introduce elements of safety into mountaineering. These procedures were based on experience gained during the club's early years and on techniques developed by European alpinists. Ropes and ice axes now became standard pieces of safety equipment. And it was upon techniques worked out at this time that mountaineering has developed down to the present.

The Mountaineers also furnished the first four guide service managers in Washington. In the words of one of their number, Joseph Hazard, they introduced "business methods and safe party guidance" to the sport. In the years to follow, members of the Mountaineers would develop formal courses in climbing and wilderness survival, out of which would emerge the classic textbook in the field, *Mountaineering: Freedom of the Hills*, first published in 1960.

Under the inspiration of the Mountaineers and the Federation of Women's Clubs the conservation movement took root. Creation of Mt. Rainier National Park in 1899 became the region's first bow toward conservation. Mountain recreation at the park and the steady development of the Snoqualmie Pass recreation area (accessible by train) soon drew attention westward to the Olympic Peninsula, a virtually unexplored wilderness. The Federation, as early as 1904, sought support for a national park — "Elk National Park". The Mountaineers summer expedition there in 1907 inspired the club to request the state's congressional delegation to introduce legislation for national park status. These efforts were crowned by lame-duck president Theodore Roosevelt's Executive Order establishing a national monument within the national forest in 1909. Attempts to cancel this designation by the Olympic National Forest supervisor and the district office were rebuffed before 1911. That year Congressman William Humphrey introduced a national park bill, setting off a tussle that lasted until 1915, when President Wilson reduced the boundaries by one-half. By this act the lowland forests in the national forest were freed up for harvesting. Confidence began to wane in the conservation values of the USFS, occasioning a visit to Seattle by Chief Forester Henry S. Graves to meet with the Mountaineers and the Federation. Graves promised trails in an attempt to relieve the pressure for park status.

The two conservation groups responded by passing a resolution in May 1915 for national park status; to this both Mountaineer member and commercial photographer Asahel Curtis and the Chamber of Commerce strongly protested — as they would consistently in the years ahead. Controversy over establishment of a National Park Service and the war diverted attention from these efforts for the time being. Not until 1933 would the struggle to establish an Olympic National Park resume.[2]

Beautifying the City . . . For Eternity?

Seattle was a coal and wood-burning city throughout the period. Even as a youngster in the 1920s and 1930s the author recalls the smells of the coal smoke-laden air in winters, of dense fogs filled with pollutants cast up from thousands of homes; all this added to particulates contributed by the dozens of sawdust-burners in the Salmon Bay area and industrial smokestacks scattered south of Yesler Way. But, unlike the present day, the mountains remained clearly visible whenever the clouds lifted. A brownish veil did not then accumulate with successive sunny days. Views of the mountains, of the waters, and preservation of existing city woodlands were what the Board of Park Commissioners attempted to retain before it was too late. What they managed to accomplish by the time America entered World War I is largely what the city has today.

The Seattle Board of Park Commissioners was established in 1884, when David Denny donated the Seattle Cemetery to the city. Near Westlake Avenue and Denny Way in the regrade, this tract would be renamed Seattle Park after the coffins were removed, and finally Denny Park. As with the city itself, the commissioners had no power of condemnation that would allow them to acquire private land for public purposes. Nor did the $100,000 budget the commissioners had in 1892 allow them to buy land outright; they urged that the budget should be at least $500,000 if they were to make progress. In this year they were allowed to appoint a park supervisor, E. O. Schwagerl, whose "master plan" demonstrated both wisdom and foresight.

He "selected" as the best grounds "suitable for public pleasure" the stretch of shore land between Bailey Peninsula and Madison Park. He considered this to be the "grand link between the two great parks on Lake Washington"—the "real heart and center of the magnificent system ˙.˙. [and] that at the earliest practicable moment the boulevard between Yesler avenue and Madison street be made." Whether Schwagerl's conception inspired Assistant City Engineer George F. Cotterill is not certain. But as chairman of the Paths Committee of the Queen City Good Roads Club, he mobilized and supervised volunteers in the construction of twenty-five miles of bicycle paths stretching along the shores of Lake Washington, practically encircling the city and extending into the suburbs. It was largely upon this route that the Olmsted Brothers would develop a city-wide plan for parks, playgrounds, and boulevards, beginning in 1903.[1]

The purchase of two large tracts in 1900, Woodland and Washington parks, inspired the commissioners to seek professional advice. Woodland Park, which had been acquired and platted by Guy Phinney in 1887, was sold to the city for $100,000. Woodland would inherit Leschi Park's zoo population in 1903 when the Seattle Electric Company no longer saw a profit in maintaining it. But (according to the *Argus*) the Company simply gained revenue by transporting zoo-goers to Woodland Park.

Street railways had begun developing commercial parks attractions as early as 1887, running one line to Lake Union from downtown, then others to Leschi and Madison in 1888. Leschi was reached by a cable car on Yesler Way, carrying recreationists from the shore of Elliott Bay over Profanity Hill, then about two miles across residential districts, before steeply descending to the park on the shore of Lake Washington. From Leschi people could see a sweeping panorama, the Cascade Mountains, extending from Mount Rainier, sixty miles south, to Mt. Baker, slightly more than one hundred miles to the north. Beach cottages as summer homes lined the shores in both directions from the park. Abutting Leschi Park was Madrona Park to the north. Uphill from the beach of the latter (where there was a hotel and boat launching facility) was virgin forest through which intertwined rail-protected footpaths.

Madison Park originated from twenty-one acres that John J. McGilvra, set aside to attract customers of the Madison Street Cable Car Company that he and other realtors were promoting in 1890. Developed into an amusement park, its centerpieces were a 500-seat capacity pavilion, a long stretch of beach, a boat house, a

Puget Sound Maritime Historical Society

Figure 8: Madison Park, about 1905. Smoke from excursion boat obscures view of Webster Point and Laurelhurst.

ballpark that was home to the Northwest League baseball champions, and a racetrack. Cruises departed from Madison for trips around the lake. McGilvra accommodated long-term summer vacationers by constructing platforms on which wall tents could be set up. (Woodland Park followed this practice as well.)

However, the park was intended as a promotion for real estate development. For his part, McGilvra limited building construction to cottages from which he derived revenue in the form of annual rents—the *Star* labeled the enterprise, the only fiefdom in Seattle. (The McGilvra Estate at last sold the remaining lots to the city in the 1920s.) Not content with developing Madison Park, McGilvra pressed the Puget Mill Company throughout the 1890s to donate land extending from about 31st and Madison Street to Union Bay to the city. Finally, the company, wanting to construct a water main on one of its subdivisions, exchanged sixty-two acres in that ravine area for city construction of the main. This area became Washington Park.

Attesting to the popularity of these amusement parks—all of which began as private enterprises that were later purchased by the city (after they no longer proved profitable)—theater magnate, John Cort, built a six-story Casino at Leschi in 1892. He drew on his downtown theater for vaudeville acts at the park; its stage was second only in size to one in San Francisco.

Following Cort's lead, George K. Beede built the Madison Park Pavilion. Both Beede and Cort began by offering family entertainment, but their facilities soon became beer halls once their owners found ways to circumvent the licensing requirement. The Madison Park fairground doubled as a race track, and as late as August 1911 a "running and harness race" was scheduled. Its main backer was former King County Sheriff, Edward Cudihee. He was convinced that horse racing could be done "independent of the betting ring."

Evidence challenging Cudihee's assertion could readily be found at The Meadows, a racetrack south of Seattle near the Duwamish River. The *Argus* charged in 1908 that the Meadows ". . . race track is the worst gambling hole that has ever been opened in the county of King . . . . Men lose their all at the races, and women lose more than the men . . . their souls. Young boys, too."[2]

Madison Park was refurbished for the 1909 Alaska-Yukon-Pacific Exposition, and renamed the "White City Park." After that event, Seattle Electric Company fell into a dispute with realtors along its routes. Then, in 1919, the city purchased the neglected operation; as a part of the deal, they acquired Madison Park. Seattle's purchase of other amusement parks followed similar patterns.

Alki Beach was one of Seattle's commercial parks that was not at first accessible by street car, but by water instead. The *Argus's* Chadwick, who had pleaded for development of Alki as a summer resort in 1900, recalled in 1909 that only a "few summer camps" were there in 1900. But, if there were few camps, people nevertheless traveled over by boat during the day. In 1901, an estimated 2,000 people ferried daily to the beach, and a comparable number went by small steamer. An amusement park and natatorium attracted visitors, some of whom camped on the beach in tents. By 1902 Alki had become so popular that a trolley extension finally offered a land route alternative. By 1909 Chadwick saw ". . . everything . . . from log camps costing many thousands of dollars, to the cheapest kind of loneliest tents. Farms have been invaded." A former mosquito-infested haven had become covered with campsites and cottages. One observer described the scene: "for three solid miles shacks and camps and cottages are so near together that it practically amounts to one solid block."[3]

In addition to the major parks described above, the city had acquired smaller parklands by donation and purchase. However, nothing linked these pieces of real estate together as parts of a unified whole. This, the Park commissioners decided to do. In 1903 they contracted with the Olmsted Brothers of Brookline, Massachusetts—the pioneer and foremost landscape architectural firm in the country—to develop a comprehensive plan for the city. One of John C. Olmsted's primary goals was to provide a park or a playground within one-half mile of every home in the city. In its recommendations the Olmsted Brothers contended that "much can be done if public sentiment is aroused favorably, and if owners do not try to obtain every cent possible for the needed land, but are helpful and cooperative." While urging the acquisition of as much land as possible that had views of the water, the mountains, and woodlands, the Olmsteds cautioned commissioners that the plan could be implemented piecemeal.

The Olmsteds began work on their plan at Bailey Peninsula, to the south on Lake Washington, and linked the other elements along a boulevard and parkway system. The boulevard was to run northward along the lakeshore to Mount Baker beach, then proceed upland over the "Yesler Slide" area, then return to the lakeshore at Leschi, past Madrona Park, from where it would meander toward Washington Park at 31st and Madison, passing through the park in the direction of Woodland Park.

There would be spurs to Green Lake and to Queen Anne Hill, crossing from there to Interbay, thence to Fort Lawton, a distance of about twenty miles. Extensions would be made to Beacon Hill Park, for a "meadow park," another from Washington Park to Volunteer Park via a boulevard to be named Interlaken. From Washington Park there would also be an extension past the University of Washington grounds along Union Bay. Above Yesler Slide there was to be a boulevard at "Rainier Crest" along 31st Avenue.

To the southwest, there would be a Duwamish Parkway extending from Beacon Hill. An extension to Magnolia Bluff would be approached from a scenic drive that circumnavigated Queen Anne Hill. This plan would, in its general outline, be the nearest approximation to a city plan for the rest of the century. (In 1936, John C. Olmsted would return for the last time to plan the Washington Park Arboretum as part of a Works Projects Administration venture.)

With justification, Roger Sale points out the Olmsted plan's elitist inspiration. The street railways brought the blue collar families to commercialized sites: Madison, Madrona, Leschi, and Alki—tawdry Madison Park was bypassed, and Alki thankfully stood on the periphery. The parkways, "speed ways" (really, bridle paths for the horse set), and boulevards were for those who could afford carriages and automobiles (which were just coming into vogue). These major scenic transportation routes connected wealthier residential neighborhoods, dotted with their admixtures of architectural style: Tudor, barn-style, colonial, pretentious colonnaded plantation styles, roomy box-frame, and plain brick. This clear class-oriented philosophy within the plan was reinforced by a playground system linked to it. Playgrounds were primarily the haunts of working and lower middle-class families.

When the commissioners got the city charter revised in 1904 (by using the newly won initiative technique for governmental change), they removed the Park Board from city council control. Now, the formerly dispersed agencies concerned with parks, playgrounds, parkways, and boulevards were brought under the board's jurisdiction. Its operating budget was to come from ten percent of the monies received for all licenses, fees, and fines, plus "not less than three-fourths of a mill of the annual tax levy." The board was off and running: voters successively approved bond issues of $500,000 in 1906 for land acquisition, $1 million in 1908, $2 million in 1910, and $500,000 in 1912. These actions provided the essential seed money necessary to implement the basic part of the Olmsted plan.[4]

While the 1911 Bogue Plan for the comprehensive development of Seattle would "build" conceptually upon the Olmsted Brothers' vision, it was the Olmsted Brothers' plan, in reality, that underlay whatever beautification the city would undergo in the future. In the absence of the Olmsted plan, the city would have had no coherent blueprint for the future at all. Its growth would have been dictated entirely by commercial considerations, and would have followed the pattern of what happened around Lake Union, where there are no public amenities whatsoever. Lake Union became the quintessential industrial lake, a parking lot for "Liberty Ships" between the wars.

With respect to the 1911 Bogue Plan—which the voters rejected in March 1912—two of its main features were pre-empted even before voters acted. First, the downtown University of Washington tract had become the effective northward portion of the city center by 1912, and business offices were beginning to collect there, away from the congested Yesler area. The latter would remain unaffected by the furor over the Bogue plan. And, since the existing "civic" center and business offices of the major corporations were already in the Yesler area, the two formed a complement to one another. This reality seemed not to have impressed the Bogue planners in the way it should have. Second, in respect to the Port of Seattle, it was already in the process of developing the harbor without any special reference to the Bogue plan.

Spurred by a desire to spruce up the city in preparation for the 1909 Alaska-Yukon-Pacific Exposition, in possession of the power of condemnation, and in control of its own the purse strings, the Park Board acquired the Bailey Peninsula ("Seward Park") and Ravenna Park by condemnation, and Madrona and Leschi parks by purchase from the Seattle Electric Company in 1909. By this time, the company had found park maintenance an unrewarding headache; population had expanded to their amusement parks, and other means of transportation were becoming more widespread. And seizing upon the initiative of Port of Seattle president, Hiram Chittenden, the board secured shore land from the state legislature in 1913.

While Chittenden was preoccupied with acquiring shore lands for commercial management by the Port of Seattle, the Park Board wanted these emerging shore lands to come under its jurisdiction. The board also took advantage of unemployed workers, hiring them frequently for clearing projects on many of the unimproved holdings.

The Seattle Park Board also assigned a top priority to the creation of Lake Washington Boulevard: "on account of the rapidly increasing land values of Lake Washington property, it would be best to secure as much water frontage and boulevard right-of-way parallel with the lake as possible." By 1913 there would be twenty-five miles of improved roadway—of the estimated fifty miles total—essentially following Cotterill's old bicycle path.

As to playgrounds, the board reported in 1909 that: "Up to two years ago very little had been done toward developing playgrounds." The board responded to "popular demand for recreational facilities," improving the four existing ones and placing men and women supervisors at each location during the summers. All of this activity was consonant with the objectives of School Superintendent Frank Cooper: healthy children contribute to a healthy and efficient society. By the end of 1912—the high point of expansion—Seattle possessed twenty-eight parks, twelve improved playgrounds (out of a total of twenty-two) four field houses, and Alki Bathing Beach.[5]

Part II

Urban
Turbulence
Underway

8

City Politics, 1904-1910

Mayoral Administrations of
Ballinger, Moore, Miller, and Gill

"The years 1900-1904 seem to mark the nadir of the reform movement in Washington"—in the eyes of one historian of the period. Actually not much in the way of reform had been accomplished even before Populist Governor John Rogers's death in 1901, the first year of his second term. Whatever the chief executive's intentions, the newly elected legislature had been overwhelmingly Republican and had opposed every measure he introduced, such as railroad regulation, the centerpiece of his Populist program. When Henry McBride succeeded to the governorship he, too, pressed for a commission, but was defeated by the railroad lobby. In their efforts, railroad interests enlisted the services of influential Walla Walla banker Levi Ankeny. Both he and Seattle's Samuel Piles wanted to become United States senators. Through the auspices of railroad lobbyist and ex-governor John H. McGraw, Ankeny agreed to support Piles's senatorial election by the state legislature when it assembled in 1905. In return, Piles promised to support Ankeny's candidacy in 1909. In a written agreement, Piles also pledged his support for the lumber manufacturers' objective of enlarging the Interstate Commerce Commission in an effort to dilute its allegiance to the railroads.

To get their own senator elected, the King County Republicans promised to support railroad commission legislation that would be satisfactory to Ankeny's eastern Washington constituents. For its part, the railroad lobby was willing to accept a regulatory commission, but only one appointed by a friendly governor.

This, the lobby would get under Governor Albert Mead (1904-1908), a man who owed his 1904 election to the lobby and to James J. Hill's Washington Political Bureau Chief, J. D. Farrell. Farrell's first step was to short-circuit unfriendly Republican Governor McBride's re-election. His second was to put forward Mead's candidacy, a politician in whom Farrell had confidence. These arrangements were made with the assistance of a compliant legislature.[1]

At the state level, it was the railroad domination of the legislature, the Republican party, and even leadership in the conservative wing of the Democratic party in which Farrell's support could be found. This combination drove liberal members of both parties to join in passing reform legislation in Olympia from 1907 through 1911—actions paralleling a similar "insurgency" at the national level. Within city government, reform forces tended to coalesce, forming short-lived organizations, such as the Citizens' Non-Partisan League, the Municipal Ownership Party, the Civic Union, the City Party, and the Public Welfare League. These local constituencies were preoccupied with establishing publicly owned utilities: the water supply, electric power, the street railways, sewage and garbage disposal, paved streets and sidewalks, and public amenities in general.

In the first few years of the century there was even greater pressure for municipal ownership of Seattle's street railways than there was for electrical power—the latter seemed a foregone conclusion, a natural second step once the Cedar River water supply problem had been resolved.

Although municipal ownership advocates could cloak themselves in the raiment of high moral purpose (because the franchises were considered by many to be at the foundation of political corruption), those who stood in opposition to vice in its open-town form could attract more public attention. After all, their purpose was the suppression of activities that were not only corrupt but also "evil." Newspapers could wax eloquent about vice and police corruption. But as to municipal ownership, even the King County Republican Party's 1900 platform carried a plank advocating a municipally owned plant to supply street lighting and public buildings. In the early twentieth century it was vice in the form of prostitution, liquor, police bribery, and gambling that riveted public attention.

The whole panoply of corruption and the police protection it received, appeared to threaten the preservation of middle-class family and social values. Rallying to Decency's cause were members of the local clergy, prohibitionists, women's groups, owners of small businesses, young professionals, and even some trade unionists.

The "enemies" of this crusade were often, if not usually, found also to be opponents of municipal ownership who also favored the continued protection of vested property rights in vice operations. To overturn things as they were would undermine the entire structure for those who had become accustomed to exercising political power.

The overtones of morality easily became associated with a wide range of other social and political issues. By attacking vice conditions, reform elements also attacked those opposed to municipal ownership, direct legislation through the process of initiative and referendum, regulation of labor conditions, workmen's compensation, non-partisan election of judges, and the like.[2]

Disgust with Mayor Humes's open town policy, led to a grand jury investigation in 1903 and to a recommendation that the mayor and police chief both should resign. But the two men hung on until the election of strait-laced Richard A. Ballinger (1904-1906), who had the crucial backing of the downtown business elite. Ballinger would only slightly "close down" the city. At the same time, he lent support to employers in their opposition to unions, and he remained cool to overtures made by municipal ownership advocates. The *Argus* noted that, only in the closing days of his administration did Ballinger "[screw] down the lid," thereby putting his successor on the spot. The Republican mayoral candidate, John Riplinger, promised to close down the town, while his opponent, William Hickman Moore, pledged to enforce the law against slot machines.[3]

After successfully mobilizing citizen protest against the City Council's granting of an exclusive franchise to the Seattle Electric Company for a streetcar route along Westlake Avenue in 1905, the Municipal Ownership League tried to restrict the granting of franchises in the future. The league next joined with the Workingmens' Party to establish the Municipal Ownership Party. Together they opposed the Citizens' Alliance that had been organized by the Seattle Electric Company's Jacob Furth (first in 1901, then again in 1904).

The Alliance opposed the union shop, boycotts, and picketing, thereby underscoring the essential unity of its membership on these issues. Members of the Protestant clergy also vigorously championed municipal ownership as a means of minimizing graft and as a way to improve service. With the Democratic Party abstaining, the Municipal Ownership Party backed the candidacy of William Hickman Moore. He won, but only by fifteen votes. A known Democrat, Moore earned the endorsement of the *Times* (the *P-I* supported the Republican candidate, John Riplinger)—but Editor Blethen supported all the other Republican candidates, refusing to endorse Riplinger because of his closed town advocacy—or so Harry Chadwick alleged. The *Argus* editor attributed Moore's victory to the "labor vote which believes in municipal ownership": "thousands" of these working men lived in the north end. Not surprisingly Moore lost the First Ward.

Going down to defeat in this election was a bond issue for a street railway; it had been opposed by the Seattle Economic League, headed by Thomas Burke and John H. McGraw. The proposal lost by about 1,400 votes. Significantly, a Sunday closing law passed, along with voter approval of a recall measure; this legislation would first be used in 1911 to recall Mayor Hiram Gill.[4]

Mayor Moore's administration (1906-1908) was characterized by strict enforcement of the law closing saloons on Sunday. The *Argus* feared entertainment would be Moore's next target, taken from a list drawn up by the Ministerial Federation. However, Moore did not proceed to close down gambling houses until the waning days of his administration, just before the February 1908 primary election.

Civic improvements received high priority during Moore's term. But in their execution, City Engineer Thomson continued to face Harry Chadwick's wrath for having no general plan. Chadwick pleaded for a commission or "an engineer, or several of them," to counter Thomson's control of the Board of Public Works—to no avail.

Chadwick also charged that several councilmen were connected to a construction combine that, in turn, fixed prices and distributed work. In fact, Seattle's ward system promoted local improvements by means of pork-barreling, so his suspicions were well-founded. Moore also managed to alienate much of his labor support by opposing the Socialist Party's free speech movement in 1906-1907. Given the tensions that many of these policies generated among his 1906 supporters and the narrowness of his victory in 1906, Moore's re-election appeared out of reach.[5]

Heading into the 1908 election, the Municipal Ownership Party became the City Party; it aimed for direct legislation as a means of combatting corporate control of city government. As a spin-off, the *Star*'s political correspondent, Joe Smith, organized the Direct Legislation League, which led a petition drive for inclusion of initiative and referendum propositions on the ballot; over Hiram Gill's objections the council approved their inclusion. Also on the ballot would be a proposition to have franchises submitted to voter approval.[6]

Seattle's 1908 election was the first to be held under the direct primary law. John F. Miller, opposed William Pitt Trimble in the Republican primary. Trimble campaigned on a promise to fire R. H. Thomson, thereby earning *Times* support. He also tried to use guilt-by-association tactics, making much of the fact that, as a lawyer, Miller had gamblers as clients.

In his campaign Miller promised to continue enforcing the Sunday closing law, claiming that people would not tolerate an open town. He said he would remove the restricted district—but did not say to where. Miller won the Republican primary by picking up support in the residential neighborhoods.

At this point, the Democratic Party entered the campaign, along with the City Party. Moore had their backing and that of the Ministerial Federation. But, as it turned out, he became a victim of his own legacy. As mayor, he had done nothing to remove the red light district, and had only recently begun to close Chinese gambling houses and lotteries, "which have always been said to be the best source of revenue to a grafting administration." Blind pigs still existed in the parks. So, although Moore had done more than previous administrations to establish a closed town, he had not gone far enough—or so it seemed.

Vice became the dominant issue in the 1908 campaign, not municipal ownership. Blue-collar workers, who voted for Moore previously, found vice more tolerable than their former middle-class allies; and, finding Moore hostile to free speech demonstrations, they turned out in sufficient numbers to elect Miller. The *Times* and *Star* supported Moore; the *P-I*, Miller. Miller won by over 5,000 votes.[7]

Equally significant, however, was voter approval of a measure establishing a superintendent of public utilities to oversee franchises. This legislation also required that the city's franchises be approved by referendum vote—another step toward "home rule." Voters in outlying districts overwhelmingly supported these bills because they suffered special neglect at the hands of the franchised utilities.

Ballard's population, for example, was rapidly expanding, causing one Electric Company official to inform managers in Boston that ". . . I am afraid we will have to do something for this section the first of the year . . . [in connection with both street car service and electric rates]." The company also had constructed new trackage and purchased a fleet of new cars to serve the crowds expected to visit the Alaska-Yukon-Pacific Exposition held on the University of Washington campus. This seemed only to whet the appetite of promoters and the neighborhoods for more. Writing to the Boston office again, in December 1909, the company official declared "There is a very strong attempt on the part of the real estate promoters and business people to have us extend many of our lines and open up new territory. . . ." With such rising expectations there was no winning; the pressure on the company would continue to grow.[8]

Mayor Miller had come under fire for being unable to rid the city of the restricted district. In May he indicated its closure "will take some time to accomplish . . . [it] will be necessary to house the poor unfortunates who constitute the colony." In mid-July he promised to close "the lowest houses"; but he also indicated there might be a need for a restricted district somewhere. Harry Chadwick needled him for not closing businesses in question above the Deadline on First and Second avenues and on Pike Street: "There assignation houses [are] everywhere. There are restaurants with closed boxes, and lodging houses above easily reached by back stairways. . . ." He also pointed out conditions in the south part of the city. Under this prodding Miller set September 1 as his starting date, expecting that the time period would be sufficient to allow the denizens of the "colony" to go elsewhere.

This they did. But to Chadwick's dismay, he learned that "some four hundred of the most disreputable women [scattered] through the lodging house section" and elsewhere uptown and into the residential areas. He noted that crib houses had been changed into "parlor houses." After missing his September 1 deadline Miller set another, December 1. On that day he closed down the district, once again, accelerating the scattering effect. To this situation he responded: "The sooner a new district is prepared the better." His offer to establish one was ignored. By mid-May 1909 the *Argus* claimed, "Mayor Miller appears to have made a fizzle of handling the whole [restricted district] affair. . . . [Now,] some of the old places [have] opened up again." And although both the mayor and City Council agreed on the need to segregate "it," the question was "where?" As to the police department, the *Times* accused its chief, Irving Ward (who Miller appointed after firing Wappenstein), of having lost the confidence of his personnel; rumors that the chief was about to be replaced became a source of much disobedience, according to the *Times*. With this scenario as a backdrop, Seattle approached its 1910 election.[9]

The 1910 City Election

The 1910 election was essentially a contest between two Republicans, A. V. Bouillion and Hiram Gill. Bouillion, a city official and member of the Board of Public Works, allied himself with insurgents wanting to reform the party. Gill had been president of the City Council and had consistently opposed municipal ownership of utilities, taxes for city projects, and labor unions. He enjoyed the support of party regulars who saw no need for change. Mayor Miller's noteworthy failures in managing the restricted district, once again, made vice the campaign issue. What should Seattle do with, or to, the restricted district? Allow it to spread uncontrolled over the city, which seemed to be the effect of Miller's policies? Should it be reestablished? These were the questions that had to be answered.

The primary was feverishly contested between Gill and Bouillion, with Gill being charged with responsibility for flooding once-vacant lodging houses in the First Ward. Men were thought to be "colonized" there by William Hurley on camp cots at fifteen cents a night; then transported by taxis and autos to the registration office at the Prefontaine Building. Grand jury detectives flagged an estimated 700 individuals for arrest should they try to vote on February 8.

Gill's finance committee chairman, Miller Freeman, countered these allegations by declaring: "The large number of representative business men who are working for . . . Gill should be a guaranty that the campaign is conducted on clean lines. The attacks [on] Mr. Gill are an insult to every decent citizen in Seattle." Gill, always ready with newspaper copy himself, asserted with hurt innocence: "I don't understand . . . why everyone seems to think that the day after my election I am going to open a dance hall and faro bank on Pioneer Square, and keep it running all night for the next two years."[1]

Members of the clergy objected to Gill's claims that he was a defender of civic morality. The Reverend Mark Matthews of the First Presbyterian Church declared that 1,763 voters from his congregation would go for Bouillion; Reverend George Cairns of Temple Baptist urged his parishioners to do likewise. Other ministers pressed their men to vote, but not for Gill (ex-mayor Moore was running on the Democratic ticket, and had regularly had support of the clergy). The Seattle Federation of Women's Clubs also made it clear where they stood after the primary, during which they succeeded in closing down the Dreamland Dance Hall, an alleged source of prostitution.

Notwithstanding the opposition, Gill won the Republican nomination 17,436 to 14,299. In the process, he lost support of the reform element when Bouillion and Austin Griffiths, seeking a cessation of "machine rule," swung their backing to Moore. Moore, who received a paltry 1,536 votes to win the Democratic primary, lost to Gill in the runoff, 18,012 to 14,703. Gill's victory was sweetened by the election of Republicans to all council seats that were up for election.

Seattle's 1910 election witnessed the largest number of voters registered and voting (legal or not) to that time. But of greater significance, it marked the end of the city's ward system; future Seattle elections would be held on an at-large basis and would be non-partisan as well.[2]

Since Gill had campaigned for a segregated vice district, the imposition of one would, in the view of McClure's reporter Burton Hendrick, give vice concessionaires "almost a legal standing," thereby protecting them from police harassment. Hendrick saw Gill's support as coming not only from vice operators, but also from bankers, "Public Utility Corporations," as well as the *Times*, the *Argus*, and Freeman's *Town Crier*.

In Gill's own words: "[The segregated district] will be the most quiet place in Seattle. . . . The restricted district under me will be located in a place where men will have to go out of their way to find it."[3]

1911: Reform Forces Coalesce

The year 1911 marked a high point of reform accomplishment both within the city and in the city's relationship to the state legislature. The 1911 Washington Legislature began meeting in January, just as a campaign to recall Seattle's Mayor Hiram Gill reached a crescendo. Women, although a political force previously, were able to vote for the first time; a long fought-for workmens' compensation bill would be enacted; enabling legislation for the formation of port districts would pass; and a public services commission would replace the former railroad commission. However, the new body lacked authority to regulate municipally owned utilities.

The latter two pieces of legislation were of critical importance to advocates of home rule. The fight for legislation authorizing the formation of port districts and movement for a public service commission each had its own distinctive history; the timing was right for them to come together in this particular year.

Tempering the surge for reform was the expectation that Seattle would soon benefit from the expansion of trade as soon as the Panama Canal was completed. Because of this expectation, elements in the business community, who were normally hostile to reform of any kind, supported some of these efforts, most notably labor legislation and the formation of port districts.[1]

Gill's election had stimulated reform forces to join under the leadership of the Public Welfare League (PWL), which was organized at the Commercial Club June 16, 1910, just three months after the mayoral election. The Commercial Club itself had supported municipal ownership, public amenities, and moral uplift. It was viewed by some of the downtown establishment as opposing anything the Chamber of Commerce advocated.

The PWL declared in its articles of incorporation that it would:

> advocate, encourage, assist and procure the enforcement of all laws in King County and ordinances in . . . Seattle; to secure the suppression of public vice, [to conserve] the morals of the young; to encourage provision of public recreation; to encourage honesty and efficiency in public service; to secure economy and fidelity in the disposition of public funds; to secure the punishment of all officials who neglect to enforce the laws . . . to invoke the recall against all city officials who violate their oath of public office. . . .

The Clean City Organization merged with the PWL, bringing with it three reports resulting from its own investigations. The Ministerial Federation lent its strong organizational backing, and the Reverend Mark A. Matthews (who is often credited with playing the major role in Gill's recall) brought along his huge Presbyterian congregation.[2]

The Municipal League had been spawned in 1910 out of this local opposition to control of the city by members of a downtown elite who were unwilling to share power. In conjunction with this opposition, they also protested against the typical urban blight associated with police-vice racketeering that Muckrakers were exposing in other cities.

Unlike the single-issue and single-election organizations of a few years earlier, the League saw itself as permanent and addressed a broad spectrum of identifiable municipal issues and problems. It sought to draw into its membership a wide range of people: small businessmen, professionals, members of the clergy, and labor leaders. Together, they hoped to confront the city's problems in a rational, non-partisan way. Its members were discouraged from using the League as a stepping-stone to public office. And, since Seattle's topography tended to promote neighborhood exclusiveness, the League aimed to coordinate the polyglot neighborhoods in common efforts toward shared goals. Its membership reflected this.

Most League members were Republicans; about half were originally from the East, while the rest came mainly from the Midwest. Women were excluded from membership. The majority of the organization's members were comfortably middle class and supported restrained, free enterprise, as well as efficiency and economy in city government. To accomplish these goals, vice and corruption had to go. Where business was found to be in alliance with the various social evils, standing in the way of opportunity and obstructing civil amenities sought by the rest of the population, it had to be regulated.

Organized labor was to be similarly subject to regulation if and when it became abusive of its power. The League's structure reflected these concerns: committees on budget, health and sanitation, harbor development, and city planning were created.

As mentioned above, the league's membership was broadly based: Joe Smith was, for instance, a political reporter who frequently exposed corruption in the pages of the *Star*; the Reverend Mark Matthews headed the largest Presbyterian congregation in the nation and was a self-righteous moral reformer with a Georgia Populist background. But as his power increased, Matthews developed a conservative bias as he associated more with the downtown elite. Another clergyman, the pacifist Reverend Sydney Strong, a Social Gospel Congregationalist, and Rabbi Samuel Koch were members, engineers Reginald H. Thomson and George Cotterill, attorneys James Haight and Bull Mooser C. J. France (the League's first president and, shortly, legal counsel for the Port of Seattle), Austin E. Griffiths ("father of Seattle's playgrounds"), J. Allen Smith of the University of Washington, and small businessmen like Oliver Erickson also belonged.

Besides coalescing on reform issues and sharing a general moral stance, most members found that the city's existing power structure hampered the most efficient use of available resources; so they were susceptible to the preachings of efficiency experts who were then becoming the rage. In 1910 and early 1911 these elements joined to oust Mayor Hiram Gill from office.[3]

Upon his election Gill reappointed Charles Wappenstein as chief of police (he had been Mayor Moore's chief, but was dismissed by Mayor Miller). "Wappy" was a suspected grafter, and Gill, with the ardent support of Alden Blethen, had declared Seattle an open city. Wappy was instructed to implement the plan. The chief soon met with two leaders of the vice rackets, Clarence Gerald and Gideon Tupper and cut a deal: Wappy was to be paid ten dollars per month for each prostitute in Gerald's or Tupper's employment; there were about 500 prostitutes then in Seattle whose addresses were known; police kept a close watch on them and kept track of their whereabouts so that they and their chief would not be cheated. While Tupper regulated the larger brothels, his partner ran much of the gambling, buying the Northern Club, which ran continuously on a three-shift basis; barkers embellished the carnival atmosphere.

Under these conditions, which attracted nationwide publicity, syndicate vice operators and independents flooded into the city to partake of the largess. But, for that very reason, and also because many brothels continued to operate uptown as they had in the past, vice got out of control. The restricted district could not be contained, and Gill's promise to make the social evil obscure now appeared to many, especially members of the Public Welfare League, to be a flagrant and willful lie for which he could not escape responsibility.

McClure's Hendrick reported:

> The city seemed to have been transformed almost magically into one great gambling hell. All kinds of games simultaneously started up, in full public view. Cigar stores and barbershops did a lively business in crap-shooting and race-track gambling, drawing their patronage largely from school boys and department-store girls. . . . All over the city "flat-joints," pay-off stations, and dart-shooting galleries were reaping a rapid harvest . . . in the thirty or forty gambling-places opened under the administration of Hi Gill.

Things appeared to be going so well that Tupper and Gerald formed a corporation, the Hillside Improvement Company, to develop a resort on Beacon Hill with a five-hundred-room brothel as its centerpiece. To spread the building over a city street, builders applied to a sympathetic City Council and got a fifteen year lease. Although it was completed the building only showed how far the city had sunk in sin. Thunderstruck, the population was embarrassed into action by the Public Welfare League in October. Erastus Brainerd, editor of the *P-I*, and a feuder of Alden Blethen, announced, "Gillism has allowed the enforcers of the law to enter into lewd partnership with breakers of the law. . . . It has fostered and encouraged a species of governmental and official favoritism wholly at variance with the spirit and genius of American political institutions and American law."[4]

The *Star* castigated "Gillism." As for the *Argus*, Chadwick declared Seattle still to be the cleanest city on the coast; that the *P-I* was hounding Gill for his role in defeating John Wilson's senatorial candidacy; and Blethen was fattening on the "pickings." He praised Gill for being even-handed; furthermore, he pointed out that not until Gill announced in favor of municipally owned docks did the downtown establishment begin withdrawal of its support—symbolized by dock-owner, Laurence Colman's heavy financing of the recall campaign, using the *P-I* as his chief organ.[5]

The Public Welfare League began circulating petitions October 8 for the mayor's recall. Gill immediately left for Alaska, and William Murphy, president of the council, sought cover in Idaho. Max Wardall ascended to Murphy's position, and became acting mayor, as well. After reading the PWL reports Wardall fired Wappenstein, and had the acting chief close down a number of the offending houses. The council then established its own investigating committee.

When Mayor Gill returned from his sudden trip to Alaska he reappointed Wappenstein as Chief of Police. When enough signatures were gathered on the petitions to initiate a recall, Gill asked Circuit Court Judge Cornelius Hanford for an injunction. Hanford obliged, but was overruled on appeal. The city headed for a bitter campaign.

Gill's strategists, sensing the inevitability of a recall election, and hoping to have it occur before the the onset of woman suffrage, sought an early election. Gill was thwarted by the opposition, which chose not to deliver its petitions until mid-December, too late to avoid the effect of the female vote. The PWL next chose one of its members to run against Gill, a real estate man with a "progressive" reputation, George W. Dilling.[6]

Parallel with the vice and corruption charges against Gill were allegations that he was in league with the Seattle Electric Company against City Light. Electrical system growth provided the incentive for removing the electrical department from the jurisdiction of the Water Department in 1910. Mayor Gill, who, as president of the City Council, had consistently opposed municipal ownership, appointed a former Seattle Electric Company employee, Richard Arms, to the superintendency of the new department.

At the SEC, Arms had been superintendent for overhead lines. Many had expected the appointment to go to James D. Ross, who had served well under Thomson's leadership, both of whom shared a vision of Seattle's industrial and commercial future. The *Star* accused both Gill and Arms of being underlings of Jacob Furth after Arms had failed to get the Ballard street lighting contract once City Light had already set up the poles. Arms also had rejected several lucrative contracts, but had extended service to one expensive outlying area. When an investigation by the council committee reported the misfeasance of Arms these facts only added to Gill's troubles.[7]

Dilling had served in the Legislature in 1903, and, according to an SEC memorandum, ". . . took part in several fights against granting privileges to corporations . . . but he is not in favor of Municipal Ownership as a principle." It was predicted he would fire Arms for ". . . ruining the business of the City Lighting Plant [allegedly] acting under the direction of and to the benefit of this company." The writer reported to the Boston office that the *P-I* was accusing the company of herding its employees to vote for Gill, accusing the company of charging "exorbitant" rates, as well.[8]

Women played a major role in the 1911 election, coalescing under the Seattle Federation of Women's Clubs. Having just gained the franchise, and given the issues of vice and corruption and the narrow margin of victory for Dilling, their vote was critical. When added to the vote which the clergy was able to mobilize, Gill was assured of defeat. Of the 23,000 registered women voters 20,000 voted; Dilling won by a 6,000 plurality. In its survey of nationwide newspaper opinion the Literary Digest found substantial unanimity in crediting Gill's defeat to the female vote. The Oregonian declared: ". . . it was proved that the so-called business man in politics who believes that gambling, drinking, prostitution, and free-and-easy public conscience spell industrial prosperity, is grossly mistaken."[9]

While the *P-I* and the *Star* attacked Gill, of the weeklies only the *Union Record* blasted him; the *Town Crier* and *Argus* supported his policies, convinced, along with Alden Blethen, that vice was not controllable, and also that it represented property that deserved due process protections, foremost.

In the aftermath, a grand jury heard evidence about police receiving payoffs from gambling and vice operators, and for failing to enforce the law. Attention was focused on Wappenstein, whom Dilling had promptly replaced with Claude Bannick. Bannick proceeded to close down the vice establishments. And although Alden and Clarence Blethen were indicted along with Wappenstein, only the latter was convicted and sent to the Washington State Penitentiary at Walla Walla.[10]

9

The City in Transition

Dilling's Administration

Mayor George W. Dilling was able to finish out Hiram Gill's regular term of office by focusing on reorganization within the Police and Lighting departments. However, developments in other areas of city government continued apace. Of primary importance was the campaign for the "Bogue Plan" for a civic center and for harbor improvements.

Following on the heels of Dilling's election came the Harbor Island controversy and the 1912 city election highlighted by George F. Cotterill's candidacy for mayor and the re-emergence of Hiram Gill as a political force.

By 1911, Seattle's downtown finally began to take shape, especially in the vicinity of the University of Washington's Metropolitan Tract, under the dominating influence of John F. Douglas. In effect, Douglas's activities caused the Bogue Plan for a civic center to be bypassed, just as the port commissioners, under Hiram Chittenden's leadership, superseded harbor development under the Bogue Plan with a scheme of their own. The "city beautiful movement" died as a result.

Mayor Dilling had previously accused his rival Gill of conspiring with City Light Superintendent Richard Arms on Stone and Webster's behalf. After Arms resigned, Dilling appointed Chief Lighting Engineer James D. Ross, as superintendent. The mayor instructed Ross to go after downtown customers by appointing two additional solicitors to stalk the area. Ross was also told to seek line extensions north to Ballard and to Georgetown in the south. For its part, Seattle Electric Company responded quickly by mailing 71,000 "folders containing arguments and statistics to combat . . . [the municipal ownership] policy [one to each registered voter]." The company was not about to roll over, not by a long shot.[1]

Following the advice of the National Electric Light Association, Seattle Electric and its private utility cohorts, had Senator David H. Cox introduce legislation to place all public Washington utilities under the jurisdiction of a state commission. But there were too many "home rulers" in the legislature, and the Public Services Commission bill that passed exempted municipally owned utilities from such regulation. Seattle Electric executives complained bitterly. They saw their company losing business because the Seattle Lighting Department offered lower rates. Unfortunately for Seattle Electric Company, its rates were registered with the Public Service Commission and, therefore, were public knowledge; the Lighting Department's rates were not. This frustration was expressed by Seattle Electric's superintendent, W. J. Grambs, on October 2, 1911. Writing to H. T. Edgar in Stone and Webster's Boston office, he said:

> . . . the City schedule is so designed as to lower the KWH rate automatically as a consumer's load factor increases. This results in a consumer always paying practically the same per kilowatt of demand and the rate adopted by the City was so designed to produce practically $65.00 per kilowatt year, while our rate is fixed and does not vary with an increased load factor . . . I don't see how we can hold our residence customers when they realize that they can save from 50 [cents] to $1.50 per month using the City service. . . . The City has given good service.

Bringing municipally owned operations under Public Service Commission control became a goal of private utility forces in the Pacific Northwest. Grambs had been encouraged after the bill's passage when City Councilman Oliver Erickson, introduced an ordinance to reduce City Light's residential rates over Ross's objections. Ross explained that residential customers were already being served at a loss that was made up by sales of commercial lighting and power. Erickson even called together his own claque, which the *P-I* accused of "mob conduct." Although Erickson could not muster more than one other vote in favor of his proposal, a smaller rate decrease was conceded. Company Sales Manager H. M. Winter encouraged Grambs in September by reporting that Ross ". . . is desirous of finding some means of blocking Councilman Erickson's efforts [at taking the referendum route for his ordinance]."

At this time, Ross feared losing his new job if he antagonized Erickson. Grambs and Winter, for their part, hoped to modify the Public Service Commission Act and to have Ross seek protection from Erickson under cover of the commission. Ross was not, however, prepared to take such a desperate a step. That Erickson's political ambitions appeared paramount at this early stage seems clear—he had contested William Hickman Moore for the Democratic mayoral nomination in 1910 (and had received less than a thousand votes). Then he won a council seat in 1911 in the city's first at-large election. Thus, the rate reduction episode marked the beginning of antagonism between the two men that intensified until Erickson finally overreached himself in an effort to destroy Ross in 1931.[2]

Mayor Dilling received mixed reviews for his performance as Seattle's chief executive. The Seattle Electric Company reported to its Boston office in July that, "Among the conservative element the conviction is growing that Dilling is one of the best Mayors Seattle has ever had." The fact that he vetoed an ordinance limiting passenger loads on its street cars (partly in light of increasingly frequent accidents) drew the company's applause. And when a recall movement was started against Dilling for not instituting certain jail reforms, and when the names of four councilmen were added to the recall list, recalling the mayor suddenly seemed too frivolous. Seattle Electric Company officials rallied to Dilling's support.[3]

The catalyst for the recall effort was to be found within Erickson's claque, many of whom were disappointed in the City Council's failure to endorse the rate reduction proposal. All three daily newspapers opposed the movement for the political instability it promised, and the undertaking collapsed.

Notwithstanding his general performance in office, Dilling's support of City Light posed a problem for Seattle Electric. When the mayor led a tour group of 1,200 citizens to City Light's Cedar River plant in August, several Seattle Electric Company employees were among their number. One, S.C. Lindsay, reported to Grambs that if the crib dam does not wash out, the plant is superior because of its simplicity. Another wrote that the site itself was "ideal," the power plant "well-arranged," the operators "attentive" and "well-informed"; and despite skepticism about Ross's own oil switches, he was impressed with a Ross-designed "bench board" to control the switches—"very cleverly worked out." In summary, they saw that the plant required a smaller work force to operate; it could be enlarged at minimum expense; and the management was ". . . going ahead in an intelligent and aggressive manner." For Seattle Electric, this intelligence must have seemed particularly gloomy because the company was steadily losing business to the competition. Yet, some lesson might have been learned from information in a December 1911 memorandum that a residential rate reduction by the company had "positive effect." It did not register, apparently.[4]

Meanwhile, Mayor Dilling was compelled to take action on another front; he had to do something about the restricted district. In this undertaking, the appointment of Claude Bannick as chief of police proved of great benefit to him; in fact, Dilling could not have found a more incorruptible public servant to enforce the law.

Bannick soon established a reputation for vigorous, even-handed enforcement that consistently placed him at the top of lists of candidates for chief of police whenever a new mayor took seriously the matter of law enforcement. Soon, Bannick's enthusiasm for the job grew to the point where Dilling finally asked him to relax his "iron hand a bit." To this Bannick asked for the order to be put in writing. Robert "Bobby" Boyce, then writing a column for the *Argus* and Gill's former secretary, predicted the new chief would stay.[5]

With Dilling acting like a "lame duck," in the fall of 1911, candidates began to line up for the spring 1912 city election. The business candidate for mayor was Republican Thomas Parrish; he had served as county assessor and as a member of the Washington Tax Commission. He promised little more to voters than a business-like administration. George Cotterill, known as a leader of the prohibition forces, for his key role in getting the vote for women, and for other reform legislation, also decided to run. Then, former mayor Hiram Gill threw his hat in the ring, as did Socialist candidate Hulet Wells.

Confident that Gill could be beaten in the finals, Cotterill, focused his attention on defeating Parrish in the primary. The *Argus* reported that only Gill was attracting crowds whenever he spoke. (Gill predicted that even Wells would get more votes than Parrish; he was right). Gill won the primary in a landslide, running about 10,000 votes ahead of Cotterill. But Cotterill won in the final election, getting votes from Wells's constituents as well as those of the "moral" middle class.[6]

Legislation: More Common Ground Found

One of the high points of statewide labor reform legislation in the early twentieth century was passage of the Workmen's Compensation Act. Another was eight-hour-day legislation for women, which was passed once workers in the fishing and canning industries were exempted.

Washington's Workmen's Compensation Act would become *the* national standard it was so well written. One of the reasons for the legislation's success, it will be remembered, was that lumbermen and mine owners had joined with organized labor in efforts to reduce mounting liability insurance rates and litigation costs. In addition, the new governor, Marion Hay, gave high priority to workmen's compensation legislation.

Lumbermen, led by the St. Paul and Tacoma Lumber Company's Everett Griggs (president of the Pacific Coast Lumbermen's Association) had another reason for sponsoring the bill—to siphon off increasing radicalism among timber and mill workers. Governor Hay supported this sentiment, as well. He appointed an Employers' Liability Commission to draft a bill. Attorney Harold Preston wrote the legislation, working with a labor and an employer representative. In the legislature, lumberman Mark Reed and Govnor Teats of Tacoma shepherded the bill through, though not without opposition.

A sticking point proved to be a clause providing for "first aid"; it had to be sacrificed to get the act passed. Separate accident funds were provided for forty-seven different occupations; payment rates were graded according to occupational hazards, thereby giving employers an incentive to develop safety programs. Payment by employers into the compensation fund was compulsory, and payment for injury was to go directly from the Insurance Commission to injured parties, thus eliminating insurance companies and lawyers from the process.

Washington was one of the first four states to enact eighthour and a minimum-wage laws for women. The former was given a boost when the United States Supreme Court declared an Oregon ten-hour law for women constitutional in 1908 (*Muller vs. Oregon*). Although the Washington State Federation of Labor, the Federation of Women's Clubs, and members of the clergy failed to get such legislation passed in 1909, the state's granting of woman suffrage in 1910 lent impetus to their effort.

Advocates met resistance from legislators who were sympathetic to industries where large numbers of women worked: fruit picking, processing, and canning, and fish canning. Legislators agreed to exempt these industries as a concession to the coalition of orchardists, agriculturalists, and fruit and fish canning interests. But all other industries employing women were affected. In Seattle this included, among others: laundry, garment, bakery, candy, telephone, restaurant, and hotel workers.

In a 1912 challenge to this legislation, the Washington Supreme Court rejected an employers' argument that their right to due process had been violated (State vs. Somerville). The court also found that the law was within the police powers of the state for protecting the health of female laborers. In 1913, the legislature passed a minimum wage bill as a capstone to this protective edifice.[1]

Not all efforts to enact legislation during these years could be categorized as "progressive." For instance, the Joint Legislative Committee of the State Federation of Labor, the Grange, and the Farmers' Union made an ominous attempt to have a law passed that barred aliens who were ineligible for citizenship from owning land in Washington. This endeavor was aimed primarily at Japanese immigrants. The Federation feared the loss of white jobs and the lowering of pay scales. Many white farmers also resented competition for available land and in truck crop production. For their part, residents of Japanese descent were not content with being held down as a wage-laboring class. Instead, they bought and improved land, often pieces of property that Caucasian farmers chose to ignore; they invested in hotels, cafes, import houses, and other small enterprises. Those European Americans who felt threatened by these activities would finally get their repressive legislation enacted in the 1920s.[2]

Out of the 1911 legislative activity, the work that had greatest immediate significance for Seattle was the passage of a bill authorizing counties to establish port districts.

City Beautiful, the Waterfront, and the "Interests"

Between 1910 and 1913 several factors converged to affect the city's future. The "city beautiful movement" stalled after a splendid beginning. Under the tactful guidance of General Hiram M. Chittenden of the U. S. Army Corps of Engineers, the Lake Washington Canal finally progressed beyond the drawing-board stage when construction began in 1911.

Meanwhile, the Washington chapter of the American Institute of Architects, after pressing for eight long years for a "Civic or Administrative centre" and for a general plan for city development and improvement, succeeded in getting Seattle to establish a Municipal Plans Commission. Out of this effort would emerge Virgil Bogue's plan for comprehensive city development based on two central features, a civic center and harbor development—the latter having a "Bush-type" terminal at Harbor Island as its centerpiece.

Under the leadership of John F. Douglas's Metropolitan Building Company, the University of Washington's downtown tract became an effective city center by 1912, despite the fact that the City's administrative offices remained fixed near the Yesler area at the south end of the business district.

Voters elected the city's first set of Port Commissioners in September 1911, each of whom was strongly in favor of municipal ownership; each also had definite ideas that ran contrary to those of the established business interests about how the Seattle waterfront should be developed. And it was the municipal election of March 5, 1912 that brought these simmering issues to a boil.

The Lake Washington Ship Canal controversy emerged from an earlier canal-scheme battle that came to a head between 1900 and 1904. At that time, a proposal to run a waterway through Beacon Hill to Lake Washington lost out to the northern route connecting Lake Washington to Lake Union en route to Salmon Bay at Ballard and Shilshole Bay on Puget Sound. One of the key issues held over from the earlier controversy was the fact that Lake Union's water level was nine feet lower than Lake Washington and Salmon Bay was a mud flat at low tide. Those two bodies of water would still have to be brought to the same level as Lake Union.

After some urging from city business interests, the Army Corps of Engineers undertook a study in 1903-1904. While conceding the canal's feasibility from an engineering standpoint, they reported that no economic benefit from the project could be foreseen. So, in November 1905, the Corps recommended against construction. The city would have to look to its own resources for the time being.

Not until 1906 did anyone make a serious effort to construct the canal. Then, James A. Moore, a well-known promoter who was responsible for much downtown construction and known for his extensive financial commitments, proposed that a waterway and a wooden lock be built under his auspices; after three years he said he would donate it to the United States government. His projected cost was to be only $500,000. First, however, the federal government would have to grant King County the right-of-way, leaving the county free to contract with Moore.

When Hiram Chittenden, Seattle district engineer for the Army Corps of Engineers, was asked for an opinion by his chief, he declared that Moore's lock would not last more than five years, that it would be too narrow, and that the project would cost twice the estimate. Chittenden urged postponement of congressional action, but to no avail. The Chamber of Commerce had already dispatched former governor John H. McGraw to Washington, D. C., to lobby for the enabling legislation. In pressing for government support of the canal at this time, chamber leaders had a hidden agenda. They expected the volume of traffic through the new channel to become significant enough to convince the federal government to upgrade the project on its own. In the apparent absence of opposition from the Army Corps of Engineers, a right-of-way bill was signed June 11, 1906.

Now, since he was obligated to build the facility, Chittenden was faced with the problem of circumventing Moore's insubstantial plan and coming up with a viable alternative. Historian of the Seattle District of the Army Corps of Engineers, Robert Ficken, reports that Chittenden began by shepherding influential citizens on cruises around the area to demonstrate the engineering infeasibility of Moore's idea. These proved effective. In a December report to his chief, Chittenden recommended a system with two locks, one larger than the other, with the smaller one intended to accommodate Seattle's "mosquito fleet" and small craft; he also preferred construction of masonry locks.

The key to the project's success, and politically its most troublesome problem, was site location. Should it be situated at the lower end, near the Narrows at Shilshole Bay, or at the upper end in Salmon Bay? If located at the lower end, Ballard mill properties probably would be flooded. In early March, Chittenden suggested that the Chamber appoint a board of engineers to decide, but within the next few days events moved fast.

The Chamber overcame mill-owner resistance by guaranteeing that their land would not be inundated; together, the chamber and mill owners got the state legislature to pass a bill on March 18 authorizing the organization of an assessment district for "River, Lake, Canal, or Harbor Improvements." Then, Thomas Burke was sent to Washington, D. C., on behalf of the Lake Washington Canal Association to persuade the War Department to allow revenue collected through this assessment to be put at Chittenden's disposal. Moore, now in over his head, assigned his rights to the Association on May 6.

On May 28, Chittenden assumed full control of the operation, or so it seemed at first. He gave a copy of his plan to *P-I* Editor Erastus Brainerd for publication as a special article. In the piece, Chittenden concluded in favor of the Narrows site. The Chamber supported his recommendation in a resolution issued on July 10. This action was followed by a public meeting on July 17.

According to City Engineer R. H. Thomson, the opposition at the meeting came from the Ballard mill interests represented by the Seattle Cedar Lumber Company's "McEwing," who, when queried by Thomson, admitted that mill owners were really opposed to the canal outright, because, as Thomson sarcastically put it: ". . . the passage of vessels would disturb [them] in the quiet and peaceful possession of the bay for rafting, booming, and storing logs."[1]

Meanwhile, a viable coalition against the canal scheme in general began to take shape. As *Railway and Marine News* described it in its January 1909 issue: ". . . big shipping interests . . . almost to a man, are in favor of the Duwamish improvement to Black River. . . ," Lake Washington's outlet. Railroads were building into the vicinity, and the area was being promoted as an ideal spot for industry and warehouses. For this purpose, widening and straightening of the Duwamish channel were essential. If there was to be money spent, this was where the coalition wanted it spent. Thus, they persuaded the Washington courts to declare the assessment law unconstitutional and to prevent the King County Commissioners from issuing the necessary bond.

Railroad lobbyists also were able to persuade the Manufactures Committee of the Chamber of Commerce to join them in opposing the canal, and in advocating instead the manufacturing development of the Duwamish Valley where the cheapest sites for factories existed:

> . . . except for its low and wet condition [it] is ideally situated for manufacturing . . . and it is readily available for transportation. [But the land is still too expensive. Therefore, the city and Port of Seattle should] condemn and purchase a tract of land . . . preferably on the east side . . . [for a distance of two to four miles] and put it in condition for the erection of manufacturing buildings [so that the cost of an acre would be about $6,000].

The Duwamish coalition emerged January 1911, filing a taxpayers' suit in the names of E. F. Blaine and Gerald Frink challenging the $750,000 bond issue for harbor development.

Railway and Marine News countered accusations leveled by City Council members that railroads were behind the suit by declaring that the canal was unnecessary. In addition, the publication argued that the canal would only increase the civic tax burden and drive several manufacturing plants out of Ballard. *Railway and Marine News* went further, accusing the council of threatening to deny a franchise to the Oregon-Washington Railroad & Navigation Company for the laying of tracks to manufacturing plants in the Duwamish area.[2]

While the Duwamish issue shaped up as an alternative to the

spending of tax revenues on the canal, the chamber went to work. First, the body compromised with mill owners, offering to support lock placement at the upper site. Simultaneously its members promised support to the Duwamish interests for waterway funding. The chamber concluded its effort by running a bill through the Washington Legislature providing $250,000 for canal construction.

Now Chittenden had to reverse his position on the canal site because, as he expressed himself confidentially to Erastus Brainerd of the *P-I*, he feared not getting the canal at all if he were to persist with his preference. He thought that the community would become too divided and then Congress would refuse any appropriation. However, Congress relied on the engineer's December 1906 report anyway, abruptly terminating the controversy by opting for the lower site at the Narrows. To appease mill owners, Chittenden recommended the use of $100,000 from assessment revenue to compensate them for any damages. There was a precedent for this, as R. H. Thomson recounted:

> In 1898, when canal work was done, the Stimson Mill Company was compensated for prospective damages with $40,000, Seattle Cedar Lumber Company with $16,500, and the town of Ballard with $7,500—no damages were sustained, but the money was kept anyway because no one in authority gave a try. [3]

Still, the canal controversy carried into 1910. By then, Thomson, who probably was closer to the in-fighting than anyone, congratulated Senator Samuel Piles for getting the Senate to accept the canal bill. But he accused, ". . . certain persons owning or interested in existing wharfs along a portion of Seattle's waterfront, and who, for the sake of maintaining wharfage rates exorbitant in price, oppose construction of this important work." Complicating Thomson's efforts and those of Chittenden were discussions between an Army Corps of Engineers officer, a Major Kutz, and a "timber jack" named Ives from the Stimson firm. Thomson claimed the talks encouraged the mill owners to hold out for the upper site and ultimately for compensation.

In his own lobbying, Thomson worked with Frank Terrace of Orillia (in the White River-Duwamish Valley) to mobilize area Granges in favor of the canal as a flood control measure—by lowering Lake Washington, the Black River would dry up and relieve the farmers of a major cause of inundation. [4]

During the year, $500,000 was raised from local sources for purchasing right-of-way and for excavation. Construction finally began on September 1, 1911, nine months after Chittenden's retirement and one week before he was elected to the Seattle Port Commission.

The two locks were completed in 1916 and passage between Lake Union and Shilshole commenced. When the canal opened formally on July 4, 1917, construction budgets tallied $1,055,000 from the county, $2,051,000 from the state, and $5,861,000 from the federal government. Seattle's potential harbor now included Lake Union and Lake Washington. Lake Union became an industrial basin; farmers from the east and north of the Lake Washington now had better market access; shoreline along the lakes was recovered both for recreation and commercial development; freshwater access was provided for the storage and wharfage of commercial and recreational craft; and a less expensive means for the trafficking of logs, lumber, oil, and other commodities was provided.[5]

The City Gets a Center . . . and More

Early twentieth-century city planners were fascinated with ideas of engineering efficiency. In this regard, Reginald H. Thomson, Seattle's city engineer was no different. In fact, he was a leading proponent of the idea that engineers could accomplish wonders if they were left unimpeded to work out their designs for the future. He was also at the forefront of municipal ownership advocates who believed that efficient development of Seattle's utilities was being blocked by utility and railroad franchises.

Thomson claimed that, as early as 1893, he had successfully thwarted James J. Hill when the railroad magnate decided that the Great Northern should place its terminal out in the tide flats and then build out to it. Thomson had argued that such a project would interfere with overall requirements for draining the tidelands for future industrial development, proper drainage of the uplands, and that other railroads would follow Hill's precedent and build independent terminals as well. Thomson wanted to prevent the City Council from granting a series of franchises to railroad companies to lay tracks at right angles to the course of the city's growth, and therefore at right angles to what would soon be arterial traffic patterns. The city engineer, as shown above, succeeded, but not without inviting biting criticism like that of Harry Chadwick, who accused him of being a witting or unwitting tool of both the Seattle Electric Company and of the Hill interests.[1]

Thomson also claimed that in facing up to Hill, he forced the GN to tunnel under the downtown to reach its final destination between Smith Cove and Shilshole Bay. After the turn of the cen-

tury, the GN did construct the tunnel, but not without a prolonged fight with the Northern Pacific over a critical piece of the
waterfront, the so-called "ram's horn."

That dispute ended when the two roads, under continuing
pressure from the Chamber of Commerce to replace an existing
ramshackle frame structure, agreed to build a union passenger
terminal at 2nd Avenue and King Street. The chamber, despite the
inevitable presence of Hill's "satrap," Thomas Burke, complained
to Hill in October 1901: "the passenger facilities of your companies
at Seattle are inadequate, poorly arranged for the convenience of
the Railroads and the comfort of their patrons and with surround-
ings calculated to create erroneous impressions on all incoming
travellers . . . and are altogether incommensurate with the dignity
and importance of a city of 100,000 people and are insufficient
recognition of the business provided by its citizens. [We urge you
to establish a Union Passenger Station and the Chamber of Commerce will use its influence] to obtain from our City Government
such franchises, and vacations [as you need]." The chamber apparently did not want to seem entirely ungrateful to Hill for all the
good he had done for Seattle. Not until 1906 would the Union
Station be ready, just as the Union Pacific's Oregon & Washington
Railroad Company sent out its own terminal plans for bidding—
to become known as the King Street Station.[2]

Picking up from the account in chapter two (in which his
overall development plan was sketched), it is clear how far
Thomson had proceeded toward its fulfillment by 1912. Regrading,
hill removal, filling in the tidelands, and harbor development became his top priorities. First Avenue was leveled between Pine
Street and Denny Way in 1898; Western and Railroad avenues,
near the shoreline, received the fill. They would get tons more as
the western half of Denny Hill was steadily sluiced and conveyed
downhill during the first years of the new century. (The eastern
half of Denny Hill remained between downtown and the south
end of Lake Union.)

Beacon Hill prevented easy access from downtown to Lake
Washington, the Rainier Valley, and points south. To establish a
route, part of the hill had to be cut through—remember that
Semple's Seattle and Lake Washington Waterway Company was
washing the western slope into the tidelands. Undaunted, the Engineering Department cut two routes: one via Jackson Street to
12th Avenue, and a second, deeper cut, through the hill at what
became Dearborn Street; the latter was done in conjunction with a
bridge at 12th Avenue that was 110 feet above Dearborn. Hydrau-
lic methods learned in Alaska were used in these excavation

projects, and the operators also usually came with Alaskan experience. The work was completed by 1912.

To the east of the Denny Hill remains, Westlake Avenue was regraded to course from downtown along the western shore of Lake Union toward Fremont and Ballard—later part of the route for the city's first ill-fated attempt to launch a street railway, its "Division A" line. A parallel regrading project routed Fairview Avenue along the southern tip of Lake Union and north near the east shoreline toward the University of Washington. This work was finished by 1911.[3]

But Thomson was not alone in preparing Seattle for its seemingly destined supremacy among Pacific-Coast cities. Army engineer Chittenden, as noted above, was in the process of laying the foundation for industrialization, as he treaded carefully through the minefield of conflicting economic interests, all seemingly bent on maximizing individual profit rather than the city's welfare. Certainly James D. Ross of City Light made his contribution; and the municipally-owned electric plant, of which he was head, was but an expression of popular sentiment.

Thorstein Veblen, in his classic study, *The Engineers and the Price System* (1921), must have had men like these mind; each in Veblen's phraseology was concerned with "matter of fact" knowledge and its application; and they found commercial concerns to be a hindrance because of their vested interest in the status quo.

Thomson joined hands with the Washington State Chapter of the American Institute of Architects in promoting a civic center plan that would have moved government buildings northward; land had been regraded under Thomson's direction partly for this purpose. Such a center would attract new building construction northward, all within the existing 200 foot building height limit. Skyscrapers at the south end of the business district need not be built in this event, and rentals could be kept in check in the process. By the same token, Thomson hoped this move would relieve pressure on the south-end business group to eliminate the height restriction to allow skyscrapers to be built near the Yesler Way business core.

These south-end interests, in anticipation of the need for a modern court house, convinced county commissioners to buy land near Third Avenue and James Street in 1903. They wanted L. C. Smith to build a skyscraper on his adjacent holding once the height covenant in that area had been eliminated. This action, they believed, would tie business development to the Yesler area. Smith applied for a permit in October 1910 on the declared premise that the civic center would remain where it was. The City Council lifted the restriction, and the forty-two-story Smith Tower was begun in November 1911. Court house construction remained in abeyance because an attempt by the county commissioners to get voters to approve funding failed in September 1911—and temporarily, with it, their version of the civic center.

On another front, in 1908 architect A. Warren Gould presented to the Seattle Commercial Club an improvement plan having a civic center at the city's heart. The center was to be located in the northern regrade area surrounding Fourth and Blanchard. Fearing that, in the absence of a comprehensive plan, all of the regrading would have been done without purpose and subsequent growth would be a form of anarchy, the Washington chapter of the American Institute of Architects (AIA) organized a Municipal Plans League in January 1909. With its allies: the Commercial Club, Chamber of Commerce, and "the valuable assistance of Scott Calhoun," a charter amendment was drafted for establishing a Municipal Plans Commission to be voted on in the 1910 election. The charter amendment was overwhelmingly approved, and a Municipal Plans Commission was established to carry out the work. It began with a decision to allocate 150 square miles for the project and to conceive of a city with one million people. (Thomson was named commission head.)[4]

Thomson dominated the Municipal Plans Commission. His candidate to direct the planning was Virgil Bogue, a man with a temperament similar to his own. Both saw topography as an obstacle to be overcome, not to be accommodated. One of the other two candidates was John C. Olmsted, who had designed Seattle's parks and boulevards in 1903, and whose pioneer landscape architectural firm had designed the grounds of the University of Washington campus. These two elements represented the quintessence of the "city beautiful movement" in Seattle. Olmsted, by predisposition, designed in a manner that took advantage of the natural landscape. He was, clearly, not a Thomson man, because he would plan with nature, not against it. In the fight over municipal ownership of the city's Cedar River water supply in 1895, Thomson declared his unadorned utilitarian bias: "I have always opposed contracting debts for municipal luxuries such as Boulevards and Parks and other wild and vicious speculations." Olmsted didn't stand a chance.

Bogue readied his plan by following the Gould formula for the most part, and he added provisions for harbor improvements. But a mandatory clause was included which was to prove damaging in the bitter campaign that followed: that once the proposal had been adopted, it "shall become the plan of the city." How rigid this admonition might be was heralded in August 1911 when the AIA urged voters in the upcoming September election to vote against two bond issues because they would "jeopardize the integrity of the Bogue plan." One of these two issues was sponsored by the Washington State Fine Arts Association for a museum and auditorium at the site of the old Providence Hospital; the other was for a new court house that was sponsored by south-end business interests. Both issues were defeated. The Municipal Plans Committee approved Bogue's plan at the end of September.

In a public airing prior to the March 1912 election, only two organizations supported the Bogue Plan: the AIA chapter and the Municipal League—the latter containing a large contingent of engineering efficiency advocates. The League charged the "Landlords Trust" with trying to keep rents high by concentrating the business district in the south end. The most devastating criticism came in a pamphlet from the Civic Plans Investigation Committee (CPIC), which questioned the wisdom of topping the regrade with fourteen to thirty feet of fill dirt, the slicing off part of Queen Anne hill, and the enormous expenses to be incurred in the process, amounting to more than $100 million. Then there was the seeming mandatory feature about commitment—that the Bogue Plan had to be accepted as a whole, not piecemeal. To the distress of pro-Bogue forces, much was made of this aspect of their proposal. They tried to counter by pointing out that while the plan was a "master plan," it could be implemented on a pay-as-you-go basis—but there must be conformity with it. They tried to argue that it was flexible and inflexible at the same time.[5]

But the real trouble in trying to promote voter interest in the Bogue plan was the eclipsing of it by the Harbor Island terminals issue on the one hand, and by what had been unobtrusively happening to the University of Washington's downtown property.

At the time, University of Washington's Metropolitan Tract was being developed by the Metropolitan Building Company under the direction of John F. Douglas. What formerly had been a troublesome and puzzling problem for downtown business interests had become the city's retail and hotel center under his management by the spring of 1912. Intermingled with department stores, smaller shops, and hotels were office buildings and apartment houses. The vested interests so recently established there assured opposition to the Bogue plan would come from the most influential portion of Seattle's business community: that in the south end and that in the newer part to the north. Bogue Plan supporters apparently failed to grasp the uptown project's significance because of its recent development.[6]

For many years, the school's ten acres had been left largely undeveloped while becoming surrounded by an increasingly urban landscape. The land belonged to the University of Washington, having been donated to Washington Territory in 1861 by Arthur Denny and other pioneers whose lands abutted on his property. The donation was contingent on the land being used for educational purposes by the school. Having declared that the tract was no longer suited to the development of a modern institution of higher learning, the Washington Legislature appointed a committee in 1891 to locate a new university site and to clarify the terms of the original donation. The site of the present university was acquired, 355 acres in all. When the first building had been completed in 1894—Denny Hall—the original location was vacated, except for the original building and the Armory.

In subsequent years, as the regrading progressed on First, then Second, and then Third Avenue, the old university building was left standing twenty-five feet above street level. With regrading of Fourth Avenue progressing along the site by 1905, the University of Washington's Board of Regents' failure to cooperate with the project was becoming an embarrassment. (The Chamber of Commerce in 1901 had even proposed to the regents that they consider making the plot into a central park, but without effect.) This obviously important piece of university property—between Third and Fifth avenues, bordered by Seneca to the south and Union on the North—clearly, was not being utilized.

But it was not as if the regents had ignored the situation. Unsuccessful in their efforts to sell the land in the 1890s, they leased it in 1900 to J. C. Levold. However, Levold failed to execute the terms of the lease; nothing was built and the regents cancelled the agreement accordingly. In 1901 the regents sold a strip of land along Third and Union to the federal government. Then in December 1902 the ubiquitous local developer of the downtown, James A. Moore, leased the property for a period of thirty years. To get construction going, he formed the University Site Improvement Company. His first project was the construction of a new building for the *Post-Intelligencer*, a four-story brick structure.

While that work progressed, Moore decided to construct temporary buildings that he could rent as a source of current revenue; the regents immediately ordered him to tear them down. In another effort to remedy his cash flow problem Moore then asked for an extension of the lease to fifty years to enable him to realize profits that were not possible under the existing agreement. The regents approved the extension in November 1904 and got a guarantee from Moore that he would complete the *P-I* building. Frustrated further in his efforts to improve his financial position, and overextended by his spread-eagle investments, Moore sold his lease to a group of local capitalists who were brought together by John F. Douglas.

Douglas had come to Seattle in 1900 by way of Park River, North Dakota, and the University of Minnesota Law School. He joined with a classmate, Warren D. Lane, and a brother-in-law in practice; he also engaged in construction on the side. (Lane would become a City Councilman and established for himself a pro-municipal ownership and pro-union record. He remained a stockholder for only a short time.) The stockholders in the new venture, the Metropolitan Building Company, were mostly lumbermen; and the first two buildings completed were almost exclusively devoted to office space for regional lumber firms.

The Metropolitan Building Company with its eighteen stockholders was incorporated in July 1907 to take over the Moore leasehold; but prior to that date, Douglas already had two young architects—John M. Howells and I. N. Phelps Stokes of New York—prepare a "master plan" that would have a conceptual unity. By the time the regents formally accepted the leasehold transfer in March 1908 Douglas had already publicly announced his new plan for the metropolitan site as a "city within a city."

Immediately, work began on the first building, to be named after the principal stockholder and company president, Chester F. White. Office space was being rented simultaneously. While the White Building was going up, work on an adjacent structure was started, to be named after another stockholder, Horace C. Henry, who had made most of his money in railroad construction. Both buildings were completed in 1909. In the process, the twenty-five foot obelisk that crowned the original university building was leveled, and the four columns at its entrance, were transferred to the new university grounds. The regents had denied Moore an opportunity to erect temporary buildings to earn current income while permanent his buildings were going up. But, when Douglas petitioned them to allow the construction of temporary structures for rental, they approved. They saw that Douglas, unlike his predecessor, was serious about developing the property.

Douglas had originally planned for a department store, expecting to entice one of the existing ones: the Bon Marche, or Frederick and Nelson, or McDougall and Southwick, or the Standard Furniture store, but none was interested. He also planned a hotel, but hotels were not steady sources of revenue, while office rentals were—as he pointed out in the December 1909 issue of the house organ, *Metropolitan Bulletin*. Adding to his configuration, and giving it a balance was the Cobb Building, devoted exclusively to medical and dental offices. While proudly pointing to the "Lumbermen's Club" formed by his coterie of renters, Douglas boasted also of the elitist social clubs situated along Fourth Avenue: the Seattle Athletic Club, the Rainier Club, the Metropolitan Club, the Elks Club, and the College Club. The prestigious Arctic Club lay nearby at Third and Columbia.

While the Stuart Building (named after stockholder E. A. Stuart, founder of the Carnation Milk Company, known for its evaporated milk) was abutted onto the Henry Building in 1910, a novel departure from the original plan was made. The company built a theater, the Metropolitan, at University Street between Fourth and Fifth avenues. Like the somewhat native-elitist quality that Douglas was imbedding in the downtown Seattle community, the Metropolitan Theater was classy. It was opened amidst great fanfare on September 30, 1911, under a contract with the Klaw and Erlanger Circuit.

What Douglas had accomplished was nothing less than the establishment of a city center—though not a "civic" center—something Seattle had previously lacked. Because this happened concurrently with the development of the Bogue Plan, which aimed to establish a civic center north of the existing downtown, the Bogue planners were defeated from the start. Douglas had already built a city center, and what gave it first life was the cohesiveness with which the real metropolitan residents fought the Bogue Plan.

As it turned out, the pro-Bogue forces were also pre-empted in their hopes for a Bush-type terminal at Harbor Island. Seattle voters, on September 5, 1911, had approved creation of the Port of Seattle, and they had elected three strong municipal ownership advocates to the new Port Commission. Commission president, Hiram Chittenden, began the planning by writing to his counterparts in other seaport cities; but he was to be temporarily stymied by the chicanery of Port legal counsel, Scott Calhoun, working with Chamber of Commerce representatives to set up a Bush terminal at Harbor Island under private control, with an added incentive that deferred rents, along with other incentives to make it an attractive investment for private capital—at taxpayers' expense. The story of how this came about follows the "Epilogue."

Epilogue

With the Metropolitan Tract assuming fuller proportions on completion of the White, Henry, and Cobb buildings, and the addition of the posh Metropolitan Theater—each a "permanent" structure as defined by the original lease—J. F. Douglas's dream was becoming a reality. For his Metropolitan Building Company board of directors he had chosen individuals who had achieved the pinnacle of business or professional success in the city. These men intermingled with other downtown leaders in prestigious gathering spots such as the Rainier, Arctic, College, and Ivy League clubs. A number of board members moved to the Highlands on the northern outskirts of the city when it was established in 1909. (In the mid-twenties this golf-residential community would serve as a model for the exclusive Broadmoor Golf Club just west of Madison Park). In Neal Hines's words, those who made up the company's board or who became closely identified with its mission, were individuals "whose names would go on banks or buildings or who would be shaping or polishing a still-formative Seattle. . . ."[1]

In 1915, the Stuart Building was joined to the White and Henry buildings to form a single complex occupying the entire Fourth Avenue side of the block between Union and University streets. Ten "temporary" buildings (structures with seven-year life spans as defined by the lease) included a short-lived YWCA building, the Seattle Art Company, the Olympic Motor Car, the Metropolitan Garage, the College Club, and the Hippodrome (an auditorium). From the first, the White-Henry-Stuart Building attracted lumber firms as tenants. Railroad companies added offices, followed by so many lawyers that Douglas supplied them with a convenient reference library. According to Hines, Douglas "wanted tenants of the 'best class'—lumbermen, shippers, merchants, builders." And he catered to their needs in such a way as to contribute a class cohesiveness that might well not have been accomplished without his special elitist and managerial sense. The esteem he attached to these tenants was reciprocal; he was often toasted by occupants for what he had accomplished.

With secure self-assurance, he continuously pressed the University of Washington's Board of Regents to modify the original lease, sometimes presenting them with *faits accompli* that presumed their acceptance—until William Winlock Miller joined that university body. Miller led the fight against accepting the Arena Building because it did not meet requirements for a permanent structure. It was Miller, followed by a number of University of Washington Alumni Association officers, who first reminded members of the Board of Regents that they served as trustees for the university, and not the Metropolitan Building Company.

Tensions between the regents and Douglas would stem from the latter's imperious drive to modify the original lease on terms which he believed were essential to attract investors. For buildings classed as permanent (those costing at least $500,000, that were fireproof, and made of concrete and reinforced steel construction) he tried—though unsuccessfully—to let each have a fifty-year lease. (The general lease of the company itself would expire in 1954, at which time the buildings were to revert to the university.)

The Port of Seattle versus Private Interests

By 1910 a strong sentiment was growing for a municipally-owned port. The rest of the city was taking a form suited to a population that expected prosperity to flow through the Panama Canal: electric rates had been halved as a result of establishing a municipally-owned electric plant; the city's topography was being reformed to accommodate new industry and to facilitate commerce; the Lake Washington Canal was about to become a reality; and the city's population growth was plateauing after surging for more than a decade. Under these circumstances, it is not surprising that the waterfront should get special attention—commerce was the reason for Seattle's supremacy on Puget Sound, and many expected the city to achieve coastal hegemony as well. Oddly, the very downtown interests who were ideologically opposed to public ownership as an unwarranted intrusion into their free enterprise system became supporters of public ownership, if only in a fit of pique. Many had become unhappy with the way railroad interests hampered port development, and they became angry with the way these interests flaunted their political power.

Miller Freeman, founder of the *Town Crier*, expressed the strategic situation well in the weekly's first number, September 3, 1910: "Cheap industrial acreage is necessary to give stability even to the value of our present tidelands and primary waterfront [along with] provision of auxiliary dockage." He saw the canal as being essential to enlarging this acreage. By the end of the year, the weekly lobbied the public on the second strategic factor in an article by C. C. Closson: "The Bush Terminal—A Lesson for Seattle." New York was portrayed as having achieved its shipping supremacy by the private development of its waterfront, giving it "a public character"; the Bush Terminals were primarily responsible. These factors would interweave with the Bogue plan and the plans of the Port commissioners in the months ahead, all within the following legislative backdrop.[1]

When George F. Cotterill was elected to the state Senate in 1907, he sponsored a bill that passed by a large majority for improving public facilities for shippers. In addition, his bill created a public commission to implement a suitable program. But Governor Mead vetoed the bill at the prompting of the Great Northern interests. In response, the Seattle City Council quickly established a Harbor Lines Commission in 1908 to gather information about ports in other cities.

The 1909 legislature passed a bill that established a Duwamish Improvement District to enable voters to act on a bond issue for dredging the Duwamish River; it also established a Lake Washington Canal Association for the dredging of that channel. Such bonding carried with it the power of eminent domain.

In 1910 voters approved both bond issues. But the railroad and lumber interests, fighting the threat of lowered wharfage rates and other competition from a public corporation, challenged the right of the legislature to set up improvement districts. The State Supreme Court sustained their objections, thereby throwing the whole matter into confusion. But in their challenge, the opposition alienated traditional sources of support: conservative businessmen, the Chamber of Commerce, the Commercial Club (which normally opposed whatever the Chamber wanted), and the newspapers. All wanted a modern port and would choose municipal ownership in desperation should that eventuality become necessary. A committee of the Seattle Chamber of Commerce and the Seattle Commercial Club was formed and reported late in 1910 in favor of municipal ownership.

Responding to this initiative of the downtown business interests, the Corporation Counsel, City Engineer Thomson, and his former assistant, Senator Cotterill, joined in framing an appropriate bill for the 1911 legislature—one that would allow counties to establish port districts while getting around the Supreme Court's decision invalidating local improvement districts. Their strategy was to set up a municipal corporation with broad governmental powers that the voters could vote into existence. The bill passed the House overwhelmingly, squeaked by in the Senate, and was signed into law June 8, 1911.

A special election followed in September for establishing the Port of Seattle and for choosing three commissioners to carry out the program. A screening committee of the Commercial Club selected three strong candidates who were known municipal ownership proponents: Robert Bridges, who had been state Land Commissioner in the Populist governorship of John Rogers, and who had been a union organizer in the coal mines; Charles E. Remsberg, a Republican, judge, and businessman; and General Hiram Chittenden, who was uncontested because of his reputation for integrity and sound judgment, and for his handling of the Lake

Washington Canal controversy. The Port was established with a vote of 13,771 to 4,538, and Bridges and Remsberg won overwhelmingly over the candidates put up by the waterfront interests. The *Town Crier* began hammering on Bridges immediately because of his declared socialist principles.[2]

Probably, what drew public ownership advocates and traditional conservatives together as much as the latter's disgust with the overreaching railroad interests was the generally depressed economy and the expectation that once the Panama Canal was completed Seattle would be in a stronger position to exploit the commercial potential, but only if the city had a better port than the railroads were willing to provide. Public ownership would enable the city to make improvements by voter approval of bond issues instead of waiting upon the railroads and other private owners to do so, if and when they saw prospects for their profit—service to the city was not their primary goal. A publicly funded port, by way of contrast, would broaden the profit base, spreading the wealth around, as it were. This was, perhaps, the binding element of the municipal ownership movement.

In this same month, the City Council accepted the Bogue Plan for the comprehensive development of Seattle. At the September 26, 1911, meeting of the American Institute of Architects R. H. Thomson spoke in celebration of the council's action by comparing Seattle with Paris and Washington D. C., stressing the inherent logic in the Bogue plan. He concluded "in truth the development of the City of Seattle in the past as well as in the future would be said to be the result of the Bogue plan." There seemed to be no doubt about its resounding acceptance by the voters. Kenneth MacKintosh, president of the Municipal Plans Commission, followed Thomson to the podium. He chose to emphasize that part of the plan relating to harbor and shipping facilities, while allowing for the popular appeal of its civic center feature. Scott Bone, Brainerd's replacement as *P-I* editor and a District of Columbia emigre, compared Seattle's prospects favorably with that city. Capping the evening's festivities was a talk by the featured guest, Virgil Bogue, himself.[3]

Part of Bogue's plan had been the creation of a great central harbor with diverse facilities, and the conversion of Lake Union into an industrial lake. It was the Harbor Island part of the Bogue Plan that downtown business interests liked. They wanted that area developed by private capital completely after seed money had been provided through issue of municipal bonds. The Chamber of Commerce, in looking at Harbor Island terminals, saw "promise [of] an early impetus to the commercial and industrial growth of the port." It prophesied coastal supremacy for the city by developing it "along the general plan of the Bush Terminals [and by having the Port of Seattle enter] into a lease with some responsible and competent party to build and operate the entire plant." This ebullience would lead the chamber to make itself foolish before the end of the year. In effect, the chamber and specific interests within it, were attempting to narrow the base from which profits were to be derived just after having uncharacteristically joined forces in the community at large to get approval for port facilities that were partly, municipally owned. The story of how this happened follows.[4]

One of the first tasks of the newly elected Port Commissioners was to draw up comprehensive plans for the harbor's development. To start with, voters had given them $750,000 toward canal work, $600,000 for work on the Duwamish waterway, $50,000 for the Cedar River project, and $25,000 for a "city dock." With Thomson now acting as port engineer, the commissioners planned a $3 million facility; but instead of choosing to submit that large a bond issue for voter approval, they elected to build only one of the piers costing but $500,000. Voter confidence was expected to follow if that were successful; then they could get the entire project done in due time. Moving conservatively and deliberately, Chittenden wrote to the Bush Terminal Company and to other ports for information. His Bush letter was received by R. F. Ayers, a vice president for advertising. Ayers replied to Chittenden in October 1911, adding to the general information, that a Charles Fenn was interested in getting some Eastern capital together for developing Harbor Island. Ayers followed this letter with another, telling Chittenden that Fenn probably preferred Tacoma—a sure way of stirring up the competitive spirit on the Sound. This was fabrication to which Chittenden did not respond. But rumors began circulating in Seattle that a "Bush" type of terminal might get built at Harbor Island—the seed had been planted a year earlier by the *Town Crier.*

Scott Calhoun, now the Port's legal counsel, became enthusiastic, and told Chittenden that he wanted to check out the rumors in New York. To get Chittenden's approval he had Alden Blethen join in their meeting on December 25, 1911. Chittenden consented, but on condition that Calhoun make no commitment on the Port's behalf, while reassuring Bush representatives that the Port would not interfere with the Bush plans for Harbor Island.

Unknown to Chittenden, however, were the prior negotiations Calhoun had undertaken involving dedicated opponents of municipal ownership: Thomas Burke, Chamber of Commerce president J. D. Lowman, and J. S. Gibson, president and general manager of the International Stevedoring Company.

So, when Calhoun arrived in New York he met with the "New York parties" and consummated an agreement; the three Seattle men noted above endorsed it. It would commit the Port to a $5 million bond issue and to construction of facilities for private developers. When Calhoun returned, he arranged a meeting with Blethen on January 26 at the Chamber of Commerce, at which an explanation of the "Gentlemen's Agreement" (alternately, later, "tentative" agreement was used interchangeably) would be given. To overcome the Port Commission's resistance to accepting the agreement, Blethen coordinated publicity with Scott Bone of the *Post-Intelligencer*; the city was greeted on the morning of January 27 with the headline: GREAT TERMINAL FOR SEATTLE . . ." On page two Calhoun expanded on the front page coverage by exclaiming what it all meant for Seattle's future prosperity at the expense of San Francisco's. The *Times* followed in the evening with more of the same, uncharacteristically supporting a bond issue for public improvement: "The project will involve a bond issue. But more than half the amount . . . will immediately be spent to begin the construction of a *Bush Terminal on Harbor Island*. . . . The Bush people have made their proposition. The matter is now in the hands of the newly-created Port Commission." This statement was an outright falsehood. Ayers was the only "New York party," and he no longer worked for Bush because Seattle businessmen had contributed $25,000 to his support while he barnstormed for public approval of the project. At a large meeting at the chamber on the twenty-eighth, Calhoun denounced the Commission for foot-dragging, and he resigned as its legal counsel to work with the Ayers group.[5]

Chittenden, in the meantime, had responded to the well-spring of sentiment that was building for port improvements by increasing the original bond request from $500,000 to $2 million. Now he chose to add two propositions amounting to $5 million. He worded the bond proposal so that if the Ayers group could not raise their own personal bond, the Port could invalidate the partnership with Ayers. Blethen and Ayers could not force Chittenden to change the wording. Only Robert Bridges, of the three Port Commissioners, campaigned directly against the Harbor Island project. The *Town Crier* charged Bridges with being "the most dangerous factor in the opposition to the terminal plans." By this time the focus of the coming election had shifted almost completely away from the Bogue plan to the Harbor Island issue.[6]

Thomson, decided to remind Burke that he was not a law

unto himself. After receiving a message from Thomas Burke, who was still in New York, that the "terminal proposition must be adopted substantially as agreed upon," Thomson retorted on February 7: First, the state constitution limits the lease of harbor lands to thirty years; second, that the state constitution prohibits the lending of credit to a "private institution," thereby invalidating the provision for seven years of free rent; and the "demand that all construction shall be done by the Fuller Construction Company, who shall be paid cost plus ten per cent [violates state statutes requiring competitive bidding]." He reminded Burke that as to a subway to Harbor Island, this was a city matter, not within the Port's jurisdiction. Thomson concluded: "Now, Judge . . . this proposition has, from the beginning, been put up to the Commission as a "strong arm proposition. . . ," leaving Burke gasping at Thomson's impudence, no doubt.[7]

Bush terminal supporters became temporarily unsettled when it was rumored that Irving Bush had not been involved in any of the negotiations. And while the *Town Crier* conceded that the Ayers group need not be the only one to build the terminal (the Port might even be allowed to do it), the *Times* opposed this pusillanimousness by standing rigidly by the Pacific Terminal Company—as the Ayers group was now called. Blethen contended that "no one can question the ability of the Pacific Terminal Company" with its array of "respectable business men," financiers, and other experts.

Amidst great fanfare, Ayers arrived in the city on February 20 to sign the agreement that Calhoun had negotiated; appropriately the chamber building was the site of the scene. The terminal forces remained undeterred even by Irving Bush's announcement of the twenty-fourth, in the *Town Crier*, that his company "has no connection with the terminal enterprise of Mr. Ayers; that no arrangement has been made for the interchange of traffic with the proposed Seattle terminals, and that Mr. Ayers was in the company's employ less than two years, in charge of certain lines of advertising." The *Town Crier* took the same defensive line as the *Times*, asserting, "such men as J. D. Lowman, Scott Calhoun, Joseph Blethen, and William W. Chapin, after careful investigation in New York City, satisfied themselves of the responsibility of Mr. Ayers and his associates and financial backers." However, the weekly tempered its defense by advising Ayers to "clear up the situation, [otherwise] it will be far better to vote against all [harbor] propositions."[8]

As election day approached the Municipal League plaintively pleaded for a "Square Deal for Bogue Plans." Chittenden, in the

February 24 *Municipal News*, argued that such a plan would save the city money in the long run; and that it was only "directive in character," not "mandatory," as characterized by its opponents. Since development toward a population of one million will occur, Chittenden argued, it should be orderly but need only be implemented by stages. However, the tract for the civic center ought to be acquired as soon as possible. In the same issue, the *News* quoted from an article in Harpers Weekly stating that Seattle had a chance to avoid the "predicament that hampers New York." Then, in the March 2 issue of the *News*, Chittenden published a critique of the rival Ayers plan, beginning with the statement that the company itself would not operate the facilities, but would lease out operations. He explained that the "company is to have a free hand to exploit the leasehold for its own profit; that it is to pay no taxes on the property; that there is no guarantee that the company will spend the $600 million it says it will; and its insistence on a substantial deferral of rental payments might even prove illegal." The port president added a warning that if the company failed, the Port District would have to assume its financial obligations; he pointed out that the likelihood of such an occurrence was high, as Ayers offered no "security." He concluded by claiming that there was no proof that the Ayers plan was superior to that of the commissioners.[9]

As to the "Bogue Plan," it had practically slipped from view by the time the March 5 election rolled around. A survey of newspaper coverage dramatically shows this. The *Times* front page carried a large sketch of the terminal dream; beneath it followed an article under the column heading "Terminals Plan Endorsed by Leading Business Men." Ayers was quoted as saying that whichever Puget Sound port received the terminal would control fifty percent of the trade. If Seattle lost out, industrialists would desert to Tacoma. The Bogue Plan was not mentioned on page one, and it would have taken a real effort to find it elsewhere in the issue. Like the *Times*, the *P-I*'s front page featured a terminal sketch, a two-part illustration projecting future growth that might occur if the $5 million Harbor Island bonds are approved and the inevitable depression that would result if the issue failed at the polls. The *P-I* carried its own version of the *Times*'s "Tacoma horror" story, but added the fear that land values would drop if Seattle workers departed for Tacoma. Interestingly, the *P-I* contributed the thought that "Harbor Island will remain in the hands of private individuals at an exorbitant figure." The article was furnished by the Chamber of Commerce. The *P-I* chose neutrality on the Bogue plan.

and Salmon Bay, the commissioners filed a suit before the Interstate Commerce Commission. The railroads chose to agree rather than face ICC hearings. However, implementation came only after the end of the belt line controversy that extended from 1915 to 1917; each bond issue for the belt line was rejected by the voters.

To pump up voter adrenalin, Tacoma rivalry could always be used . . . and it was.

With the Bogue Plan rejected by the voters in March 1912, and the Port of Seattle bonds thunderously approved, there remained one disputed item: siting of the courthouse. Was it to be at Fourth and Blanchard or at Third and James? Lacking confidence in resubmitting a bond issue to site the building at Third and James, the county commissioners met with Mayor Cotterill to discuss his proposal for a joint county-city building. Tentatively agreeing, they co-opted A. Warren Gould of the pro-Bogue forces to design the building, a strictly commercial type, without "civic center" linkage. Gould was excommunicated from the American Institute of Architects soon after.

The pro-Bogue group formed the Seattle Civic Center Association to combat this project. Charles F. Gould had expressed disbelief at the April 10, 1912, meeting of the American Institute of Architects that the voters had really rejected the kind of civic improvements represented by the civic center part of the Bogue plan. The new association was sufficiently influential that it persuaded the commissioners, on October 1, to submit both locations to the voters in November. After a heated one-month campaign, during which the association lambasted the south end "monopolists" while neglecting to point out that $950,000 would not nearly cover the cost of construction, the voters overwhelmingly favored the Third and James site, 35,768-16,565. Construction began in June 1914.

Richard C. Berner is founder of the University of Washington's University Archives and Manuscripts program (1958-84) and author of the award-winning book Archival Theory and Practice in the United States: A Historical Analysis *(1983). He is in the process of writing a multivolume history of twentieth-century Seattle.*

Figure 9: Heating up the rivalry with Tacoma as the controversy over Harbor Island obfuscates the Bogue Plan for the city's comprehensive development.

The *Seattle Star* carried no reference to the Bogue plan on page one, but it did urge voters to vote "No." The *Star* claimed an "eleventh hour surrender" by the Ayers promoters, quoting the group as conceding to mounting criticism, and to suspicion of the tentative agreement, saying "We don't care who builds the terminals. . . . The port commission [is] free to do as it pleases in case the bonds carry." Chittenden finally had agreed to support the Harbor Island bonds on condition that the Ayers group make this concession.

The two major weeklies, the *Argus* and *Town Crier*, also smothered references to the Bogue plan with coverage of the Harbor Island bond propositions. The latter claimed the commissioners had not dealt fairly with the "people," and asserted that Calhoun had been given power to negotiate a contract during his New York mission. The *Argus* displayed oval portraits of Alden Blethen and Scott Bone with Harbor Island in the background. Its two-column editorial conceded that although $5 million was a lot of money, it would be wisely spent; besides, the property would revert to the city in sixty years. The editor added "the so-called civic center plan is also lost in the shuffle and fails to elicit a mention [in the dailies] . . . Anyway the Bogue plans will keep."

The *Municipal News* opposed the Harbor Island bond proposition on grounds that it was too big to be considered without more careful deliberation. Beyond this, according to the paper, pressure to have the measure approved cast doubt on its validity.[10]

On March 5, voters overwhelmingly approved all eight of the Port of Seattle bond propositions, totalling $8.1 million. The Bogue plan was resoundingly defeated by a margin of over 10,000 votes; it failed to carry in a single ward. In contrast, park bonds passed by a margin of almost two to one. Whereas parks were natural adjuncts to neighborhoods, an extravagant civic center almost certainly ran counter to this sentiment. Another issue that passed was the bond issue for acquisition of both the Hebb and Cushman sites for City Light. The Seattle City Charter was also amended to give the Port Commission power to control waterfront streets.

Chittenden set the tone for what was to follow after the bonds had passed by assigning top priority to condemnation proceedings at Smith's Cove. He announced that the commission is not in any way committed to the plan as proposed by Ayers and his associates. . . . [But it is] conceded that the [gentlemen's] agreement will not be seriously considered. The Commission is unanimously against it." Port Engineer Thomson resigned because he had opposed the Harbor Island propositions and now wanted no part in the work of implementation; besides, he yearned for the fresh air of Strathcona on Vancouver Island.[11]

Epilogue

After the March 5 election the *Times* and *P-I* kept pressure on the commissioners to sign a contract with the Pacific Terminal Company. Finally, one was signed over the strenuous objection of Commissioner Bridges on August 23, 1912. He contended that, since the company had not yet signed articles of incorporation, it had no legal standing; it was a company without assets, and it was not an operating company. In proceeding in this direction Chittenden had a different strategy, one that depended upon the company's ultimate default.

When Ayers could not raise a surety bond, Chittenden's gamble paid off. He then took steps to invalidate the contract. Next, he prepared measures for a June 1913 election that asked the voters to cancel the two Harbor Island bonds he had added in 1912. In their place he substituted a new $3 million bond to develop East Waterway and Smith's Cove facilities. Voter disillusionment with the stealthy maneuvering of the Ayers promoters, combined with their undiminished enthusiasm for harbor development, led to approval of Chittenden's adroit, cool-headed actions. Unfortunately this political maneuvering exacted a price on his already failing health. In addition, he incurred the hostility of Commissioner Bridges, who then proceeded to gain the presidency of the Port Commission for himself. Chittenden retired in 1915; a year later he stood in opposition to Bridges when he tried to get voter approval for a belt line railroad.[1]

Interestingly, after the voters authorized the transfer of funds from the Harbor Island project following the failure of the Ayers group, it became public knowledge that steamship companies had preferred the construction of an East Waterway terminal site all along; they had been shut out by the Ayers supporters and chose to remain silent during the controversy. At any rate, they were happy with the outcome. Reflecting their approval, the *Railway and Marine News* also switched its support to the East Waterway choice of the commissioners.

Early in 1914 the Port Commissioners announced that the city would build two cold storage plants, one for apples and the other for fish. The latter was to provide local fishermen with an alternative to the monopolistic pricing of the private plants. The private owners railed against these "visionary plans," and filed a taxpayers' suit to block sale of the bonds. The State Supreme Court ruled in favor of the Port in 1915.

Frustrated by the large number of seemingly useless railroad switches required to get cargo to and from the ships, and by the financial expense thus incurred, the Port Commissioners appealed to the State Public Service Commission in 1914 to force rate reductions. Railroads were accused of charging $9.00 for switching to the Port docks, and only $3.00 to private facilities. And when the railroads refused to establish a "common-user" line between Smith's Cove and Salmon Bay, the commissioners filed a suit before the Interstate Commerce Commission. The railroads backed down, choosing to cooperate rather than face an ICC hearing. However, these changes were implemented only after the belt line controversy subsided; every bond issue between 1915 and 1917 for a belt line was turned down by voters.[2]

With the Bogue plan rejected by voters in March 1912 and the Port of Seattle bonds thunderously approved, there remained but one disputed item on the civic agenda: siting of the court house. Was it to be at Fourth and Blanchard or at Third and James? Lacking confidence in resubmitting a bond issue to site the building at Third and James, the County Commissioners met with Mayor Cotterill to discuss his proposal for a joint county-city building. Tentatively agreeing, they co-opted A. Warren Gould of the pro-Bogue forces, to design a structure, a strictly commercial building without "civic center" linkage. (Gould was excommunicated from the American Institute of Architects soon thereafter.)

The pro-Bogue group formed the Seattle Civic Center Association to combat this project. Charles F. Gould expressed disbelief at an April 10, 1912, meeting of the American Institute of Architects that voters had really rejected the kind of civic improvements represented by the civic center part of the Bogue plan. This new association was sufficiently influential to persuade commissioners, on October 1, to submit both locations to the voters in November. After a heated one-month campaign, during which the Association neglected to point out that $950,000 would not nearly cover the cost of construction for its proposed building, while lambasting the south end "monopolists," the voters overwhelmingly favored the Third and James site, 35,768 to 16,565. Eventually the commissioners got the construction underway in June 1914.[3]

Thomson Reflects on the Cost of it All

When R. H. Thomson left the Port Commission to regain his health through outdoor exercise, he became consulting engineer for laying out Strathcona Provincial Park on Vancouver Island; but he kept in touch with events in Seattle. Writing to Virgil Bogue in November 1913 when the *P-I* had just blasted the Port Commission for alleged outrageous expenditures (stating that this conduct would not have been condoned if Bogue and Thomson were present) Thomson commented:

> The trouble with Seattle is: That they have gone improvement and expense crazy and the whole cry of the town is, and has for years been, spend money; spend it for something, and anyhow, spend it. . . . The *Post-Intelligencer*, would apparently, have been perfectly satisfied if the Port Commission had followed its advice and paid fabulous sums for the lands over on Harbor Island, and backed with public money the scheme of exploitation put forward by the New York crowd. . . . It seems to me that the final question as to the Seattle's Port development will hang on the attitude of the great railroads to the Port, in the matter of freight rates.[1]

10

Politics and Labor: The 1912-1914 Interlude

Mayor Cotterill Meets the Colonel Head-On

Colonel Alden J. Blethen captured the city's largest newspaper circulation for the *Seattle Times* by combining his own brand of super-patriotism with a choleric temperament and an antipathy to anything that smacked of radicalism or challenged the divine right of private property. This admixture was fired by an ego that bordered on the megalomaniacal at times. But in the opinion of Harry Chadwick, Blethen simply practiced "yellow journalism." At any rate, Blethen's reportage established a new benchmark for triggering vituperative vendettas that seldom has been equalled. One such outburst led to what became known as the Potlatch riot of 1913.

Indicative of Colonel Blethen's temperament is an account published three days after the riot by E. H. Wells in the *Seattle Sun's* July 21, 1913, edition:

> When the *Times* building was burned out a few months ago owing to somebody dropping a cigarette stub in the waste paper in C. B. Blethen's upstairs office, the *Times* sought to make capital out of the incident by alleging that red handed anarchists had tried to destroy the paper because of its loyalty to Old Glory. . . . And the *Times* staff got up on the roof . . . and [shot] bombs in the air . . . raising Ned in an effort to parade their patriotism.[1]

The Potlatch Riot itself cannot be understood outside the context of the city's politics of the preceding two years. During that time, the Colonel supported Hiram Gill in the recall election of 1911, and made clear his dedication to the inevitability of urban vice. Blethen also believed that efforts to suppress vice brought with them the inevitable violations of constitutionally protected rights of private property—worse than a sin. Above all, he found inconceivable the exertion of police power for any purpose other than the protection of private property.

As noted above, from December 1911 until the March 1912 election, Blethen was also deeply involved in opposing the Bogue Plan and in supporting a Bush Terminal for Harbor Island. In these efforts, he joined with the *Post-Intelligencer's* Scott Bone and was backed by the Chamber of Commerce.[2]

The March 1912 election decided the fate of the Harbor Island terminal and the Bogue Plan; it also decided the issue of who was to succeed George Dilling as mayor. As outlined above, Gill received about 10,000 more votes than Cotterill in the primary. But he lost because "moral" middle class voters (the church-going element) and a bloc of Socialists that previously backed Hulet Wells also supported Cotterill.

Cotterill, on the prohibition-vice side, planned only to enforce existing laws; he played heavily on his pro-municipal ownership advocacy and the need to keep the city's utilities free from control by the State Public Service Commission. As a senator in the 1911 legislative session, Cotterill had been instrumental in getting legislation passed that exempted municipally owned utilities from control by the commission. As noted above, he also played the key role in enacting the port district law. As a former Populist, and still a single tax proponent, it was not surprising to find him to be an outspoken supporter of former Populist state land commissioner and trade unionist, Port Commissioner Robert Bridges, on whom much media enmity was focused.[3]

Blethen, consistently lampooned Cotterill over the years, denounced Robert Bridges, and just as regularly ridiculed R. H. Thomson. Thomson, having been called a "semi-criminal" by the Colonel, had been repeatedly thwarted in his libel suits against the *Times*, allegedly by the newspaper's use of various legal ruses.

Colonel Blethen also pursued Hulet Wells, who he linked with "IWW-red flag anarchists."[4] In 1913, socialism's popularity was peaking nationally, and in Washington it was stronger than in most states outside the Northeast and Wisconsin. In June of that year, an IWW-led strike in Paterson, New Jersey, reached crescendo proportions after a spectacular New York City parade organized by Oregon's own John Reed.

It was within this larger political setting that Colonel Blethen linked Wells with the Industrial Workers of the World, despite Wells's known opposition to the radical organization's promotion of dual unionism and rejection of political processes. Reportedly, Blethen was a tearful patriot and notoriously prone to making wild declamations that his conduct during the Potlatch would underscore. The Gill recall election, the recent spate of reform legislation, woman suffrage, City Light's success, now the creation of a Seattle Port Commission that blocked his dream of a publicly subsidized harbor project appeared too much for Blethen to accept.[5]

After Seattle's March 1912 election, and with May Day only a few weeks away, Socialists obtained a permit from the new mayor to stage a parade. In an apparent effort to frame Wells, a raid on the paraders was staged in which the United States flag was seized and torn. In the course of this action Wells was heard to call Old Glory a "dirty rag." The *Times* headline read: "Denouncing Flag As Dirty Rag May Cost Wells Citizenship . . . Chief Examiner of Naturalization Bureau Takes Up Alleged Statements of Socialist Mayoralty Candidate."

Wells claims in his autobiography that, at the time, he was at work on his City Light job, and that the flag in question was quickly taken to a nearby saloon where it was photographed in the company of *Times* reporter, M. M. Mattison. It was Mattison, then, who concocted the story about Wells "waving a red flag." Wells sued for libel and ultimately won, but not until 1916, after Blethen's death.

The initial judicial proceedings, before Blethen's friend Judge John Humphries, became such a farce that Wells was inspired to write a play while waiting for the case to wend its way through a legal tangle that only well-financed lawyers can weave. His drama was called *The Colonel and His Friends* and was based quite literally on his trial transcripts. Handbills printed by The Red News Wagon announced its opening at the Moore Theater on July 27, 1913.[6]

With Blethen and Humphries portrayed as buffoons in the vein of Gilbert and Sullivan operetta characters, there was sufficient cause to suppress it in Blethen's view. But Mayor Cotterill was given to allowing free speech even by anarchists. Not only that, but Chief of Police Claude Bannick had been conducting raids (usually without warrants) on property devoted to the promotion of vice—the Colonel resented this deeply too. The prospect of the play being given, combined with Blethen's pent-up hostility to Cotterill, stimulated the *Times*'s editor to wage a demagogic campaign to confront the mayor and his damnable policies, even to unseat him if possible, and to crush Wells in the process.

But then Blethen had more salt rubbed into his wounds when

COTTERILL ATTEMPTS TO SUPPRESS TIMES

TRIES TO SHIFT BLAME FOR LAST NIGHT'S RIOTS

MAYOR AND POLICE CHIEF ARRESTED

MOB AT WORK ON RED SOCIALIST QUARTERS

Printed with permission of *The Seattle Times*

Figure 10: The Potlatch Riot of July 18, 1913, showing the trashing of Socialist Party headquarters and burning of files and furniture.

a grand jury called to investigate corruption among county officials wound up disrespectfully indicting him and his son Clarence for libel. The injured party in question was a Socialist, John Jarvis. Jarvis had been accused of absconding with fund-raised money, fleeing the country, and then obliquely trying to link Wells to the whole mess. In response to the indictment, the *Times* headline of June 18, 1913, read: "*Times* Editors Indicted For Libelling Soapbox Orator"![7]

Seattle's annual Potlatch celebration began four weeks later on Wednesday, July 16. Secretary of the Navy Josephus Daniels, then on a Pacific Coast tour, was feted throughout the week; he gave speeches, it seemed, on the hour. Thursday evening's address was before a group of business and professional men at the elite Rainier Club.

Cotterill introduced Daniels, who later disclaimed any knowledge of the extent of Wobbly influence in the region—and of the menacing symbolism of the red flag—innocently referred to the red flag as a stop-signal for trainmen. While Daniels was orating uptown, pacifist Annie Miller spoke from her soapbox to a large crowd near Occidental and Washington streets. During her speech she was heckled by three sailors who took over her stand. When she tried to get it back, so the story goes, she was threatened by one of them. Then, someone looking like a dude came to her defense, reportedly shouting at the sailors, "You'd hit a woman, would you?"

At that point, two soldiers tried to help their outnumbered comrades. In the ensuing melee, the soldiers and sailors got the worst of it before police arrived. The servicemen were arrested (One was reported by the *Times* as being a Sergeant Wallace from Fort Flagler, and later to have died from his wounds. This was proven to be a complete fabrication.)[8]

This scuffle was calmly reported by the *P-I* and *Star*, and not at all by the *Sun*. The *P-I*'s mid-page column headline ran, "Three Soldiers Assailed By Mob, Saved By Police. . . . Aided By Two Sailors Until Emergency Arrives." Its article continued: "[the soldiers from Fort Flagler] heard a woman speaker abusing the army and navy. . . . Suddenly a man in the crowd saw them and shouted 'Here are three of the ____ now.' Someone struck Wallace and the fight started." As to the *Sun*'s Friday edition, its headline read: "Judge Humphries Changes Another Grand Jury Report." (This concerned Blethen's request that Humphries delete any reference to the Italian-American Club in a grand jury report of November 21, 1911—no reference to the Thursday evening fracas. Request obediently granted.)

In contrast, the *Times* used the coincidence of Daniels's presence in Seattle and the scuffle involving the servicemen to promote a riot by misrepresenting Daniels's speech. The paper's main headline read: "Daniels Denounces Tolerance of Red Flag." A column head declared: "I.W.W. Denounced by Head of Navy, Attack on Soldiers and Sailors . . . Scores Executive Who Fosters Lawless Mobs . . . His Brilliant Castigation of American Mayors Excites Unparalleled Demonstration of Enthusiasm." Mattison's article under the headline stated:

> Then reaching his peroration he pointed to the American flag over his head [and began his denunciation of mayors who permit the display of red flags] . . . This country has no place for the red flag and it has no place for the believers in the red flag, he exclaimed.

From Mt. Rainier National Park, Daniels wired his denial of the *Times* report: "The reference I made to the red flag and the statement that the red flag meant danger, was the same one as originally made by me at a banquet . . . at Washington City a few days ago. It had no reference whatever to local conditions in Seattle."[9]

Mattison also indicated that Thursday's event would not go unnoticed, and that police have been warned "a large force of enlisted men in the city on leave would circulate about the IWW headquarters this evening." Indeed, as the *Times* reported the following day, the demolition of IWW and Socialist quarters and destruction of The Red News Wagon was "carefully planned" by the soldiers and artillerymen. And once they started, paraders joined them to continue the wrecking. The *P-I* reported: "The rioters planned the attack at a time when the police department was busy with street throngs watching the Potlatch celebration." In its story, the *P-I* estimated that about 3,000 civilians followed the group of soldier-sailor wreckers.

The *Sun*'s Saturday headline ran, "START SECOND RIOT", then gave its account, much like the *P-I*'s. The Sun carried a blast by Governor Lister, who accused Blethen of wrapping himself in the United States flag. For its part, the *Times* prominently showed the event, apparently to distract readers from believing that anyone appearing so patriotic could not possibly tell a lie. Mattison gleefully reported:

> The smashing of chairs and tables, the rending of yielding timbers, the creaking and groaning of sundered walls, and above the rest the crash of glass of the windows on the east side all blended together in one grand Wagnerian cacophony. And all the while the crowd outside just howled and cheered. It was almost more joy than they could stand.[10]

The *Sun* reported, on the July 19 that:

> Col. Blethen made several dashes into the alley in the rear of the *Times* building between one and two o'clock and gesticulating wildly, unburdened his opinions upon the police department to the police stationed there to enforce the mayor's order. Before that he had been trying to make a speech to the assembled mob.

That Mayor Cotterill was disturbed by the riot that his arch-enemy had promoted is not at all surprising. He ordered all saloons closed, stopped street meetings, and ordered the *Times* to stop its presses until Potlatch festivities ended. Immediately, Blethen asked his friend, Judge Humphries, to enjoin the mayor and Police

Chief Bannick from enforcing these edicts. Humphries obliged, as usual. Blethen's justification for appealing to Humphries was that the mayor and Bannick were conspiring to injure the *Times*. Humphries also issued a blanket injunction to open the saloons on appeal of six saloon keepers protesting the arrest of "nearly 40" of their number. When the mayor and Bannick requested modification of the injunction, the judge refused. Instead, he prepared bench warrants to serve on the mayor and his police chief.

Sun editor, E. H. Wells (no relation to Hulet), made much of Blethen's frequent use of Humphries, to the exclusion of other available judges, when he sought injunctions. Humphries also made the order not returnable by the mayor or chief until July 23, and admitted that this did not give either a chance to answer until then.[11]

Humphries's order read: ". . . everyone is restrained from taking any action or doing anything to interfere with the printing or distribution of the *Times* until the further order of the court." The *Times*, near day's-end on Saturday, finally got out a late edition with a headline and sub-lines: "Cotterill Attempts To Suppress *Times* . . . Tries To Shift Blame For Last Night's Riot . . . Mayor And Police Chief Arrested."

Below the headline appeared a half-page photograph of the destruction scene bearing the caption: "Mob At Work On Red Socialist Quarters." On page two, a column head boasted: "Anarchy in Seattle Stamped Out When Sailors Get Busy"—the anarchy referred to was freedom of speech that had been permitted by Cotterill, not the anarchy promoted by Alden Blethen. The article claimed the riot was "carefully planned." Page three capped off the account by proclaiming that: "Union Man [Abe Ransom] Plants Stars and Stripes Over Hall of Reds . . . Says Won't Works [IWW members] Are Working Man's Enemy."

Sunday's edition one of the *Times* was decked out as usual with Old Glory—despite a law which prohibited use of the flag for commercial purposes—and quoted Judge Humphries: "I want to tell everybody that American born people are not going to permit a lot of irresponsible foreign born men and women to come here and ruin this country." (Cotterill had emigrated from England).

There was no successor riot, but during the following week, on July 23, both the *Sun* and *P-I* reported that there was no "Sergeant Wallace," that his real name was Boehmke, and that he was not dead, contrary to the *Times* story. The *Sun* accused Blethen of using the faked death report to start another riot, but by then, military authorities were cooperating with the police in quieting matters.

And what about Hulet Wells and his play? On the same day, July 23, the *Sun*'s leading headline read: "Judge Humphries Would Disbar Author of 'Colonel and His Friends.'" Humphries appointed a committee of four, including a Blethen lawyer, Frank Hammond, the Prosecuting Attorney, the Bar Association's disbarment man, Alfred H. Lundin, and Charles K. Poe to investigate. Lundin quickly resigned in apparent disgust, given the charges, which included authorization for issuing an injunction to prevent production of Wells's play, and disbarment of Wells for belonging "to a society, namely the Socialist Party, which is inimical to the present form of American government."

As the tension wound down, Humphries was reported on July 26 to be planning to issue a blanket injunction forbidding "street speaking" since neither the chief nor mayor intended to do so. Not to be outdone, Blethen futilely tried to initiate a recall campaign against the mayor.

Not unexpectedly, owners of the Moore Theater decided not to stage *The Colonel and His Friends* for fear of the theater's demolition. Wells was similarly disappointed in his efforts at getting it staged in Tacoma; in fact, it was never staged. But Wells's claim that Blethen fomented riot and disorder to prevent the farce's presentation must figure in any account of the Potlatch Riot.

Ironically, according to Wells, the IWW had decided before the 1913 Potlatch began not to hold street meetings (they had been holding them freely all along, so a suspension would have been no real sacrifice). This raises the inevitable question of would there have been a riot if the declaration had been made public? Unfortunately, the line of inquiry really begs the question. First, the IWW never would have made public such a policy because it would have been an admission of accommodation to "the system"; it would have been a denial of a standard tactic used by the organization. Second, given Blethen's increasing hostility to Cotterill's permissiveness concerning radicals, their street meetings, and demonstrations, which only added to the editor's recent political frustrations, it is doubtful that Blethen could have held himself in check. Potlatch provided him with an ideal opportunity to mount his counterattack.

Industrial Relations: A Case in Point

By the beginning of the twentieth century labor unions in the Pacific Northwest were finally able to challenge unilateral control over wages and working conditions by industrial employers. In their struggle against this authoritarian control, they sought the right to represent wage earners within an employer's jurisdiction and to bargain for them as to wage scales, hours, and working conditions. To carry out this mission, union leaders and organizers sought protection under the constitution for their freedoms of speech and association. If successful in their efforts, they could set up closed shops within the area's industrial plants, thereby insuring job security for their members. Inside the factories, different crafts could then be represented as specialization, technological change, mass production, assembly lines, and "scientific management" became commonplace. In Seattle, shipbuilding during the World War I provided an example of this process, just as the automotive industry did in Detroit.

Nationally, the National Association of Manufacturers was the leader of the open shop forces. Robert H. Wiebe in his *Businessmen and Reform* notes that Eastern and Midwestern chambers of commerce tried to keep at arms-distance from such outright advocacy. As discussed above, the Seattle chamber also sought to do so for a time. But in 1910 the organization passed a resolution supporting the open shop concept; in 1913 its membership was reminded of this action. Subsequently the chamber lent support to the Employers' Association and, after the General Strike of 1919, to the Associated Industries of Seattle. To entice outside investors into the city after the General Strike, the Chamber of Commerce trumpeted proudly that Seattle was "open shop."

The dynamics of the business-labor struggle is well-illuminated in the case of Stone and Webster's Puget Sound Traction, Light, and Power Company. It must be remembered, however, that it is but one case in point.[1] In the early twentieth century, Stone and Webster was among the largest of Washington's urban employers. On the one hand, its paternalistic policies were in advance of the time in many respects. A Stone and Webster Club of Washington held annual picnics to which more than 2,000 employees and their families trekked. Entries were sent monthly to the Boston headquarters for inclusion in the *Stone and Webster Journal*. The company had a policy of promoting from within each of its subsidiaries. Nearly all of the Seattle division heads had come up through the ranks. At employee instigation, an Electric Club was established, which met monthly for smokers and to hear talks on technical subjects; presentations usually were given by qualified employees. An employees Beneficial Association rounded out the picture of a happy, corporate family.

All of this beneficence, however, existed in an open shop environment. The company rigidly adhered to a policy of absolute employer control of the work place. The employees purchased job security by sacrificing their freedoms of speech and association. At Seattle Electric, employee loyalty had to come first.

The company operated the city's street car system under a franchise, accounting for seventy-four percent of its revenue in 1911; its light and power business in the city brought in another twenty-two percent; its coal mines at Renton accounted for almost all the rest, plus supplying the company's steam plants at Georgetown (and later, the Shuffleton plant at Renton); and a very modest income came from hauling freight on its traction system.

Seattle Electric underwent a reorganization in 1910, and emerged in 1912 as the Puget Sound Traction, Power, and Light Company, combining the Seattle-Tacoma Power Company, and the Pacific Coast Power Company. Alton W. Leonard was transferred from Stone and Webster's Minneapolis operation to head up the PSTP&L.

By the time Leonard left Seattle for the Boston headquarters in 1931, he had become one of the most flatteringly portrayed, and certainly one of the most photographed, of the city's citizens. He was rivaled in this regard only by City Light's J. D. Ross. Playing the two men off against one another made good newspaper copy because their rivalry was intense; it colored the fabric of city politics for many years.

In 1904, Seattle Electric had locked out workers at the Renton mines when they rejected a company wage offer. Attempts by a labor mediator, working on behalf of Renton citizens and about 200 miners, failed to bring the company around. Instead, strikebreakers were brought in and housed at newly constructed bunk houses. The miners' resistance was soon broken. Many, in fact, left for jobs elsewhere. The open shop was easily maintained.[2]

Seattle Electric's electrical workers and trainmen were a more difficult matter. To deal with them the company had a Secret Service Department, the mission of which was to plant "inside men" to work among the employees whenever union activity stirred. The department also hired special agents who would join the unions, infiltrate the leadership, promote disruption, and report regularly to the company. At one stage, eleven such agents were in the International Brotherhood of Electrical Workers (IBEW) Local 77, in which "[we] have the help of such floating notorious characters . . . as 'Red Handling, Hot Wire Daly, Walk-out Jones, and Monte Ladd'. The chief occupations of these men have been . . . . starting strikes, walk-outs, and trouble of all kinds pertaining to labor's activities." (This kind of program was a national standard among large scale employers.) In reviewing the company's labor policies for a Portland firm in 1913, PSTP&L's traction head, A. L.

Kempster, observed that ". . . we have [not] allowed any of our railway linemen to affiliate with the union among our conductors and motormen."[3]

Competition with City Light also complicated Seattle Electric's situation because the rival's employees were unionized and their organization was recognized. In the International Brotherhood of Electrical Workers (IBEW), Local 77, they would organize boycotts against Seattle Electric's customers, place Stone and Webster on the "unfair" list when they could, and lobby small businesses to contract with the City for their light and power as soon these businesses themselves became unionized. It was Leonard who instituted the policy to dilute its rival's advantage.[4]

A strike against Seattle Electric in 1910 aborted, reportedly because of confusion caused by the company's reorganization activities. On completion of the merger at the beginning of 1912, however, the IBEW renewed negotiations with backing of the Central Labor Council. Leonard refused to negotiate and he refused to stop discrimination against union workers. Not only that, but the merger brought consolidation of many operations. In turn, the work force at Georgetown was reduced from about 250 workers to 127, then to 112 by July and 103 in November. Undoubtedly union members and sympathizers were the first to go. To combat the company, the IBEW's Pacific District Council head, J. Morganthaler, ordered a strike vote of the Seattle, Everett, and Bellingham locals. They struck the first week in January 1913. But the company reported that only eleven of its Seattle employees were affected and said "they regret leaving."[5]

To effect state-wide collaboration among employers the PSTP&L actively supported the Employers' Association of Washington. And, to give broad effect within the utilities industry, coastwise, it instigated creation of the Pacific Coast Utilities Association in 1913. On March 31, 1913, the Employers' Association issued a general letter to "various business men" in the city warning that the closed shop had driven off eighty percent of San Francisco's manufacturing. "It will paralyze the industries of Seattle." Following this alert, the Employers' Association sent out a nine-page letter on May 6, declaring that employers must have absolute authority in the work place. The publication asked, "Is it feasible to effect an organization of the utility companies on the Coast for mutual protection against the aggressions of labor unions?" The letter referred to the split in the IBEW between the McNulty and Reid factions; the former being dominant in the East, and the latter on the West Coast.

What made this split particularly exploitable was the action of the American Federation of Labor in withdrawing the Seattle Central Labor Council's charter for its refusing to negate IBEW local charters. The letter concluded, "This, then, would seem to be an opportune time for us to organize." The IBEW strike of early 1913 fell afoul this factionalism, enabling A. L Kempster to boast to the Boston office that infighting had ". . . occupied their time to the exclusion of plans and efforts to injure us." That the strike failed is understandable.

On the same day, May 6, Kempster reported to the Boston office that representatives of PSTP&L had met with representatives of the Washington Water Power Company, as well as with Portland Railway, Light, and Power Company officials, agreeing ". . . to maintain the open shop with reference to the electrical workers." He explained that the IBEW had gained agreements with a number of California and British Columbia utilities. Furthermore, the IBEW was pushing for legislation to change the construction of ". . . overhead lines, stations, and substations . . . [and to establish worker qualifications for linemen] which would have put the operating companies at the mercy of the unions in case of a strike." It all sounded like preparations for a war. Kempster quoted colleague Grambs " I fear it will be only a short time before the Unions will be in full control of the situation . . . [unless the open shop is maintained]."[6]

In response to the organizing effort, the British Columbia Electric Railway Company promised cooperation. And following Grambs's advice to bring in the larger Pacific Northwest companies before approaching those in the "south," the "Byllesby interests" in Tacoma were brought into line. It all seemed propitious, as the Pacific Gas and Electric Company faced a strike and seemed ready to collaborate.[7]

H. W. Kerrigan, who headed up the coastal association, considered the "card system" that he developed to be the key to operational effectiveness. The cards, which his office used in placing each worker, contained an employee's work history. The card also gave his office ". . . a list of picked emergency men, who are not already employed by a member, and who are available, should a strike or lockout occur. [This card system is] the only near insurance against strikes to be had."[8]

Factionalism in the IBEW continued into 1914, inflamed, when necessary, by Kerrigan's agents. He bragged in June 1914, "In fact, we have already two factions in B.C. and Seattle, fighting each other tooth and nail. We have gone so far as to have the Reid-Murphy crowd in this city take up the question . . . to put the McNultyites out of power, of putting the Seattle Electric Company

[sic] on the fair list." He promised, further, that should any of the unions try to force Stone and Webster into agreement ". . . we will take this means of disrupting their forces . . . ." They voted thirty-five to nine to put Stone and Webster on the fair list. The company would reappear and be removed from the "Fair List" over the coming years, depending on the strength of the City Light faction.[9]

Not entirely satisfied with Kerrigan's regular reports, because they seemed only to be "cullings" from the nation's newspapers, and being satisfied that the local Employers' Association would do the job, A. L. Kempster advised Leonard in October 1914 that he was withdrawing from the Pacific Coast Utilities Association. As for the Employers' Association it had instituted its own card system and an employment bureau.[10]

Labor Movement vs. Employers' Association

In addition to contending with Colonel Blethen's riotous attempts to unseat him as mayor, Cotterill found the Employers' Association ready to give battle on another front as the Teamsters began a long strike against the Team Owners Association. This strike had begun a few weeks before the 1913 Potlatch celebration. The strike ultimately went through several stages before being settled by Cotterill's successor, the reformed Hiram Gill. Before examining this sequence of events, it is important to understand the strike's general setting.

The year 1912 signalled an upturn in the city's economy. A. L. Kempster, in his regular reports to Stone and Webster's Boston headquarters, pointed to the opening of industrial sites just to the south of Seattle's city limits, in the Duwamish River area, as part of a process of "some well capitalized concerns from the other towns to the South"—meaning Portland for the most part. Sears and Roebuck announced its intention to build at First and Lander; Swift and Company, to start a butter plant at Second and Jackson. Kempster drew attention to the Oregon-Washington Railway and Navigation Company's withdrawal from Portland of its trans-Pacific business in wheat and flour, shifting four of its direct lines to Seattle, and two to Tacoma. As a measure of change, March flour exports from Puget Sound now exceeded those of New York. The region's millers reported that three times as much flour was exported from its ports as from Columbia River ports; over ninety percent went to the Orient, and the amount was more than one million barrels over that shipped in 1911. The city could now boast of five flour mills, the recently completed Fisher mill, being the coast's largest, with Albers not far behind.

Kempster pointed out that lumber shipments from Puget Sound ports were the largest since 1906. However, rail shipments of lumber were hampered by a lack of cars to carry the wood. Farmers were expected to earn $25 million more than in 1911, with apple production up by 325 percent over 1911; much of the crop was handled through the Port of Seattle's new cold storage facilities. The railroads expected to ship 18,000 carloads of fruit worth about $18 million.

Although the fish pack from Puget Sound and the Columbia River was down from 1911, that of southeast Alaska was up, a trend that would continue. Most of the Alaska fish packers had their headquarters in Seattle, handling an estimated 100,000 tons of fish products annually. The railroads predicted about $13 million worth of fish would go eastward on their rails.

As though to cap off this recovery, the Great Northern Steamship Company announced that the SS Minnesota had brought in the largest shipment of raw silk on record, 1,937 bales.

Kempster then took pains to list the largest of Seattle's employers, either by individual company or by industry. They were:

Company or Industry	Employees
steamship companies	5,000
woodworkers	3,000
steam railroads	2,500
breweries	2,000
coal mines	2,000
laundries	1,700
flouring mills	500
Denny-Renton Clay and Coal Company	900
Seattle Dry Dock and Construction Co.	800

As though setting the stage for the conflict to come, issues of the September 1910 *Town Crier* (then in the first month of publication) argued that San Francisco was losing out in competition with Seattle because the Bay City was a closed shop town, while Seattle could still boast an open shop status. This situation was not to endure for long. The outcome would suggest that factors, other than unions, were more significant in determining which city was to dominate. By the time Seattle achieved hegemony, it, too, was a closed-shop town.

This was the setting in which the Teamsters Union and the Employers' Association collided. It was refined by the immediate turmoil generated by the Potlatch Riot and by Blethen's abortive attempt to see Mayor Cotterill recalled. Because the economy was on the upswing, there was a relative labor scarcity. Unions pressed the advantage given them by this labor shortage, while the association battled to see that labor relations be conducted in the framework of the open shop.

Teamster Local 174 struck Globe Transfer Company in June 1913. Soon, however, the strike would extend throughout the city's teamster trade and it would not be settled until May 1914. In the struggle, the Teamsters became a main focus of the Employers' Association's open shop campaign after the Seattle Team Owners Association showed signs of signing an agreement.

Local 174 had tried bargaining with the Team Owners Association in 1909, but without success. But in 1912, the union succeeded in signing contracts with fifteen firms and had harmonious relationships with them, although recognition of the union as the official bargaining agent had not been won. Heartened by these successes, the union tried again in 1913 to bargain with the Team Owners Association. This time they were rebuffed. So, on June 14 the union chose to open negotiations with Globe; but the talks came to nothing, and the strike began.

Although the closed shop-open shop issue had not been raised, the Seattle branch of the state Employers' Association began putting pressure on all teamster owners who had union contracts; Eyres Transfer was the first, then others fell in line. Strikebreakers were brought in by the team owners, but strikers were generally successful in coercing drivers to return to the barns with their teams, claiming "no violence." So successful was the union that owners and the Employers' Association finally persuaded the ever-compliant Judge John Humphries to issue an injunction to prohibit picketing.

The atmosphere was further charged by a petition drive to recall Sheriff Edward Cudihee for his deputizing of men who were picked and paid for by managers of the strike-bound Renton mines of Stone and Webster, as well as by Ballard lumber and shingle mill owners. The Ballard mill owners bragged that there had been no successful strike against them in twelve years. At the time there was one in progress; it began in April 1913. To break it owners employed strikebreakers.

The teamster strike continued to be effective for the rest of the year, despite some violence. In fact there were times when the union appeared to be winning. Then, on December 19, Ben Angel, a strikebreaker for the Seattle Drayage and Storage Company, "emptied his revolver into a crowd that surrounded his wagon," wounding at least three strikers.

The team owners now began to complain about the lack of

police protection, just as the Central Labor Council decided to concentrate its forces on this strike. These increasing tensions and Mayor Cotterill's seeming indifference prompted W. J. Grambs, Secretary of the Employers' Association, and superintendent of lighting for the Seattle Electric Company, along with about twenty team owners and four other representatives of the association, to schedule a meeting with Mayor Cotterill for December 22. Grambs opened by accusing the mayor and council of being dominated by the unions. Cotterill responded by banning Grambs from the meeting, although it required a police escort to oust him.

Just when many team owners were preparing to sign contracts, the Employers' Association stepped in declaring for the open shop. The association took over negotiations by threatening unionized owners with retaliation if they resisted the association. The *Town Crier* expressed the concern of the Employers' Association when it insisted that the open shop-closed shop was the issue because the dispute over wages and hours would lead inexorably to union recognition, then to the closed shop.[2]

Four thousand people assembled at Dreamland Pavilion on January 16, 1914 to protest what had become an open shop campaign. After Judge Humphries enjoined the Teamsters from picketing, arrests of striking teamsters began in earnest. There would be thirty-five such arrests, either for loitering or for interfering with strikebreakers by March. And, although two team owners bolted, all others were kept in line by threats that the Association would go into business against them if they caved in to the union.[3]

At the same time, the violent tactics of some teamsters had a negative effect on public opinion. A special agent planted in the Seattle Central Labor Council (SCLC) by the Pacific Coast Utilities Association discovered that the council itself was aware of this problem. The spy reported to his bosses that the Electrical Workers Local 77 business agent warned that such tactics were becoming counter-productive. According to the electrical workers official: "We see the mailed hand in the silken glove of Mr. Furth . . . [and that tactics should be changed to gain the confidence of the business men of the city] . . . or I can see the beginning of the end of all your municipal plans . . . your street railway [whose construction is near completion] and your city light plant."[4]

But if we are to judge by the two-to-one vote favoring a $2.75 per hour minimum wage for workers on local improvement projects in the March 2 election, the public's sympathetic response to organized labor seemed to remain unaffected by the teamster strike. And, among churchmen, Mark Matthews was pretty much alone in his advocacy of the open shop as the American Way. More typical it seemed was the attitude expressed by Arthur Carpenter, editor of *Church Life*, when he advocated arbitration, beginning with the notion that "Organized employers should in all fairness recognize Organized Labor."[5]

Seattle's new mayor, resilient Hiram Gill, quickly appointed a conciliation committee on March 28. This action was objected to by Association spokesmen, who contended there was nothing to arbitrate. On April 25 the committee recommended that the Teamsters return to work under the owners' terms, but urged the owners not to discriminate against the strikers when rehiring. After considerable writhing within the Central Labor Council and among the strikers, the strike was called off because of the impasse and the negative effects of public inconvenience.

It was a clear victory on the surface for the Association. But in light of the coercion the Association brought to bear on its membership, it was hardly a victory for the free enterprise system. Then, most owners signed with the union once they were out from under the domineering pressure of the Association during the strike. As for the union's position, all arrested strikers were acquitted. One writer on Seattle politics of the period regards the March election as marking the emergence of a class consciousness among the "upper class of labor"—the skilled workers who were in unions; they undoubtedly felt their job security and living standards were threatened by the open shop campaign.[6]

The Bon Marche, the city's largest department store, had been on the unfair list since early 1913 and the boycott against the company appeared to take its toll, although management refused to talk with the union. The Bon opened in 1890 and occupied a full city block at 2nd Avenue between Union and Pike streets. Between 1,000 and 2,000 workers were employed annually over the years. In 1913, the company began work on a building occupying the entire block between 3rd and 4th avenues and Pine and Stewart streets, its present location. Following the intervention of the Employers' Association in the teamster strike, the Bon began displaying cards in its windows boasting of its membership in the Association. A strike against the Bon, which had been called off in April 1913, resumed on January 23, 1914, in response to the Bon's declaration for the open shop—which had never been at issue as far as the union was concerned.

Related to the Bon's stiffened resistance to unionization was the Chamber of Commerce's declaration for the open shop principle at its February 2, 1914, meeting. The Chamber had announced this principle in 1910, but now reasserted it: "every effort possible should be made to maintain [the open shop] and the Chamber of Commerce pledges to use its influence towards that end." The SCLC appointed a joint strike committee. Then the Women's Card and Label League (of the SCLC) joined in the picketing and implemented a boycott. By late May, the Bon caved in and allowed its clerks to join the union and bargain with the Retail Clerks Union.[7] By late May, the Card and Label Leagues decided to form a state federation to coordinate lobbying, boycotts, and educational work.

The effectiveness of these leagues is indicated by the legislation they helped to enact. As early as 1911 they lobbied for the eight-hour-day law for women workers and the eight-hour law for workers on public projects. That the State Federation of Labor and SCLC leaders considered their role to be crucial is underscored by the inclusion of a Card and Label League page in each issue of the *Union Record*. Appreciation was shown for their role in May 1914 when the SCLC voted unanimously to organize women barbers through the male union; but not without having to persuade the Barber's council representative that no matter what the union's policy was there was "no good reason to exclude women" from the union.

It was, it appeared, always the Card and Label League that would do the leg-work in initiative and referendum campaigns. The July 1914 campaign for a universal eight-hour day offers only one example. The leagues also took the lead in organizing parades and demonstrations. With Card and Label League backing Mother Jones addressed a May 30, 1914, protest parade in which an estimated 7,000 to 10,000 participated.

At that May 30 demonstration, they protested militia violence conducted against miners in Calumet, Michigan, as well as the mid-April massacre of miners, women, and children at Ludlow, Colorado, where militiamen burned a miners' tent colony and then opened fire without warning on the defenseless crowd. Soon after the Ludlow killings, the *Union Record* began to devote a page in each issue to news submitted by District 10 of the United Mine Workers and to national mine news. The Card and Label League led in this kind of propaganda work.[8]

By 1914, industrial relations were in such turmoil throughout the nation that Congress appointed an Industrial Relations Commission to investigate and report its findings. The *Town Crier* greeted its appointment as a "campaign against employers." The paper declared the "Commission is dominated absolutely by the most radical of the labor element of organized labor." It believed the congressional commission was "boosting" the union cause. Mayor Gill, who had never been a union proponent, nevertheless, testified that it was employers who were more likely to start trouble than unions.[9]

This ferment in industrial relations, brought on by union growth and the threats it posed to the absolutist/paternalistic employer class, caused an ambivalence among members of the socially conscious middle class members and, significantly, among the judiciary. The former supported reform in general. That staunchly middle class organization, the Municipal League, nicely portrayed this uncertainty during the longshoremen's strike and lockout in 1916 when its publication, its *News* complained that the cause of violence and wharf fires could be attributed equally to both sides. But then it asked longshoremen to cease such activity; the publication refrained from making a similar request of the Waterfront Employers' Union.

Some members of the judiciary began to show signs of resisting the traditional rubber-stamping of every injunction request submitted by employers against their striking employees. In September 1915 Judge Kenneth MacKintosh, for example, dismissed an injunction and suit brought by the Employers' Association on behalf of the Jacobi Delicatessen because no damages could be determined. That same month, he also threw out a suit brought by the Victor Theater.

Judge James T. Ronald also decided such cases on their merits and was often favorable to labor. Judge Albertson seems to have won labor's confidence because workers volunteered him as a potential mediator in a Teamster's strike. On the other hand, Judge Mitchell Gilliam behaved in a traditional way, granting an injunction ordering the Motion Picture Operators Union to cease interfering in any way with the conduct of business by the Electric Theater in October 1915. This period of transition within the judiciary would not fade until passage of the Norris-LaGuardia Anti-Injunction Act of 1932.

In spite of these subtle shifts in sympathy in favor of organized labor, the Employers' Association continued to provide legal aid to the afflicted businesses, to threaten those firms that chose to abide their union contracts, to encourage unionized companies to break union contracts, and to operate a "blacklist." When the Labor Council decided to enter the free enterprise system by purchasing and operating the Mutual Laundry, the Employers' Association took measures to sabotage the effort through control of its membership.[10]

During this period, the Central Labor Council was not solely preoccupied with the Employers' Association. In line with its concern about the threat posed by the influx of southern and eastern Europeans who might undermine the existing wage structure, it began to focus attention on the miserable exploitation of immigrant workers employed on the construction of Sunset Highway near Issaquah.

Two Seattle contractors, Pat McHugh and Henry Brice had

set up tent-colony company towns for their Italian, Russian, Greek, and Austrian workers in defiance of current standards for public health and working conditions. The *Union Record* covered the situation in April and May 1915 when the Russians in Camp 10 struck and then got other camps between Renton and Issaquah to follow.

Conditions were so incredibly bad for the workers that Issaquah citizens formed a committee to feed the workers. Contractors worked their crews ten to sixteen hours a day, a direct violation of the eight-hour on public projects law. Brice was arrested on this count, and the authorities began looking for a subcontractor named Peter Chantilis. Even the conservative King County Commissioners agreed that the law should henceforth apply to subcontractors like Chantilis, and that contractors should not circumvent the law by the ruse of subcontracting for workers.

Although the Labor Council may have been concerned about the exploitation of newly arrived Caucasian ethnic groups (those not yet integrated into the organized labor movement) it reacted to the employment of Asian laborers in a different way. The Council saw Asian immigrants as threats to labor standards that the SCLC was working hard to establish. It was outraged when the Butler Hotel fired all of its "working girls" and replaced them with "cheap Japanese labor." The *Union Record* claimed this was done to spite the new minimum wage law which was to take effect in August 1915. Altogether hotels fired 2,000 workers and Japanese residents were substituted for them after passage of the act. By late July, however, the Butler fired the Japanese workers and rehired its former employees at the new minimum wage.[11]

The 1913-1914 Teamsters strike was significant because it focused attention on the Employers' Association and that organization's determination to keep Seattle in the ranks of open-shop cities. In their struggle, the strength of the opposition became apparent. One of the Association's officers, John V. Patterson, an executive of Seattle Construction and Drydock Company (successor to Moran Brothers Shipbuilding Company), fought tooth and nail keep unions out of the shipyards.

The Laundry Owners' Association and other employers also were in collusion with the Employers' Association for the same reason. The fortunes of the open shop movement, which had existed since the turn of the century, ebbed and flowed with the ups and downs of the local economy and the labor supply. As the economy revived under the stimulus of wartime production spurred by fighting in Europe after 1914, the inevitable shortage of labor temporarily defeated the Employers' Association. Seattle became a closed shop town until after the effects of the 1919 General

Strike, just when the economy headed toward a downturn in 1920. From then, until 1934-1935, Seattle, like most other large American cities, became an open shop bastion.

The Legislature and the City, 1913

Although activity in Olympia in 1911 marked a high point in the history of Washington legislative reform, legislators in the 1913 session seemed ready to continue the trend. Much "sociological" legislation—as it was then called—was introduced at the opening of the 1913 session. The *Seattle Sun* (which began publication on February 3, 1913) inquired into the reason for this unusual spate of altruism, and found that lawmakers attributed it to the granting of suffrage to women. On the list of this kind of legislation were: a minimum wage for women and minors, a teachers' pension bill, one for mothers pensions, another to establish vocational schools, one to support destitute women, an eight-hour law for underground coal miners, liquor bills, a "red light" law, and bills to protect workers from employment "sharks" (for-fee employment agencies).[1]

That the women's influence on legislation after 1911 should occur should be no surprise in light of the past record of women's' clubs, in particular that of the Federation of Women's Clubs. Louise Beck wrote in 1904 that "the work of all women's clubs in the city, even those most given over to self-culture study, is strongly tinted with altruism. . . . We are learning self-control, for the woman who rules in club work has learned to rule her own spirit. We are learning a new regard for the rights of our neighbors. . . . Seattle clubdom is a mixed affair. Mixed to our liking."

Beck also outlined the Seattle federation's program. The federation, which consisted of two or more delegates from each affiliated group, discussed and acted on matters of public concern such as: civic improvements, playgrounds for children, a juvenile court system, workers accident compensation, free kindergartens, consumer protection, the need for uniform child labor laws, eight-hour laws, and forest preservation were among their concerns. They lobbied legislators zealously, and joined forces with other groups favoring the same kind of legislation; often this meant cooperation with the State Federation of Labor, the Ministerial Federation, and other reform groups. Some laws got passed that they had promoted; most did not. But once women got the vote, legislators could not ignore them, frequently, lawmakers complained of the heat women applied.[2]

Helen Ross, the *Town Crier*'s columnist for women's clubs,

wrote in 1913, that these organizations proliferated as the "woman question" has grown in number. She counted more than 2,000 club women, and twenty-seven federation affiliates. "Now there is not a club in the Federation which is not engaged in some altruistic work. . . . There has been scarcely a movement for civic betterment to which the club women have not lent their support." Consequently, city officials paid them heed. (Ross would soon complain about this altruistic emphasis).[3]

One major piece of legislation that passed with the strong support of women's clubs was the "Iowa Red Light Law." This statute prohibited the existence of districts that had been restricted for the conduct of prostitution. It followed a report of the Reverend Ralph Atkinson and two other ministers who repeated a tour of the red light district they had taken three years earlier. On their second trip, the clergymen found the city to be "clean," and they credited Police Chief Claude Bannick for bringing about the change. And, although the Chamber of Commerce objected that the rights of private property were being violated without observing due process, the state Supreme Court upheld the law as a proper exercise of police power.[4]

Of vital importance for the city's future, physically, was the fate of the shore lands to be uncovered when Lake Washington was lowered. A bill had been introduced by Senator William Wray that would have given these shore lands to the upland owners. In anticipation of the lake's lowering, private parties had bought most of the upland property from the state in 1909 and the Chamber of Commerce supported the bill. The *Sun* claimed that Jacob Furth, N. H. Latimer of the Dexter Horton Company, and the Northern Pacific Railroad were the powers behind the legislation. Port Commission president, General Hiram Chittenden chastised the chamber for its support of the bill, claiming that it would "give absolutely without expense, to a small group of owners—most of them wealthy organizations or individuals—the important industrial and commercial sites around the shores. . . . It thus proposes to lock up in speculative ownership the last remaining opportunity in this port for providing cheap sites for commercial and industrial purposes." Chittenden cited the enormous price the Port of Seattle had to pay for lands acquired at Harbor Island and at the south end of Lake Union. As an example, the *Sun* pointed out the purchase of Lake Union shore land from the state in 1908 by J. M. Clapp for $15,952 on a ten-year contract, and selling it to the county for $87,482 in 1913.

But, if Chittenden was concerned about providing cheap industrial and commercial sites, the Park Board also had its priorities. The board wanted parkways and boulevards along the shore, filling in more elements of the Olmsted parkways and boulevards plan of 1903. Board members went to Olympia hoping to amend the bill to protect these lands, which were integral to the city's long-range plans. They were only partially successful. The House approved a substitute bill giving the upland owners land out to a depth of sixteen feet of water at the new level; but with the following stipulation: The upland owners were to get this land only after the state land commissioner had made public reservations for streets, alleys, dock sites, and after the park board had laid out parkways and boulevards. The Board dedicated the land between Mt. Baker Park and Rainier Beach for this purpose. (The three-mile stretch between Seward Park and Rainier Beach, however, fell into the hands of private developers.)[5]

City Politics and Municipal Ownership

As the area's economy began its recovery in 1912, bank clearings for the year showed an increase of $50 million over those in 1911, and continued to increase in 1913. Gold discoveries in the Shusanna District spurred a provisioning trade keyed to the latest rush. Shipyards were busy with both new construction and repair work attuned to the annual springtime provisioning of Alaska. A. L. Kempster reported to the Boston office that the Alaska salmon pack would see a record year. Not least of importance in the Alaska picture, according to Kempster, was the federal government's decision to build the Alaska railroad by guaranteeing protection of private investment, so badly needed ". . . to restore active trade between this city and the territory." Investments that had been withheld were now expected to pour forth.

In addition, a general increase in immigration generally stimulated business, filling apartment houses to capacity and triggering a housing shortage.

Kempster, also reported that lumber and shipping interests were "flourishing"; 100 million board feet of fir lumber for railroad car construction helped. Employment at the Seattle's new Sears store soared responsively to these signs of life as the company expanded its work force from 110 to 858. Store management began demanding better street car service to meet its needs. And, in anticipation of the Panama Canal opening, the Kosmos Line inaugurated its trans-Pacific service. A. L. Kempster observed that businessmen are looking forward to the canal opening with "firm optimism."

Responding to this flurry of activity, J. D. Ross requested a bond issue of $425,000 in October 1912 for building a steam plant at the south end of Lake Union to attract industry and to meet any emergency at the Cedar operation where a masonry dam was being completed. He did not have to wait long. Timely voter approval was forthcoming in the March 1913 election. Ross also sought an inter-tie with Tacoma's municipal plant as its Nisqually dam neared completion. But, as Kempster reported to Boston, the company had its Tacoma engineer speak to that city's chief engineer, and successfully warded off the inter-tie.

In the March 1911 municipal election voters approved an $800,000 bond issue to purchase the failing Seattle, Renton, & Southern Railway, an independent that ran from Renton into the city. However, when the owners upped the selling price to $1.2 million the City Council decided to divert the money to construction of a line that looped from Third and Pine toward Lake Union, then along the canal to end at Fourteenth Northwest, where an existing Ballard line terminated. The city had entered the street railway business with its "Division "A" line, completed in May 1914. But, the State of Washington had to bail out the effort by purchasing $300,000 in bonds when no takers came forward. As to the Seattle, Renton & Southern, it went into receivership in 1913 and each offer of the City to buy it was rejected by the receivers.

When Seattle was offered the Highland and Lake Burien Line in 1913, it accepted, after company owners decided it was wiser to give the line away than to dig the tracks out from under a massive landslide; this became "Division C" of the Municipal Street Railway. Division C would operate at a loss, serving the sparsely populated Burien area. The city's investment in excavation, repairs, rolling stock, and car barns never paid off.

These successful bond issues in support of municipal enterprises (including one that put the city into the garbage collection business), plus one that failed to get the City into the telephone line, raised vociferous opposition from the *Times*, the *P-I*, and the Chamber of Commerce, all of which contended that tax support of these enterprises inhibited private investment. They also contended that City Light was operating at a loss, and that its Camp 2 at the Cedar River dam construction site was being extravagantly run. This would mark the beginning of a continuing barrage against City Light in particular; one to which Ross would just as regularly argue the contrary by showing how the department's surplus was being plowed back into plant expansion and improvements that would lead directly to lower rates being charged, not only by the city, but by the PSTP&L as well.

As to the Port of Seattle, at the end of 1913 President

Chittenden issued a progress report: The Central Waterfront wharfs and accompanying warehouses were to be completed in 1914; Smith's Cove dock—the world's longest—would be ready in June; the Salmon Bay facility was already producing revenue; the Lake Washington ferry would be in full operation by spring; and about half the land had been purchased for the East Waterway terminals. In addition, contracting for construction of a 1,500-foot wharf and a one-million case capacity salmon warehouse had been undertaken. Clearly, the Port of Seattle was moving rapidly to fulfill its promise.

The initial bitterness felt by the Chamber of Commerce, the *Times,* and the *P-I* at losing the battle for Harbor Island waned as Seattle's trade steadily increased. The turning point seems to have been the voters' defeat in June 1913, of a proposition to increase the number of commissioners from three to five. In A. L. Kempster's words: "to curtail the power of the individual members." He reported to Stone and Webster in Boston on June 20 that the *P-I, Railway and Marine News,* and *Pacific Fisherman* have switched their support to the East Waterway project. Soon the Seattle would be the leading port on the Pacific Coast.[1]

11

The Economy, 1914-1920

An Overview

As Seattle emerged as the leading shipping port on the Pacific Coast in the second decade of the twentieth century, the long-sought manufacturing base for the economy finally became a reality. The trouble was that Seattle's precipitous manufacturing growth was dependent on a wartime industry—shipbuilding. The sudden demand for vessels brought on by the outbreak of war in Europe only masked the fact that national and regional shipbuilding were in a fragile condition, allegedly due to the relatively high wages paid to shipyard workers. With Japan embarking on its own massive shipbuilding program, competition was bound to become acute. Added to this problem after 1918 was the surfeit of ships owned by the Shipping Board, for which a market had to be found. The alternative was to moor these surplus vessels in "graveyards," like the one found in Seattle's Lake Union.

Seattle's shipbuilding industry during World War I, like the aircraft industry during World War II, spawned numerous, associated manufacturing ventures. In the case of shipbuilding, these included boilermaking, a host of metalworking operations, companies that provided lumber for deck planking and superstructures, and the supplying of raw materials to those yards still building wooden ships. According to the 1918 Port of Seattle *Yearbook*, the city had 1,300 manufacturing plants employing 50,000 workers; but shipyard employees accounted for 35,000 of that total. Combined, their payrolls were about $5 million per month (a large proportion this amount went for housing, in the opinion of the

shipyard employees. They believed they were targeted by landlords for paying premium rents because of their relatively high
wages).

The Skinner and Eddy yard, one of nineteen in Seattle, set the
pace for rapid expansion. Organized in 1916 by the two major
owners of the Port Blakely Mill Company (which they leased to
the Dominion Mill Company during the war), this facility launched
its first ship in September of that year. Its first launching (and first
in the nation) for the Shipping Board occurred in late November
1917. Between January and April the yard launched eight more
vessels, setting a national record. The Seattle Construction and
Dry Dock yard was first leased by Skinner and Eddy, then was
purchased outright in June 1918. This acquisition was accompanied by a $100 million contract with the Shipping Board. By the
end of the war in November 1918, this yard produced more ships
for the Shipping Board than any other yard in the nation. That all
of this activity had an enormous, distorting effect on the economy
is understandable.[1]

As to Seattle's lumber industry, once the great strike of 1917
had been settled and the eight-hour day was accepted in March
1918, it was hampered less by supply than by the difficulty in
finding transportation for its products. The Federal Railroad Administration (FRA) limited the number of rail cars allocated to the
hauling of lumber and prohibited Seattle shipments from traveling east beyond Chicago. To make this policy clear, the FRA issued an edict in April 1918 requiring that one government car be
loaded for every two loaded for commercial purposes; and then
the Administration furnished "very few" orders to fill its allotted
cars, according to A. L. Kempster. As to the possibility of
waterborne lumber shipments, commodities of higher unit value
than wood products normally were given preference.

Seattle lumber mills found their biggest market in the region;
one customer being the fledgling Boeing Airplane Company, which
was delivering one plane a day to the government. In addition,
local shipyard demands and a regional housing shortage provided
a large and steady outlet for wood products; building permits
issued for small-housing construction in January 1918 were reportedly the highest in nine years.

In other areas, however, Seattle promoters did not always
take full advantage of opportunities as they presented themselves.
When, for instance, the city became the nation's largest importer
of vegetable oils in 1917 and 1918, instead of triggering investments in soap-making plants and other manufacturing that utilized these oils, storage tanks were constructed and tank cars built;

the tanks to hold oil until it was ready for shipment; the cars to transport the liquid to factories in the East. Accentuating this lack of foresightedness, Japan resumed its use of the Suez Canal route for shipping most of its vegetable oil after the war ended since it was destined for the Atlantic seaboard anyway. *Railway and Marine News* complained strenuously about this lack of investment initiative. The same situation existed for raw silk, which was Seattle's largest single import.

In the "value added" category of Seattle's manufactures for 1919, foundries led the way with over $15 million; wooden shipbuilding followed with $6,882,124. And although the federal census listed six steel shipyards, it separated out no product values. But the amount must have been at least double that of the wooden yards, since 1919 was the best year of all for the steel yards. On the other hand, contracts for wooden ships, were among the first to be cancelled after November 1918.

Lumber and timber products followed shipbuilding with slightly over $6 million; then printing and publishing with almost $8 million added value, which was divided between job printing and publishing ($3,388,460) and newspaper and periodical publishing ($4,225,755); then flour-milling with over $3 million; followed by products consumed locally for the most part, such as bakery goods, and confectionery items. Foundry products, of course, were heavily dependent on the shipyards for their market.[2]

Waterborne commerce, while steadily increasing before 1914, boomed during the war period. Total imports in 1914 were worth $89,339,742; exports, $65,260,205. By 1916 these values expanded to $259,550,106 and $152,879,213 respectively. By 1917 they jumped to $377,991,955 and $221,599,000 respectively. Expansion continued through 1919, when the figures climbed to $455,184,862 for imports, and $294,887,045 for exports. A slackening occurred in 1920, the value of imports dropping to $374,936,169 and exports to $213,087,028.

What were the major characteristics of the commodities traded? Taking the 1917 figures as representative domestic imports totaled $109,097,093. Included were over $39 million worth of commodities received from Alaska; almost $44 million from California; over $5 million from the Philippines; from the "Fishing Banks," $1,638,791; from Hawaii $575,238 worth of commodities; and the Mosquito Fleet brought to the city more than $18 million worth of goods.

Major commodities traded with Alaska were (in thousands of dollars):

Imports		Exports	
salmon (canned)	$19,976,000	machinery	$3,106
gold dust	11,763,000	meat	2,146
concentrates	1,166,134	tin plate	1,336
halibut	600,931	tobacco	670

Major commodities traded with California were (in thousands of dollars):

Imports		Exports	
gasoline	$9,592,166	flour	$3,494
fuel oil	6,805,716	salmon	2,002
sugar	4,946,495	wheat	1,880
tobacco	2,688,450	canned milk	1,008

Single staple products dominated the other domestic imports: From the Fishing Banks almost all of the total was halibut ($1,425,320); similarly, Hawaii's exports were nearly all pineapple ($566,999); from the Philippines $4,842,093 of the total was hemp.

Domestic exports totalled $69,543,458, with $32,488,942 going to Alaska; $16,657,938 worth to California; $16,789,155 of value to Puget Sound points; and $3,238,704 worth to the Philippines. Hawaii imported $368,719 worth of general goods of which lumber totalled $83,490, coal $79,464, and box shooks $53,363.

Foreign imports in 1917 totalled $268,894,862 with $187,648,717 worth coming from the Orient. Of this total raw silk made up $100,699,498 of the value; soy oil $30,004,455; hides $5,188,285; tea $4,257,903; camphor $2,456,406; and peanut oil $1,794,719. Another $45,249,138 worth of commodities came from the East Indies, of which $34,842,300 was in crude rubber, and $7,203,138 was in tin. From India came $12,081,307, half of which was in the form of jute and jute bags, and $3,936,882 as crude rubber—for these two regions the relationship was only for the "duration." British Columbia shipped goods worth $22,312,823 of which gold coin and bullion were worth over $13 million, copper blisters worth $4,522,221, explosives worth $1,137,136, and paper $1,028,630. Miscellaneous small amounts were imported from the other trading partners with whom commercial exchange was just beginning; it would resume after the war when full advantage of the Panama Canal route would finally be realized.

Exports to foreign markets were valued at $152,055,542 with the Orient receiving $122,812,254 of the total; British Columbia $10,188,231 worth; Siberia receiving $7,377,245 of value; India $4,358,887; and the East Indies $2,710,431 worth of commodities.

Great Britain managed to buy $2,624,497 mainly in the form of wheat, canned milk, and salmon. Even France imported $551,464 worth of flour after importing nothing in 1916—due undoubtedly to Germany's submarine warfare. India's imports were valued at $4,358,887 of which steel made up $1,108,366, canned milk $529,298, and tin plate another $498,759. The East Indies took $2,710,431 in value, of which canned milk made up $924,002 of the total, cigarettes $432,595, and steel $252,091. Siberia's imports were valued at $7,327,245, including "spelter" (zinc) worth $1,954,843, raw cotton at $1,587,193, cotton at $565,396, and machinery at $404,126. Australia's imports of $211,062 included lumber valued at $81,145 and salmon at $59,677.

Since the Orient (Japan and China) and British Columbia normally were the two most important foreign trading partners during the period from 1915 to 1920 it is useful to compare their relative position in terms of tonnage handled, and peek at the figures for 1921.

	Foreign Exports		Foreign Imports	
	Orient	B.C.	Orient	B.C.
1915	18%	15%	43%	34%
1916	39	36	40	36
1917	66	15	46	33
1918	79	6	54	27
1919	75	10	46	38
1920	54	9	40	47
1921	67	6	18	65

Taking only the Oriental trade and comparing its dollar value relative to all imports and exports, and in relation to only the foreign imports and exports from 1904 to 1932 is helpful in assessing its importance as well as its characteristics.

	Foreign		Relative to all Imports
	Exports	Imports	& exports
1904	74%	23%	17%
1909	54	87	19
1913	41	84	24
1914	38	80	25
1917	80	60	51
1920	80	88	41
1922	62	94	48
1924	66	94	43
1926	62	93	39
1929	51	94	34
1932	33	88	16

The figures for 1904 are for the period before heavy importations of raw silk were being made, and they show exports (mainly to Japan) were three times larger than imports. A reversal had set in by 1909—as noted earlier. Raw silk had become the basis of the trade, the main source for obtaining dollars to help build Japan's growing industrial economy. As will be shown below, the relative importance of the Oriental trade declined in the 1920s as the trade through the Panama Canal opened up markets in the Gulf of Mexico, the Atlantic seaboard, the United Kingdom, and Europe. Heavier oil imports from California also contributed to the declining overall importance of Seattle's Oriental trade.[3]

When the Suzuki Company, a shipping and commercial firm, moved its headquarters from Portland to Seattle in January 1917, it was part of a trend: the Pacific Coast Steamship Company had done so previously, and so had the Union Pacific operations when it transferred the Washington-Oregon Railroad main offices to Seattle and built a depot next to the Union Station. Suzuki's eight steamers were the means for getting Seattle into the vegetable oil business in such a big way, reportedly spawning the world's largest vegetable oil terminals, the largest operated by the Rogers Brown and Company. Prior to 1916 these oils had not been imported through Seattle.

Significantly, the nature of apple exports, which would become a major commodity after 1924, underwent two vital changes. Deprived of a developing European market, growers concentrated on selling their crops in the United States. But until that time growers depended on Eastern buyers for financing, and suffered the consequences. By 1918 Seattle bankers decided to compete and began to finance the growing and harvesting of the crop, which was worth about $20 million by A. L. Kempster's estimate. After the war, these relationships stabilized as the European market re-emerged.[4]

While the importance of canned salmon, flour, lumber, and wheat have been generally recognized as Seattle's major commodity exports, the significance of canned milk has been overlooked. It figured heavily in the Pacific Rim trade, and as an export to California. During World War I, Great Britain also imported a significant quantity of canned milk. The main source of supply probably was the Carnation plant in Mount Vernon, situated on the Skagit River, and brought to Seattle on stern-wheelers and by rail.

The transportation pattern that characterized Seattle in the 1920s was established during the war years. While shipping by water and rail would continue throughout the year, there were seasonal peaks of activity. The first came with the annual opening of Alaskan waters in the spring. It involved re-supplying the territory, outfitting those going there for jobs, outfitting the fishing fleet sailing from Salmon Bay, and readying the region's fish canneries.

The second peak occurred in the fall, when lumber shipments by rail were heaviest and the summer wheat harvest had been prepared, either for direct shipment or to be processed at local mills for export to the Pacific Rim and California. By fall, canned salmon was also ready for shipment by water and rail. Exports of fruit crops, principally apples and apricots, also contributed to the late-year commerce.

The Dark Side of the Economy: Unemployment

Unemployment in Seattle peaked during the years 1913 to 1915. Only crude estimates of its extent can be made because statistics on the phenomenon were not gathered at the time. But unemployment was, nevertheless, clearly observable. The United States Industrial Relations Commission, for example, published a report that found unemployment to be a critical national problem. For its part, the State Federation of Labor and the Seattle Central Labor Council agreed and pressed for wide circulation of the document. The federation then began collecting actual statistics by use of a questionnaire; and the SCLC started a "Seattle Forward Movement" directed at organizing the unorganized, including the hoboes and transients (in part to compete with the IWW) and to seek legislation for the eight-hour day as a means of spreading the work.

During the early years of the twentieth century Washington's main cities became havens of refuge for seasonal agriculture, logging, construction, fisheries, and canning workers. In these industries approximately two-thirds of the wage earners were affected by seasonal layoffs. As a result, the number of people out of work in Seattle, Spokane, Tacoma, and the state's other cities increased dramatically between November and March.

Not only did unemployment bring social problems for which these municipalities were unprepared, but private employment agencies took full advantage of the situation. The seasonal nature this work proved ideally suited to such firms; there were more than 100 in the state. Abuses became so flagrant that by February 1913 Mayor Cotterill lobbied with the state Labor Commissioner to prevent employment agencies sending workers to the Gray's Harbor lumber town of Cosmopolis, "where there is either no work or conditions are such that the man can't work." Fraudulent practices became so widespread that the 1913 legislature passed a law to abolish private employment agencies and to encourage the creation of a public employment office. (The Employers' Association challenged the law and the United States Supreme Court declared it unconstitutional in 1916.)

According to the *Seattle Sun*, agencies would advance transportation fare to a prospective worker, but would hold personal baggage until the agency was paid back, thereby forcing men to work to retrieve their belongings. In response, Seattle established a public agency at Third and Jefferson, which, by December 19, 1913, registered 1,300 workers for employment.[1]

In order to feed and house the large numbers of unemployed in the city, Mayor Cotterill converted the former Providence Hospital into the "Liberty Hotel." E. H. Wells of the *Sun* congratulated the mayor for this effort. But not all were fortunate enough to find a spot in the Liberty Hotel; women, for instance, were not allowed there.

In the absence of an appropriate city agency, the police department was assigned jurisdiction over workers without jobs who roamed the streets. Police Chief Claude Bannick assigned officers to "look after the unemployed men and women" by jailing them for idleness. This practice provoked Wells, to object that "Idleness is not a crime [and police should instead] keep closer tab on the criminals of this city." Although the Liberty Hotel remained open, its limited facilities were inadequate, to say the least.

Other city policies served to exacerbate the problems faced by destitute workers without jobs. On many homes of the unemployed and poor the Health Department posted notices to vacate. After Gill's second election, the Health Department also took action to shut down a "camping resort" for the poor at Alki Beach declaring it to be unfit for habitation. The SCLC futilely protested, and tried to get Mayor Gill and the council to act. Gill responded at an applauding Conference of Charities and Corrections meeting that the unemployed were out of work due to their own improvidence and "brutish drinking habits." He continued, asserting that these "bums" must not be given any money for their work except their "board and flop" at the Liberty; a meal at two to four cents is sufficient for them.[2]

Henry Pauly, manager of the Liberty, presented a different perspective to a more sympathetic Municipal League audience. He countered Gill's slap-dash comments with an impressive set of statistics and commentary that were printed in the *Municipal News*. Pauly pointed out that hotel residents worked in and around the hotel, or on land-clearing projects for which he was able to contract and which were paid for by issuance of meal tickets worth twenty-one meals for every two days worked. Furthermore, these men labored on city and county projects without pay. Between November 18, 1914, and February 18, 1915, they worked 5,238 hours, earning enough to pay back the $5,200 lent to the hotel by the City and County. The League also took pride in the effectiveness of the city's free employment office in finding jobs for many of the unemployed.[3]

In the early twentieth century, unemployed working women faced even greater difficulties than their male counterparts. To begin with, the Liberty Hotel was for men only. Two hundred unemployed women who petitioned the new YWCA for beds, were told there were none available. And although plans were made to form a Women's Unemployed League to publicize the plight of women without jobs, nothing came of it.[4]

As many civic leaders saw it, unemployment was not altogether a disaster. George Zinn, secretary of the Chamber of Commerce's Charities Endowment Bureau, told business leaders to take heart; as he reported in September 1914, the unemployed have an association for land clearing projects in winter at "reasonable prices . . . the idle men who do not seek work will be compelled to move on, in accordance with plans already agreed upon by the city and county authorities."[5]

From the perspective of the unemployed, theirs was a desperate situation. The threat of starvation and need for clothing became so acute at one point that a group of men raided local produce stands for food; others stormed the Salvation Army headquarters and stole clothing after they had been turned away earlier.

The Central Council of Social Agencies responded to this pitiable situation by appointing a committee to study the problem and to try to provide work, "if possible." The King County Board of Commissioners voted $1,000 to assist the council in its work.[6]

The rate of unemployment declined in 1915 as the lumber trades revived at mid-year. Simultaneously, shipping in general picked up; the Osaka Shosen Kaisha Line added four vessels to its roster. In response to the unsettled world situation triggered by World War I, area shipyards now ran at capacity. Until the end of 1920, a labor shortage would be Seattle's major problem, not unemployment. World War I proved a boon to the city's economy.

12

City Politics, 1914-1915

The Setting

During the last months of 1913, two issues absorbed the public's attention in Seattle. One was the Employers' Association open-shop drive; the other was an increase of vice activity and alleged police corruption. Mayor Cotterill made clear where he stood in relation to the association when he expelled its W. J. Grambs from a December meeting to deal with the Teamsters' strike, and in his confrontation with Alden Blethen over the publisher's right to promote riots. But the mayor was unable to deal with the vice problem. The Seattle *Sun* ran a series of exposes in late October 1913, claiming a ". . . scandalous increase in gambling and other evils," contending that Chief Claude Bannick ". . . has been deceived by some of his subordinates, [holdovers from Wappenstein's force], who were not in sympathy with the closed town policy. . . ." The council was accused of issuing licenses to "cafe-saloons without dissenting votes when the entire membership . . . knew of the shameless orgies that were nightly carried on in those resorts." The *Sun* tried to separate Cotterill from responsibility; the *Times* questioned the charges themselves and opposed cafe-saloon regulation under terms of the Red Light Abatement Law as a violation of property rights.[1]

Earlier, Councilman Austin E. Griffiths had criticized Cotterill and Bannick for permitting police raids on hotels and cafes without cause—and without warrants. Cotterill had vetoed the Griffiths ordinance, spelling out police powers, including the requirement for using a warrant. Griffiths pointed to the 17,078 arrests made without warrants in 1912, and to the dismissal of 5,699 of the ensuing cases—examples of police violations of the constitutionally protected rights of free speech and assembly: "They dictate what meetings will be held. They seize a printing press, confiscate papers and shut up the business and then decide how it shall be run to suit them." It seemed clear that such abuses of police power provided untold opportunities for shakedowns and payoffs.

Whether the shower of criticism from friend (co-prohibitionist Griffiths and the *Sun*) and foe alike prompted Cotterill to announce that he would not seek re-election is unknown; but when he chose instead to try to unseat Senator Wesley Jones, ten people lined up by the end of January for a chance to succeed him as mayor. Hiram Gill unblushingly decided to run, this time as a closed-town advocate.[2]

The year 1914 also saw unresolved industrial-relations issues, that had lain dormant since early in the century, come to a head. The 1913 teamsters strike was still in progress. There would be other strikes during the year: the Bon Marche strike; another by 200 men against the Pacific Coast Steel Company in Youngstown in January that was lost in February. A new sheriff would replace Cudihee, against whom the Central Labor Council had started a recall campaign for his complicity in providing Ballard shingle-mill owners and the Stone and Webster Renton mines with deputies named by employers. The mine workers' union, Local 2116, would be disbanded after a lockout. All of this activity led A. L. Kempster to report optimistically at the end of February 1914: "The employers of the Puget Sound district are more closely associated than ever before and are a unit in advancing the policy of the open shop."[3]

Unemployment was viewed as the crucial problem facing organized labor in 1913; it reached 30,000 statewide by the end of the year. The tight job market threatened the wage scales unions were slowly achieving; linked with this concern, unions began a campaign to restrict immigration. Employer organizations opposed placing restrictions on immigration and heightened their open shop campaign at the same time. Both policies were aimed at lowering wage scales and allowing the employer full authority over working conditions. Nevertheless, union membership for both the State Federation and for the SCLC continued to climb. While the Employers' Association's declaration of class warfare would set the tone of industrial relations for the next six years, the prohibition issue would assume major proportions by the time the voters decided the matter in November.[4]

The battle for dominance between City Light and Stone and Webster also took a twist in November 1913 when the Boston-based company applied to a sympathetic Board of County Commissioners for the "perpetual exclusive franchise" for providing light and power to all unincorporated areas in King County; this request was in direct conflict with Ross's expansionist plans and also the state constitution, which specifically prohibited the granting of such franchises. By the end of 1914 City Light would face a new crisis, but J. D. Ross narrowly would escape its worst effects.[5]

The city's very own street railways were nearing readiness, after debris had been cleared away from the Division C tracks and $75,000 of garbage funds were used to complete the Division A line. Both would be operational by the end of May; almost immediately they began losing as much as $2,000 a month.[6]

During that last week in May 1914, Anna Louise Strong returned to the city with a Child Welfare Exhibit that she had organized for the United States Education Office, and had been showing throughout the country. Despite minimal media attention, the exhibit drew an average 6,000 persons daily, concluding with an attendance of 40,000 on May 31. The exhibit was an outgrowth of the child welfare movement that had resulted in child labor legislation that focused on hygiene, recreation, education, and other factors bearing on child development.[7]

Helen Ross, a columnist for the *Town Crier*, trumpeted the "Passing of the Shrieking Sisterhood" when Beatrice (Mrs. Henry) Lung was elected president of the Seattle Federation of Women's Clubs. Mrs. Lung vowed to keep the federation out of politics, unlike her predecessors who had been active in getting legislation passed that favored women and children. Lung claimed such activity brought much "discredit" on the federation and had obscured its good works: "we will go back to self-culture to a great extent—that sort of thing which our club women have largely despised during the last few years and discarded in favor of so-called altruistic work. . . . The Federation will do much toward raising the general cultural level in the community."

In keeping with the *Town Crier*'s editorial policy, Helen Ross wrote articles objecting to the minimum wage bill, to arbitrating the teamsters strike, sternly objecting to unions in principle, and opposing municipal ownership of any kind.[8]

At the University of Washington, Colonel Blethen's vendetta against President Thomas Kane led to the chief executive's dismissal in January 1914, essentially for Kane's defence of academic freedom. On the other hand, many faculty thought that Kane had not gone far enough.[9]

At least three architectural landmarks were completed in Seattle during 1914. One was the forty-two-story Smith Tower—"tallest in the West." Another was the Young Women's Christian Association building at Fifth and Seneca. The Pantages Theater (later called the Palomar) at Third and University Street and designed by B. Marcus Priteca was the third.[10]

City Politics, 1914

A historian of Seattle's reform support, Mansel Blackford, rates the 1914 city election as a watershed. He sees the previous coalition of the "upper class of labor" with the middle class as breaking up. In the primaries, among the mayoral candidates, Gill logged 23,419 votes; Trenholme only 11,897, beating out Socialist Richard Winsor by a slim 380 vote margin; Austin Griffiths garnered a mere 9,087. Gill convincingly defeated Trenholme by about 14,000 votes in the runoff, losing only the 10th ward, and running up huge margins in the labor wards. That Trenholme was openly backed by the Employers' Association undoubtedly brought out the labor vote due to the association's open shop drive.

In Robert Saltvig's judgment of this mayoral campaign, reform as an issue failed to catch voter interest because "economic and moral issues were [not] joined." When they had been in the past, Moore had been elected Mayor in 1906, Cotterill went to the state Senate in 1909, Dilling defeated Gill in 1911, and Cotterill defeated Gill in 1912.

Despite tough accusations made by Griffiths against Gill in the primaries (assertions that Gill's law firm profited from defending white slavers, gamblers, pimps, and saloon keepers) Gill appointed Griffiths his police chief, as if to challenge him to put up or shut up. Although Griffiths resigned in November to run as a Progressive for Congress, he accomplished a great deal in the time he headed the police department. Officers were forbidden to enter places of business except on police errands; many of the city's dark alleys were lighted; police maps were made to better concentrate on heavy crime areas; and conditions at a detention center known as the Stockade (near Jefferson Park) were radically improved. Stockade inmates were provided educational and lecture programs on secular subjects; inmates now maintained vegetable gardens to feed prisoners and to supply other city departments. In addition, women's quarters were completely segregated from areas where men were incarcerated. In later years, when running for other offices, Griffiths pointed with pride to his achievements as chief of police.[1]

Among the issues facing Seattle residents in 1914 was a new city charter. In fact, freeholders had been elected to frame a new city charter so that it could be voted on in July. The document they created proposed a city manager form of administration that would neutralize the mayor's office by making its occupant president of the city council and head of the police department. Beyond these responsibilities, the mayor retained the power to appoint several board heads. The mayor would receive a salary of $5,000 a year, the city manager $12,000.

Changes outlined in the charter would also mark a return to the ward system which had been abolished by the voters in 1910 in favor of city-wide voting for each office—there were to be thirty wards.

Elmer E. Todd (who would later become an officer of the *Times*, and was chair of the League's Freeholders Committee, as well as a member of the City's Charter Revision Commission) addressed the Young Men's Business Club, accusing the *Star* and "certain labor interests" of leading the opposition. The *Star*, he said, was "misleading uninformed voters." Threatened by change, he urged termination of what he saw as "domination" of the city's government by groups who previously had been powerless to affect an alteration of the traditional exercise of power.

"Efficiency" was the objective of civic administration in Todd's view and in that of a majority of League members.

Efficiency would be helped by a charter provision that would enable administrators to bypass the Civil Service Commission and hire and fire at will. Even though, Todd made no mention of J. D. Ross, City Light forces collaborated openly with the Labor Council against the Employers' Association and Chamber of Commerce.

Ross was always sensitive to any attempt—and there would be many—to dilute his control over City Light policies; he consistently saw the hand of the "power trust" as their source. The Municipal League found the talk about bringing engineering and business efficiency particularly appealing, and supported the proposal.

When the vote came in June 1914, the charter revision went down to defeat by a two-to-one margin, due in large part to Ross's efforts to mobilize public opinion. It would not be his last such fight—the League continued to look upon professional city management as a key to de-politicizing municipal government, and would try again in 1925. As for Ross, he could always count on organized labor's support because both he and Labor had a "common enemy"—the Electric Company.[2]

Seattle Endorses Prohibition

The Prohibition Movement as an effective force for change came later to Seattle than to other cities in Washington. Although Everett had voted to become "wet" in 1912, overturning an earlier dry law, Bellingham remained "dry," and twenty-eight counties prohibited the sale of alcoholic beverages outside their cities and towns. Six counties were altogether dry. From 1909 to 1912 there had been 220 local option elections resulting in 140 prohibition victories. And, although the Washington Legislature defeated a local option amendment in its 1911 session, lawmakers passed to voters an initiative and referendum amendment. The latter, combined with the winning of the franchise for women in 1910, laid the groundwork for a statewide abolition of alcoholic-beverage sales. In the second decade of the twentieth century, this campaign would center in Seattle where voter sentiment had not yet been tested.

Meanwhile, formidable opposition to the prohibition movement was already lining up: the *Times*, *Post-Intelligencer*, *Town Crier*, *Argus*, and the Chamber of Commerce were in the forefront. In contrast, anti-saloon forces lacked major newspaper support. But they did have the formidable Presbyterian zealot, Mark Matthews, who began holding daily revival meetings in October 1914 as election day approached. The historian of the state movement, Norman Clark, writes that the city "quickly became the [center of the] most anguished conflict between the evangelical churches and the business community in the city's history." Seattle's traditional conservative alarmist, Thomas Burke, argued that prohibition would put 8,300 men out of work at a time when a depression already was in progress. Advertisements paid for by brewers urged moderation in alcoholic consumption, not prohibition. Trade union locals in the provisions trades were understandably opposed and formed the Anti-Prohibition Labor League to combat activities undertaken by union locals favoring the initiative. The Prohibition Labor League appealed to the executive board of the State Federation of Labor, which had been cooperating with dry farmer organizations for a decade, mainly through the Joint Legislative Committee. The board unanimously voted to support the League after a bitter internal fight. James Duncan, leader of the Seattle Central Labor Council, a radical member of its Metal Trades Section and a persistent advocate of industrial unionism, was also a staunch prohibitionist. For many years he would remain in opposition to WSFL leadership partly owing to the prohibition issue.

On election day, November 3, 1914 the issue brought out the

largest vote in the state's history. The initiative won, 189,840 to 171,208; 94.6% of the electorate voted, a state record never surpassed. Seattleites favored prohibition by sixty-one percent, a larger margin than in any other city in the state. In the judgment of Norman Clark "the middle classes in the country and of the city had united in a great effort to control their environment, and the lower classes, who lived mainly in the cities, opposed them." The law took effect January 1, 1916.[1]

Municipal Ownership Gains Ground

As the date for the Panama Canal's completion approached, at least two Seattle groups became increasingly anxious about the waterway's impact. For their part, labor unions feared an influx of cheap labor from southern and eastern Europe. The business community, on the other hand, wanted to prepare for this hoped for source of cheap labor. Big corporate interests like Stone and Webster, the railroads, and the maritime trades certainly entertained with some glee, the notion of driving down wages and, perhaps, breaking the unions. The extent to which their attitude was shared by the rest of the business community is unknown. But if the lowering of wages could be achieved without turmoil, they would probably have welcomed it. Then there was the rising expectations of J. D. Ross and his supporters; they were sure of the boom to come. In part, their city-building plans were framed with that in mind.

If city-building were to continue, in Ross's opinion, City Light needed new sources of power to attract industry with cheap electric rates. The first step in this process involved replacing the original Cedar River wood crib dam with a masonry structure. At the prodding of Councilman Oliver Erickson, and urged on by Reginald Thomson, and his successor, City Engineer A. H. Dimock, Ross conceded the initiative to these three men. Unfortunately, construction went ahead before a thorough examination of soil conditions in the river bed had been undertaken. Earlier reports completed by two University of Washington geologists, Milnor Roberts and acting president Henry Landes, indicated that the glacial bedrock under the Cedar ran in the direction of Snoqualmie Falls. Further, their work indicated that after a dam had been constructed, water from its reservoir would seep in that direction.

R. H. Ober, superintendent of the Buildings Department agreed with findings by Roberts and Landes, and would eventually lose his job as a result. Most of the project's advocates were, however, caught up in the enthusiasm of the moment and ignored this cautionary advice. Thomson and others, while expecting some leakage in that direction, believed that it would gradually be staunched by a natural process called "clay puddling."[1]

Although construction on the masonry dam proceeded at full speed, the City's lighting and engineering departments continued to search for additional sites for the production of hydroelectric power. They agreed that the Hebb site on the White River and the Cushman site on the Skokomish River in the southeastern Olympic Mountains offered the greatest potential. In 1912, voters had already approved a bond issue for acquiring the Hebb site by a large margin and the Cushman location by a narrower one. After completing his investigation, Ross chose Cushman, and then proceeded to campaign for voter approval for permission to raise condemnation money to implement the project. In addition, funds for construction of a steam plant at the south end of Lake Union were approved by the voters in March 1914.

Prospective condemnation of property at the Cushman site excited both the supporters and opponents of City Light from early January until the March 2 election. As expected, the traditional opponents of municipal ownership, the *Times* and *Town Crier* objected, playing down the hydroelectric potential of the Skokomish and arguing that Seattle did not need more electric power. At the same time, they claimed the "Electric Company" was already acquiring additional sites to meet any future demand. Furthermore, they argued, electrical power could not be transported from the Skokomish site to Seattle. To top it off, they accused City Light of operating at a loss.

Indicative of the intensity generated by the issue were the debates beginning in January among members of the Municipal League. The league had appointed a special committee to investigate the matter and to submit a report and make recommendations. In mid-January the committee recommended that the league oppose the Cushman condemnation. Formal debate followed with Harry Ballinger claiming that, since the Electric Company was in the process of expanding its operations, there was no need for City Light to build new facilities. It was improper to compete with private enterprise anyway. He was opposed by George E. Wright, who argued the opposite position. The 200 members who were present at the meeting voted overwhelmingly for acquisition of the Cushman site.

Going along with the league, was the Commercial Club, which represented many small businessmen. Unfortunately for City Light, not enough people turned out to validate the proposition on March 2; a three-fifths majority was required.[2]

Councilman Erickson, undaunted by the defeat, considered resubmitting the issue to the electorate again in November, but changed his mind. Instead, he pressed for the extension of electric power services to the north and south ends of the city and outside city limits to the Duwamish valley. At the time, both areas were served by the Electric Company. Ross was predictably supportive of the plan; but Mayor Gill was unalterably opposed to extending to areas outside the city, pointing to the possible purchase of supplemental power from the Schwager-Nettleton Lumber Mill. Erickson's proposal met defeat in council in November, although that was not the end of the matter. Debate dragged on into December once Corporation Counsel James Bradford pronounced the extension legal.

City Light's precarious political situation was underscored when the Cedar River power source nearly dried up just when the Lake Union steam plant became operational in mid-September. But that was nothing compared to what was to come when the masonry dam was completed on November 1. As predicted, it did not hold water; at least, not for long. By mid-December there was no water left behind the dam. Defenders of the clay puddling process must have been convincing, however, because Ross weathered the initial hullabaloo. (The issue of seepage did not die out until the late 1920s and it was used to nag Ross on numerous occasions.)

Perhaps the immediate clamor subsided because Gill reappointed Ross on December 20, over the howling protests of the *Times* and *Town Crier*. These newspapers kept up an attack on both City Light and Ross all year long, apparently expecting Gill return to his old habits. But Ross was not only lucky in the short run, but in the long run as well. For the critically thin margin on which City Light operated became all too apparent during World War I, just when the federal government needed all the electric power it could get.

Deciding that it was cheaper to file for a site on federal land than to buy privately held property for hydroelectric generation, Gill persuaded the City Council in late December to pursue development on the Sauk and Suiattle rivers; both were in the Mt. Baker National Forest. An appropriate resolution was passed. During discussion no mention was made of possible Skagit development because Stone and Webster held a licence for development in that watershed.

In January 1915 competition heated up when the Company purchased rights to 3,000 acres on the Skagit River and to water rights on the Baker River. Stone and Webster accompanied these acquisitions with an announcement that no construction would occur at either location until there was sufficient industrial demand in Seattle. Unlike Ross's strategy, which was to create a market, Stone and Webster apparently preferred to let the market create itself.[3]

The Port of Seattle

The long-awaited Panama Canal opening occurred on August 15, 1914. As expected, railroads serving the area began losing traffic. Would they have to lower rates to meet the competition? They were not sure. But by July, the month before the canal opened, there were indications of what the future would be like. *Railway and Marine News* reported that:

> The regular steamship lines have taken from rail carriers almost the entire eastbound movement of canned goods, dried fruit, wine, etc., and the railroads principal losses on westbound traffic have been pipe, wire, steel, metals, drugs, chemicals, dry goods, pianos, and general merchandise. . . . The heaviest loss to the railroads westbound has been sustained in dry goods and cotton goods moving from New England, New York city [*sic*], State mills, Pennsylvania, and the South. All Pacific jobbers and many large department stores are shipping by the canal, and strongly endorse the service.

Six months after ships began passing through the waterway, its effects on overland commerce in the United States were apparent. About forty-one percent of the cargo passing through the Isthmus of Panama was between American ports; over twenty-one percent was between the Pacific Coast and Europe. About twenty-one percent was between the west coast of South America and Europe, as well as U.S. ports on the Atlantic. About twelve percent of the canal's commerce was between the Far East and the Atlantic seaboard. In order of tonnage, the chief commodities affected were grain, nitrates, coal, refined petroleum products, lumber, and cotton.[1]

Although 1915 did not promise exceptional opportunities for Seattle trade when it began, by year's end it proved to be the best in port's history. For the first time, the dollar value of trade in the Washington Customs District exceeded that of San Francisco. To what extent this was due to the canal route is uncertain because World War I also provided vigor to the economy. However, in the 1920s, the canal played a crucial role in developing area trade with the Gulf states, the Atlantic seaboard, the United Kingdom, and Europe. World War I provided a special short term stimulus, as well as a distorting one, as seen in the sudden boom in the trade with India, Southeast Asia, and Vladivostok.

In Seattle, little of this traffic passed through the Port of Seattle's facilities. According to the *Railway And Marine News*, most imports and exports passed over private docks and wharfs belonging to steamship companies or railroads. Still, *Railway and Marine News* editors accused port commissioners of operating at a loss and cutting wharfage rates to lure business away from private operators. The *News* also accused the commissioners of adding no new business to the port, only taking it away from private operators unfairly. In view of the *Railway and Marine News* editors, all the new facilities and those under construction were unnecessary: "It may be years before a ton of coastwise traffic moves over any of the publicly owned docks. . . ," they argued. Besides, they saw the city's bonded debt growing beyond acceptable limits. Representing the private operators, the editors applauded a bill then in the legislative hopper that would, not only enlarge the Port Commission from three to five, but would alter its complexion by giving three positions to King County officers. Private operators had regularly sought and gotten support for their projects in the county lying outside Seattle, so this ploy was not unexpected.

The Port Commission, however, looked to the future and planned accordingly. That future came quickly, as a result of the war, and the Port's facilities would make a crucial difference in Seattle's competition with San Francisco. And although it was threatened by adverse legislation that would have done away with the existing governing body, commissioners focused their efforts on getting voter approval in the December 1915 election for a belt-line railroad.[2]

As noted above, railroads always had been a part of the entrenched power structure in the city. With railroads owning most of the waterfront land, the Port of Seattle was forced to undertake expensive condemnation proceedings to acquire property. The commission also had problems with the railroads in another way. Early in 1914 the Port of Seattle appealed to the State Public Service Commission over the discriminatory switching rates charged by railroads, accusing the companies of levying $9.00 for cars hauled to the Port's docks and only $3.00 to private ones. Adding to Port of Seattle woes, the railroads also refused to cooperate by improving switching facilities on Railroad Avenue. Commissioners felt they had no choice but to bring the case before the Interstate Commerce Commission for the purpose of establishing a common-user line between Smith's Cove and Salmon Bay.

In the end, railroads serving Seattle chose to agree with the commissioners rather than face an ICC hearing. But implementation of the agreement came only after what became known as the belt line controversy.

Persistent obstructionism by the railroads only made Port of Seattle commissioners more firmly committed to public ownership; this was particularly true of the commission President Hiram Chittenden. He took to the stump to defend and to articulate the public's interest in harbor and shoreline development. In 1913 he protested against the acquisition of Lake Washington shoreline by upland owners when the water level was lowered. In this case, he and the Park Board won a partial victory. But Port of Seattle opponents got the 1915 legislature to pass bills that would severely curtail the Port Commission's effectiveness.

One bill would have gone so far as to transfer the power to fix wharfage and dock rates to the State Public Service Commission; it was defeated by one vote in the Senate only after Chittenden mobilized the Municipal League, the Public Ownership League, and Commercial Club to lobby against it. The measure to enlarge the commission that had failed to pass in the 1913 legislative session, was reintroduced in 1915 in order to dilute the power of public ownership proponents on the commission. Clearing the Senate by a vote of thirty-six to three, it sailed through the House after only a ten minute discussion, just long enough to add an amendment restricting the Port's bonded indebtedness to what it was already, $5.7 million. Lister signed the bill after refusing to hear the arguments against it of Port lobbyists.[3]

The Port of Seattle's fate was now joined with that of the labor movement, home rule proponents, and prohibitionists. These groups collaborated in a spectacular referendum campaign in 1916 to undo the handiwork of the overreaching 1915 legislature. Six acts that directly affected these organizations were suspended by voters in the 1916 general election.

Aiding support to the Port's cause was a sudden upsurge in harbor activity beginning in mid-1915. Although Seattle was two days closer to the Orient and to Vladivostok than San Francisco, it was the Port's facilities that made the real difference. Seattle had the terminal space, San Francisco did not; it had the equipment also, such as a heavy-duty Gantry crane to handle locomotives and other heavy cargo. The wharfage and warehouse rates were also cheaper—to the dismay of private operators. The results can be seen in the dramatic increase in the dollar value of Seattle's exports and imports: $117,228,797 in 1915; $360,526,940 in 1916; $485,289,158 in 1917; and $597,180,914 in 1918. In the euphoria of prosperity, traditional sources of opposition to the Port of Seattle were quieted, except on the issue of belt-line railroad. In this case, the ideologues won out.

Indicative of the decline in opposition to Port-related matters was support given by the Chamber of Commerce, the *Times*, and *P-I* to a huge bond issue submitted by the Port in 1918—$4,490,000. Nearly $2 million was for construction of a second pier at Smith's Cove, paralleling the first one, which was the world's longest; another $1,250,000 for extending the first pier; and $1,250,000 to purchase land on Harbor Island. The voters approved the bond request.

As to the belt-line railroad, the commissioners were anxious to reduce switching charges that were related directly to the excessive switchings required to get a car transported from the main rail lines to the waterfront piers. To correct the problem, voters were asked to approve a belt-line railroad proposition in the December 1915 election. But prior to the election, Chittenden resigned his seat, and the commission lost its key spokesman in the process.

Although a majority of the voters favored the belt-line railroad proposition, the margin of support was less than the required sixty percent. The belt-line proposition was resubmitted successively and defeated by a narrow margin each time. It appeared on the ballot for the last time in March 1917; once again, traditional opponents lined up against it in defense of the free market system—despite solid evidence that belt lines at San Francisco and New Orleans had not injured private enterprise there. When the Port Commission tried to build one anyway, the Chamber of Commerce sued and the state Supreme Court ruled against the Port in 1917. Soon after this decision, railroads lowered their switching charges and granted the Port of Seattle common-user privileges on the tracks.[4]

Two events affected Seattle's commercial picture in late 1915. First, landslides closed the Panama Canal in November. This was expected to benefit both the railroads and Puget Sound ports. Second, the Panama Canal Act required American railroads to divest themselves of their interests in steamship lines by November 4. A complicating factor in this divestiture requirement was a clause in the Seamen's Act of 1915, which mandated English-language literacy among a high percentage of the crews on ships flying the American flag.

As the November 4 deadline approached, many steamship companies changed ships from United States to foreign registry to escape the act's requirements. The Great Northern sold its *Minnesota* to an Atlantic shipper (the *Dakota* had irretrievably run aground in Japanese waters); the Pacific Mail Line (of the Southern Pacific

Railroad) sold its ships rather than continue—no more ships of United States registry would be operating in the Pacific. Announcement of San Francisco's loss of the Pacific Mail Line emboldened Frank Waterhouse and Company to open trade with Vladivostok, provisioning the Tsarist armies. Eight vessels entered this trade in October, claiming overseas tonnage, ". . . alone, greater than that of the Pacific Mail vessels recently withdrawn from the Oriental trade." Waterhouse acted as the Union Pacific's agent in setting up this trade.[5]

The University and the City

The year 1914 opened with the firing of University of Washington President Thomas Kane in January. Kane's dismissal had been in the works for many years because of his unwavering defense of academic freedom. For this, he came under suspicion from the regents who seemed to see the advocacy of change, the open and free expression of ideas, and intellectual inquiry as manifestations of anarchy. J. Allen Smith, while not the only liberal on the faculty, was a principal source of tension; although philosophy professor William Savery's relativistic teaching about religion, without providing a special primacy to Christianity, hardly endeared him to regents who also believed that indoctrination and education were the same thing.[1]

The *Times*'s Colonel Blethen had been particularly alienated from Smith because of the active role his students had played in the Gill recall campaign in 1911. They had served as petition circulators and poll watchers (Gill had later almost initiated an investigation to test the eligibility of those students who voted). It was also Smith's students who led the opposition to the regent's acceptance of the Blethen chimes in 1912. The chimes controversy attracted attention throughout the Northwest and among civil libertarians who sided with the students against the man they all loved to hate—Alden Blethen.

Kane's banning the *University of Washington Daily* during the student protest against the chimes added to the unpopularity he had earned among students during the 1912 presidential campaign when he imposed the "gag rule." So, in 1913, without the support of faculty and students, which he previously had enjoyed, Kane found himself vulnerable to the traditionally truculent Board of Regents.

In October 1913 the regents, belatedly acted on a motion passed at their June meeting asking for Kane's resignation. The president rebuffed them in December, whereupon he was fired, effective January 1, 1914. This action produced turmoil on campus throughout much of 1914. During the ensuing controversy, the regents admitted that they had requested Kane's resignation three years earlier when he had opposed their attempt to ban political speakers from campus. Kane also had allegedly adjourned a regent's meeting at one point to prevent Smith's dismissal.

In his December response, Kane noted that the very existence of the regents as a notoriously reactionary body served to goad students and faculty. He was quoted in the *Star*:

> The department of political science has been the cause of considerable displeasure on the part of the regents, and yet it is one of the strongest features of the university. Some people don't seem to understand that a student can listen to both sides of a question and then decide for himself.
>
> They want to eliminate the radical side and give only the conservative. It is true that study and investigation lead to progressive views.

Governor Lister had opposed Kane's firing, feeling that he should remain in office at least through the 1913-1914 term. But the regents prevailed. Thereafter, Lister removed four regents who were primarily responsible for Kane's dismissal.

With Kane's firing, a campaign against student radicalism at the University of Washington was stepped up, infused by fear of the growing influence of the Industrial Workers of the World. During the chimes controversy Blethen had rhetorically written, asking if it were possible "that the IWW have invaded the University of Washington . . . why wouldn't it be well for the Legislature to enact a law that every student seeking the benefits of this great educational organization should be compelled to make an oath to support the Constitution [federal and state] . . . before entering the University at all." Such a bill was actually introduced by a legislator from Aberdeen, where the IWW was particularly menacing; it never came to a vote.

Nat U. Brown, writing in the *State Capitol Record*, estimated that "about 10 per cent of every graduating class gets out into the world chock full of socialism. . . ." Besides Smith, he singled out one his proteges, instructor Teresa McMahon, who after graduating from the University Washington, went to the University of Wisconsin for doctoral work among a faculty who were members of Senator Robert LaFollette's brain trust. These were scholars who had helped break the control of Wisconsin's government by railroad and timber interests. One lumberman wrote to the University of Washington Board of Regents that he was sending his children to private schools because Smith and McMahon had been giving public lectures supporting the eight-hour day initiative amendment, which, if passed would "bankrupt the state." Professor of Geology Henry Landes was named interim president while a search for Kane's successor was begun.

Kane left a strong foundation at the University of Washington on which his successors would build. In his twelve years as president, student enrollment climbed from 601 to 3,340; faculty numbers correspondingly increased from 33 to 194. The introduction of new programs in marine studies, forestry, mining and engineering contributed to the University of Washington's growth. By implementing these practical programs the school was also becoming integrated with the economies of both the city and state. In addition, the university served as a training ground for skilled labor that would be fed into the professional and white-collar labor pool of an expanding economy. Yet, the Washington Legislature remained impassively ungrateful by continuing to deny the perennial requests for new buildings, and to make faculty salaries competitive with those at comparable institutions.

On the eve of Kane's firing, the regents approved one last recommendation, that for establishing a school of commerce, an action that had the hearty support of the Chamber of Commerce— seeing that the initial job of training men (at least) for business careers would be shifted from the business community to a publicly funded institution.

Landes had earned widespread popularity among students and faculty; he was their candidate for the school's presidency. The fact that Blethen also supported his candidacy, somehow did not diminish their enthusiasm. But Lister and the regents wanted someone of national stature; this meant looking into the labor pool in the East.

The candidate who appealed to the three-man Regent's search team was Henry Suzzallo, a protege of Columbia University's president Nicholas Murray Butler. But Suzzallo's appointment was held up by an article that appeared in the Northwest Journal of Education that linked Suzzallo with an alleged attempt on the part of the "reactionary" Butler to control American education.

Columbia's liberal philosophy professor, John Dewey, came to Suzzallo's defense, claiming that Suzzallo would be a "college executive of a new type, and the movement for a more democratic control of college institutions will have received new impetus." When Suzzallo's only serious rival, James Rowland Angell, rejected the job, regents settled on Suzzallo, being partly persuaded by the argument of former University of Washington president Graves that Suzzallo is a "man who can get hold of people, and can get around the state to rouse them educationally and ethically." He would do that and then some when World War I opened unexpected opportunities.

The Legislature and the City, 1915

[F]or the first time in years we have a decent legislature, made up largely of businessmen . . . [who] are looking at things not from a sentimental standpoint, but from a purely dollars and cents point of view. [Lumberman Edwin G. Ames of the Puget Mill Company to F. H. Peavey, 8 March, 1915; quoted in Joseph Tripp, *Progressive Labor Legislation*, p. 139.]

While the Employers' Association spread its protective wings over the activities of a variety of employers outside Seattle, its efforts tended to be concentrated on the lumber industry. Areas of greatest concern were mill towns like Everett, Centralia, the Grays Harbor and Olympic Peninsula towns, and the Port Blakely Mill Company on Bainbridge Island . The Shingle Workers Union (having been provisionally authorized by the AFL to organize lumber workers, had been involved in a strike/lockout in Centralia since the summer of 1914; Everett witnessed a similar situation. The Centralia strike would end in March, by which time so many strikers had emigrated that only fifteen picketers remained—too few to continue. Seattle workers and citizenry in general were kept informed of the association's statewide open shop campaign by the *Union Record*.

It was against this backdrop of labor unrest and home rule issues that the business-dominated legislature began its work in January 1915. Its goal was threefold (since there was no real opposition):

1. to defeat or undermine municipal ownership of utilities and ports;
2. to render the labor movement ineffective;
3. to destroy the direct legislation process.

When the legislature had finished, its goals seemed largely accomplished. Democratic Governor Ernest Lister only partially impeded the lawmaking process. If much of the legislation affected Seattle it was because much of it was directed at Seattle-generated issues. In the first category of bills, City Light and the Port Commission were affected. Senator Howard Taylor almost got a bill passed that would have prevented a new utility from competing with an existing one unless there was a "public necessity." In these cases, the Public Service Commission would decide—its composition had always been controlled by the Republicans, and usually a private utility man or men, directly represented private utilities on the body. (Two members of the commission's property evaluation survey team had been with the company before accepting appointments; another former employee was then engineer for the commission; Commissioner George Lee had also been with the company, according to Kempster).

Under the legislation, the commission also would control rates. Furthermore, under the original bill, a municipality would have to purchase an existing private utility rather than compete with it. While the Taylor bill was defeated as a single piece, nevertheless its certificate of necessity segment was passed, thereby, diluting "home rule."[1]

To block expansion of municipal utilities the "Renick Budget Bill" was passed. According to its provisions, cities would be prevented from using surplus funds designated for one agency to support work desired by another agency whose funds were insufficient. As noted earlier, the Municipal Street Railway had to borrow from the garbage fund to finish construction of the ill-advised Division A line. But the Municipal Street Railway was in debt to other departments as well. Its substations, also, were about to be transferred to the Lighting Department. Then, under the inspiration of the Chamber of Commerce, Senator Frank H. Renick introduced a bill that would prevent this action. After its passage Seattle Comptroller Harry Carroll refused to sign warrants needed to pay the railway's employees.[2]

To limit competition with Stone and Webster's street railways even further, Colonel Blethen of the *Times* was able to get a bill passed that required bonding of jitneys and the regulation of their routes and hours. The company's A. L. Kempster had been recording a steady decline of about twenty percent in revenues, estimating that the jitneys were taking about sixteen percent of the traffic by running ahead of its cars and scooping up passengers who would pay their lower fares; even private cars were entering the field according to Kempster. After the Supreme Court approved the measure, there was a considerable drop in the number of jitneys—a $2,500 bond was too steep for most; by May only about 250 jitneys were still in service.[3]

As to the Port of Seattle, Kempster proudly reported to Boston that pressure from voters in King County, outside Seattle, were responsible for a bill to enlarge the commission to five members (including non-Seattle members), and to transfer rate-fixing authority to the Public Service Commission. This would prevent the Seattle Port Commission from setting its own rates in competition with the privately owned waterfront warehouses (the Port had reduced rates by at least thirty percent since it began operations.) Kempster expected it to make "impossible . . . any additional capital expenditures requiring bond issues." This measure also struck at home rule, and like the Renick bill, was a referred bill to be voted on in the 1916 election.[4]

The 1915 Legislature also passed a bill containing an anti-picketing measure that was potentially devastating to the labor movement. Since employers, whatever their personal disposition, were disciplined by the Employers' Association to refuse arbitration or conciliation by a public authority, strikes were often the only recourse left to the workers in dealing effectively with organized employers. The strike and boycott were also the only effective ways of informing the public of the issues, since the press could not be depended upon.

As it was, the power to strike was usually enjoined by the courts whenever an employer lodged an appeal. So pleased was the Association with the work of this legislature that it declared in its Legislative Bulletin Number 6,

> No legislature of this state has ever been so attentive to the wishes and demands of the taxpayers as the members of the present session. In almost every case no action, favorable or against any of the many bills that have been introduced has been taken by members without first ascertaining the wishes of their constituents.[5]

The Association's ecstasy was to be short-lived, however, because Card and Label Leaguers led a successful petition drive to suspend the law's implementation; it, too, would be voted upon in 1916—Lucy Case, lobbyist for the State Federation of Labor, filed 52,000 names with the Secretary of State on June 9, more than enough.

In the lobbying against the bill, the first crack in the labor-farmer alliance surfaced when, in the Joint Legislative Committee, the State Federation of Labor failed to convince the Grange and Farmers' Union to oppose the bill. Farmers pleaded ignorance of union issues. At Central Labor Council meetings some union leaders then spoke against the farmers' abdication and threatened unilateral action in the future.[6]

To deal with an attempt of the Laundry Owners Association to get the 1915 legislature to exempt laundry workers from coverage under the eight-hour law, Alice Lord was appointed to lead the fight in Olympia. (Laundry workers' salaries averaged $5.87 per week, they were on call at all times, and were prohibited from joining a union.) Joanna Hilt, a union worker, testified that she had been fired and blacklisted; and that owners had coerced their employees to sign the petition requesting their exemption from the law's application. This lobbying blocked passage of the bill, but the blistering fight that ensued showed the temper of this legislature.

One event that may have had a significant effect on the legislature's actions was a Eugene V. Debs speech in Seattle at the end of January 1915. The perennial Socialist presidential candidate addressed an overflow audience of 3,000 at Dreamland, where most mass meetings and fund-raisers were held during those years.

Lending added credibility to Colonel Blethen's view that the University of Washington was a hotbed of radicalism, a lecture series on "The Problems of Labor" began; it would be followed by a series on municipal government. These lectures were given at the Labor Temple each Sunday evening. Beside the speakers one would expect (like J. Allen Smith, William Savery, Teresa and Edward McMahon, and Joseph K. Hart) was zoologist Trevor Kincaid. Even University of Washington president Henry Suzzallo lectured, speaking on vocational education—a matter of concern to the Central Labor Council and many in the general public.[7]

In its euphoria the 1915 legislature also passed an amendment to the workmen's compensation law which was intended to thwart attempts by the WSFL and liberalized businessmen like Representative Mark E. Reed to abolish the onerous hospital fee system. Under this scheme, workers paid one dollar or more per month into a hospital fee fund. Employers contributed nothing, nevertheless they administered the funds. The practice of collusion between employers and physicians became so widespread that Governor Marion Hay had risked his re-election in 1912 by supporting abolition the fee system. He lost to Democrat, Eugene Lister, who failed to come up with recommendations acceptable to both groups.

As a result, the WSFL began an initiative campaign in 1914 to establish a "first aid fund," which would impose the entire expense of first aid on the employer, would eliminate a waiting period before compensation, and would eliminate the employers from an administrative role. Governor Lister was promised the backing of the employers' "Stop—Look—and—Listen League" in his effort to produce a compromise measure if he would oppose the initiative. This, he did. The proposal was defeated in the November 1914 election.

Lister, now depending on Employers' Association support during the 1915 session, appointed a commission to come up with remedial legislation acceptable to employer groups and unions. Representative Reed, worked closely with the commission to develop a more just "First Aid Bill," one which would require equal contributions and, administration by a commission. The Employers' Association, however, decided to oppose any compromise, and, instead, it had Senator John Kleeb (representing the lumbering counties of Pacific and Wahkiakum in southwestern Washington) draw up a bill that passed both houses. But its contents were so outrageous that Lister vetoed it. (A compromise bill did get enacted in 1917.)[8]

Soon after the legislature adjourned in March, two ominous events occurred. One was an abortive drive to organize trainmen of Stone and Webster; it resulted, for the moment, only in a mass meeting and attempts to tie up the street cars. However it clearly indicated that the immediate future lay with union organizers once war production assumed paramount importance.[9]

The second event involved Seattle's longshoremen. Perhaps, feeling encouraged by the anti-labor stance of the 1915 Legislature, the Waterfront Employers' Union of the Pacific Coast reduced the wage scale by twenty-five to thirty-five percent without informing the longshoremen. Employers up and down the coast simply told workers that there were plenty of unemployed who are willing to work if they are not. When the longshoremen in Vancouver, B. C. quit the International Longshoremen's Association called a sympathy strike and boycott along the entire coast. In Seattle the Employers' Association hired strikebreakers for the waterfront employers. The *Union Record* claimed that thugs and provocateurs were being used, and it complained about the arrest of three union men.

Police Chief Lang called a conciliation meeting with the employers and recommended that hiring be done on an alphabetical-rotation basis to minimize unfairness in hiring, he was rebuffed. The ILA even contended that the IWW was scabbing, and when the manager of the Hotel Liberty reported that 125 men who had recently arrived from Portland were "missing" the suspicion seemed confirmed. Chief Lang promised that "no scabs shall be recruited from this source"—meaning the IWWs. After more than a week of this strife the longshoremen returned to work with the understanding that it would be on the same terms as before the lockout. Most employers honored these terms but the Pacific Coast Steamship Company did not. This firm gave preference to scabs in hiring and used them as straw bosses as a reminder of who was boss. At the annual meeting of the ILA in San Francisco the union decided to resume union negotiations with the Waterfront Employers' Union, but with a deadline in mind. The objectives were a uniform wage scale on the West Coast and jurisdiction over loading and unloading. No mention was made of the hiring issue, although it would become the loaded one for the next forty years.[10]

Part III

Toward Wartime

13

1916: Improvement . . .
for a Time

News Briefs

On January 1 Mayor Gill personally opened the year 1916 for the city by rigorously enforcing the state's new dry law on the first day it went into effect. The homes of aviation pioneer William E. Boeing, cement manufacturer John Eden, and mill owner David E. Skinner, were raided without proper warrant and their private collections of assorted spirits confiscated. Gill's Dry Squad would catch headlines for numerous such raids throughout the year. For his part the mayor was frequently pictured in the press with shirt sleeves rolled up and an axe in hand doing his duty.[1]

The ranks of Seattle's unemployed declined as the economy improved in 1916, although industrial relations became more turbulent, highlighted by prolonged strikes and lockouts involving longshoremen and steamboat workers. The ubiquitous Employers' Association even tried to protect the general public from seeing the horrors of the workplace by applying to the Seattle Censor Board to suppress the showing of the film "The Eternal Grind," starring Mary Pickford, and depicting sweat shop conditions.

At the annual January meeting of the State Federation of Labor, State Labor Commissioner E. W. Olson reported that job tenure had increased "remarkably" since the abolition of for-fee employment agencies. He also reported that, in cooperation with the

Federation, he had been successful in excluding "Orientals" from fish canneries and also in enforcing the eight-hour law.

In its unrelenting quest to exclude Asians from the job market, the Central Labor Council succeeded in displacing Oriental porters in all saloons, cafes, and restaurants. The council then organized the remaining "American citizens" into a local of the Hotel and Restaurant Employees Union.[2]

Hovering darkly in the background in May 1916 was the specter of a shingle weavers strike against the state's holdout lumber barons in Everett. To block further inroads on the industry's open shop front, Everett mill owners decided to break the union. They prepared for the task by gaining absolute control of the Everett's town government and constabulary. What began as a strike developed into a struggle over of free speech and assembly, an issue specifically tailored to the tactics and bravery of the IWW. It ended in the infamous "Everett Massacre" of November 1916.

Seattle was the staging ground for most IWW activity and, in Judge James Ronald's courtroom, it would host the subsequent trial of seventy-five Wobblies who were accused of murdering two Everett deputies. Defence attorney George F. Vanderveer would earn his reputation as "counsel for the damned" by the time the trial ended on May 5, 1917.

Dry Law Takes Effect

Enforcement of Washington's dry law flushed out a colorful cast of characters who participated in a drama heralding things to come after the entire nation went dry in 1920. Norman Clark, historian of Washington's prohibition movement, points out that the 1916 state law was not strictly "bone dry." An individual was allowed to import as much as two quarts of hard liquor or twelve quarts of beer each twenty days, providing a permit had been acquired from a county auditor. Lines at auditors' offices around the state were impressive on the first day, and by August as many as 18,000 permits were issued. In addition to the permit system, an illicit trade began to flourish once the legislation's loopholes were spied out. Demand outran supply, driving up prices for bootleg booze to five dollars a quart by December.[1]

This scenario was a setup for that consummate actor, Mayor Hiram Gill; if nothing else, he provided good newspaper copy. Clark reports the devastating axing and trashing of stores and restaurants by him and the Dry Squad. Two restaurants lost $20,000 in fixtures. Even arch-prohibitionist Reverend Mark Matthews criticized the heavy-handedness of the enforcers for their raids on private homes and clubs such as the Rainier Club, of which he was a member. Matthews thought the law was made to look too offensive, but there were some who suspected that his wealthy friends inspired his complaint—he was now far removed from his populist past.

Not without notice, thirty-five new "drug stores" opened for business during the first three months of 1916. One of these establishments was the Stewart Street Pharmacy, owned by the Billingsley brothers, Logan and Fred. After successfully resisting bootlegging charges several *Times*, they fell victim to Gill and the Dry Squad one day when a truckload of liquor was being unloaded at the store; not only was the liquor destroyed but also the store's interior itself. Gill responded to the Billingsley's protests by announcing his willingness to take a chance with a jury should the brothers press their claims for damages.

Instead of testing Gill's will in court the Billingsleys organized a "mock-up" company to engage in shipping liquor from Cuba to Canada. This liquor found its way south and into the hands of the two brothers; they bootlegged it. But, in pursuit of this line of business they found themselves in competition with an ex-policeman, Jack Marquet, who already had a corner on the market. Violence followed, ending in a shootout at the Billingsley warehouse in July, leaving two dead.

But there were good things about prohibition. Business in general picked up, and although war-induced prosperity was the primary cause, business people were inclined to credit the new law for diversion of money into bank accounts and toward the purchase of household items and clothing—wages that previously went to the saloon, so it was believed.

In this setting, two initiative measures were scheduled for voter action in the November general election. One, Initiative 18, would have allowed hotel dining rooms to serve liquor. The second, Initiative 24, would have permitted the manufacture and direct sale of beer to consumers, thus bypassing bootleggers. While Alden Blethen did not live to see the abhorred law go into effect, his successor at the *Times*, Clarence Blethen, did; and he was persuaded that the law was justified on economic grounds, seeing the big improvement in business. Harry Chadwick of the *Argus*, who had voiced opposition to the law when it was still being debated, now opposed its repeal, although he favored the brewers' initiative while protesting the hotelmen's bill as special interest legislation—one might call it "class legislation."

Scientific arguments against the ingestion of alcohol now began to reinforce the earlier, moral ones. Abstinence was equated with a longer, saner life and efficiency in the workplace. Correlations were also shown linking liquor with criminal behavior, prostitution, and poverty. During the year, nearby Oregon enacted a "bone-dry" law, under protection of the Webb-Kenyon Act of 1913, that legalized state interference with interstate liquor traffic. Once the United States Supreme Court ruled this act constitutional in January 1917, the way was paved for more bone-dry legislation and ultimately nationwide prohibition.

Industrial Relations Intensify

Seattle's first and largest steel shipyard, the Seattle Construction and Dry Dock Company, began the year 1916 with its regular work force out on strike. On December 6, 1915 the Boilermakers Union and the Shipbuilders Union led a walkout of about 400 workers. Besides demanding a twenty-five percent pay increase and double pay for overtime, the unions wanted to deal directly with foremen on hiring, and to cease having to find work through the employers' Metal Trades Association. In the absence of arch-open shop leader J. V. Patterson, David Rodgers agreed to union demands. (Rodgers would transfer his accommodating personnel policies to Skinner and Eddy Shipyards during the war, helping that yard set efficiency records.) When Patterson returned, he abrogated the agreement and put the men on piece work, forcing resumption of the strike. Strikebreakers were imported, and arrests of strikers were a regular occurrence. The Central Labor Council described the situation to federal authorities, pointing to the use of untrained strikebreakers and the inevitable faulty workmanship that it claimed led to the sinking of a ship, the *F-4*, off Hawaii, with loss of life. Not until mid-June was the strike settled, with the company acceding to union demands.[1]

While this strike ran its course, Mosquito Fleet workers organized themselves into an industrial-type union, the Puget Sound Steamshipmen's Union, affiliating with the Sailors Union of the Pacific in February. About six weeks later, in late March, the union led 500 workers out on strike, asking for union recognition and wage increases of five to fifteen dollars per month.

Anticipating the strike, the Puget Sound Navigation Company (PSNC) imported Blacks as strikebreakers and imposed a lockout. Violence flared up resulting in the strikebreakers being accused of stabbings. For its part, the PSNC threatened any companies that signed union contracts with competition on their runs. To get unity of action, all of the affected unions in the maritime and shipping trades federated as the Seattle Waterfront Federation. Reportedly the federation had almost half of the employers signed up by mid-April.

After the annual meeting of the International Longshoremen's Association in Seattle in May 1916 the waterfront workers all along the Pacific Coast went out on strike. Besides a wage hike, the union demanded that pay be effective from the time employees are ordered to report in, and that they be guaranteed at least two hours pay if, after reporting, there was no work. They also asked for a nine-hour day and that gangs working in the holds be of no less than eight men. Temporary settlement was reached in early June when the Seattle Port Commission, under the influence of Robert Bridges, conceded to the demands. Also, many of the smaller companies in the Mosquito Fleet had signed up. But not the PSNC, whose determined leader, Joshua Green, set about threatening smaller firms that had conceded. By September the union claimed 800 members and fifteen contracts, but the PSNC still held out, aided in December by Judge Mitchell Gordon's banning the use of a strike banner advertising the company as "unfair."[2]

When the longshoremen resumed their strike in June it merged with the steamboatmen's strike. The longshoremen's action was more violent and complicated, due to intransigence of the Waterfront Employers Association of the Pacific Coast. The Association recruited Filipinos and other Asians, as well as Blacks, as strikebreakers. It was a common practice calculated to inflame unions, which had banned these races from membership, and which had pressed for restrictions against Asian immigration. However, T. K. Sasaki of the Japanese Labor Association, assured the Labor Council that his organizations would not furnish strikebreakers.

A crisis was provoked when a Black shot and killed one of the strikers. Mayor Gill then appointed special police in the pay of the employers to infiltrate a Central Labor Council protest meeting at Dreamland, July 2. The mayor tried to justify the action by claiming that San Francisco was trying to get the city's commerce. Some steamship lines also boycotted the public docks because the Port Commission had made concessions to the union and because they congenitally opposed public ownership and regulation.

The Municipal League's offer to mediate the strike was rejected by employers. And, when Governor Lister was asked to bring in the militia to maintain order, he refused. After the Association frustrated the efforts of federal mediator Henry White, Captain Robert Dollar urged fellow businessmen to hire thugs to beat up strikers. He then initiated a campaign to raise $1 million for an open shop drive on the coast. Seattle businessmen subscribed $200,000 to help out. Further aid to the employers came from the judiciary in mid-July, when Judge Jeremiah Neterer enjoined the ILA from picketing the Alaska Steamship Company.

Outbreaks of violence, including minor dock fires, were inevitable in this setting and they occurred with increasing frequency as time passed. Into this picture stepped the Municipal League making an appeal for moderation. It began by blaming both sides for the trouble, and asking each to "stop it!" Although acknowledging that the cause of the fires was undetermined, the public undoubtedly would attribute them to "Organized Labor"—so, it seemed to the editors of the *Municipal News*. They proceeded to act as though the union was solely to blame.

The *News* also struck at the union for defying a court injunction that led to the arrest of sixty-nine strikers; this was "anarchy." The *News* claimed that "peaceful picketing" was not at issue, but "wrongful acts" were, by causing the "destruction of the business of the plaintiff." Leaguers could not accept the fact that only by collective action could workers deal with the combined force of an individual employer's capital and the overwhelming authority of a group of employers acting in unison.

Employer militancy was not uniformly rewarded, however. By the end of July, the largest grain shipper on the coast had signed a union contract. Black strikebreakers struck for the union scale and won at the Milwaukee Dock in Tacoma and the Grand Trunk Dock in Seattle. Mayor Gill reversed himself, characteristically, by warning businessmen at a Chamber of Commerce meeting in early August, that he would not use police to help them establish an open-shop town. Federal mediator, William Blackman, also arrived at this time to try his hand; but his offer was initially rejected by the Waterfront Employers' Union. However, since the city had been losing commerce, the Chamber of Commerce was given authority by the WEU to act on its behalf. Blackman was allowed to mediate; by the end of September he succeeded, and formally announced settlement on October 4. This was not the end, however, because the employers refused to live up to the agreement's terms. The Central Labor Council began conducting a sympathy strike vote in early October, but the steam had gone out of the strikers and they were gradually reabsorbed into the work force as port activity picked up.[3]

As a postscript to the strike, the *Northwest Enterprise*, in its May 9, 1924 issue claimed "It was largely through [James Roston's] efforts that the 1916 longshoremen's strike was broken." Prior to the strike Blacks could not get work on the waterfront because of ILA resistance. "Peace" was made with the ILA "on condition that men who worked could join the union and remain at work." Roston had organized the American Federation of Labor and Benevolent Protective Brotherhood and also the Northwest Stevedores and Trucking Association during the 1916 strike. He operated a real estate business after the strike until the 1921 stewards' strike.[4]

Reflecting in the February 1917 issue of his *Railway and Marine News*, editor Kenneth Kerr claimed, "No greater victory for the employers was ever recorded. Not one point was gained by the striking longshoremen. Other men took their places." He boasted that by October sixty percent of the original strikers had left the waterfront and the remaining ones ". . . abjectly crawled [back] . . . begging for work at a greatly reduced rate . . . ."

The Everett Massacre and Seattle Labor

Organized labor in Seattle was gradually drawn into the statewide Shingle Weavers strike that had begun on May 1, and became centered in Everett—due largely to the intransigence of mill owners there: future governor Roland Hartley, David Clough, Joe Irving, and Neil Jamison, allied with banker William Butler (brother of Columbia University president, Nicholas Murray Butler, whose protege, Henry Suzzallo, was president of the University of Washington). Although half the state's mills had signed union contracts, the Everett mills stood solidly opposed, ready to break the union. They uniformly rejected the request to restore the wage cuts made in 1914, although Clough had promised to do so in 1915. So much for promises!

The Everett Commercial Club, a broadly based community organization, conducted its own investigation of the strike, blaming it for the 1914-1915 recession and urging that the town become an open shop bastion. Social Gospel ministers, liberal businessmen, unionists, and reformers resigned in numbers, leaving control of the club in the hands of mill owners; its president, Fred Baker, was one of them. By mid-June strikebreakers were being recruited by employers and pickets were being posted by the union. Everett historian, Norman Clark, records: "the waterfront bristled again with barbed wire, bunkhouses, searchlights, guns, and armed guards." Class war had been declared, and the union found itself an unwilling belligerent. Pluralism was not congenial to the mill owners; their model for the ideal society was the company town, and they sought to establish one in Everett.

In July, the Seattle IWW office took notice of events taking place just to the north—which, up to this time, had been moving quietly to a head. Wobbly leaders in Seattle decided to take an active role, also, to bolster the organization's decimated membership. A successful IWW organizer, James Rowan, was brought in for the organization drive. He traveled to Everett and spoke on July 31 and was arrested by Sheriff Donald McRae. Throughout early August this scene was repeated, over and over again. The IWW's plan to flood the Everett jails as they had done at Spokane during the 1909 "free-speech fight." McRae countered by blockading the town at all major points of entry, using Commercial Club members as deputies. On August 22 the sheriff ordered all Wobblies to leave Everett. To test McRae's edict Rowan and about twenty others organized a visitation from Seattle; they were arrested in turn as each spoke. Tension grew to near riot proportions, abated by a respected union leader, Jake Michel. The arrested group from Seattle was shipped back to the city. Immediately they set about raising free-speech funds and recruiting volunteers for a return engagement. While a federal mediator was in Everett to get the true picture, IWW speakers were neither molested nor arrested; but after his departure, tensions resumed and events tumbled on their seemingly predetermined, fateful course, leading to the "Everett Massacre."

In late September, McRae headed off another invasion by a Seattle Wobbly contingent which had hired a tug out of Mukilteo; the owner was severely beaten by the half-drunk sheriff; the Wobblies were thrown in jail for nine days before being returned to Seattle. This continued violence, directed at the "outsider"-Wobblies became so extreme that Ernest Marsh, head of the State Federation of Labor and of the Shingle Weavers, spoke out in the dissenters' defense—although he abhorred the IWW both for its advocacy of dual unionism and for the negative impact of Wobbly agitation on the labor movement. He ridiculed "the professional and businessmen who have allowed themselves to be buncoed into a private standing army." He called for a mass meeting of Everett citizens to acquaint them with the facts. This did not occur. Instead, picket lines thinned as McRae's blockade proved effective. Then on October 31, an IWW "soldiery" of forty-one men left Seattle and docked in Everett, where they were singled out by McRae, backed by more than 200 deputies. They and were then carted off to Beverly Park where they were savagely beaten. The sadism of McRae and his deputies was graphically described by one of their number, mill owner, Joe Irving: "We took down their pants and beat them with Devil's Club—you know, the plant with the heavy stalk and poisonous thorns .˙.˙. and made them run the gauntlet."

With the newspapers silent, Marsh called for a mass meeting to calm the growing hysteria, assess the situation, and to organize some of the majority of Everett citizenry who tried to dissociate themselves from the Beverly Park brutalities. Acting independently, and short-circuiting Marsh's pacifying efforts, the IWW called for a protest demonstration for November 5, hoping to create a major confrontation on the free-speech issue. The Seattle editors of the *Industrial Worker* declared "the entire history of the organization will be decided in Everett." After a boisterous send-off at Seattle, about 200, mainly IWW's, sailed on the ill-fated *Verona* to Everett where they were met by Sheriff McRae and his armed companies of volunteers who had been training for weeks, anxious to apply their new skills in just this kind of class confrontation.

What followed is known as the "Everett Massacre," which will not be recounted here; but Mayor Gill let it be known how he thought Seattleites should understand what happened: "In the final analysis it will be found that these cowards in Everett, who, without right or justification, shot into a crowd on the boat, were murderers and not the I.W.W's. . . ."—Gill was no friend of the Wobblies, and he had an ambiguous record on unions. The mayor's sympathies earned him the wrath of the *Times* and *P-I*, doubly, when he personally distributed tobacco to the IWW inmates.

The aftermath of this infamous event pre-occupied the labor movement for the rest of the year and into early 1917. On January 21 nationally famous militant Elizabeth Gurley Flynn and local Socialist, the popular Kate Sadler, addressed a mass meeting at Dreamland to raise defense funds for the jailed Everett Wobblies. Mass meetings, reportedly were held throughout the state for their defense. When the trial began on March 5 Judge James Ronald was praised by the *Union Record* editor, Harry Ault and Anna Louise Strong for his fairness in jury selection and for his conduct of the trial.

Convinced there was a "plot," one of the *Union Record* staff writers disappointedly confessed to having found none after three weeks of trying. Just as George Vanderveer ended his devastating cross-examination of the prosecution witnesses in a court room packed with reporters from most of the major daily newspapers in the country, Woodrow Wilson declared war on Germany on April 6.

Chief defense attorney Fred Moore, followed Vanderveer to argue his case. But his arguments placing the trial in the context of the class struggle were presented before an empty court room. Popular attention switched to the war. The key defendant, Thomas Tracy, was found not guilty; charges against the others were dropped accordingly. Vanderveer would soon find himself defending Hulet Wells under the Espionage Act for distributing anti-conscription literature before the act was passed.[1]

Also on the Labor Front

While tensions in industrial relations on the waterfront dominated the public's attention before the Everett turmoil, the Teamsters and the Team Owners Association calmly signed a three year contract. The union claimed every teamster in the city was union; and the union had broadened its base to include auto truck drivers as the trend away from horse-drawn transportation seemed unmistakable. And, after the Employers' Association had been skirted by the team owners and union in Seattle, they turned on an open shop drive in Bellingham, provoking a teamster strike there in May. The *Union Record* accused the Association of trying to draw in the Seattle teamsters into a sympathy strike; if true, the Association failed.

Labor peace reigned in Seattle theaters also. On the eve of a threatened strike in January 1916, against the Coliseum Theater an agreement was signed with the Greater Seattle Theaters. The Coliseum would open with Puget Sound Traction, Power, and Light electricity, but A. W. Leonard, of the company, agreed to bargain with the union. He agreed that union electricians would no longer be barred from working for the company, in return for the end of the union's discrimination in favor of City Light.

Meanwhile, the Central Labor Council's stab at free enterprising—the Mutual Laundry—was going strong at year's end despite efforts by the competition to block Mutual's purchases of supplies and machinery. Success breeds success: Two "laundry girls" married two laundry men.[1]

The City vs. the Legislature's Referred Acts of 1915

The acts passed by the 1915 legislature pre-occupied pressure groups as the electorate moved toward the 1916 general election. At its January 1916 annual meeting the Employers' Association urged its members to contribute money to defeat efforts to overturn the anti-picketing bill—it had been suspended from taking effect because of the successful initiative campaign of the State Federation of Labor. The EA then sought an injunction to prevent circulation of the initiative petitions being sponsored by the Joint Legislative Committee on the measure. The Association's injunction request was refused and the State Federation and the Central Labor Council began a house to house canvass for signatures to make up for time lost in the court. But, when the petitions were finally submitted to Secretary of State, Howell, the Association persuaded Howell to intervene to cloud and obstruct their placement on the ballot; Howell was supported by the Supreme Court, which overturned a ruling of a Thurston County judge that the court could not interfere with the legislative process, but must rule afterward on appeal. On this authority, Howell was able to change the wording of the preambles of each initiative to suit the Association. One of the Association's members, the Puget Sound Traction, Power, and Light Company, even threatened to fire any of its employees who signed the JLC petitions.[1]

All eight pieces of legislation that were being referred to the voters were conceived to overrule the reforms enacted by the 1909, 1911, and 1913 legislatures in particular. There were actions that impeded the initiative and referenda process, that prevented municipal corporations from competing with private ones, that thwarted peaceful picketing, that applied the prohibition law unequally to social classes, and disallowed people the vote if they owned no property. For example, Referenda numbers 3 and 4 would require everyone to sign petitions in the registration offices, and before the registration officer—if he could be found, and if the registration office were not whimsically closed. (This paralleled the registration laws in the former Confederate states.) The "Whitney convention bill" restored the caucus-primary in place of the direct primary, and it practically would eliminate independent candidates. The anti-picketing bill needs no comment as to its class bearing. The certificate of necessity requirement, already referred to, was aimed to obstruct municipal ownership and home rule. So too, the Port bill. Number 24 would allow hotel dining rooms to serve liquor (few blue collar workers frequented such hotels). The Renick budget bill, like the certificate of necessity bill, was intended to obstruct municipal ownership by tightly circumscribing municipal fiscal management. The constitutional amendment requiring a property test for voters was a transparent piece of class legislation.[2]

The Municipal League's recommendations to the voters illustrates a middle-ground of opinion, and also its persistent romancing of "efficiency"—as though practitioners of efficiency had undergone a purifying revelation. In tune with its original advocacy of municipal ownership as a counterweight to abusive monopoly power, the League opposed the Certificate of Necessity Bill, and the Port Bill. But it favored the Budget Bill which deprived municipal governments of flexibility in managing their budgets and diluted home rule at the same time. Interestingly, the League rejected the majority report of its committee on the property qualifications for voters, and it accepted the opposition represented in the minority report. It took no position on the anti-picketing measure, although it had previously displayed a bias against the long-shoremen in their recent strike by ripping in to them on the dock fires and ignoring the waterfront employers, while acknowledging that both parties were probably to blame. It chose neutrality on the amendments to the prohibition law also.[3]

While the *Times* despaired that church leaders would probably urge their congregations to vote against all eight measures, it conceded defeat on the prohibition amendments. And, when the Washington Federation of Women's Clubs was accused, on the basis of reports emanating from its "altruistic" ex-officers, that it also was against the referenda, the new officers quickly asserted that federation's neutrality.[4]

Voters resoundingly defeated all eight measures. While the anti-picketing bill lost by only 97,370 votes, the hotel drink bill lost by a margin of 215,036; and the margin of defeat on the others ranged between 130,000 and 155,000. The remoteness of the legislative will from that of the voters was clearly demonstrated. But the inability of the voters to affect legislation of the type they had indicated by their voting, would continue through the period. However, these same voters would coalesce with these same legislators on anti-labor and anti-civil liberties laws once the nation entered the war in April 1917. But, the legislators in 1921 would repeat much of the disputed legislation of 1915, and with comparable results . . . once again, reflecting their distance from their voting constituencies.[5]

The University, City, and State

When Henry Suzzallo took over the presidency of the University of Washington on July 4, 1915, from acting-president Henry Landes, he found 3,225 students enrolled for the fall term—less than half the number at comparable institutions. Also, the state ranked eighteenth nationally in expenditures per student in higher education. The university had few graduate students; this led to its being denied membership in the prestigious American Association of Universities. Suzzallo saw as his first task the education of the city and state as to the potential the University of Washington had as a city, state, and regional resource.[1]

The new president launched himself quickly on a tour of the state, pronouncing that the university would be "a scientific institution, grouping scientific men and interests"; the school would bring new, "practical truths" in which "the public is interested," not merely "theoretical truths." By mid-November he reportedly had visited twenty-five towns and had made 110 speeches, stressing the need to "intellectualize" engineering, forestry, and agriculture to better serve practical goals.

All of Suzzallo's effort would contribute to that seemingly neutral objective, "efficiency." He took the opportunity to mobilize the alumni also during this public relations stunt. But, while gaining statewide recognition for the university and for higher education in general, Suzzallo managed to ruffle sensibilities in the eastern Washington by insisting that the University of Washington should become the training ground for the professions other than agriculture, while Washington State College in Pullman should intensify its efforts to become a great agricultural school. His condescension was colored by the appointment of Ernest O. Holland to the presidency of WSC in 1916. Holland was a former student of Suzzallo's and the two men were close friends. Unfortunately, Suzzallo's ebullient self-confidence tended to bloat his paternalistic feelings toward his former student. The above-mentioned statewide tour preceded Holland's ascension to the presidency, and gave Suzzallo a big advantage obtaining badly needed funds from the legislature—inevitably, at WSC's expense. Not only financial support was at issue, but the curriculum as well; Suzzallo did not want WSC to develop professional schools outside the area of agriculture. He argued that duplication of programs was an inefficient use of state funds.

Even before the arrival of Suzzallo and Holland at their respective schools, the Washington legislature had established its Commission of Educational Survey to examine the state's higher education system. The commission had contracted with the United States Bureau of Education to conduct the survey. The two surveyors assigned to the task began their work just as Suzzallo assumed office, and were half finished by the time Holland took up his duties in Pullman—another advantage for Suzzallo, because the surveyors regularly called upon the UW president for advice and information, and they spoke a common jargon of "efficiency." Not surprisingly, the April 1916 report favored the UW by showing that it was under-supported relative to WSC. The commission accepted the bulk of the surveyors' recommendations, but allowed WSC to retain its pharmacy program and school of mines. The commission also recommended that the UW should receive about twenty percent more millage than WSC. And, if the commission's recommendations to the legislature were not enough, Suzzallo would further benefit from Governor Lister's employment as a teacher of accounting in the university's extension division during the spring and summer of 1915; the governor tended to identify more with the university as a result.

It was the 1917 legislature that would act on the commission's recommendations. The relative significance of the educational survey report may be judged from Frank Dallam's coverage for the

Town Crier. Dallam claimed that the two most important pieces of legislation before the session were the first-aid amendment to the industrial insurance law, and action on the higher education survey report. (Republicans dominated the legislature: thirty-seven of the forty-two senators, and eighty-three of the ninety-seven representatives.)

Suzzallo spent most of his time in Olympia, pushing the university's cause, and drawing on survey data to substantiate his arguments. While the legislature gave the UW less millage than the amount recommended by the commission, the school's position relative to WSC was improved dramatically. To deal with higher education on a continuing basis the legislature decided to establish a Higher Curriculum Board. As to curriculum of the moment, the legislature turned that matter over to the governor after being frustrated in its attempts to work out a satisfactory compromise. Lister accepted the job on condition that his decision was to be final. He then granted the UW exclusive right to offer instruction in law, architecture, forestry, commerce, journalism, fisheries, marine and aeronautic engineering, and library economy. WSC was granted exclusive instruction in agriculture, veterinary medicine, and economic science as it related to agriculture. Duplication was permitted in liberal arts, pure science, pharmacy, mining, civil, electrical, mechanical and chemical engineering, home economics, professional training of high school teachers, school supervisors and superintendents. An agreement was also reached to place the medical school in Seattle should there be a future need for one.

Concurrent with Suzzallo's political maneuvering at the state level were similar initiatives within the university itself. While he would inherit the always troublesome J. Allen Smith and would deal meanly with him when the time came, first call on his skills was the long-standing feud within the School of Education.

When Frederick E. Bolton was appointed dean in 1911 it had been without consultation of two key faculty, Joseph K. Hart and Herbert G. Lull. Further, Bolton's predecessor had been removed by President Kane for his involvement in an attempt to force Kane out. Bolton promptly took over Lull's responsibilities for the summer program, gave one of Hart's courses to a recruit, and denied Hart a promotion. The school was in such turmoil that Acting-President Landes recommended the dismissal of all three men, and the Regents concurred, but indicated that Suzzallo could have the last word. Suzzallo did.

Hart was suspected, along with Smith and the McMahons (Teresa and Edward), of being socialists—a source of discomfiture in the university's relations with Seattle's downtown business establishment. Hart also pressed for what is now called "participatory democracy" in the administration of the university.

Suzzallo reported to his mentor and role model, Nicholas Murray Butler, that "a group of radicals were ruling the faculty and the students by sheer aggressiveness." Suzzallo held conferences and set his plan of action: Hart was dismissed not because he was a "Socialist and a radical [but] because he could not cooperate in the university." Hart's cause was not helped any by his editorship of the *Northwest Journal of Education* when it published an article alleging that Butler was trying to take over the nation's higher education through his intellectual offspring, of whom Suzzallo was one and Holland another. Suzzallo believed Hart had written the article. When Hart requested and got a hearing from the newly formed American Association of University Professors that organization concurred in the firing, believing that conditions in the school alone justified the action. Dismissal of Lull was easier. Suzzallo then reappointed Bolton as dean. Notwithstanding, Suzzallo really controlled the school, since education policy and teaching were his strengths, and this was a period of major transition in education in which he wished to play a key role.

Although Suzzallo would have preferred to dismiss J. Allen Smith, and he did threaten to do so if Smith continued his public lectures on controversial issues, Smith was unmoved. Reportedly, James Duncan of the Central Labor Council (where Smith was often featured and Suzzallo himself had already lectured) intervened on behalf of Smith. Suzzallo chose to isolate Smith by breaking up the Department of Political and Social Science, leaving the former and establishing a Sociology Department and a School of Commerce—the latter was mandated when the Regents approved the creation of the commerce program on the eve of Kane's dismissal. Smith was left the lone member of the Political Science Department. To head the School of Commerce Suzzallo brought in Carleton Parker from the University of California; Parker had been impressed by the two new faculty that he had recommended: Rexford Tugwell and Stephen I. Miller. He saw in them, and in Suzzallo, a strong future. Parker also worked closely with Suzzallo in the State Council of Defense during the war, arbitrating labor disputes—Suzzallo served as chairman of the defense council.

One other feud, that between the head of the Physical Education Department, D. C. Hall, and women's physical education instructor, Jessie Merrick, was resolved by creating programs for each sex. This change was suggested by the university's new Dean of Women, Edith Coldwell, appointed by Suzzallo in 1915 to replace the recently deceased dean. She was a long-standing friend of the president, one in whom he placed much confidence.

Not all of the new president's time was spent resolving unpleasant legacies. Professor Hugo Winkenwerder was allowed to consolidate university lands to develop a demonstration forest. And, for fisheries professor John N. Cobb the president acquired permanent land at Friday Harbor for the marine biology station.

All of these actions and measures received wide approval, and Suzzallo became one of the best-known figures in the state in the process. That the University of Washington would, itself, become a center of more favorable attention than in the past, was inevitable. World War I and war preparedness on campus reinforced this trend. He began in January 1916 by countering the Student Anti-Drill Society's protest against the existing compulsory drill requirement by meeting with the group's leaders, then presenting their brief to the faculty. The latter, compliantly chose to retain the drill, and he "abided" by their decision. So did the students.

Part IV

Wartime

14

War Preparedness and War in the Schools

Notwithstanding the continued fighting in Europe, war preparedness measures were resisted by the School Board and by the Seattle Central Labor Council, usually allied with the Parent-Teachers Association, the Federation of Women's Clubs and the Municipal League. An outbreak of hyperbolic patriotism, many feared, would have disastrous consequences for civil liberties and the labor movement.[1]

The School Board was pressured as early as 1915 to allow military training in high schools, but Socialist member Richard Winsor convinced the Board to keep it out. Then, in the spring of 1916, the board allowed a recruiter to speak to high school students, thereby arousing the State PTA to propose a resolution opposing military training in the schools. In May the Federation of Women's Clubs protested against "military addresses . . . or any addresses of a political nature in the public schools." The Board also refused a request from the Northwest Business Men's Preparedness League to allow pupils to march in a preparedness parade. The School's medical inspector even tried to get the board to introduce marching drills into the physical education program. By the end of 1916, however, the board agreed to require physical training in all grades, without associating the term "military" with the subject.

School Superintendent Frank Cooper, resisted these pressures throughout the war, as well as during the preparedness period. In these efforts, he could always depend upon veteran board member Winsor and, beginning in January 1917, Anna Louise Strong. Strong's first resolution presented before the board was against the introduction into the schools of anything smacking of militarism; only Winsor supported her. When the nation became a belligerent in April 1917, the U.S. Army asked the Board to introduce its School Guard program into the curriculum in the form of an after-school military drill. Cooper opposed on practical and academic grounds: already overcrowded buildings, undesirability of wearing distinctive uniforms, incursions on pupil time, and he questioned its educational value. The board overruled him, and the program was introduced. Still, the board supported Cooper in his efforts to keep recruiters out of schools buildings and in attempts to obtain lists of militarily eligible students.

After the United States entered the war, the Seattle School Board lifted the traditional ban on outsiders when it allowed the Red Cross to use the sewing classes as a supply source. Fund drives followed, and some classes were integrated into the war effort on the Home Front. These intrusions into the classrooms, would serve as a precedent for the board intrusions into the curriculum after the war.

One particularly nettlesome group with which educators had to deal was the Seattle Minute Men, a paramilitary organization endorsed by the mayor and chief of police as being a respectable extension of local government. The Minute Men were a group of business and professional men organized primarily to suppress any effort to "embarrass" the government in prosecuting the war. Potential targets of their wrath included Wobblies, political radicals, pacifists, much of the militant labor movement, but also teachers and principals with German names. Also targeted were teachers who resisted indoctrinating their students with patriotism according to Section 232 of the School Code which required them to "impress patriotism" upon their young minds.

Under pressure from the School Board, Frank Cooper listed fifteen "alien" teachers, and then followed up by enacting a policy to employ only "American citizens" in the future. One teacher was fired because, as a conscientious objector, he refused to register for the draft; another for telling students that both sides were equally to blame for the war. One grade school teacher was fired for not

answering "correctly" all the questions in a patriotism questionnaire issued by the King County Council of Patriotic Defense—
although she was later reinstated because she was found to be
simply ignorant of the issues.

Altogether, six teachers were dismissed as a result of Minute
Men diligence. The once deliberative Municipal League whole-
heartedly supported these actions (they even purged the Reverend Sydney Strong from their membership for his pacifism in an
action that violated their own due process rules.) Such was the
distorting effect of war-generated hysteria. Since Cooper opposed
all these intrusions into the educative process he, too, came under
suspicion. His cause was not helped by his known friendship with
Principal Otto Luther of Queen Anne High School, whose very
name gave the super patriots cause for suspicion. In June 1918, the
Minute Men would become a division of the American Protective
League, a paramilitary organization operating under the umbrella
of the federal Justice Department.

Two other issues figured in the school system's troubles with
war enthusiasts. One surrounded newly elected board member
Anna Louise Strong; the other involved selection of Ginn
Company's two European history texts written by James Harvey
Robinson and Charles A. Beard. Strong was well known for her
pacifist views, having written articles in the *Seattle Daily Call* and
the *Union Record* against conscription prior to the war entry. She
testified for Socialist and union activist, Hulet Wells, during his
spy trial (for activities executed before passage of the Espionage
Act), and for sitting with Louise Olivereau as moral support during her trial for violating the Espionage Act.

At voting places on election day in December 1917 Spanish-
American War veterans (a major manpower pool for Minute Men
recruits) began collecting signatures for Strong's recall. With the
required signatures gained, the recall voting was staged with the
city-wide election on March 6, 1918, at a time when a Grand Jury
was investigating fifty-seven treason and sedition cases, and only
three days before the Justice Department began rounding up IWWs
for possible deportation. That she mustered 21,447 votes against
the majority 27,167 in this hostile setting indicates how evenly
divided the city was on the issue. That mayoral candidate Ole
Hanson had to beat the drum of Americanism to narrowly defeat
labor attorney, ex-corporate counsel, and 1916 Progressive Party
candidate for governor, James Bradford, also indicates the growing polarization in the city.

Nationwide, there was opposition to the Ginn textbook series
for its alleged pro-German bias and because Robinson had do-

nated $100 to an IWW defense fund, and Beard appeared on a list of German "sympathizers." Cooper had been trying for three years to get the School Board to adopt the series and finally succeeded August 15, 1917, only to be met with the board's refusal to buy the books. When Ginn withdrew part two of the series in summer 1918 it only proved to critics that they must have been right all along. Cooper even considered abandoning general history in the high schools until the board changed its mind. He then wrote a letter to the board stating that the real issue was whether the judgment of professional educators was to be respected or negated. The Board responded by appointing a stacked Textbook Committee that included the ubiquitous Thomas Burke (national liaison for the Minute Men), John W. Roberts (Minute Man activist), banker Worrall Wilson, Anglophile University of Washington professor, O. H. Richardson, Librarian Judson T. Jennings, and a W. R. Hawthorne. The committee advised the Board not to buy the series until the revised edition became available for examination. The Seattle School Board gladly followed this advice.

Industrial Relations
and the War

The Growth of Patriotic Fervor

If friction among members of the School Board and between the board's majority and professional educators grew during the period from 1914 through 1918, they were but a pale reflection of tensions at large in Seattle. Board conservatives were businessmen, preoccupied with "economy" and "efficiency." Possessing attitudes that were spiced with patriotic fervor, they were individuals who often confused indoctrination with education. Their counterparts in the social macrocosm were open shop advocates, men who confused social reform with "class" legislation. What they really intended was that "their" class should rule and they should be held accountable only to themselves by means of self-regulation.

We have witnessed lumberman, E. G. Ames's expression of relief when discovering the distinctively business orientation of the 1915 Washington Legislature. Symptomatic, also, was A. L. Kempster's comment to his Boston associates that, "The tendency of city and county officials from all over the state to congregate at the capitol during sessions of the Legislature is becoming more pronounced at each session and Seattle and King County have more than their share of these self-appointed advisors to the state." It all depended on who was doing the advising. Particularly alarming was the electorate's use of the initiative and referendum to overturn eight of the 1915 legislature's acts passed with the help of the business lobby. Political control was not as easily exercised as it had been in the past—not with all the reform legislation in place: the direct primary, woman suffrage, the popular election of senators, the initiative, referendum and recall, plus numerous pieces of social legislation that accompanied the opening up of the political process.[1]

In addition, there was that minority of Winsor and Strong on the School Board, officers who ignored the need for economy and efficiency; they looked instead on schools as institutions for ameliorating social inequality by blending a broadly based education with special social programs that would provide disadvantaged youngsters with opportunities for greater social equality. This minority of two mirrored stresses accumulating outside the schools. They were irritatingly pro-union and pacifist; they wanted to protect civil liberties when the nation seemed clearly to be in mortal danger from within and without. But, like many others, they found that civil liberties would become perishable commodities in the ensuing three years.

By 1917, rapid changes began to occur in the economy that critically affected social and industrial relations. And, although two sensational trials early in the year—the first of Mayor Gill, Sheriff Hodges, and Police Chief Beckingham for allegedly for accepting police protection money from bootlegger Logan Billingsley; the second of the Everett Wobblies—the real catalyst for change occurred on the waterfront.

Shipyards were running at capacity and shipping was stretching the harbor's ability to handle it all. Except for three yards (Seattle Construction and Dry Dock, Edgar Ames, and the Duthie Shipyards), union recognition prevailed, setting wage standards that drew workers from other occupations.

Two thousand men were hired by Seattle Construction and Dry Dock in March; Ames landed a Cunard contract in March for nine ships and increased its work force from 500 to 3,000 men. The day war was declared in April 1917, Skinner and Eddy Shipyards executed one of the largest real estate deals in the city's history when it purchased fifteen acres on the waterfront for $1.5 million. In June, the company added the Centennial Flouring Mill's property for $600,000 (the mill built a new facility). In January, Suzuki and Company transferred its headquarters from Portland, thereby adding eight large steamers to the Puget Sound fleet. In May, Frank Waterhouse purchased twelve acres near West Waterway for his new terminal. On the freshwater side, as the Lake Washington Canal neared completion, Libby, McNeil, and Libby announced plans to build a wharf on Lake Union. The waterfront hummed with activity; with the formal opening of the canal on July 4, 1917, freshwater facilities would extend the waterfront by many miles. In its June 24 edition the *Times* presented a table showing that 336 1/3 acres of land edging Elliott Bay and the lakes had been sold in the year in response to the burst of ship construction, shipping, and opening of the Lake Washington Canal. That 100,000 people turned out for the waterway's opening ceremony attests to the significance of the event.[2]

Of special significance was shipbuilding's effect on the city's street railway systems; both the PSTP&L and the Municipal lines had to carry the workers to their jobs. And, since the United States Shipping Board's Emergency Fleet Corporation (EFC) contracted with Seattle yards for its ships, the EFC could—and would—exert pressure on the city administration to provide the necessary transportation—for which neither the company nor the city were prepared.

Out of this transportation crisis there would result: the City's deeper miring in the quicksand of street railway ownership—to the relief of the company; and with it, there would emerge the central issue of municipal politics and the economy for the next fifteen years.

Tensions Accumulate

The crisis in industrial relations during the first half of 1917 simmered; it boiled continuously in the last half of the year. While the Chamber of Commerce and the Commercial Club set aside their differences and merged in early January, the Seattle Central Labor Council and the Grange joined forces in a drive for a bond issue to support a publicly owned market. The SCLC wanted it to reduce the high cost of living by cutting out the middleman, while the Grange was satisfied with eliminating the middleman. But the SCLC also betrayed its phobia toward aliens, who they wished to exclude from the labor market—they opposed the existing "Pike Place Public Market" because it was "monopolized by Japs and Italians." And, just as the Municipal League began to boast of successes in the public employment office (for which the league had played a key role in effecting legislation), the United States Supreme Court declared the 1915 statute unconstitutional. Altogether, 47,995 men had been "supplied with work by the 'male department'"—no mention was made of women in the *Municipal News*.[1]

Finally, late in January, the Steamboatmen's strike was called off after ten long months of fighting mainly with the powerful

Puget Sound Navigation Company. But wage increases were granted and the union reported that it had 700 members (only 10 "traitors") and that union men were being rehired while "stool pigeons" were being laid off. (Remember, that most owners had been willing to sign with the union, but they had been coerced by Joshua Green to resist and to break any contracts already signed.)[2]

In mid-January about 100 streetcar men walked off the job at the King Street Passenger Terminal, asking that their twenty- to twenty-two-cent hourly pay be raised by a whopping ten percent—they wanted pay that was equal to that received by common laborers ($2.75 to $3.00 a day). Federal mediation was sought. And Mayor Gill was asked to supply police to patrol the passenger yards.

Women also took action to affect the conditions of their employment. Given the labor shortage and the steady attraction of women into the industrial labor force, the time appeared ripe to deal with the laundry owners. When the Seattle Federation of Women's Clubs came under the presidency of Viola G. (Mrs. Thomas) Crahan she took aim in December 1916 by organizing clubs for the women laundry workers. Wages in this line of work averaged $5.87 weekly, and conditions described earlier still prevailed. Finally, in mid-June, 900 laundry workers went out on strike.

Five laundries quickly signed with the union, but just as suddenly they felt the rough hand of the Laundry Owners Club. This association had a "holding committee" with power to take over and operate any plant owned by one of its members who recognized the union. Two owners were testing this authority in the court. Public sentiment transferred to the strikers when the club tried to fine L. V. Williams of the Peerless Laundry for violating the owners' agreement. At this point, the strike became a lockout. Strikebreakers were brought in, but they soon joined the union, swelling membership to 1,550 by the end of June. By July 12, the strike was won, and 27 laundries began paying the union scale: $9.00 a week for apprentices, $10.00 for journeymen.[3]

While all this union activity was taking place, the Washington legislature excitedly passed what was called an anti-syndicalism bill. Since the law-making body was dominated by employers (many directly representing their own interests) it is not surprising that it would take advantage of the "Wobbly Horrors" largely manufactured by the press, and pass a bill that was directed against unions in general. The state's union leadership tried to distinguish the aims of law-abiding, peaceful labor-employer relations from the objectives of the IWW—the one big industrial union that eschewed political processes and sought to revolutionize society by means of the General Strike.

The IWW's ambivalence toward creating formal organization of any kind affected the union's efforts; Wobblies could not and would not sustain any strike action nor link one strike action with another—leading to the General Strike. Regular trade unionists considered this kind of activity to be disruptive to the labor movement.

Union Record editor Harry Ault, was an outspoken "red" Socialist whose editorials pleaded against unionists' joining the IWW—"dual unionism." And J. G. Brown, president of the embattled Shingle Weavers, claimed it was impossible to make progress in fighting the lumber barons because of the disruptive tactics of the IWW. These efforts to put the IWW at arms' distance from the union movement persuaded Governor Lister to veto the anti-syndicalist bill for the time being.[4]

A continuing dilemma posed for the AFL leadership in the state and city was how to defend the constitutional right of free speech and assembly of Wobblies and avoid being associated with them in the popular mind. This "guilt by association" is just what the employer groups and their support in the press tried to imprint on the public. A hysterical sense of patriotism was fed by the largely anti-union press which found in the war a veritable hothouse for pursuing open shop objectives and a return to the good old days before 1911.

War on the Home Front

Although the United States entered World War I in April, the course of industrial relations already in progress ran without interruption. A lockout by sign company Foster and Kleiser was followed quickly by a settlement. When the "hell hole of Seattle," the Washington Iron Works, refused to put its workers on an equal footing with those in other, similar plants, 200 employees walked out. The Metal Trades Council asked the State Defense Council to investigate.[1]

When the United States became a belligerent on April 6 the Seattle Central Labor Council sent President Wilson a telegram protesting the war declaration. Downtown, at almost the same time, a man named Captain Bunn addressed a Harvard Club audience of businessmen, claiming an "internal industrial revolution" might be upon us within 48 hours, and that he had twenty-five businessmen in training at American Lake for the event—shades of the vigilante business and professional men deputized by Sheriff McRae against the Wobblies in Everett.[2]

At the same time, the Municipal League betokened the drift toward total war, when it asserted that "the time for debate has ended. . . . We will encourage others to be loyal and will stamp out disloyalty wherever we may find it." The League would oppose any criticism of the nation's war effort—this meant the Central Labor Council and other organizations and individuals with whom it had cooperated in the past.

In July the League, acting on advice from its Committee on the Conduct of the War, requested that Governor Lister call a special session of the legislature to amend the militia code so that it could engage in "necessary secret work" and define acts that hinder prosecution of the conduct of the war, such as strikes, pacifist protests, and the like; all of which directly affected the labor movement in Seattle. The League even wanted to give the governor power to declare martial law when dealing with disloyalty and to establish internment camps to corral those rounded up. At the end of 1917 the Employers' Association asked the governor to call a special session of the legislature to force alleged industrial slackers to work or go to jail: "no one should eat bread in the sweat of another man's brow [and] Such idleness breeds disloyalty, treason, sedition, anarchy, and vice. . . . The legislature should enact a law to make it a criminal offence . . . for any able bodied man to remain willfully idle." For industrial relations, the war had made bedfellows of the moderate League and the predictably reactionary Association.[3]

April 15 saw 4,500 people meet at Dreamland to protest the threatened hanging of Tom Mooney for an alleged role in the bombing of a San Francisco preparedness parade. At the end of the month, the Carnation dairy plant was struck and pickets were posted outside its Seattle offices.[4] Early in May, when rumblings of a longshoremen's strike were heard by the Seattle waterfront employers, they voluntarily raised wages five cents an hour to head off the strike. Milk Wagon Drivers also won a brief strike.

The shortage of workers suggested that there would be many more "victories" for organized labor. More workers were turning toward unionization to improve their respective lots. In the face of this shortage the *Times*'s Joseph Blethen, spoke out for unrestricted Oriental migration. The Central Labor Council was joined by the Municipal League in opposition to this importation of "coolie labor"—it had wage standards and working conditions to maintain.[5]

The Trainmen's Strike

The bad reputation of the Puget Sound Traction, Power, and Light Company had not improved by 1917; its labor policies remained harsh and uncompromising, although more amendable under A. W. Leonard than they were under the irreconcilable, less adroit, W. J. Grambs. Of no help was the company's deteriorating traction service. The *Municipal News* charged the Traction Company with being a "tramp" for its outmoded and inefficient service; instead of improving its operations and equipment to meet the competition from the jitneys the *News* accused the company of trying to regulate the jitneys out of business, all to "protect its capital. . . . There is nothing sacred about the Traction Company's capital."

The company came under fire not only for its abysmal operations, but also for its labor policies. The Streetcarmen's Union, using the rising cost of living as an opening, had achieved almost 100 percent success in organizing. It tried to open negotiations with A. W. Leonard in June, but these efforts were rebuffed. When two union men were fired and others were threatened, the men struck the company on July 16, just as the statewide lumber strike began.

Following its earlier attack on the company for inferior service, the *Municipal News* chose this occasion to blast Stone and Webster for refusing to recognize the union, for reneging on its franchise obligations to pay the city two percent on its gross revenues, and for not paying its proportionate share for the canal bridges—these were all signs of "internal disorder."

The company began importing strikebreakers, arming, training, and housing them at its Georgetown facility. No cars ran from Tuesday through Thursday, but it planned to run ten from its North Seattle car house on Friday, providing they received police protection. But when thirteen of the policemen assigned to the task refused to ride cars with strikebreakers, they were discharged by Mayor Gill. With so little protection, the company chose to run only two cars to test the climate of public opinion. When the cars bearing the strikebreakers arrived at a point near Yesler and Washington Street, violence began; the final tally registered about twenty injured, two cars demolished, and several arrests.

A citizens' petition with 4,000 names urged reinstatement of the discharged policemen, and donations for their defense were collected.

Kempster reported to Boston on the 28th that the strike is now ". . . a test of wits rather than a test of strength though we have placed in our Georgetown shops some 500 strikebreakers and are prepared to operate . . . on short notice. . . . The city administration has not shown much desire to be caught between the opposing lines of the Company and the strikers during the last week." Kempster blamed the shipyard workers for pressuring the company's trainmen to take advantage of the labor shortage, by organizing: "our men" have been "stampeded."

Leonard asked Mayor Gill and the City Council to request federal troops, but, instead, Governor Lister was called to the city to help restore operations so that the shipyards, in particular, could continue running at capacity. The governor responded by appointing Henry Suzzallo (in his capacity as chair of the State Defense Council) the head of an arbitration board. The company's Leonard decided to recognize the union and to agree to the arbitration decision on wages, hours, and working conditions. The strike was won by August 2. In late September the board determined that its self-imposed guideline was that a living wage must be paid for those in public employment, a novel policy for the time. The board's report and award was issued, granting a "comfort wage," five days annual sick leave, and two days of "recreation" monthly. . . . But, in Kempster's view, the company came out well, not having to concede an eight-hour day, and losing only those employees who were trouble-makers anyway.[1]

One more old union target was struck after the Trainmen's strike when the Meat Packers Union walked out at the Frye plant in early August demanding ten hours pay for eight hours' work and the elimination of the "compulsory boarding house" requirement by which the men were required to eat at the company boarding house. After one week, the strike was won, and other packers fell in line. There would, however, be more strikes before years-end.

Twelve thousand shipyard workers struck the non-union yards at the end of September; not until October 22 did they agree to arbitration. Telephone workers, inspired by the example of the laundry workers, had signed up with the Electrical Workers union by early August, becoming Local 42-A. No pay increase had been given by the employers since 1913, and they rejected the demand for one in 1917, charging that such an action would be "unpatriotic." So when the "hello girls" struck all along the Coast in October, amidst much public sympathy, it was no surprise. But, when the coast-wide strike was called off by federal promises to help out, Local 42-A resumed its walkout November 2 when federal promises proved unproductive, only to succumb to more promises couched in suitable patriotic rhetoric. A mediation agreement in early December gave them "two-thirds" of their demands, according to the *Union Record*.

The Candy and Cracker Workers also took action when 400 walked out in September. They were joined by Teamsters in a sympathy strike against the same employers. But the employers got a court injunction in a landmark case—the St. Germain Bakery case—in which it was determined that the recently-passed federal legislation, the Clayton Act, did not apply to disputes confined within a state's boundaries.

Domestic workers also became active in 1917. Alice Lord, business agent for the Waitresses Union, began organizing "house-maids and domestic help" in mid-September with the help of Ida Levi. With membership growing, an employment office was opened at the Labor Temple. Women began entering the male trades: as machinists, shipyard workers, taxi drivers, and other lines. But, because they were hired for the same jobs as men, but at lower pay, they thereby threatened the union scale. The Central Labor Council countered this threat by getting a ruling from the Industrial Welfare Commission giving women the right to receive equal pay for equal work. Unionization became the prevailing force.[2]

Most of these 1917 strikes took place only after the conclusion of the most sensational strike of the period, one that allowed employers and self-styled patriots to exploit the Wobbly "menace" to the full. This was the great strike in the logging camps and lumber mills that was so serious that the federal government had to be brought in to settle it. These actions set the pattern of labor relations in the industry until the New Deal.

The Great Lumber Strike of 1917

Seattle became the center of activity for the period's most significant strike, that of lumber and shingle workers. What began as a protest against miserable working conditions changed into a demand for the eight-hour day as the primary goal. It started in April in eastern Washington and in the Idaho panhandle, where the IWW assumed leadership. In western Washington the AFL had been organizing, and had set a July 16 strike deadline. Initially, the IWW held off joining in the strike, but once it clearly had broad support, the organization ordered its members to fall in line two days later. They concurred in making the eight-hour day the main issue. 20,000 men walked off the job in mid-July when the employers refused to negotiate, and also refused arbitration. Since the lumber industry was the IWW stronghold, and because lumber was essential for the war effort—particularly spruce for airplanes—the lumber barons used both the "Wobbly horrors" and the appeal to patriotism to full advantage.[1]

No agencies of government or the employers would deal with the IWW because they were convinced of the IWW's revolutionary aims. Instead, Wobbly leaders were simply rounded up and jailed. By the end of August, unable to generate a general strike, the IWW decided to strike on the job by slowdowns, sabotage, and assorted acts against productivity. This left the strike in AFL hands.

Although J. G. Brown, president of the International Shingle Workers Union, claimed to be organizing the strike, the Seattle Chamber of Commerce insisted it was run by the IWW. The IWW basked in the Chamber's accreditation. Despite mediation efforts by the State Defense Council, the strike continued into the fall. Longshoremen lent a helping hand by refusing to handle any lumber produced in any of the ten-hour mills.

When the IWW "called off" the strike in early October, and rumors floated about that the strike was lost, Brown insisted the eight-hour day was being won and the strike was still on. Moreover, he claimed things were moving in the right direction, with Governor Lister declaring for an eight-hour day standard and with the National Defense Council asking the lumbermen to concede it. Not lost sight of was the fact that the lumber industry was the only industry that was not operating on the eight-hour-day standard, and it was the only major industry to successfully resist unionization — as Edwin G. Ames boasted in a letter in which he admitted trouble with the IWW, "but no organization [of the AFL] has ever successfully controlled the industry in the Northwest [either]."

The pattern of labor-management relations that would become acceptable to lumbermen as an alternative to worker controlled unions, is one that was finally established in early 1918. It would last until undermined as a company union by the National Industrial Recovery Act in 1933. It is the pattern of employer-controlled unions, alongside corrupt unions run by racketeers in league with employers, that prevailed generally until New Deal reforms. How the pattern developed in the lumber industry is instructive.

Lumber was needed for buildings at army cantonments, for wooden ship hulls and deck planking, for special housing for war workers, and spruce was required for airplane construction (in Seattle this meant the Boeing company). Getting to the rarely logged spruce posed a special problem for loggers because of the difficulties of access and technical problems concerning its cutting. It was a problem that the University of Washington's School of Forestry helped solve.

Also, logging was generally unpredictable because the IWW exerted predominant influence in the woods. Contributing to the IWW's influence was employer intransigence; as a group, employers insisted uncompromisingly on unilaterally dictating the terms of employment as though it was an immutable, divine right. While they found the war offering golden opportunities for making unusual profit, they were under government pressure to grant the eight-hour day and to improve and sanitize logging camp and mill town life in order to stabilize production.

So determined were the lumbermen to prevent the effects of unionization from spreading that they arranged for the drafting of workers they blacklisted. The employers were certain, however, that if they met the competition for labor by accepting the eight-hour-day standard, they would simply go bankrupt.

Into this situation was injected the Spruce Production Division of the War Department, and its civilian arm, the Loyal Legion of Loggers and Lumbermen (the 4 Ls). Professor Carleton Parker, of the University of Washington, an advisor to Henry Suzzallo in his capacity as head of the State Defense Council, and widely respected as a mediator of labor-management disputes, prepared reports for the Council. One of these appeared in the *Atlantic Monthly*, and it down-played the importance of the IWW's, contending their menace was being exaggerated; that its syndicalist preachings appealed to the casual/seasonal worker because the employer-as-villain was their everyday experience, and their experiences with local police and civil authorities confirmed their suspicion that government was the handmaiden of the employing classes. Parker argued that the federal government must step in to guarantee lumber production by stabilizing the industry. This was to be done by year-round employment, by providing lumbermen access to remote spruce stands, assuring them a fair profit, and improving working conditions in accordance with recognized standards of decency.

War Secretary Newton Baker, to whom Parker was already known, was impressed with these recommendations as the means to get needed lumber production. When Lieutenant Colonel Brice P. Disque reported in September to the War Department for assignment to France, he was sent to Baker who knew of Disque's familiarity with lumber situation. And Baker's secret agents (who had been employed by lumberman Alex Polson before the war) had reported that the Wobblies were planning a general strike in the woods on January 1. It was necessary to head off the action. Enter Disque. When asked for his opinion, Disque recommended following suggestions outlined in Parker's reports. Baker then persuaded Disque to accept assignment in the Pacific Northwest, knowing that Disque was respected by lumbermen, by the AFL's Gompers, and even by many Wobblies. The historian of the 4 Ls,

Harold M. Hyman, provides all the essential details in this background and for the subsequent events leading to final settlement of the issues on March 1, 1918.

According to Hyman, Disque reviewed the situation and the options available to him as an Army officer. These were: to engage soldiers to work alongside civilian workers, and to provide an allied civil organization involving workers and lumbermen to cooperatively deal with working conditions and wages. The first assumed the form of the Spruce Production Division (SPD); the second, that of the 4 Ls. The first would assure a steady flow of lumber; while the second would deal essentially with developing the reforms needed to pacify the workers and to mollify recalcitrant lumbermen like Edwin Ames of the Pope and Talbot enterprises, the Everett phalanx of irreconcilables, and the lurking Employers' Association. Gompers' approval was essential; Disque brought Gompers around on the SPD in early November, diminishing the 4 Ls idea (he really wanted the Legion to disappear altogether because it only complicated his work at this stage).

With Gompers in the fold, he was given the go-ahead to organize the division. But on returning to the Northwest he found that key lumbermen had been actively promoting the Legion, and that Parker and a Lieutenant Crumpacker, acting under prior orders from Disque, had written up guidelines for Legion organizers to follow. Faced with these unforeseen accomplishments at the scene of action, Disque had to recognize the Legion. Soon, it became the "primary instrument of Army policy" and not the SPD, according to Hyman. And, as Robert Tyler points out in his *Rebels of the Woods*, the 4-Ls filled a vacuum left by the failures of the IWW and AFL to establish negotiations with the lumbermen. In Tyler's words, "the government found itself creating its own labor organization" so that the lumbermen could legitimize any agreement they would negotiate. The only requirement was that they would not negotiate unless they could control. The 4-Ls fit the bill.

The needed work force, an estimated 38,000, including 5,000 soldiers was not readily forthcoming, however. While recruits to the SPD were not entering its ranks, the Legion grew, but under domination of the lumbermen. Disque managed to persuade the lumbermen that each camp's Legion secretary—the liaison for all the parties—be an army person and not one of their own employees. Organizing of the locals got underway in early December, establishing 400 Legion locals and swearing in some 20,000 civilian members. This remedying of the labor shortage and the loyalty declaration success rate impressed even Edwin Ames, who resisted any dilution of employer authority. Along with other lumbermen he began promoting the idea of transferring all power to Disque in matters concerning spruce production.

While the War Department was convinced that only the introduction of the eight-hour day could solve the labor shortage, Disque persuaded War Secretary Baker to hold off while he proceeded to work with the lumbermen, who by now placed full confidence in Disque and transferred their hostility to Parker and Suzzallo, to whom they attributed responsibility for the threatened reforms. Under Ames's guidance, the Lumbermen's Protective League formed a committee to resist imposition of the eight-hour day. The members were heartened by news from Disque that they could expect no IWW trouble this season.

So inspired, they concluded that no reform was needed to prevent strikes. The committee met with Disque in Seattle on January 27. They agreed to let him decide when to impose the eight-hour day, should it be necessary. Since Disque wanted to expand the SPD and 4 Ls into eastern Washington and Idaho at the urging of the lumbermen there, and since Felix Frankfurter of the Raw Materials Board had resisted funding that operation, Disque used his new authority to persuade Frankfurter to give in as a way to get the needed lumber. Given the funding to expand his empire and with it the prospect for remedying the labor shortage with the eight-hour day, Disque returned to negotiate with the lumbermen's committee.

Over their heads loomed the rumor that a labor board was about to be created that would impose a solution if Disque and the lumbermen did not. To bring recalcitrants like Ames and future governor Hartley in line, Disque induced some of the larger operators to introduce the eight-hour day in mid-February. Adding to this pressure was the growing recognition that if Disque were not to spread the SPD and 4 Ls along with the eight-hour day, then the industry would have to confront the AFL. At a meeting of the lumbermen in Portland on February 27 and 28 Disque and his allies among them, persuaded members to accept the eight-hour standard as an alternative to the AFL. Ames and other resisters walked out, but the die had been cast.

16

The University
and the War

University of Washington President Henry Suzzallo commemorated the city's and the university's entry into World War I at an Arena rally of more than 8,000 people on April 7, 1917. He made it clear that traditional freedoms had to be put aside: "There is no place for further debate." To this sentiment the normally tolerant Municipal League shouted an "amen."

He quickly got the United States Secret Service to "watch all men in the German Department and all members of German birth or descent." During the war he also received reports from the "volunteer secret service" in his role as director of the State Defense Council, and he organized a comparable service on campus. Professor F. W. Meisnest was forced to step down as chairman of the German Department after speaking out publicly against United States entry two months before that event and for delivering a lecture, "Germany is Faust, not Hamlet," in which he hoped to introduce some understanding of Germans. Suzzallo appointed a faculty committee to determine whether treason had been committed. Though it found no basis for such a charge, the president, having decided ahead of time that the embarrassing Meisnest had to be replaced as chairman, did so. He did, however, retain him on the faculty for the time being.

Enrollment in University of Washington German classes

dropped precipitously, leading to three faculty resignations, Meisnest included. So enduring was the resentment against Germans that Meisnest was not reinstated in the department until 1927, two years after Suzzallo himself was fired.

Suzzallo acted not only to keep his faculty in line during the war by means of surveillance, but he also mobilized the student body and adapted the campus to serve the war effort. On one hand, he cautioned students not to enlist immediately, but to consider, instead, whether they could render better service by pursuing their studies and later apply their knowledge and skills at a higher level. Nevertheless, thirty percent of the male students enlisted, about 600 in all. Since this was part of a nationwide pattern, and because President Woodrow Wilson shared the concern expressed by Suzzallo and other university presidents, he had his cabinet devise a scheme to offer an alternative to premature enlistment: the Student Army Training Corps.

Recruits for this program began arriving in September 1918, just in time to do battle with a deadly influenza epidemic, and only a few weeks before the armistice. Providing basic education quickly for these recruits became a primary goal for the university. Construction of temporary buildings and tent platforms to accommodate soldiers, sailors, and marines was not begun until October, just when the full force of the epidemic hit.

The campus was quarantined; the third floor of the former Women's Dormitory was converted to serve as an infirmary on upper campus. Here, 346 patients were treated, and only two deaths occurred. But facilities on lower campus—home of the naval recruits—were woefully inadequate: outbreaks of food poisoning, sleeping on the floors, cold tents, all complicated the cures. Thirty-three deaths resulted from the 1,700 cases that were treated. A dismal and depressing statistic in the home front's war record.[1]

17

A City Headed for Crisis

The Beginning of the Crisis

Toward the end of 1917 and overlapping 1918 a number of international developments affected life in Seattle; but coloring everything were events associated with Russia's Bolshevik Revolution in early November. The State Federation of Labor fretted over what effect these dramatic changes would have on the labor movement in general and the AFL in particular. American Federation of Labor officials were well aware that their Washington affiliate's attempts to alter existing socio-economic relationships were bound to come under suspicion.

The Seattle Central Labor Council applauded the revolution, thereby splitting from its own state leadership and alienating most of its remaining middle-class support within the city. Area newspapers brooded over the diversion of German armies from the Eastern to the Western Front once the new Bolshevik government sued for peace and concluded an armistice agreement in December 1917.

Local officials increased the level of intensity with which citizens and "alien enemies" were pursued for interfering with the war effort. Symptomatic of this paranoia was the zeal that characterized a second raid by police and their vigilante supporters on Socialist and IWW offices in November. In the atmosphere of the time, it became easy for the general populace to link the Bolshevik Revolution with the aspirations of America's more radical groups and individuals. But organized labor in general fell under suspicion as well, if for no other reason than its goals seemed by many to be an unknown quantity.[1]

The *Shilka* incident in late December 1917 portrayed the temper of the time. Newspaper headlines on December 24, 1917, ran: "Rifles and explosives found on Russian ship [the *Shilka*]. Believed plot to arm IWW or to start voyage as Pacific commerce raider . . . U.S. naval officials believe it is to foment uprisings in the U.S. . . . Committee runs ship . . . Crew members are the worst kind of Bolsheviks and anarchists". Twenty-one alleged IWW members were rounded up, "most of them Russians," when they started a demonstration at the pier. The Associated Press claimed the *Shilka* might be involved in an "international plot to overthrow organized government; there was also a "mysterious" cargo—which proved to be mainly licorice root. By December 29 even the *Times* admitted that fears were unfounded.[2]

Into this situation came a new police chief to replace the embattled Charles Beckingham, who, with fast-fading Mayor Gill, was blamed for Seattle's being declared off-limits to about 40,000 Camp Lewis soldiers by General Henry Greene. Greene feared for the health of the soldiers in, once again, wide-open Seattle. When veteran Spokane law enforcement official, Joel F. Warren, replaced Beckingham on December 11 he declared "undesirables, whiskey, and seditious preachers must go. . . . Bootleggers, we will hammer hard . . . the whiskey game is the meanest and worst that this city has to combat." For the moment, top priority would go to restoring Seattle's respectability and to bringing the soldiers' dollars to the city's merchants in the process.

Moving quickly, the police chief uncovered a "booze plot" in which members of the Dry Squad were caught wholesaling whiskey from the vast stores that been accumulating from their raids. Sergeant Comstock and ten other officers were arrested. Restored to respectability by this bold stroke, Greene lifted his ban on January 8, 1918; it had lasted forty-seven days.

Radicals, alleged and real, would get foremost attention in the future. Gill would survive impeachment petitions; but in January he was disbarred for one year, accused of unethical soliciting of law business by the State Board of Examiners.[3]

When Gill chose to run one last time in the February primary, he finished a poor third, behind arch-opportunist Ole Hanson and tested Progressive James Bradford. The count was 23,241 for Hanson, 11,738 for Bradford, and 8,121 for Gill.

All three men campaigned for municipal ownership. But while Gill ran on his not-so-good "moral" record, and Bradford on a solid Progressive platform that included respect for civil liberties, Hanson unfurled the flag, adopted the stance of a super-patriot and anti-radical, and made good use of a well-worn letter from one of the unions lauding his reform leadership in Washington's 1911 legislative session.

The Washington State Federation of Labor leadership backed Hanson, as did the *Times, Post-Intelligencer,* and *Town Crier.* The *Argus* found Bradford "far superior," thereby joining company with the Central Labor Council and Gill. Bradford lost 32,202 to 27,683. This was also the election in which School Board member Anna Louise Strong was recalled by a narrow margin, despite a hostile press and her outspoken pacifism—she was not yet a political radical, but merely an advocate of the Social Gospel. Apparent in this election was the polarization that had occurred in the city during the past seven years; moderates had either been driven to extremes, or else they had become discouraged and apathetic.

But as far as Thomas Burke was concerned glad tidings abounded at the end of 1917. Two new steel shipyards were to be built; "Government Labor Agents" were to "gather" 15,000 skilled mechanics from the East and an additional 5,000 workers for accessory industries. Burke boasted that "Puget Sound will be the location of the greatest shipbuilding industry the world has ever seen"; therefore, the 20,000 mechanics should be considered a permanent addition to the work force.

The Chamber of Commerce quickly appointed architect Charles Bebb to head up a housing committee to plan accommodations for these newcomers. None too soon, for shipyard workers threatened to strike because of exorbitant rents in general and the alleged surcharges landlords exacted from them. The Metal Trades Council appealed to the Shipping Board and local and state authorities. The board assigned Carleton Parker in late January to conduct a cost of living survey.

When Parker concluded that only an 8.25 percent cost of living rise had occurred since October 1, including a ten percent rent increase, the Board refused to allow a pay increase. The Metal Trades Council then sent representatives to Washington in late March to protest. Events that followed would lead directly to the General Strike in February 1919.[4]

Meanwhile, the Seattle Central Labor Council started the new year by sending a note of sympathy to Soviet leaders in support of the revolution. The following day, January 6, twenty men dressed as sailors and two in civilian garb, wrecked the Linotype and other machines at the Piggott Printing Plant, where both the *Union Record* and *Daily Call* were produced. The six workers were forced at gunpoint to lie face down on the floor under threat of death. Police response was dilatory, but civilians identified the two leaders and authorities were cajoled to arresting them: G. Murl Gordon, an Employers' Association operative, and G. Fred Drake, a veteran strikebreaker. It turned out that the Chamber of Commerce had hired Gordon and Drake for the job. Both men pleaded innocent on grounds of insanity and mental irresponsibility and were acquitted. The *Call* soon ceased publication and one of its writers, Anna Louise Strong, joined the *Union Record* as feature editor.[5]

Two strikes continued into 1918: the Candy and Cracker Workers strike, and that of the Butchers Union. While the former boasted of new unionized candy shops springing up employing former strikers, the Butchers had a tougher time of it. In early December, 700 packing-house workers struck the Frye, Carstens, and Bartons plants. When the Master Butchers Association allied with the packers, the strike became a lockout. Events in Tacoma followed a similar course. The *Union Record* reported that Frye ("Kaiser" Frye) had imported twenty-two Chinese and 100 Blacks as strikebreakers, housing them at the plant. Reportedly, dozens of Black strikebreakers were leaving the plant and the union offered to accept them as members.

When packing houses in Chicago, Kansas City, and Omaha resolved labor disputes that were going on simultaneously, the Seattle union offered to settle on the same terms, but the federal mediator announced the local packers were adamantly opposed. Finally, the butchers called off their strike in late May, but not before their union built its own cooperative packing plant and formed the Cooperative Food Products Association, probably inspired by the success of the Mutual Laundry, a union laundry cooperative.[6]

Longshoremen faced uncertainty over whether or not waterfront employers would live up to terms of their settlement. In mid-January the National Adjustment Board "abolished the employers' hiring hall and 'card-rustling' system," effective July 1, 1918. After that date, hiring would be done through halls operated by the International Longshoremen's Association, at the docks, or at employers' halls operated under Shipping Board jurisdiction.

The ILA threatened a strike in mid-April at the same time that a federal mediator tried convincing employers to grant a wage increase. (The employers refused to talk with any committee of workers, only with Carleton Parker's successors.) In mid-September, the federal representative took over the employer's hiring hall, and "henceforth"—but not really for long—all longshoremen would have to be hired from the government-controlled location. The union quickly stepped up its organizing; on October 5, 500 new members were initiated. Waterfront employers countered by ignoring the government hall. Instead, they hired through the Northwest Stevedore and Truckers Association (NSTA) and proceeded to fire union members. The NSTA was primarily an organization of Black waterfront workers headed by James A. Roston. In the 1920s it would become the Colored Marine Employees Benevolent Association, supplying strikebreakers and non-union employees as needed. (Blacks were basically excluded from ILA membership at this time; consequently, this was one of the few outlets for Blacks to work on the waterfront, casual as it was.)

By late December, however, the federal authorities got employers to hire through the government hall. But the future for amicable relations along Seattle's waterfront appeared dim. When the "settlement" finally did occur, it was on waterfront employers' terms in 1921 (under a plan devised by University of Washington instructor, Frank Foisie). Foisie would engineer employer strategy and tactics for the next decades; until employers came to realize they were really victimizing themselves and ports along the coast by their stubbornness and their insistence that Bolsheviks controlled waterfront unions.[7]

On February 9, the Justice Department sent Clarence Reames to Seattle to organize the prosecution of IWW members and others suspected of violating the Espionage Act. Reames, a Medford native, had been the United States Attorney for Oregon, where he had established a solid reputation for going after "neutrality violators." He would have plenty of cases facing him. Due in large part to the exuberance with which Minute Men pursued suspicious characters, Seattle's jail could hold no more. Indicative of what constituted sedition and spying in the eyes of the Minute Men is the following case list for May 1 to November 1, 1918. Cases included: 399 alien enemies, 1,114 for passport applications violations, 707 as a result of loyalty reports to government, 677 disloyal citizens, 938 Liberty Bond and Red Cross slackers, 1,198 IWW agents, 990 pro-German radicals, 451 alleged spies or German agents, 449 people making seditious utterances—altogether there were 10,042 cases and 1,008 arrests. It is understandable that Reames found many of them unindictable; but he did conduct proceedings vigorously when he believed he had the slightest chance of winning. He also found that he had to restrain Minute Men from coming directly to his office with evidence that would not stand up in court.

On March 2, following on the heels of the establishment of the eight-hour day in the lumber industry—a measure calculated to remove a reason for IWW agitation—the Labor Department ordered a round-up of "alien disturbers in the Pacific Northwest . . . whether I.W.W.s or not . . . [they] shall be confined for deportation," adding more to Reames's case load. The *Times* reported that "civic organizations and employers urged the establishment of a detention camp at Puget Sound to accommodate 3,000 men".

By the summer of 1918 the IWWs were driven out of the woods by the combined action of the soldiers of the Spruce Production Division and the 4-Ls, plus a succession of roundups by federal and local authorities. As an organization, the IWW practically ceased to exist. But many drifted to the cities where the demand for labor outran supply, and employers were less fussy about one's background. The result in Seattle was the infusion of more radical militants into an already radical-leaning union work force. Seattle had become a union town, to the dismay and frustration of the Employers' Association. Soon, Reames found himself under heavy attack from the Central Labor Council, which sent a resolution to President Wilson asking for Reames's removal. This action was, in turn, opposed by State Federation president, William Short, who termed the resolution "nonsensical," further accentuating the split of the state labor movement.[8]

These repressive acts by governmental forces and the government-blessed vigilantes contributed to a growing militancy within Seattle's labor movement. Throughout the year, demonstrations and mass meetings were held protesting the Tom Mooney case in San Francisco. Most of organized labor—even the conservative State Federation of Labor leadership—were convinced that Tom and Rena Mooney and their cohort, Warren Billings, had been framed by the Employers' Association and the San Francisco Chamber of Commerce. If the Mooney conviction was upheld by what labor believed was a prejudiced court, then all organized labor would be threatened. Setting the tone, a parade ten-blocks long was held in early February, terminating at Dreamland. The following week the Card and Label League organized a mass benefit attended by an overflow crowd.

In early August, 4,000 gathered at the Arena for a meeting presided over by outspoken Socialist Kate Sadler. The Mooney case brought labor together as nothing else had done before. Even the British labor movement protested. Demonstrations continued through the fall, one to hear the released Rena Mooney.

After Armistice Day in November 1918, the Central Labor Council voted 155 to 0 to request Governor Stephens to pardon Mooney. Stephens had postponed action until after the November elections, and finally commuted the sentences from death to life imprisonment. That became *the* issue to protest, at least until events leading to the General Strike overtook the Mooney affair. Ironically, the Mooney protests deprived the Seattle labor movement of its more conservative leadership during the days before the strike referendum got underway—they were in Chicago at a Mooney conference.

From April 1917 through the General Strike period and continuing into 1920, the Seattle Central Labor Council asserted its independence, much to the dismay and embarrassment of State Federation leadership. The SCLC catalyst was James Duncan, its secretary, feisty advocate of industrial unionism, leader of the Metal Trades Council (which controlled the shipyard unions), and staunch pacifist and prohibitionist. Duncan was one of the main speakers at a mass meeting held at the Moore Theatre in mid-August 1918 under auspices of the Russian Workers Council of Seattle. Duncan, along with others, spoke in favor of Soviet recognition and in opposition to American military intervention; a resolution was sent to President Wilson.

Under Duncan's leadership, the Metal Trades Council urged the President to dismiss Colonel Disque, of the Spruce Production Division, because he was allegedly responsible for the breaking up of Timberworkers' Union meetings by local Defense Councils, and for his insistence that the 4-Ls be the only legitimate organization for Timberworkers' to join. Since AFL president Gompers was an admirer of Disque and saw the SPD as an ally in removing the disruptive Wobblies, this independent action was frowned upon by state leaders. And, when the WSFL joined with the Grange and Farmers Union on their Joint Legislative Committee to support most of the platform of the National Non-Partisan League and a set of candidates, it faced a separate ticket sponsored by the SCLC. This led to the demise of the JLC in September.

Hulet Wells observed from his position as a former president of the Central Labor Council, as the 1912 Socialist candidate for mayor, as a wartime shipyard worker, as a soon-to-be member of the General Strike Committee, and soon-to-enter the McNeil Penitentiary:

> One of the features of the Seattle labor movement at this time was the rise of an aggressive left wing which in 1919-1920 was to attain majority strength in the Central Council, expressing itself in the general strike and pronounced sympathy for the Russian Soviet. . . . The radical labor sentiment which existed in Seattle at the close of the war was not typical of the country as a whole.[9]

The Erosion of Civil Liberties

All of the strike activity and the dramatic increase in union organizing among workers on the periphery of the labor movement took place in a setting in which wartime hysteria led an apparent majority to focus their attention on domestic unrest instead of the actual conflict. Local press coverage, with exception of the *Union Record* and the *Daily Call*, insured this focus. The *Union Record* reflected the anti-preparedness and pacifist stance of the Seattle Central Labor Council. But it was IWW notoriety that enabled the press, the Minute Men, and state and federal agencies to move on opponents of the war with seemingly widespread popular approval.

Civil liberties historian, Albert Gunns, ventures that "it was probably safer to be a German agent in the Northwest than to be a Wobbly". Labor historian, Jonathan Dembo, claims that all of organized labor was tarred with the IWW brush, even by the reputedly pro-labor *Star*, which was trying to establish its own legitimacy under the guise of Americanism. During the General Strike the paper would hawk the Americanism line.[1]

Governor Lister established the State Secret Service in August by contracting with a private New York City detective agency for services. Locally, the IWW had been singled out as being responsible for the lumber strike; most had been driven from the woods to the cities. Seattle gatherings of Wobblies, radicals, and others had been attacked in the early months of the war by mobs that included soldiers and sailors.

Civil liberties that were presumably protected by the first ten Constitutional amendments—the Bill of Rights—quickly were eroded under the inspiration of President Wilson, who, ironically, aimed to make the world safe for democracy. Particularly bitter for veteran reformers must have been the realization that it had been only in the previous decade that Bill of Rights guarantees were seriously implemented. Those lost during the war would not to be regained and expanded until the New Deal of the 1930s. Again, it would be in association with a resurgence of unionization and in an atmosphere of broad social reform. It is no accident that those who oppose reform often use oppression to cement their position whenever they have the power to do so. The key to maintaining such power when it is won, is to establish a compliant judiciary that will at least tolerate violations of the Bill of Rights, if not actively promote those violations.[2]

Seattle's first victim to lose civil rights was Socialist and former President of the Central Labor Council Hulet Wells. Wells was arrested before the Conscription Act was passed as he was taking the copy of an anti-conscription leaflet of the Anti-Conscription League to the printer and bundling them for distribution.

Only the Socialist members of the league were arrested. Wells and his colleagues were tried in the spring of 1917, but the jury refused to convict because the draft law had been passed after the arrests; therefore treason, as such, could not be proven. Motions by defense attorney George Vanderveer to have the charges dismissed were, however, ignored, and the trial was rescheduled for February 1918. Anna Louise Strong, president of the League's predecessor organization, the American Union Against Militarism, spoke tellingly in Wells's defense by divulging that a group of middle-class pacifists had ordered and paid for the printing of the offending leaflet, not Germans instigators as reported in the *Times*, *P-I*, and *Star*. When the second Wells trial took place, all such mitigating circumstances would be brushed aside. Vanderveer would be in Chicago defending Wobblies who were rounded up in a nationwide sweep of all IWW headquarters by the Justice Department on September 5 and in November 1917.

Caught in the mass arrests at the Seattle IWW office was Louise Olivereau, typist and active pacifist. She had begun mailing mimeographed circulars to draftees urging them to plea conscientious objection. Requesting the Justice Department return of some seized pamphlets, she was arrested instead, and indicted on nine counts covered by the Espionage Act of June, 15, 1917.

Refusing legal help, Olivereau eloquently conducted her own defense, but to no avail. Nor was the presence of Anna Louise Strong at her side any help. She was found guilty on December 1 and sentenced to ten years imprisonment at Canon City, Colorado. (She was released in March 1920.) Strong's appearance with Olivereau, provided Strong's School Board opponents with the emotional flux they needed to get her recalled from the Board in March.[3]

Strong's father, Sydney, a minister at the Queen Anne Congregational Church, also fell victim to the war hysteria. A founder of the Municipal League, he was to be expelled before the year was out. He had organized and presided over an August 16 meeting sponsored by the American Emergency Peace Federation, seeking repeal of the draft law. A near-riot at the meeting was provoked when police tried to arrest Socialist Kate Sadler.

Reverend Strong next moved against militaristic church-goers when he participated in the Conference of Christian Pacifists in Los Angeles on October 1. Three conference leaders were arrested for conspiracy, and they became the first case—a losing one—for the new National Civil Liberties Bureau, later to become the American Civil Liberties Union.

Leaving Los Angeles after being subjected to police and Home Guard harassment, Strong was detained by police in Cleveland, but was released to attend a national meeting of Congregational Churches at Columbus, Ohio.

Meanwhile, the *P-I* mistakenly reported his arrest in Los Angeles. This erroneous information was used by two Municipal Leaguers to petition for his ouster from the League. Without waiting for clarification, and violating its own rules of due process, the organization voted seventy-three to twenty-one for his removal. If the formerly moderate Municipal League could be overtaken by war hysteria, it is not hard to imagine how the less well informed among the populace responded.

Not content with Strong's removal, the League demanded that he be jailed, as well. Strong fared only slightly better with the Seattle Ministerial Federation for his remarks at the Columbus meeting comparing the Wobblies to early Christians—a judgment he gained in working with the seventy-three Wobblies arrested for their role in the Everett Massacre. These remarks had also been used by those seeking his ouster from the League. The federation acquitted Strong only when it determined that his argument was not in violation of the spirit of Christianity.[4] The fever of anti-radicalism that swept the Municipal League was, however, more than a passing phenomenon; under the heading of "radical" came issues and individuals formerly considered upright and proper. The reform organization supported prosecution of the war at any price.

It was not long after Strong's demise that two other founders were ousted. Port Commissioner Robert Bridges and City Councilman Warren D. Lane met the same fate when they joined the Non-Partisan League, an organization, initially of North Dakota farmers, that not only wanted a host of agricultural reforms, but also harshly opposed the war and conscription. As liberal members drifted from League membership under the corrosive power of war hysteria, new, more conservative people took their place. But almost simultaneously, between 1914 and 1919, membership declined from 1,282 to 610.[5]

Federalized Vigilantism

Foretelling the domestic repression of civil liberties was the widespread citizen and government support lent to quasi-paramilitary organizations such as the Minute Men. The Minute Men were given increasing latitude to operate as quasi-deputies of the city's law enforcement agencies. By mid-year 1918 they became part of a federal quasi-paramilitary operation known as the American Protective League.

The American Protective League was formed—or "recognized"—on the eve of America's formal entry into the European conflict. It filled a manpower void in the Federal Bureau of Investigation and was recognized by the Justice Department as a volunteer arm of the department. It also supplied automobile transportation to federal agents in their pursuit of German spy suspects—in the absence of such assistance agents relied on the local street cars.

The APL was the brainchild of Chicago outdoor advertising businessman Albert Briggs. In February, he had offered to provide manpower and automobiles to assist Chicago's bureau chief in attending to the huge backlog of complaints by citizens who busily had been reporting suspects. When the offer was reported to headquarters, the FBI chief, A. Bruce Bielaski, eagerly accepted both volunteers and cars. Bielaski also increased his national field staff from three hundred to four hundred agents, and requested help from local police officials.

Heartened by this federal initiative, Briggs proposed a nationwide network of such volunteers to work under the Justice Department. Bielaski lent encouragement in a March 19 reply to the Chicago office. President Wilson, responding to the renewal of submarine attacks on American shipping and accumulating reports of German spy and sabotage activities, called Congress into special session, determined to go to war. Briggs was received by Bielaski during these tumultuous days, and was given the go-ahead by the chief, aiming at cities with heavy alien populations.

Briggs set about organizing his Chicago operations in offices donated by utility magnate, Samuel Insull; his recruits were drawn from his contacts in the business community in major cities—presumably because they could be trusted. Nascent organizations often existed already, as in Seattle, where the Minute Men operated. Briggs aimed to bring these local vigilante groups into an APL affiliation. Although such centralization would require several months, it proceeded in tandem with a proliferation of state and local vigilante groups. Since industrial plants presumably had to be protected if materiel were to flow to the front, employers and their professional surrogates dominated the APL administration. Employees were recruited as informers, but played no influential role beyond that.

Once the spy scare petered out after the first months of the war—neither an invasion from Mexico nor the bombardment of coastal cities occurred—genuine spies and saboteurs proved hard to come by. The APL next turned its attention to dealing with draft resisters and opponents of the war in general. In Seattle, the APL found experienced vigilantes in the Minute Men—when national affiliation took place in June 1918 there were already 12,000 members.

The Minute Men were veterans at breaking up Socialist and IWW meetings and destroying their offices, often cooperating with police and operating under the mayor's official sanction.

Immigration Commissioner Henry White thanked the Minute Men for their help, commenting that their victims were ". . . all bad men, as you know." At one point, when they had a backlog of 3,000 suspects to arrest, they appealed to Senator Wesley Jones to find more jail space, but the senator could get no help, due to federal preoccupation with direct prosecution of the war. The Snohomish County jail accommodated the overflow. According to Joan Jensen, historian of the APL, this impasse is what led the Minute Men to turn their attention toward the Public Schools.[1]

18

Municipal Ownership I

City Light Acquires the Skagit Site

During 1918 municipal ownership advocates "advanced" their cause significantly when City Light acquired its Skagit River dam site at the expense of Stone and Webster. Hydroelectric development at that location meant success for the Lighting Department in its competition with that holding company's Seattle subsidiary. Nonetheless, the company's tactics of obstruction began soon after the city acquired the licence. For the City, capturing the Skagit was a decisive "advance." Not so its purchase of the Stone and Webster's street railway system. The fight over a Skagit River dam—merely its beginning—reached a kind of high point in early 1918; the street railway transaction reached its climax in the closing months of the year, just as the war came to an end. These two elements—the bonded debt of the traction system purchase, and the City's determination to move ahead on the Skagit—intertwined until 1940.

In its wake, World War I brought to Seattle a period of economic expansion that was unmatched in its history. Shipbuilding triggered the development. In the space of barely eighteen months nearly 60,000 people were attracted to the city, and almost one hundred new manufacturing establishments were created where none had existed before. Moreover, shipbuilding was expected to continue vigorously after hostilities ended because the nation could, in the minds of economic planners, sustain merchant marine growth of the wartime years.

Linked with this ebullient expectation and fueling enthusiasm further, was a postulate that cheap electrical power would become *the* crucial logistical factor for those deciding to locate their industry in the Pacific Northwest. While electric power's role was generally overblown by industrial leaders and engineers of the period, J. D. Ross, of City Light, was in the forefront as an advocate.

Indicative of Ross's thinking was his expression to Mayor Gill that with a new electrolytical smelting process "we can get ore from Minnesota for steel and reduction furnaces that will supply ship building." William Sparks, a historian of City Light, observed that "even the Chamber of Commerce's most extravagant hopes for the future of Seattle were modest in comparison." The chamber, although normally an unwavering ally of the Stone and Webster interests, eventually would narrowly support the City's Skagit claim to solve the power shortage. But establishing that claim proved to be a tortuous affair.

In 1914, after investigations of the Hebb and Cushman sites had been completed, Ross chose the Cushman alternative and sought voter support to proceed with condemnation and construction. Needing a three-fifths majority, the measure failed. Search for other prospective sites went forward nevertheless. One of the three prospects was on the Skagit River. But a permit had been granted previously to the arch-enemy, Puget Sound Traction, Power, and Light Company through its subsidiary, the Skagit Power Company. Ross drew the matter to the attention of the district Forest Ranger, but dropped the matter because he had filed on sites on the Sauk and Suiattle rivers, and could not reasonably claim that City Light was being blocked out from potential sites.

Ross's first preferences for dam sites had been those at Lake Cushman and the Hebb claim on the White River; a third possibility was located at Sunset Falls on the Skykomish. The Puget Sound Traction, Light, and Power Company held a permit on the Skagit site; so that one was lightly passed over, but not for long. In mid-July 1917 the Company bought the Sunset Falls and Hebb claims and filed a synthetic squatter's claim to the Cushman.

This obstruction by the Company would lend credence to Ross's later charge that City Light was being unfairly cut off from its power sources and that the Company was merely tying them up in order to control the market. Being thus cut off, Ross cross-filed on the Company's Skagit permit, which was owned by its subsidiary, the Skagit Power Company. The latter had not done any development work since the original 1913 filing, but had been granted an extension; the time for renewal was about due, and City Light would contest it. In December 1917 a hearing was to be held.[1]

Ross had written to Northwest District Forester, George Cecil (since the site was in the National Forest) that the Company had blocked the city from prospective power sources and that the city would be unable to fulfill its industrial potential unless it had the Skagit. And, since the Fuel Administration had been urging Ross to conserve on fuel oil consumption, Ross wrote to the administrator that acquisition of the Skagit River location would allow the city to generate 25,000 kilowatts within eighteen months and lessen its demand for oil—the war was expected to last until 1920 (a copy was sent to Agriculture Secretary, David Houston, who would be a principal in the proceedings). On December 22 Houston revoked the Skagit Power Company permit, indicating that the Company had been acting in bad faith by withholding a government water site from development. The stage was now set for the City to prove its good faith.

The first requirement was to acquire a federal permit to begin dam construction. Houston, in a letter dated January 18, 1918, gave the City the right to call for bids for a temporary wooden crib dam on the lower Skagit, and the city was given a deadline of May 15 to submit a general development plan. The Board of Public Works issued invitations to bidders after approving a bond issue at its January 29 meeting. The construction companies, however, refused to accept the bonds for the Skagit because of the tightness of the bond market and troublesome need to run bond requests through the wartime Capital Issues Sub-Committee of the Federal Trade Commission.

Now the City Council had to be brought into the action. Complicating Ross's strategy was the need to secure from the City Council a declaration of its intent to develop the Skagit site. The Council was evenly split; and, although this was insufficient to override the Board of Public Works, special problems were posed by the potentiality for obstruction by councilmen Oliver Erickson, W. D. Lane, and Roland Cotterill, all three staunch supporters of municipal ownership. Erickson was brought around by Ross's promise to continue the sealing of the Cedar Dam, although Ross had given up any success for the process. Lane and Cotterill were persuaded by the new mayor, Ole Hanson, and the latter with added pressure from big brother George Cotterill. On May 21 the council voted unanimously to endorse the Public Works Board's decision.[2]

The next step was getting approval from the Capital Issues Sub-Committee. A. W. Leonard, president of the Puget Sound Traction, Light, and Power Company, had written to committee chairman, John Perrin, that City Light was only trying to take customers from the company without adding to the power supply, and would only divert material and labor from the war effort for power that was not needed. W. H. McGrath, a company vice-president, had also written in opposition, and had suggested an intertie between the two operations for the wartime period. These letters were holding up any action on the City's request, but Ross and Hanson did not realize this until Hanson wrote to urge approval on May 1. Perrin responded by asking for confirmation of the power needs claimed by Ross and Hanson. The *Times, Post-Intelligencer,* and *Town Crier* began sharply criticizing the Skagit project, combining with a majority of the bankers, and the Building Owners and Managers Association. On the City's side were entered the *Star* and *Union Record.* Ross and Hanson then got crucial support from the Municipal League; and David E. Skinner of the Skinner and Eddy Shipyards, a City Light customer, dragged grudging approval from the Chamber of Commerce to approve the bond issue.

On June 1 the Capital Issues Sub-Committee recommended that new business be shared between the two competitors by an intertie, and to postpone any work on the Skagit. The City then submitted a new proposal that attached $500,000 for a sub-station to handle the Skagit power once it was generated. This was justified as a war measure to meet the predictable power shortage. A report on the power situation in the Puget Sound area had been prepared for Ross, and it was given to Hanson for submission to the committee. Since the data contradicted that submitted previously by the Company Perrin asked banker, Manson F. Backus, to supply more information, presumably from an "independent" source. The latter was no less than the Company vice-president, W. H. McGrath! Realizing that this was only more biased information, Perrin sent a consulting engineer, S. W. Taylor, from his staff, to investigate. Taylor went directly to the Company's A. W. Leonard, to learn just how much surplus the Company had, to see about the prospect of an intertie. Ross, suspecting this would happen, hired San Francisco's city engineer as consultant. Reports from both consultants were received by Perrin, who then decided to postpone action on the City's bond proposal.

The War Department then came down hard on the City by

threatening to seize the city plant and operate it if the City refused to interconnect. Hanson met this threat by having Senator Wesley Jones submit a resolution to have the Senate impound the committee records; the Senate passed the resolution on July 13. A rehearing was then granted, and was scheduled for August 1, to decide the question solely on the basis of the region's power needs. Three reports were considered, each predicting a power shortage by the end of the year of 40,000 kilowatts. The Company offered to meet this by a dam at Sunset Falls, while R. H. Thomson recommended the Skagit as the only one with the needed capacity. The committee agreed with Thomson, and approved the bond issue for the City to begin construction at the Gorge dam site. By the time the City could begin construction the war had ended, and with it the committee's qualifying stipulations became moot. Although Ross immediately ordered an engineering survey to determine costs, the survey had to be called off once the snows began falling; it would resume in spring 1919.[3]

City Gets a Street Railway . . . Bargain or Not

While events moved toward a showdown between the shipyard workers and the Shipbuilding Labor Adjustment Board (SLAB), Stone and Webster was preparing to part with their decrepit city traction lines to the City. Its franchise limited fares to five-cents, and the payment of a fare by passengers at each transfer point did not compensate the company adequately. The company also owed the City about $400,000 for non-payment of taxes on its gross revenues for 1916 and 1917. It was appealing to the State Supreme Court for reversal of the City requirement that the company pave between its tracks on First Avenue South and Sixth Avenue West. Finally the company was facing a suit by the City for non-payment of its pro-rated share for use of Fremont Bridge and on a piece of property nearby. When the federal government ordered demolition of the Stone Way bridge, just to the east of Fremont, the company was forced to use the Fremont Bridge and be held for payment of rent, at least. But it was resisting all the way.

As for the City, it had three municipal railway lines, all operating at a loss: one, on a trestle, was up and running by the end of January along Railroad Avenue to West Spokane Street paralleling the waterfront; this hooked up with its Burien line; Division A was the oldest, linking up with the old Ballard line. Unlike the Stone and Webster lines the City lines were well-constructed.

Among outgoing Mayor Gill's last acts was to persuade the

Shipping Board to subsidize the operation of a steam railroad eight and one-half miles along the transcontinental tracks to transport shipyard workers from the north to the new Municipal line running along Railroad Avenue. But this was only a temporary measure of limited effect that the Shipping Board wanted out of as soon as possible, refusing to take over the street railways when that alternative was proposed. It would coerce the City into taking appropriate measures if necessary.

For its part the Puget Sound Traction, Power, and Light Company (PSTP&L) applied for relief from its franchise obligations, and it asked for permission to raise car fares to meet its alleged deficits. The company had been suffering a sizable labor turnover during the past several months, pointing out that in just eleven days in April 103 men had quit, and only thirty-two "qualified" ones had been hired as replacements. To meet the competition, the company was now running on the basis of an eight-hour day as well. . . . All, unexpected expenses.

It was in this setting that company president Alton W. Leonard sought and got a conference with the mayor and City Council members on May 14, 1918. He proposed that the City suspend payment of the company's franchise obligations, and he repeated the request for a fare increase. Leonard got support for his application from Local 77 of the union. But, the company did not offer to improve service in exchange for concessions. Former City Engineer, R. H. Thomson, now Councilman Thomson, suggested outright purchase of the company lines at the meeting. Leonard asked for an offer in writing. None came soon. On July 6 Hanson offered some concessions to Leonard. Partly to head off a threatened strike he requested wage parity with City line employees; but he was denied a fare increase. Leonard rejected this overture; there was no purchase offer made apparently. In August Hanson offered to lease the company lines for the duration of the war, but this bore no fruit.

Forcing a solution was the problem of transporting shipyard workers. It was made clear from the start that unless the City dealt successfully with their transportation that the government would issue no more shipbuilding contracts to the city's firms. The head of the Emergency Fleet Corporation's Housing and Transportation unit arrived in Seattle; this EFC representative was himself a traction owner from Philadelphia, A. Merritt Taylor. On September 6 they gathered with company representatives and city council members at the New Washington Hotel. Hanson, again offered to lease the lines, but combined this offer with a possible purchase in the future. Councilman Lane objected to the lease, if purchase was intended. Taylor threatened to withdraw contracts from the city, a tactic that his EFC superior, Charles Piez, would employ during the upcoming shipyard workers strike.

Leonard quickly offered to sell for $18 million. Hanson shot back a counter-offer of $15 million—apparently based on his projection of what it would currently cost to build. When Leonard reported the offer to Stone and Webster, with little delay, they advised acceptance. However, no reference was made specifically to the properties embraced in the purchase. Nor was the source of Hanson's figure really apparent.

Councilman, Oliver Erickson raised the requisite questions but he was drowned out by the newspaper barrage in favor of purchase. Councilman Lane backed him in objecting, but Erickson was the only one to reach the public, this in an article in the October 22 issue of the *Times*. Erickson contended that "as near as can be computed one-third of all the property in the county is what we are buying and it should, according to the foregoing be worth about $5,562,000." He argued that Stone and Webster had let the traction company property deteriorate with the intent to sell it eventually to the City at an inflated price after thoroughly frustrating the public with inferior service and oppressive labor policies. Harry Chadwick cautioned his *Argus* readers that both Hanson's price, and the P-I's estimate of $11,684,000 were too high. He suggested that Hanson might even use the purchase to build a political machine, beginning with the appointment of his sidekick, Thomas Murphine, as superintendent of the system.

After bitter debate, the Council provisionally approved the purchase, wanting the issue put on the November 5 ballot to get an advisory vote from the citizens. (The Armistice was only six days away, and the city was in the depths of the influenza epidemic.) The *Times*—always friendly to the Company—devoted a substantial portion of its Sunday edition to pumping up the estimated value of the property to a whopping $16,102,946; the city was getting a bargain, no question about it! This kind of publicity, plus the accumulated grievances felt by the public in regard to Stone and Webster, and the public's repeated preference for public ownership, all led to voter approval by a margin of three-and-one-half to one.[1]

Although the above is an outline of the events leading toward the agreement some note should be taken of maneuvering that is relevant to later charges and counter-charges that would emerge in the early 1920s. Erickson, in a letter to Cotterill dated November 4, 1918 (before the election), said all the newspapers except the *Times* "have shied [at publishing my argument] . . . and the *Star* turned me down after agreeing to run an answer to some of the misrepresentations published by the other side. . . . They have carried on a good selling campaign for the company . . . every avenue of publicity was closed against opposition. The Municipal League set an investigation in motion but it was quietly shut off with a flu mask. . . ."

Erickson had written Cotterill in connection with the latter's objection made to the Council that the property was worth no more than $8 million; that the power rate that the company would charge before the City could supply the power to run the railway was twice the normal rate, and the interest to be paid by the City was about twice what was justified. State Representative George Hogsdon wrote Cotterill about the five to four Council vote in which Fitzgerald's was decisive, and he suggested that Fitzgerald's follow-up campaign for voter acceptance aimed to blur the difference between the bond language of the Stone and Webster contract and that for the City's Division A street railway bonds. Fitzgerald was accused by Hogsdon of complying with the demand of the company's attorney, James B. Howe, which would have obligated the City's general fund.[2]

As to the *P-I* and *Star*, neither questioned the fairness of the price offered, instead, they emphasized the opportunity the City had before it. A *P-I* editorial of September 8, urging the citizenry onward and upward, claimed the purchase will be "the biggest job on its hands that the city has ever undertaken. . . . Clearly the price fixed upon is reasonable, not to say cheap." The only qualifier made was that the City will have to run it efficiently—which it did in fact do, within the constraints imposed upon it.

The *Star* did emphasize in its headline of November 2: "Car Line Will Be Paid For, Not Out Of Taxes, But Out Of Passenger Fares." This argument would be part of a running controversy during the ensuing years.[3]

Interestingly, the very forces that normally resisted support of any bond issues judged to be for the public benefit, saw no harm in using the public revenue to bail out a private corporation whose operations were enfranchised to serve the public, but, which was unable and/or unwilling to carry out its public responsibilities. They even defended the obviously inflated price to be paid for property that had not even been specified. In other contexts these very interests had harassed public officials—and would continue to do so—for "wasteful" expenditures and questionable decisions: R. H. Thomson, James D. Ross, and Robert Bridges were standard targets for their wrath. This street railway purchase-episode paralleled the experience of their earlier attempt to develop

Harbor Island with bail-out provisions to be funded with tax revenues in the event of failure.

"Congratulations"

When Henry Bradlee, a vice president of Stone and Webster, expressed satisfying amazement and congratulations to PSTP&L's president, Frederick W. Pratt, in Boston on October 1, one can appreciate the magnitude of the transaction. Bradlee reported that in his discussions with the company's board of directors he had learned of their discouragement with street railway business: ". . . it is hard for them to understand how such a trade could possibly have been put through [under the circumstances]." Earlier in the letter he wrote "You are sure doing some stunt, and if it can be finally put through . . . it will be a bully good trade for the Company . . . [if] we could be sure to make it stick and could obtain bonds or other security from the City, which would be satisfactory to the bankers. . . . A bond which is a first lien on the gross earnings, and which has the taxing power of the City indirectly behind it to make up the deficits in operating expenses certainly ought to be good enough to satisfy the bankers." Again, focus was on tapping the general fund for bond payments, not the system's revenue.[1]

The State Supreme Court had yet to rule on this very point of the bonds being a first lien on the general fund. The Municipal League's Fred Catlett, contributing news to the *National Municipal Review*, commented that "the Company is quite pleased with the sale [because its franchise is due to expire in 1934, and it does not expect its renewal; nor can it get a loan for the necessary improvements]." He added in a later issue that the court had ruled that the City Council was authorized to establish a special fund for debt payment, and only that fund could taxed, not the general fund. He reported that the company never questioned the adequacy of that fund. This interpretation would prove only a beginning, not an end.[2]

An Epilogue

Under these circumstances it is understandable that suspicions of fraud and bribery were rampant at the time, and they would be kept alive indefinitely by circumstantial and other evidence. An affidavit of a former head of PSTL&P's Secret Service Division, Earl V. Minich, and notarized November 21, 1923, provides some information that tends to fill in some blanks in the above outline of the transaction. At that time Mayor Edwin Brown had hoped to prove bribery and fraud on the basis of Minich's evidence, but he needed more, and that was not forthcoming. So the investigation was called off. Much of what Minich attested to as company policy in countering unionization conforms to what has been earlier described from company documents. Minich alleged that A. W. Leonard had been in constant touch with Thomas Murphine, whom Hanson had just named Superintendent of Public Utilities. Both had been friends in the state legislature; Murphine was labeled a representative for the company when he served in the Legislature. Minich claimed that the $15 million figure was given by Leonard to Murphine, to be used by Hanson.[1]

Minich, ". . . began immediately working on the labor union officers and City Councilmen . . . to further the proposed deal." The company was paying four officers of the trainmen's union and the president of the electrical workers union to swing union support of the transaction. One of Minich's agents also had men from the car barns on his payroll.

In addition, one of Minich's agents, Robert Whiting, began working directly with Leonard, after returning to the company once he had succeeded in breaking up the jitney drivers union. Whiting was assigned to work on councilmen Hesketh, Bolton, and Fitzgerald. The former two were trade unionists and had opposed the purchase originally. Whiting, working with the business agent of the trainmen's union, persuaded them to change over—the subversion of the union leadership had been going on for some time, as noted earlier.

Paralleling these activities was the publicity campaign, coupled with circulating rumors that both a shipyard and trainmen's strike would follow if the purchase was not approved. The company tentatively agreed to a wage increase, but threatened to rescind it if the deal did not go through. Then, at Leonard's suggestion, Mayor Hanson called a meeting of various union officers to explain matters. On election day, November 5, trainmen were distributing leaflets on all street cars that all street cars would be tied up if the vote was not favorable.

After the State Supreme Court approved the transaction in early 1919 it remained for the City Council to pass the necessary ordinance in March 1919. Bolton's vote was essential. So, according to Minich, Whiting was instructed by Leonard to give Bolton "another" $1,000. (Bolton, in financial straits, was living with Whiting and they shared a safe deposit box at the Seattle National Bank. Whiting had also contributed to Bolton's recent council campaign). Whiting instructed the clerk to transfer the money to

Bolton's account. Minich also claimed that Murphine, Bolton, and Councilman Hesketh were regular visitors to Whiting's office during this period, receiving money and liquor. At the time of filing the affidavit Whiting was alleged to own a yacht jointly with Councilman Fitzgerald. A substantial part of the above was reported in the newspapers covering the issue when then-Mayor Brown started his investigation.

Muddying the view of the transaction even further, and contributing to the enduring suspicion of bribery was, the role of Walter Meier. Corporation Counsel Hugh Caldwell resigned to accept an Army commission while negotiations were nearing completion—he had ordered an evaluation of the company's property in February, when the company had requested a rate increase. Meier had been Caldwell's assistant; he succeeded to the position of Corporation Counsel, and in this position he drew up the final papers. Somehow any record of the property to be acquired was either destroyed, if one was made; or none was ever made. If compiled, it was probably destroyed either by Mayor Hanson or by the Corporation Counsel.

After the war Caldwell was elected mayor partly on the strength of his promise to investigate the whole transaction. Hampering his investigation, to his dismay, was the absence of any property listing. When Meier ran for mayor in 1922 with Municipal League support, and as the business candidate, he was defeated in large part for popular suspicion about his role in the street car transaction. He became a member of the company's legal staff in the early 1920s, and chaired the Charter Revision Committee in 1925-1926, playing a role that would have led to the destruction of municipal ownership. By then he would be regularly debating City Light's J. D. Ross.

As events would unfold it became apparent that the plight of the street railway system would be used to obstruct the Skagit project and lay the ground for a takeover of City Light by Puget Sound Power and Light. The acquisition of the company's traction operations only made worse the consequences of the initial bad judgment of getting into the street railway business in the first place, when the city established its Division A line, then accepted the gift of the defunct Burien line—Division C. Both were losers.

Part V

Transition to Postwar: A Restoration?

19

Shipbuilding and the U.S. Shipping Board

Seattle's shipbuilding industry began its dramatic period of growth as early as 1914. It became Seattle's boom industry during World War I and the federal government became its chief customer. To meet the demand for more shipping, the federal government established the United States Shipping Board to coordinate production in September 1916. To promote ship construction and to oversee their use, this body then created the Emergency Fleet Corporation (EFC). Construction was stimulated mainly by issuing cost-plus contracts to builders who signed on with the corporation.[1]

In Seattle, four new yards for steel ship construction were built, along with a number of facilities specializing in wooden vessels. The latter construction provided needed stimulus to the sagging lumber market. Ultimately Seattle yards built 26.5 percent of the ships contracted for by the EFC. The work force in these facilities, along with the various allied trades, was in the neighborhood of 35,000. To recruit personnel, wage incentives were offered by some of the companies, but chiefly by Skinner and Eddy Shipyards. However, the EFC frowned on this practice because it siphoned off skilled workers from other localities. Seattle yards set production records in the process, partly by paying higher wages.

The federal government officials combined with Seattle businessmen in a campaign to recruit some 20,000 workers from the East and Midwest. In early January 1917 1,500 boilermakers were reportedly on their way. This sudden population influx made even worse the city's existing housing shortage. The EFC pressured City officials to solve it . . . or else no more contracts! This threat was taken seriously according to PSTP&L's Kempster, who reported to his Boston headquarters that several hundred businessmen were canvassing for pledges to subsidize housing construction to the extent of supplying building plans, men, and material, requiring that the buyer pay only the difference between the mortgage and the actual cost; the committee would also guarantee sale within one year for the builders. Construction of small homes that followed, was reportedly the most active in nine years.

To deal with wage differential problems and variable working conditions, the EFC established the Shipbuilding Labor Adjustment Board (SLAB), known by the name of its chairman V. Everit Macy as the Macy Board. Since the cost of living was higher in the West, the Seattle unions felt justified in having established the higher pay scale; but Charles Piez, manager of the EFC, aimed for a uniform national standard regardless of cost of living differences.

Seattle unions feared that the low scales of open-shop cities like Portland would become the norm if they did not prevail in a dispute that began in July 1917. At this time the Metal Trades Council, acting for all the shipyard locals, presented its basic wage demand of $6.00 per eight-hour day for skilled workers. Skinner and Eddy and Meacham and Babcock agreed, but the other yards did not. A strike was postponed when Edward Hurley, president of the Shipping Board, invited the Council to send three delegates to Washington to talk matters over.

Due to the chronic jurisdictional squabbles inspired by the internal administrative ambiguities within the Shipping Board, the delegates found no one in authority to whom they could address their complaints. They returned home in disgust on September 23. By then, the West Coast yards had gone out on strike and the board sent members to Seattle to conduct hearings from October 8 to 13. When the board decided to conduct hearings in Portland and San Francisco as well, the Seattle workers resisted returning to work until finally persuaded to do so by their respective international officers.

After completing its hearings, the board offered $5.25 as the basic scale for skilled workers; fretfully, it offered Seattle unions $5.50 for the basic scale. The Seattle Metal Trades Council objected because the offer was based on 1916 scales, which were considered unfair to the semi-skilled and unskilled workers, who had not been as well organized at that time; their pay was thereby disproportionately lower. The council, therefore, appealed to SLAB, sending its president, James Taylor, to Washington to argue; but the Board deadlocked, and this meant rejection. In late October, the council ordered the strike ended, despite the objections of the boilermakers, shipbuilders and marine painters. A residue of bitterness would lead to a critical strike in 1918, and then to the General Strike in February 1919.

20

Shipyard Strike to General Strike

"[If there is a general strike] it appears as if the federal government was [sic] using Seattle as an experimental station to find out just how much radicalism and unrest there is in labor, and just what to prepare for and expect in the big industrial centers in the East." From A. L. Kempster's *Weekly Letter*, February 1, 1919.

As the war was nearing its end, the nation suffered through an incredible influenza epidemic that resulted in an estimated 500,000 deaths. In Seattle this epidemic had been in progress since early October. Indicative of its severity, twenty-four deaths were reported on October 25, twenty more on the 26th, with 373 new cases reported. The Mayor ordered everyone to wear masks in public; volunteers, recruited mainly by the Red Cross, busily fabricated and distributed them. On the October 30th and 31st, stores were ordered closed.

Of longer duration than the influenza epidemic was the shipyard boom—the year 1919 would provide Seattle yards with their most significant production figures to date, despite some closures. A substantial industry before the war, shipbuilding had become the center of the city's economic activity—an industrial catalyst—and in the process it had also become the hub of trade unionism. And just as the Metal Trades Council dominated in the shipyards, it tended also to dominate in the Central Labor Council.

In his unpublished memoirs, Hulet Wells graphically depicts what it was like to work in the shipyards. After a fruitless attempt by J. D. Ross to add him to the Lighting Department payroll, Wells sought employment at Skinner and Eddy in order to sustain his family while he served his sentence for alleged espionage, which was being appealed. He expected to be recognized and rejected for employment, but a friend of his was working at the employment counter when he applied, and passed him through,

> into the howling bedlam of the Skinner and Eddy yard. . . . What a scene it was . . . a wilderness of strange machines, whirling belts and belching fires. Ten thousand men went through their motions wordlessly, for they had to shout to be heard above the din. Masts that had been tall trees moored the taut cables down which great sheets of steel went spinning to the ways. The human ant heap boiled with all the specialists that fit into the modern shipyard's division of labor: loftsmen, welders, winchmen, pattern makers, anglesmiths, riggers, riveters, bolters-up, cranemen, lathemen, furnacemen, press and machine operators, boilermakers, drillers, reamers . . . blacksmiths, machinists, electricians, molders, carpenters, and painters.
>
> Along the waterfront were the ways, where ships were sitting at every stage of construction from keel laying to launching, each launching setting a new speed record for the Scotsman who brought order out of all this confusion was an expert from the Clyde. Back of the ways was a wide open space clogged with intramural traffic, while against the street wall were ranged the buildings and shops . . . where most of the noise was generated. Here were the blast furnaces and giant shears, punch presses and table rolls. Boilers rang, planers screamed, long white-hot rods were smashed in bolt machines. Here was the angle bending floor where black men beat a tattoo with heavy sledges, and here a steam hammer thumped its measured blows. Ram presses straightened out the plates, bending rolls bent them, press brakes flanged them, and jogglers beveled their edges.
>
> Lathes of every size and shape were scattered all over the place. High overhead rolled huge cranes with little houses on them where the craneman sat peering down to catch the signals . . . Outside, small trucks rushed about with clanging loads of metal, winches creaked, magnetic cranes let fall their jangling burdens, Carborundum grinders whined and fizzed, air hammers, chippers, drills and reamers swelled the great cacophony.

To all this was added the all too-frequent ambulance sirens carting off the injured, maimed, dying, or dead. The work was not easy; and it was fast-paced. To top it off the cost of living ran far ahead of wages, and shipyard workers typically paid higher rents than others; many, being newcomers, could readily be taken advantage of due to the unending housing shortage.

In the face of these conditions, and the shortage of labor, the shipyard workers requested a wage adjustment from the Shipbuilding Labor Adjustment Board when the existing contract ended on August 1, 1918. The award was granted the first week of November, and it was greeted with the *Union Record*'s headline: "Macy Award Cuts Seattle Wages."

Remember, that the Emergency Fleet Corporation (EFC) had thwarted a threatened strike in the fall of 1917 by getting the unions' international officers to force the Seattle locals to back down and accept the SLAB award for the duration of the war. But the EFC's manager, Charles Piez, verbally had told the unions' James A. Taylor that the local negotiators could bargain separately with employers, bypassing the EFC, so long as the employers did not increase EFC financial obligations. Piez confirmed this in writing. In addition Seattle yards, spurred by Skinner and Eddy, paid higher wages than facilities elsewhere in the nation, in opposition to Piez's goal of a single national standard.

Faced with the unsatisfactory SLAB award—and after the Armistice—a strike vote was begun the last week of November. The ballots were counted on December 10, authorizing a strike. The Metal Trades Council then approached the owners, requesting $8.00 per day for mechanics, $7.00 for specialists, $6.00 for helpers, and $5.50 for manual laborers.[1]

Prior to these negotiations WSFL president, William Short, wrote to AFL president Gompers on November 29, 1918, telling him that the Seattle Central Labor Council "has gone Bolsheviki mad since the Armistice . . . and is temporarily under control of the I.W.W. . . . They are determined to have a general strike, if not over 'Mooney', then they will attempt it over something else." He continued, " . . . since the 'Mooney' agitation has started they attend the meetings in droves [overawing] the more timid [council] delegates. . . ."[2]

Negotiations began anew on January 16, 1919. David E. Skinner represented the owners, offering a wage increase that could only have been calculated to divide the workers: only the mechanics would get an increase (86 1/2 cents an hour). The MTC was not alone in finding this offer unacceptable; even the *P-I* joined the *Star* in applauding the Metal Trades Council for insisting that less-skilled workers also should get an increase.

Piez then entered the negotiations by the backdoor by telegraphing the owners, ordering them to resist union demands; if they failed, he warned, their steel allotments would be curtailed. (He had already cancelled contracts on which construction had not begun; seventy-three ships were awaiting completion and/or a further decision on their fate. But Piez was clearly implying that they might remain unfinished if things did not go his way.) *But,* the telegram was delivered to the wrong party, to the Metal Trades *Council,* instead of the Metal Trades *Association.*

A strike, now, was inevitable, since Piez had duplicitously sided with the owners. Strike notices were distributed on January 18, calling for the strike to begin on the 21st. Tacoma shipyards struck in sympathy on the same day to show union solidarity on Puget Sound. The MTC began preparations for a long one by arranging with the Central Labor Council for the care and feeding of strikers and their families.

While the owners remained unresponsive to the demands, the city health commissioner threatened to ban all public meetings due to a second outbreak of influenza. The Seattle Retail Grocers Association followed by curtailing credit for the strikers on the 24th. And, when the union-owned Cooperative Food Products Association offered to help, its offices were raided by the police under the pretence they were looking for a liquor cache. In the course of the raid police officials examined the cooperative's records.

Skinner wired Piez that a majority of workers were against the strike, and that the leaders wanted to change society. Bulletins were issued from Piez's office claiming that revolutionaries were running the strike. Piez and SLAB chairman, Macy, declared that the unions had violated their no-strike pledge—despite the fact that the war was over (but the peace treaty was long away from being signed), and despite his earlier assurance to union representative James Taylor, that the Metal Trades Council could bargain independently with owners if they chose to do so.

On January 22, the Central Labor Council's Alfred Miller (also president of the MTC), acting on his own (according to Hulet Wells), offered a strike resolution for referendum vote. It passed with little opposition, catching Wells by surprise. At this moment, the SCLC's regular leaders (Duncan, Ault, and twenty-three others) were attending a conference in Chicago called by the International Defense League to protest Tom Mooney's incarceration, and to plan a nationwide general strike if Mooney was not granted a new trial by July 4. With the relatively conservative leaders of most of the locals gone, the rank and file took control of the meeting.

Those in the Metal Trades Council dominated the proceedings. Wobblies were heavily represented in the MTC since it was mainly to the shipyards that they had migrated when driven from the woods and mill towns. The meeting was a wild one. Miller of the MTC argued that a general strike was needed to force yard owners to negotiate; it was needed to show union solidarity in the face of the owners' intent to destroy Seattle unions—that the shipyard workers had to win for the preservation of union gains made during the war. Such a set of specific objectives was ignored, however, as being irrelevant by those controlling the meeting from the floor.

Support for the general strike began to snowball the next day as the Building Laborers Union and the roofers voted overwhelmingly for it. On the 26th a mass meeting was held at the Hippodrome Arena to counter opposition charges.

Piez followed by ordering Seattle yards to plan on cancelling costs. By this action and those to follow, Piez showed that it was within his power to practically wipe out the city's flourishing shipbuilding industry, putting the lie to Judge Burke's euphoric proclamation of December 1917 that Puget Sound would become the shipbuilding capital of the world.

Union executives met on January 27, since they had not attended the meeting of the 22nd, when the strike resolution was overwhelmingly passed. According to a recent historian of the strike, Robert Friedheim, a three-way split occurred among the 120 attendees: the radicals, wanting an immediate strike; the progressives, who wanted to force the owners to openly declare their intention to re-open on an open shop basis, and thereby swing public support to the strikers; and the conservatives, who wanted to abide by existing contracts, which would be violated by a general strike—but they, too, wanted to force the owners to expressly declare for the open shop. There was no way, however, that these executives could prevent the referendum then in progress. They did agree that if a majority of the unions had voted for a general strike by February 2, they would call a mass meeting to decide what action to take next.

Newspaper coverage of developments during the week before the general strike is revealing. The two conservative dailies, the *Times* and *Post-Intelligencer*, were in marked contrast in their coverage and emphasis. The *Times* laid blame squarely on Piez, while the *P-I* stressed the radical takeover of union leadership as being the moving force. The *Times* reported events fairly directly, with minimal sensationalism, considering the magnitude of what was happening—and given its traditional phobia where unions were concerned.

The *P-I* repeatedly used scare tactics that had the effect of inflaming the situation. On the January 30, the *P-I* led off with a front page editorial, "Seattle's Labor Crisis," claiming that a majority of unions opposes a general strike; that it would represent "temporary control of the radicals over the organized work force of this city. . . . The shipyard strike was called without consent of the workers . . . [that a general strike would accomplish nothing, and shipbuilding was a dying industry, anyway. It will show] how completely the unions are under the control of their lawless masters. . . . [It will be a] Bolshevik holiday."

Both newspapers gave play to the problems and hardships that could be expected, but the *Times* tempered its speculation: That Ross was sure of maintaining electrical power for homes and street lights (and the public was well-acquainted with the power of Ross's will and of his support among union leaders)—this claim was meant to counteract the assertion of Electrical Workers business agent, Leon Green, that no exceptions would be made. On the day before the strike began, the *P-I* gave full play to Green's threat—despite the fact that by then the General Strike Committee had made public its intention to maintain these electrical services, and despite the fact that Ross could use soldiers as replacements if necessary. (Wells attributed much of the public's fear to Green's declaration).

In its front page editorial of January 31, "Turn On the Lights," the *Times* took the following contrasting line: The strike is without purpose; the EFC's flat refusal to allow negotiations to proceed except on a "certain policy outlined by the federal authority" is provocative; the owners ought to grant pay raises to common labor; and the MTC had been irresponsible.

On February 2, the day when strike ballots were tallied and actual planning got underway, the *Times* gave big play to a tentative settlement reached by the shipyard owners and the Metal Trades Council as a result of mediation efforts of a citizens' committee (the Industrial Relations Committee), coupled with the outright refusal of Piez to budge from his insistence that the strike was a contract violation—that the EFC could not "compromise on a vital moral principle."

The *P-I* gave little attention to this, while the *Times* headlined "Piez Statement Means 'Strike' Union Men Say." Moreover, the *Times* emphasized another point in Piez's statement that is crucial for an understanding of Piez's long-term motive in forcing the issue: Piez contended that labor costs must be reduced or "output" must increase if the United States is to compete in the world shipbuilding market.

The Chamber of Commerce protested to the EFC on January

30 when contracts were cancelled on ships of 7,500 to 8,800 tons, and when the EFC placed "new contracts with permanent yards able to compete with foreign builders."[3]

Given Piez's unwillingness even to discuss any terms for future negotiations until after March 31, when the existing contract would expire, the future of new negotiations did not auger well for the unions. Already Piez had instituted a policy of hiring soldiers and sailors at $4.16 per day to work on government shipyard contracts, thereby signalling his intent.[4]

Intervention of the Industrial Relations Committee came to naught—its leaders were Reverend Matthews; banker and moderate James Spangler; and anti-union Judge George Donworth. Its conciliatory efforts were thwarted by Piez and by David Skinner. The latter had been appointed to a sub-committee of three shipyard owners to bring in a wage offer. They did so; but it wired Piez directly without first consulting its parent body.

The latter rejected the offer and counter-wired Piez. Piez wired back that they should leave the settlement to him. Indicative of the suspicion of Skinner was a letter to William Todd by the manager of the Todd Shipyard in Tacoma, who asserted that "shipbuilders are suspicious of Skinner as he is continually having meetings with labor men connected with the Unions, and Mr. Ro[d]gers, when he is in town, is also getting together with them." David Rodgers, as personnel manager, had been notoriously popular among the Skinner and Eddy employees . . . to such an extent that the *Railway and Marine News* condemned him for it. But his men also had set national records, out-producing all yards in the nation.[5]

The Ministerial Federation also worked on a settlement, and telegraphed Piez on February 1 that the workers would return to work if common labor was given $5.50 per day. The *Times* had indicated on the same day that settlement hinged on the reaction of the EFC to any wage proposals for common labor. In a full-page advertisement in all the dailies on February 3, Piez stressed again his unwillingness to compromise, that America could not continue to compete, and generally to repeat his previous utterances. Further mediation efforts were called off after this assay by Piez.

In the midst of the crisis, Short wired AFL Secretary Frank Morrison, that the strike vote was "overwhelming. . . . Situation most serious in history of the movement. Community sentiment with strikers. Urge action by Piez and wire reply."[6]

During the week before the deadline, however, notoriously anti-union Edwin Selvin, publisher of the weekly *Business Chronicle*, published advertisements in the regular dailies, advocating in violent language that Seattle become an open shop stronghold, wiping out "red flag agitators in the guise of labor leaders." Although these page ads were not exactly the same as a clear declaration from the shipyard owners, they did inflame opinion favoring a general strike. (According to Friedheim, the Selvin editorial, "Spectacle of a City Committing Suicide" was the only Seattle newspaper found in Piez's files; and this probably contributed to Piez's view of the strike as revolutionary.)

There were prospects for legislative intervention, because the Washington legislature was in session. When asked by the legislature about setting up a Veterans' Welfare Commission to intervene in the shipyard strike, Suzzallo, of the State Defense Council, asserted that the strike was "one of the greatest mistakes ever made by organized labor." State Labor Commissioner C. H. Younger, added his view from Olympia by denouncing the strike leaders and urging their deportation. He did, however, temper his remarks with advice that wages of common labor should be increased. That action, in his view would end the strike, and the threat of a general strike. On the latter point there seemed to be favorable consensus. Piez could easily have averted the strike by this one easy and generally acceptable concession; but he clearly wanted a showdown that would break the unions. His trump card was the power he possessed to terminate all government contracts related to shipbuilding.

By the time the next SCLC met again, only two locals opposed the labor action. Lack of enthusiasm for the strike among the Duncanite faction lost them the leadership role they normally played. The general strike ideologues took over, inspired by IWW rhetoric about the revolutionary efficacy of the general strike.

By the time the regular union leaders had returned from Chicago the strike vote was well underway. Duncan, Ault, SCLC secretary, Frank Rust, and their allies realized its inevitability, were disturbed that no terminal date had been set for concluding it, that no objective had been determined, and that no planning had been done for maintaining essential emergency services for the public. The movement toward a general strike seemed to proceed under its own momentum. They were rebuffed by the General Strike Committee (GSC) when they proposed setting a termination date.

When the GSC did meet on Sunday, February 2, they finally began to realize that some planning had to be done at the level of emergency services after they decided to start the strike at 10:00 AM on February 6. Provisions were made for maintaining hospitals, wet garbage collection, mail delivery, and the like. Sub-committees were established, one to handle requests for "exceptions"

. . . of which there would be many. To remove an excuse for Mayor Hanson to use police as strikebreakers the committee also established a War Veterans Guard to keep strikers in line. Three hundred volunteered; and they did maintain peace. Yet, for all the GSC's success at improvising to meet these problems in the last minute, it still had not decided on the purpose of the strike.

21

The General Strike

Public notice of the General Strike appeared on Monday, February 3. Leaflets announcing the action were widely distributed around the city. One, written by strike committee member Harvey O'Connor, set the tone, claiming "Russia did it." Two leafleteers were arrested by Minute Men. But worse still, was the inescapable identification of the committee with a revolutionary purpose that it had tried unsuccessfully to disavow. Duncan and his progressive cohorts were convinced, from their long association with the Seattle labor movement, that none of the leaders had a thought of revolution. But many employers and their professional surrogates were able to use irresponsible assertions made by O'Connor and others to their own advantage.

Small businessmen and members of the middle class were clearly worried; the daily newspapers fed these anxieties. If not revolution, at least chaos and property destruction would occur. The *Star*, in its Tuesday, February 4 issue, sympathetically cautioned the labor movement that despite the "insolent attitude of the shipyard owners . . . [and] the verbosity of . . . Piez" there is no justification for the "highhanded tactics of the labor leaders to [call a general strike]." The editorial continued, warning of the inevitable failure of the strike and the absurdity of any revolutionary aims. But this advice carried little weight with strike leaders. (The *Star* editorial was reprinted in the other dailies as an advertisement.)[1]

Special Collections Division, University of Washington Libraries

**Skinner and Eddy Shipyards during
the General Strike of February 1919.**

On February 4, also, a Citizens' Committee was formed by
the leaders of the unsuccessful Industrial Relations Committee,
under the chairmanship of the Chamber of Commerce president
A. J. Rhodes. On this same day, the *Union Record* published Anna
Louise Strong's soon-to-be-famous editorial, "WHO KNOWS
WHERE!" It began with

> There will be many cheering and there will be some who
> fear. . . . We are undertaking the most tremendous move ever
> made by LABOR in this country, a move which will lead—
> NO ONE KNOWS WHERE!

Strong concluded by declaring: "And that is why we say that
we are starting on a road that leads—NO ONE KNOWS WHERE!"
According to Friedheim, this was the most important statement
justifying the strike. Strong's page-long editorial contributed to
the general fear and uncertainty. To be more certain of this effect,
the *P–I* reprinted it in full on Wednesday, February 5.

In his study, Robert Friedheim concludes: "With this editorial, Anna Louise Strong destroyed the possibility that anyone
would negotiate with labor to settle the strike. Now no individual
or group would demand anything less than labor's unconditional

surrender." Stephanie Ogle concurs with Friedheim that editor Ault did not want the editorial published when he first saw it two days earlier, but it was slipped in while he was preoccupied. He opposed the strike action, but like James Duncan and Hulet Wells, he was dragged into supporting it for the sake of solidarity once there was no turning back from the overwhelming mandate given by the members' vote.[2]

But one more announcement from the strike forces convinced many that chaos would soon occur; it related to the provision of electric power. The General Strike Committee (GSC) met with Mayor Hanson, who repeatedly implored Duncan (who was on the Labor Council's executive committee, but was not yet a GSC member) to guarantee electric power. Duncan pleaded helplessness. Hanson responded to this concern as a result of an announcement by Leon Green, business agent of the Electrical Workers Local 77, that City Light would be shut down, reiterating threats made previously. Hanson called him an "alien, slacker, Bolsheviki, and IWW." Green had no authority for making such proclamations, but neither Hanson nor J. D. Ross appeared to know this. Nor did they know that the GSC had no intention of shutting down City Light.

Unfortunately, the damage had been done; it was devastating, removing the last chance for broad public support. The *P-I* gave Green's boast headline play, along with the threat of some radical proclaimers about spreading the strike across the state.

In its official history the GSC accepted the view that the electricity issue was really a bluff between Hanson and Green:

> We had operators in the sub-stations only partially organized and could not have called them off if we had wanted to. We did call out the line men and meter men, who responded. But their absence made little immediate difference, and they went back before the strike was called off. The engineers . . . declined to [strike] and only called off their men after it was sure that city light would run anyway.

Tension between the Central Labor Council and the *Star* seemed to grow from the time when the Council passed a resolution on Labor Day 1918, exonerating Hulet Wells, the Pass brothers, and W. H. Kaufman of alleged war crimes for which they were convicted under the espionage act. Exuding self-righteous patriotism, the *Star* asserted this action was a "libel upon labor . . . and labor should promptly demand that it be revoked, and WIPED OUT." The *Star* had considered it to be the daily labor advocate before the *Union Record* began daily operations in April 1918.

According to the "official history" by the GSC, the *Star* had been the largest paper in the Northwest, but the *Union Record* had cut the *Star's* circulation by half. Consequently, the *Star's* role during the strike and aftermath must be judged in this light. Not surprisingly, the *Star*, abruptly switched from giving friendly advice like that on the Tuesday, February 4, and began an "Americanism" pitch on February 5 with a headline, "UNDER WHICH FLAG?" followed by:

> "[This is more than a general strike.] It is an acid test of American citizenship—an acid test of all those principles for which our soldiers and sailors fought and died. It is to determine whether this is a country worth living in and a country worth dying for. . . . Under which flag do you stand?"

Star editors had been uncritically super-patriotic during the war, seeming to use the late Alden Blethen for their role model. The fact that the *Star* and *P-I* continued to publish abbreviated editions during the strike exacerbated tensions inasmuch as the *Union Record* remained silent during the early days of the strike.

Not missing an opportunity, the *P-I* greeted its readers on the morning the strike began with a front page cartoon depicting the Red flag hanging over Seattle, surmounting the stars and stripes beneath it. As though this was not sufficiently dramatic, the *P-I* editorial exclaimed:

> Today is raised the issue between American Democracy and the organized forces of revolt, insurrection, and rebellion. We will let Mr. Piez settle the shipyard strike. . . . If he wants to close the shipyards and throw [the shipyard workers] into the bay let him do so—and not a few will say 'good riddance.'

The *Union Record* only rarely printed revolutionary rhetoric; Ault constantly exercised a restraining hand while allowing feature writer Anna Louise Strong a wider latitude than was probably advisable, given her romantic illusions about revolution in the United States. Ault chose to portray union solidarity as a force to be reckoned with in the economic and political arena—union strength had converted part of the working class, at least, into active participants in the democratic process.

On Monday, February 3 the *Union Record's* headline ran: "Solidarity of Seattle to be Demonstrated" . . . "Piez to be taught a lesson"; on Wednesday the 5th, "Responsibility Rests With Piez." Prominence was given, however, to Leon Green's claim that a "complete tie-up of [electric power] would shorten the strike. . . . This means that not a light in Seattle will burn tonight." The *Times* was simultaneously playing down the threat—as though confident of the strike's inevitable failure. But, the *Times's* Washington correspondent in his "Jermane's Dispatch," reported that there is ample warrant for the statement that the threatened general strike

". . . will mark the beginning of an effort of the radical elements to control American labor . . . Seattle is a stronghold of Radicals [according to AFL leaders.] Several internationals oppose the strike. If the radicals win on the Pacific Coast their control will spread.

Mayor Hanson met with the General Strike Committee on Thursday February 6, from midnight until 3:30 in the morning, to deal mainly with city services in general and electrical power in particular. He left the meeting with the assurance of full capacity operation for City Light. But one hour before this meeting he had taken measures to suppress the strike by asking the Washington attorney general and Henry Suzzallo—who were acting in place of the dying Governor Lister—for National Guard help. Suzzallo, as head of the State Defense Council, phoned the U.S. Secretary of War asking for federal troops. Hanson beefed up the police force with 600 recruits, paying them $6.00 per day, to the disgruntlement of the regular force, which received $4.25.

Elements of the army's First Infantry Division were dispatched to both Tacoma and Seattle—Tacoma, because unions there planned a sympathy strike to demonstrate worker solidarity. One battalion was dispatched to Fort Lawton to be held in reserve, while other units manned utility substations, the Navy pier, and the Ballard Locks. All this on early February 7, a Friday morning.

Not content with this degree of mobilization, Hanson proceeded to recruit about 2,400 volunteer police from University of Washington fraternities, the Reserve Officers Training Corps, and civic organizations, arming them with clubs and with firearms when they were available.

Impressed with its ability to shut down an entire city, the GSC failed to see the need for some strategic planning, such as a clear statement of the strike's purpose, a negotiating framework, and a potential termination date. At its Thursday-noon meeting, two hours after the strike began, the GSC became absorbed in tactical details: admitting Japanese workers to the unions in a participatory, but voteless role; setting up feeding stations, arranging for milk deliveries, assuring hospital operations, maintaining discipline even among Wobblies, and meeting other tactical problems as they came up. In these matters the GSC was successful, and above all, union solidarity had been demonstrated; the leaders were to claim the strike a success during the aftermath on the basis of this "solidarity."

The strike proceeded quietly: no arrests, no soap box oratory, mainly uneasy expectations. Then, late on Friday, February 7, Hanson proclaimed a guarantee of "absolute and complete protection" by the forces he had mobilized. "The time has come for every person in Seattle to show his Americanism. . . . All persons violating the laws will be dealt with summarily." A free edition of the *Star* printed the proclamation, and it was distributed by policemen, some of whom were armed with machine guns—despite the absence of any provocation.

For national consumption, and unknown to Seattleites, Hanson issued a long statement to local United Press representatives that the strike was a revolution and that he would not deal with revolutionaries. Hanson was setting himself up as a national hero, hoping to catapult himself into high national office.

But knowing that he must negotiate with strikers' representatives to end the labor action, Hanson persuaded Duncan to arrange to have the executive committee send a six-man delegation to meet with the mayor. Hanson threatened them with the prospect of martial law if the strike were not called off by eight o'clock in the morning Saturday, February 8. (Not until later that day were union leaders informed by Major General John Morrison, that only he had authority to declare martial law, not the bluffing Hanson.) With the mayor and committee at loggerheads, Duncan then persuaded Hanson to set up a meeting with the Citizens' Committee hoping that some compromise could be worked out. At three o'clock in the afternoon they met, only to agree to meet again that evening.

The committee was chaired by A. J. Rhodes, department store owner and president of the Chamber of Commerce; it included Mark Matthews, who had lost patience with the unions during the war; James Spangler, a banker and moderate, was a third member. (Rhodes would lead a reinvigorated open shop drive after the strike.) Spangler indicated there would be no need for further discussion because, "Our people have come to the conclusion that this is a revolution, and that we cannot have dealings with revolutionists."

In recounting these proceedings in July 1920 at the Chicago IWW trial (*People of Illinois vs Lloyd et al*). Duncan further reported that on leaving the meeting, Spangler said he knew the strike was not revolutionary, was a "peaceful strike, but nevertheless some of our people up there are convinced that it is." This was the last chance for a negotiated settlement of the strike.[3]

What seems unmistakable is that, at this point in the strike, the open shop forces within the Chamber, led by Rhodes and Frank Waterhouse had taken their cue from Piez and decided to break the union. These men would soon establish the Associated Industries in March for the declared purpose of making Seattle an open shop town; but it was felt necessary to keep the Chamber at a respectful distance from this single-purpose organization.

With respect to revolutionary aims, Duncan responded at the Chicago IWW trial that "There was not any word of taking over the functions of government or of doing anything illegal . . . when I was present at any [GSC] meetings"—and Duncan had made a point of attending all that he could before being invited to join the GSC.

Viola G. Crahan, who, with Duncan, W. D. Lane and others, attended the Committee of Forty-eight Convention in Chicago, also contended that, in her capacity as president of the City Federation of Women's Clubs, she was on the streets talking with strikers and the leadership six to eight hours daily, and had heard no word of revolutionary intent expressed.[4]

But, already, that Saturday morning, the streetcar men began drifting back to work. While PSTP&L was still awaiting completion of the paperwork prior to turning over its traction property to the City, Kempster reported to Boston on February 9: "We feel that the return of the trainmen to work [on Sunday] will almost break the strike as it is anticipated that many smaller unions which quit thru [sic] intimidation, will now go to work." Teamsters and other unions slowly followed.

The solid front was broken, and the *Star* led the hue and cry: "There can be no compromise on Americanism." The *Argus* chauvinistically portrayed the strikers as being the "Riffraff from Europe," and advocated army repression of the strike. The AFL leadership, having opposed the strike from the beginning, sent officers of the internationals to Seattle to pressure the local leadership into capitulation. The *Union Record* then resumed publication after foolishly depriving the unions of a voice to counter the hostile effusions of the three publishing dailies: the *Star*, *P-I*, and *Daily Bulletin*. By now much of the public was convinced that the strike was an attempt at revolution.

On the afternoon and early evening of Saturday, February 8, while the Citizens' Committee was reaching its verdict, the Central Labor Council's executive committee framed a capitulation resolution for presentation to the GSC, asserting that the object of the strike had been accomplished "through the unprecedented demonstration of solidarity." Mayor Hanson was accused in it of having impeded an earlier settlement by his threats of coercion; but, with the objective won, the strike should be called off at midnight Saturday. Duncan was chosen to present the resolution to the GSC.

Bitter and prolonged debate ensued, with Duncan and Harry Ault arguing strenuously for the resolution; but it was overwhelmingly rejected. The radicals on the GSC convinced the others that this was what class war was all about.

On Sunday, February 9, Hulet Wells—who had opposed the use of the general strike for ordinary union purposes—visited George Ryan, secretary of the county Democratic Party. Ryan, reputedly had some influence in the Wilson administration; so, Wells sought him to act as the special emissary of the Central Labor Council, while the strike would be suspended. When Wells announced this proposal at the SCLC meeting it was roundly cheered as a graceful way of ending the strike. However, this was but a brief interlude, for a small group of Metal Trades delegates blocked the plan, according to Wells.

Many of the locals met on Sunday to vote; only the longshoremen and cooks chose to continue. On Monday GSC members began circulating among the local unions only to find little sentiment for continuing; indeed, they observed a general drift back to work. The GSC then asked the executive committee for a new resolution proclaiming an official end on Tuesday, February 11.

Reflecting, in his unpublished memoirs, Wells concluded that the "loudest advocates" of the general strike were the "mass actionists," who

> formed a small but noisy fraction of organized labor. . . . One was the I.W.W . . . the other was a small number of communists who . . . were weaving romantic dreams in the belief that Russia had laid the foundation for world revolution. . . . These two factions dominated the left, but "hated each other bitterly. . . . They formed about 1/2 the [Metal Trades Council's] membership.

And that is how this ill-advised event came about. Radicals seemed possessed by a faith that somehow history was on their side, and that it would irresistibly unfold in their favor—the mystique of the general strike inspiration.

22

The Strike's Aftermath

Civil Liberties

Although the *Times* initially cautioned area employers against capitalizing on the public's embitterment against unions by reopening an open shop drive, such moderation was short-lived. The *Times* and the other dailies, the *Town Crier* and *Argus*, followed the lead of the *Star* and *P-I* and began touting Ole Hanson and Police Chief Joel Warren for having boldly faced down those involved in the General Strike. Previously, they had pictured Hanson as a clown, buffoon, and an unprincipled opportunist. On August 28, 1919, on Hanson's resignation to barnstorm the country as a Republican presidential aspirant, the *Town Crier* resumed its earlier stance, decrying his actions. The *Crier* accused him of making "political capital" from the strike and of being one of the "world's greatest advertisers." As evidence, it cited his self-portrayal in putting down the strike which:

> was begun with a well-known opposition to it among fully half the strikers themselves. . . . Government rulings were the cause of it. Right at hand was a large body of soldiers. There never was a chance for a riot or frequent affrays. The strike had lasted only three or four days, during which time there was not one affray in Seattle, not even, as the *Town Crier* recalls it, a street corner row. All that Mr. Hanson did was at the beginning to issue a proclamation that he would maintain law and order, and this he did not do until he was seriously inter-

viewed by a number of prominent business men. No sooner
was the strike broken than he was proclaimed from one part
of the country to the other. Seattle had been saved from the
torch and America from the Bolsheviki, by the good right arm
of simple citizen, loving father, the devoted husband, Hanson,
the model American. . . . [All] out of a mere proclamation
which it was in line with his sworn duty to issue." [He resigned, claiming credit for getting the Skagit site and the street
railway purchase, the latter,] made from a company which
could hardly conceal its joy in selling its assets. . . .[1]

Setting the tone for what followed in the months ahead, Chief
Warren ordered a raid on Socialist Party headquarters on February 9, arresting three men on the street for circulating the party's
newspaper. This was followed with a raid on an IWW hangout on
February 14, and the arrest of thirty-nine men because he was
"tired of reading their revolutionary circulars . . . and [I] decided
to just lock them up." Arrests like this had become traditional
under Warren. Earlier, on January 12, while the shipyard issue
was heating up, he had ordered the breakup of a parade of more
than 500 "Reds" (being witnessed by about 5,000 onlookers). He
then arrested thirteen men without charge. On January 19 about
100 Seattle police assisted Immigration Commissioner Henry White
in rounding up 316 "Russians," twenty-seven of whom were detained for investigation.[2]

During the General Strike, Warren had closed the Equity Printing Plant for printing radical literature, and on the fifteenth he
placed police on the premises to censor anything printed—the plant
manager was a leading Wobbly named Walker C. Smith. Not until
a public outcry against this violation of free speech (in which the
Star now joined, and the respected law firm of Preston and
Thorgrimson intervened), were police removed in early June. Warren had been acting, and would continue to act, under authority of
a city ordinance that gave the police chief discretion if, in his
judgment, there are actions among the citizenry that were undertaken for "unlawful purposes." It would, have been impossible to
prove in court that the chief had acted "maliciously," given this
broad legal mandate.[3]

The wartime suspension of civil liberties obviously was being
continued under terms of the Sedition Act; these actions were now
reinforced by passage of a state anti-syndicalism bill in January
1919. Under the latter, twenty-seven IWWs were being held by the
police for their ostensible leadership of the strike. When one of the
arrested, James Bruce, was successfully defended by George
Vanderveer, the twenty-four others also were freed. But Walker

Smith and two associates remained under arrest because the prosecutor thought he had a stronger case against them.

The anti-syndicalism act passed by the legislature on the first day of the session was modified at its end; but this did not deter Warren. His first arrest under the new legislation was that of James King on April 25, 1919, for collecting defense funds for the General Strike Victims Defense Committee. King was charged with "dissemination of doctrines inimical to public tranquility and orderly government." Then, on May 31 Warren broke up a meeting of 2,000, sponsored by the Union of Russian Workers—intervention in Russia was being discussed.[4]

What had become clear in all this turmoil is that the war itself was but an interlude in the struggle to organize workers, not only for more control over conditions in the workplace, but also to gain a voice in national politics and government. This pressure for change had begun as an organized protest by the nations' farmers, and now, only more coherently joined by industrial workers. It was met with resistance by large-scale employers, particularly, and their allies among the professional classes. This latter group had regained its hegemony during the war, despite short-term improvements among organized labor spawned by worker shortages. However, the outcry of the middle classes against labor's gains and federal intervention in private business through regulation and direct takeover of some economic functions, would leave the reader of conservative publications to believe that the government had gone "Bolsheviki"—the common term of political derision. This group sought a restoration not only to pre-war conditions, but to those conditions that allowed them the near-absolute control they had before all the protest began.

Under these circumstances, the question of whether legal sanction was needed to violate civil liberties, or whether it would have made a difference, is probably academic. Those who raised their voices in opposition were not were not taken seriously. Arbitrary police action became the rule. It was sanctioned by civil authorities under the rationalization that the Seattle General Strike was an attempt at revolution; therefore police actions against civil liberties were sheltered under the cloak of an ambiguous city ordinance.

Throughout the spring and summer, police continued to break up open-air meetings. Even conservatives on the Central Labor Council were outraged at these free-speech violations; they went so far as to support SCLC sponsorship of a protest meeting in mid-May at 4th Avenue and Virginia; 5,000 attended and funds were raised for the Mooney Defense Fund.[5]

Even the Health Department got into the action by closing the IWW hall in July, declaring it to be unsanitary. Not to be outdone, commissioner White arrested more than fifty Italians and Russians in May without serious charge and shipped fifty-four of them to New York for deportation (fourteen were released once they arrived.) While Mayor Hanson was out of town revealing his heroic proportions to the rest of the country, Acting-Mayor, W. D. Lane, publicly denounced these police actions. But there was no ripple effect because Hanson soon returned, puffed up and ready to continue from where he had left off.. (Before leaving the city he had dismissed labor leader George Listman from the Civil Service Commission without the required hearing, merely because Listman had provided surety for Walker Smith's bond when Smith was arrested in the Equity shutdown.)[6]

Civil liberties violations were not limited to actions by the police chief and the mayor's office. In January, the School Board had barred Socialist Max Eastman from speaking at Broadway High School auditorium, thereby reversing the 1911 policy of allowing school facilities for such public use. In early March the Board dismissed Anna Louise Strong's brother-in-law, Charles Niederhauser, for what it considered unpatriotic activities. School Superintendent, Frank B. Cooper, defended Niederhauser's teaching methods—which aimed to stimulate children to think dispassionately, and do careful research before reaching conclusions— but to no avail. Even the conservative Henry Suzzallo criticized this dismissal as being an arbitrary disregard of the facts; he contended, no university faculty would be dismissed on such flimsy evidence because Niederhauser's methods were those he— Suzzallo—advocated at the university. At this same School Board meeting of March 7, which saw the firing of Niederhauser, the Robinson and Beard textbook was also banned.[7]

Passage of the anti-syndicalism act at the beginning of the Washington's legislative session, and its revision on the last day portrays the existing climate of opinion. It represented either "collusion" or "cooperation" between the Washington State Federation of Labor and employers of moderate temperament insofar as unions are concerned. The two principals were William Short, president of the labor federation, and Mark Reed, paternalistic head of the Simpson Lumber Company and the most influential Representative in the legislature.

Reed had been able to sponsor and push through the 1917 legislature a medical aid bill that replaced the infamous hospital fee system (a fund to which only the employees contributed, but which the employers administered.) The Reed bill was one step taken to relieve tensions between employees and employers and to render radical preachings less appealing. He developed a close working relationship with Short in the process.

During the 1919 session, they met frequently, according to Joseph Tripp, historian of the state's early labor legislation. While Reed was anxious to be rid of the IWWs once and for all, so was Short. Short also wanted to neutralize employers like Edwin Ames of the Pope and Talbot firm, the Everett mill owners, and those who dominated the Employers' Association. So did Reed. Short agreed to cooperate with Reed in getting the WSFL to acquiesce in an anti-syndicalism bill in turn for Reed's supporting favorable labor actions and defeat of anti-labor measures.

Governor Lister had vetoed an anti-syndicalism bill passed by the 1917 legislature because it was too inclusive. When the 1919 legislature passed another such law, the original version forbade: "all activity which employed crime, sedition, violence, intimidation, or injury as a means of effecting any industrial, economic, social or political change." Reed amended the bill by inserting two words: "or resisting" after "effecting." Short was assured that extremists on both sides would be neutralized, and sold his colleagues on it. He also agreed to accept an "anti-sabotage" bill aimed at the IWW.

Reed then joined with Senator E. V. Kuykendall in opposing bills to outlaw strikes, to force compulsory arbitration, and to set up a police system to deal with labor unrest. Reed then got the legislature to create an Industrial Code Commission to investigate "evils existing in industrial life" and devise ways of remedying them. The commission advised creating local industrial councils to establish common ground for the conduct of labor-management issues.[8]

The future would make mincemeat of these good intentions: the ban against picketing that the St. Germain Bakery case established would be upheld by the Washington Supreme Court; and the open shop campaign would largely succeed, only to be moderated in its worst effects by recurrent labor shortages in the 1920s once the economy revived.

Dissent Within Labor

Within the union movement after World War I dissension was rampant. The progressive Duncanites, who had held the conservatives and radicals together for a decade under Jimmy Duncan's militant leadership, had lost control of the strike by being in Chicago when the radicals filled the void and took over the leadership. Furthermore, by having opposed the strike on principle, the Duncanites found it impossible to regain control. They lost to the radicals initially, and after the radical impetus waned, the conservatives then prevailed.[1]

Loss of the strike—"solidarity" hardly qualified as "victory," although it offered a face-saving pedestal for those who chose to use it—led to recriminations, right and left. Conservative locals withdrew from the Central Labor Council, leaving the Duncanites to fight it out with the radicals. Within most of the local unions factional fights between radicals and conservatives was the rule; fist fights were common. Wobblies led the radicals, often turning Central Labor Council meetings into bedlam from their seats in the gallery. So diverted was the SCLC by these internal conflicts that ongoing strikes were being run without the usual support and direction given by the council, and when the council did resume its traditional role the strikes were already lost.

The Central Labor Council was so riven that it acted against national AFL policy barring Orientals from affiliation. But, the national AFL allowed the international and local affiliates freedom to decide about Blacks. At its February 26 meeting the Council received a committee led by James Roston, representing "colored workers" complaining of discrimination against "their people," and asking that the Council use its influence to remove all barriers to their holding membership in any union. Their request was referred to the Resolutions Committee, which recommended in April that "barriers" against colored persons entering our unions be removed, and that "all locals be urged to take such steps as are necessary . . . [to provide] the same freedom for white and colored persons."

The Council concurred, and sent a resolution to the Resolutions Committee urging formation of a "pact with colored and Oriental labor." The catch was that the Council could not really compel the locals to comply; they didn't. (At the end of April fifty-seven Japanese shoe repair shops applied for a local charter in the Boot and Shoe Workers Union because the existing local would not admit them.)[2]

Deliberations within the SCLC during the spring saw the radicals aiming to unseat William Short as head of the state federation. To undermine the SCLC, they also tried to establish the Federated Unions of Seattle. And, using the unresolved status of Tom Mooney, they agitated for Seattle union participation in a nationwide general strike on July 4 to protest the Mooney conviction (later broadened to embrace defense of all political prisoners).

Further rounding out their strategy, they pressed the WSFL

also to endorse a One Big Union resolution, and agitated in support of Duncan's resolution to the AFL leadership to reorganize the federation along industrial lines. Wanting, also a medium for their radical views, they combatted Ault for control of the *Union Record*.[3]

Short won re-election overwhelmingly over the pro-OBU candidate at the June meeting of the state federation, thereby thwarting the radicals on that issue; but that result was not unexpected. Dissatisfaction, at least was registered against Short's opposition to the General Strike. The pro-OBU faction anticipated greater success with their Federated Unions proposal. Claiming that the SCLC was too busy with politics to address the economic concerns of its affiliates, the longshoremen's local had organized all of the waterfront unions into a federation and proposed that the Council promote this industrial type of organization throughout the city against AFL policy.

After a bitter debate as to whether this was "a menace to the local labor movement" a vote of 100 to forty-three declared it was, and the matter was dropped.

But, while rejecting the Federated Union proposal, the SCLC endorsed Duncan's resolution for proposing an industrial form of unionization to the national AFL. One of the strongest arguments in support of the proposal was that individual crafts in an industry bargained separately, getting different contract termination dates for each craft. This imperiled the success of any strike in a given industry because all the affected crafts could not join together without one or more of them breaking a contract whose term was yet to expire.

Contract-breaking by the unions left them vulnerable to employer attack and public opprobrium. Jurisdictional disputes among the crafts, in addition, had been a perennial problem. Also, reorganization of the AFL along industrial lines would deprive each craft of the monopoly on entry into the job market that they either had or intended to obtain. Duncanism—slowing down the radicals, and speeding up the AFL—was the main reason that Gompers and the rest of the AFL leadership considered the SCLC radical. Duncan always remained staunchly pro-AFL, as did Harry Ault; but the Duncanites remained an irritant to the national leadership and an embarrassment to Short, who found Duncan, himself, a source of bitterness during the early 1920s.

Despite Duncan's "radicalism" he played the key role in the conservative's victory over the One Big Union resolution at the June convention of the WSFL. The national AFL had threatened to withdraw the state federation's charter if the resolution passed.

He broke with the radicals, leading the SCLC to follow him; the vote was ninety-five to fifty-seven against the resolution. The Duncanites insisted on solidarity with the AFL as the only way for organized labor to succeed against the open shop drive being mounted by employers, nationwide, under an appealing rubric: the "American Plan."

To head off a move among the pro-OBU forces (centered in the central labor councils of Seattle and Tacoma) for establishing an independent labor party, Short also got the convention to agree to join the Grange and the railroad brotherhoods in a Triple Alliance "to secure remedial legislation." The Alliance's voter registration drive in August and September would scare the opposition into taking desperate measures in the fall.

The Mooney defense congress in Chicago, that had taken away the regular local leadership during general strike preparations, had agreed to promote a nationwide protest strike on July 4. Duncan and the radicals joined forces on this issue. In early April a referendum vote among all the locals was ordered. To gain public support they decided to sell tags in June, but when they applied to the returned mayor, Hanson denied them a permit, and returned the torn up request to the SCLC. In attendance at the SCLC's July 1 meeting, Agent 106, of the Associated Industries, reported that the Teamsters refused its support for reason that the strike would not be large enough to do much good; the Boilermakers, because nationwide support seemed to be lacking; and the Engineers just plain refused to participate. The strike never materialized. But the radicals maintained a domineering voice in the months ahead as polarization of industrial relations crystalized throughout the nation.[4]

Resurgence of the Open Shop Movement

> By far the most important thing in Seattle from a business standpoint, is the labor situation. The trouble, apparently beginning as far back as the Cotterel [sic] administration, is about to come to a head; labor has been fostered and sympathized with by the city government and Scrips' [sic] papers until they believe they should run the town and we think they will very soon. [February 12]. . . . We broke the Union's grip on the city and from now on, we will probably be an open shop town." [February 17]. From A. L. Kempster's *Business Conditions* Letter of February 12 and 17, 1919.

Heralding labor-management relations for the next 15 years or so, the gas company locked out union men on February 12, inviting them to tear up their union cards and work for 75 cents less a day. The Teamsters reported having trouble getting their men back at the Frye plant and at the gas company. The Central Labor Council minutes recorded many complaints of employer discrimination against the strikers, but it was helpless to act.

Adding to organized labor's woes was, first, the arrest of Ault, Strong, and other *Union Record* staffers on criminal anarchy charges—covered by the January anti-syndicalism act. Ault became diverted, while preparing for his defense, from editorial control of the paper, leaving some of the more radical staffers to write without restraint, and leaving the newspaper even more vulnerable to charges of radicalism. Next, the Chamber of Commerce urged members to boycott those businesses that advertised in the *Union Record*. The objective was to drive the newspaper out of business, because, as one of the labor spies of the soon-to-be Associated Industries of Seattle, reported: "No one can fully realize the tremendous influence this paper carries among the workers and even among a large body of small business men." Indicative, was the *Union Record*'s circulation; it surpassed that of its main rival, the *Star*. Also, in February, Seattle bankers began a boycott of the *Union Record*. And, although the Central Labor Council retaliated by establishing the Trades Union Savings and Loan Association it is doubtful that immediate relief was given the newspaper. All these actions hurt the newspaper. Then, William Short, president of the State Labor Federation, added his voice in the spring by accusing Ault of withholding federation news.[1]

The setting was perfect for reinvigorating the open shop movement. Labor scarcity during the war and the federal government, while not insisting on the closed shop for firms working on government contracts, nevertheless lent its weight toward union recognition in order to get its orders filled. These conditions combined to frustrate the open shop efforts of the Employers' Association during the war. The association was quickly replaced after the General Strike by the Associated Industries of Seattle.

The AIS was established on March 12 under the leadership of steamship executive, Frank Waterhouse. Not surprisingly, one of the first objectives was to confront the International Longshoremen's Association. In 1918 the ILA had established a closed shop on the waterfront by combining the stevedores, truckers, and checkers into "One Big Union" along the lines advocated by the IWW. On January 14, 1919 the Waterfront Employers Union signed a closed shop agreement with the ILA. But, when the ILA joined in the general strike the employers regarded the contract as broken. On March 4 the employers posted a notice to longshoremen and truckers declaring that only American citizens would be hired by them, that "any man who does not support the principles of the American government will not be employed," and that "employes [sic] individually or collectively, are invited to present for discussion and adjustment any matter of mutual interest." Disagreement occurred at the Great Northern docks April 4 when the union announced that the workers must be 100% union or the union stevedores would be withdrawn. This demand was rejected on grounds that submission would violate the policy of the Federal Railroad Administration of non-discrimination. About one-half of the union men were fired by the Great Northern and replaced with non-union men. The ILA contended that this was the opening gun of an open shop campaign, and the union was being locked out. The employers claimed it was a strike, and that "the movement was Bolsheviki in its nature"—a line of argument they continued for about thirty years.

Control of hiring became the focus of conflict. Prior to this issue the employers were required to hire men alphabetically through the union's list system; now they hired at the individual dock gates. This meant the workers had to march from dock to dock, standing in line to learn who were to be the lucky, chosen ones. University students were recruited along with soldiers and sailors looking for work at a time when jobs were in sharp decline. The strike-lockout continued until the Railroad Administration intervened in early May by ordering restoration of the previous hiring system and dismissal of the strikebreakers. This was a union victory, but one limited to the railroad docks where the Railroad Administration had jurisdiction. The ILA remained a prime target whose sway would last for only one more year.[2]

This strike-lockout experience of the waterfront employers led the Associated Industries to form a union of non-union laborers, the Associated Craftsmen and Workmen. It was funded by a wealthy AIS member, ex-Army captain, A. C. Bickford. Its nucleus was a group of American workmen—primarily ex-service men—who resented the "foreigners" and unpatriotic men having jobs they wanted. The group contended that foreigners made up sixty percent of the Seattle labor force. The organization required American nativity of its members, that no one of foreign birth be hired before them, that all labor disputes be arbitrated, and that employers be given the right to hire and fire at will. The AACW would be the waterfront employers instrument in dock disputes.

To re-establish open shop conditions that would be comparable to those before the Washington State Federation of Labor was established at the turn of the century, the Associated Industries of Seattle was to use the following tactics: coerce non-member employers to resist signing union contracts, and to assist them as needed; employ spies and provocateurs to infiltrate the labor movement; and to force the *Union Record* out of business. On the latter, the AIS continued the Chamber of Commerce's policy of discouraging businesses from advertising in the *Union Record* by impeding their operations (withholding supplies and credit, for example). Every business in the city was visited by an AIS representative to give the message. Its labor committee included Broussais Beck, manager of the Bon Marche (to whom "Agent 106" reported), C. C. Carpenter of MacDougall-Southwick Department Store, D. E. Frederick of Frederick and Nelson, Clark Nettleton of the *P-I*, C.L. Blethen of the *Times*, A. J. Rhodes of Rhodes Department Store, and H. Schoenfeld of Standard Furniture). The AIS was for all practical purposes the creature of the Chamber of Commerce. The Chamber's trustees voted in late October to oppose the closed shop, and published in three dailies a "Declaration of the Industrial Situation": ". . . every workman should have an opportunity to earn a wage proportionate to his ability and productive capacity. . . ." A referendum ballot was attached, automatically putting any non-respondent business in the questionable category.

Now, in time of peace, the Minute Men were willing to serve their original sponsors . . . employers. Having been endorsed by the Chamber of Commerce in November 1917, the organization applied for re-endorsement just before the General Strike; they received that imprimatur on February 18. The Minute Men were, apparently, working in tandem, if not directly with the AIS, for Agent 106 reported in May, the "rumor" that they had infiltrated the Soldiers and Sailors Council and moved the council's offices to their own building for closer collaboration. As a result, a new SSC was organized to replace the now-phony one.[3]

As to the shipyard workers strike, it continued into early March, when the workers returned only to resume negotiations. The time was not propitious, because the Shipping Board cancelled more contracts in early May. The Metal Trades Council was then directed by its international officers to confer with the employers, then to meet with the international officers in June to review any tentative agreement terms that might have been worked out. When the shipbuilders and the union did reach an agreement the Shipping Board rejected it, even though the federal representatives who participated in the negotiations, had approved it. After some bickering with the Board Seattle yards were allowed an increase.

At the end of March, and just before Kempster could report

for his last time (the City would take over the traction part of the company's operations on April 1) that the shipyards were back to normal, having "absorbed most of Seattle's idle labor." His successor as reporter, Donald Barnes, wrote in June that the yards were working at "war time speed," setting a new record in May—eight ships were delivered to the Shipping Board that month alone. This activity would continue, at least for the rest of 1919. The growing passivity of the shipyard workers was registered in August when Skinner and Eddy cut wages for the first time, causing not a whimper so far as the public could tell.

In this same month the street car trainmen, now under civil service, got a long-postponed wage increase, protesting its niggardly amount, but not striking. And, longshoremen accepted an increase by giving the employers control of hiring and firing.

September saw mounting tension locally, while Boston policemen went on strike, and on the 21st a nationwide steel strike began to the accompaniment of gross civil liberties violations under the cloak of the unabated "Red scare" that possessed practically all civil authorities. The steel strike lasted two months, cost twenty lives, and helped pave the way for further encroachments on Bill of Rights "guarantees." By its failure, also, the twelve-hour day would remain the norm, and the open shop would become the national standard.

Besides the closure of steel plants in Seattle, a strike of 500 tailors (including 200 women) got underway on September 15—custom made clothes were still holding their own against factory made products. (Agent 181 would report to AIS officer, Roy Kinnear, in March 1920, that 130 tailors were still on strike, over 100 were working in fair shops, about 100 had left the city, and about 100 are back at work for fourteen dollars a week).

Just as a residential housing building boom was peaking the carpenters went on strike when the Master Builders Association had refused to confer with the Building Trades Council about contract negotiations. The MBA declared for the open shop, bringing in strikebreakers for the purpose. Independent builders continued to operate, however, paying the union scale. Gradually, the workers returned, and open shop conditions became standard by the first week of November.

A gas workers strike had been going on for five weeks, but it was proving ineffective, as the company was operating at normal levels by the end of October. In September lady barbers were on strike, along with the printers. In the latter strike against ninety-seven shops the Associated Industries had threatened businesses with retaliation if they sent work to the union shops. Shipwrights were reported to be working under open shop conditions. Then, on November 1 a nationwide coal miners strike closed down the Green River region mines and those at Roslyn and Cle Elum.

As though the labor movement was not meeting enough trouble from its traditional opposition, the City Council decided to join in. In mid-October, by a five to four vote, it passed a bill making it unlawful "to organize, help to organize, give aid to or voluntarily assemble with any organization or group of persons which advocate crime, sedition, violence, intimidation or injury as a means of effecting or resisting any industrial, economic, social or political change." Although the "foreign war" had ended the war on the domestic front had resumed with renewed vigor, having all the features of a class war; the employers—at least the militants among them who had taken over the class leadership—thought of themselves as the class saviors. Councilmen who retained their senses were Erickson, Lane, and two union men: Hesketh and Bolton. It was the temper of the time. And this was before the Centralia Massacre inflamed tempers even further, helping to sustain the open shop movement.[4]

All of this local and national turmoil in industrial relations prompted President Wilson to call representatives of labor, employers, and the general public to the nation's capital in the fall, hoping to find a way towards peaceful settlement. Preceding this conference the president held a meeting in mid-September with Duncan, L. W. Buck, secretary of the state labor federation, and C. R. Cottrell, secretary of the recently formed Triple Alliance. The three described to Wilson the present labor unrest in the Northwest, the abuse and torture of Hulet Wells at McNeil Island and requested his pardon; and they suggested that industry might be best organized along cooperative lines. This meeting resulted in nothing concrete, although it was indicative of the importance Wilson attached to industrial unrest in the region. That a cooperative form of industrial organization be offered in place of the inherently strife-afflicted capitalist system also indicates how nonradical was the city and state's organized labor movement—also, how regionally insular and unique it really was.[5]

The Triple Alliance, which had been formed during the meeting of the State Federation of Labor in June, had been organizing district central committees to conduct local political races. In the March city election three labor candidates had been put up by the Central Labor Council and they had been badly beaten. The Triple Alliance was intended to help in the December elections, when two School Board members and two Port Commissioners were to be voted upon. Not only was education of workers' children important, but $5 million to be spent on building construction was of concern to the building trades, and the Port had had a union recognition policy.

An active voter registration campaign was causing some alarm among members of the AIS, but Agent 106 reassuringly reported that radicals at the SCLC the meetings were staunchly opposing the Triple Alliance—the radicals, in the syndicalist tradition, eschewed political action, hoping and expecting a revolutionary spark would soon leave capitalism in ashes. Confidently, Short wrote to Frank Morrison in early October, that he was meeting success in his statewide campaign to "combat the disruptionists," and that in six months time " we will see a radical change for the good."

Bickford, secretary of the AIS, betrayed none of the detachment conveyed by his agent. He urged opposition to the alliance and its "Red" leaders if Americanism were to be preserved; he urged employers to have their employees register and to check the registration books to make sure they do. Cataclysmic events were to threaten success of the Alliance before December.[6]

Centralia Massacre and Its Aftermath

Tensions were tightening from vigilante takeover in Centralia prior to the fateful November 11, when American Legionnaires broke into the IWW hall, resulting in two deaths and the lynching of one Wobbly, Wesley Everett. The *Union Record* appealed to its readers to postpone judgment until the facts of the Centralia Massacre were known. Clarence Blethen then organized a raid on the *Union Record* by soldiers and sailors; he even had a "dummy" account of the raid preprinted for inclusion in the *Times's* next issue. But the *Union Record* organized its own soldiers and sailors, forcing a standoff.

Blethen then took the aging United States Attorney, Robert Saunders (who owed his position to Blethen's influence) to Tacoma where he coerced Saunders into signing an order closing down the *Union Record* on grounds of sedition. Tacoma reporters telegraphed the story to Seattle so that news of impending federal raid appeared before the event took place. To head off a radical takeover, Labor Federation President Short promptly issued a proclamation urging workers to "'KEEP COOL,' Don't Start Anything. . . . Your representatives will take care of every contingency in a lawful and orderly manner."

Saunders, on returning to Seattle, was asked how long the closure would last. He said that it was only temporary and that the *Union Record* could resume publishing. When Blethen learned of this, he immediately corralled the dependent Saunders and coerced him into signing a permanent restraining order. Blethen then got Seattle's postmaster to ban the *Union Record* from the mails, thereby contributing to a loss of revenue that became an enduring financial burden and the disappearance of a voice for labor in outlying areas.

Short then rushed to Washington, D. C., and got the ban lifted after only six days. The *Union Record* had been published at a Fremont print shop in the interim. Agent 106 reported the shutdown was the "topic of discussion" at the Labor Temple; he also volunteered that employers wanted it shut down before the election because of the huge labor vote registration. The agent also reported later in the week that Ault was planning to expand the *Union Record*, but not until he had first combatted the allegedly phony Newsboys Union, which was dominated by "corner owners," and had them replaced with "real newsboys."[1]

It became clear that the three other major daily newspapers wanted to wipe out *Union Record* competition. Blethen began to buy up the *Union Record*'s newsprint supply, forcing Ault to pay higher prices than the competition. Then the *Times, Star,* and *P-I* lowered their prices from five to two cents, forcing the *Union Record* to meet the new standard—at a time when Ault needed money to fight sedition charges against himself, Strong, and George Listman. For his part, Listman was running for a School Board position on the December election. The arrest did not favor his candidacy in light of the declared hostility of the other dailies.

Fearing a loss of credibility among the rank and file AFL, Short wrote to the organization's secretary, Frank Morrison, on October 23, declaring that "Seattle is in the throes of a general open shop fight, especially in the building and printing lines.˙.˙.˙. [Please request the internationals to authorize strike action to] restore general confidence in the National Movement." After the Centralia Massacre, he wrote to Gompers that open shop forces are taking advantage by "fastening responsibility on the legitimate labor movement." He added that there was no justification for the raid on the *Union Record* because the "paper has been pursuing a rational and constructive policy for some time and I have read nothing in it in recent weeks that would justify action against it." The friction between him and Ault had ended as Ault resumed editorial control and also moved toward conservatism—inevitably so, for his being the object of continued radical attacks.[2]

Puget Sound Power and Light's Donald Barnes conveyed to Boston that suppression of the *Union Record* ". . . from a civic and patriotic standpoint . . . has been a good thing and probably will result in a thorough cleaning in the Northwest."

Indicative of the genuine uneasiness felt by business leaders at the time of the Centralia Massacre was the unrealistic fear expressed by steamship executive Frank Waterhouse at the November 13 meeting of the Chamber of Commerce. He spoke alarmingly about the potential "damage to the Chamber of Commerce building or prominent men associated with it." The trustees, at the recommendation of Thomas Burke and former Senator Samuel Piles, authorized the chamber's president to take steps to "protect the meeting place and the lives of those who are here. . . ."

Although the open shop forces had a field day after Centralia, one of their proponents, Edwin Selvin, advocated in his *Business Chronicle*, that the cure for labor radicalism was more violent vigilantism. At the request of the Metal Trades Council police arrested Selvin. His name was tacked on to the list of *Union Record* employees who were charged with sedition. On December 2, the grand jury indicted Ault, Listman, and other newspaper officers, but dismissed charges against Selvin. (Listman's opponent for the School Board position was foreman of the grand jury, Ebenezer Shorrock.)[3]

23

The Labor Movement Turns to Politics

Despite the negative repercussions of the General Strike of 1919, membership in most unions affiliated with the Central Labor Council (SCLC) grew until after June 1920. Throughout 1919 Metal Trades Section unions faced the most serious losses as a result of shipyard contract terminations. However, one-half of the SCLC unions were not affiliated with the State Federation of Labor, and most of these were small unions in which the "new immigrants" were concentrated. In labor historian Jonathan Dembo's judgment, these unions harbored most of the radical elements.

When unemployment began to spread after June 1920, these union members were hardest hit. They had resisted political action and had not been involved in the Triple Alliance campaign of late 1919. They also tended to drift toward the splinter groups of the socialists that were seeking to reestablish their foundations in the wake of the Russian Revolution and the anti-radical, anti-alien hysteria enveloping the United States. In effect, these groups had been politically neutered; consequently, it was not surprising that they advocated and used direct action. When the King County Triple Alliance revived during the year, these unionists were largely left out.

One consequence of the General Strike and the Centralia Massacre was the loss of whatever middle-class support the radical-leaning Seattle labor movement had retained. The conservative press continued attacks on the Central Labor Council for not "cleaning house" and for remaining under "Red" control. Violations of civil liberties were everyday occurrences and were accepted as normal procedures for protecting American democracy. Seattle's police, acting under the "anti-red" ordinance, would, in their sweeps of known transient and blue-collar hangouts, pick up more than a hundred suspects, keep them overnight without charging them, and retain for further questioning anyone known to be a criminal, illegal alien, or radical. This kind of police activity was, however, conducted nationwide.[1]

The open shop drive continued unabated, feeding on the public's uneasiness about the local and national strikes that seemed to threaten the America's democratic foundations. The "American Plan" of open shop advocates that had been formulated by John D. Rockefeller, was vigorously adopted by employer groups nationwide under the leadership of Judge Elbert Gary, head of United States Steel. Gary pointed the way to the future in his breaking of the 1919 steel strike.

Locally, the "Wobbly Horrors" and the 1919 General Strike combined to give the national movement a head start in Seattle. But, as a driving force, it seemed to stop abruptly in Seattle in September 1920. In Dembo's view, this cessation came about more because of the production decline and "high cost of living" than because of any union activity. However, the historian of the *Seattle Union Record*, Mary Joan O'Connell, conveys the opinion of its publisher, Harry Ault, that he and Saul Haas forced its termination when they threatened to expose the banks for their role in the open shop campaign and for their harassment of the newspaper.

Whatever the reason, most campaign objectives had been accomplished. In the years to follow, unions usually would lose whenever they tried to organize or gain collective bargaining rights. In any case, the open shop movement, which had begun just as the city was recovering from the 1893-1896 depression, had never ceased.[2]

One other wrinkle in the open shop dispute strongly suggests the Chamber of Commerce and Commercial Club's concern over Seattle's reputation for unstable labor relations played a role in this change. There were strikes after the General Strike, and although they usually had been broken and the open shop had replaced the closed shop, Seattle's reputation did not improve. Too much national publicity about putting down strikers had produced a kind of boomerang effect.

A "misunderstanding" arose in October when Associated Industries took exception to a pamphlet published by the Chamber of Commerce's Labor Relations Committee. The tract, titled *Profitism, Slackism and You: A Constructive Study of the Labor Problem*, was written by Melvin W. Cassmore of the Society of Industrial Engineers. In the publication, Cassmore contended that, although the general public had supported the employers in their open shop drive after the General Strike, "more than the open shop is wanted [to get] results in the form of labor peace and increased productivity." Cassmore argued that, although profiteering would be taken care of by the market and the courts, productivity could be increased only by cooperation between employers and employees; the general consumer would be the ultimate beneficiary. The subject needed to be approached, he argued, "with [an] open and unprejudiced mind." What he advocated was a shop committee system like that developed in Great Britain. By this system adequate provision could made "for Employees, through their chosen representatives, to meet periodically with the management for discussion and settlement of questions about industrial relations, the welfare of the industry, and its workers." Bonuses would be an integral part of the plan to provide the incentive for increasing productivity and to isolate uncooperative workers from their fellows, targeting them for dismissal.

This tract so upset the Associated Industries that its leadership requested a special meeting with the Chamber. It was held on October 19. The Chamber was criticized for its apparent choice of an alternative to the open shop, and reminded the Chamber that before the General Strike, 85 percent of the Associated Industries employers were operating under closed shop conditions, while now 75 percent were under the "American Plan."

The association claimed 2,500 members, and that through its American Craftsmen and Workmen organization of 3,600 workmen, it had placed 8,000 men in city plants. With this recitation as background, the chamber then humbled itself by declaring that it would not publish anything again on labor relations without first submitting it to the Associated Industries for approval. The chamber assured the association that it had not usurped these functions from the association. It was sorry about "the damage from publication of the Chamber report." In the future the chamber would let the Associated Industries speak for it in labor relations.[3]

In the face of losing the economic power it had acquired during the labor shortage of the war years, and in the face of the national AFL's political neutrality, Seattle labor had become restless. The Triple Alliance that was established in June 1919 was dominated by the Washington State Federation of Labor. It had struck a chord of fear among conservatives by its successful voter registration drive before the Centralia Massacre. But in the weeks following, the press and civil authorities were able to blunt the drive's effectiveness. This was attested to by the failure of Alliance-supported candidates in the December school-board and port-commission elections.

Be mindful that the middle and upper classes tended to consider all labor organizations as being radical because the prerogatives of owners of capital were considered by many to be absolute. The constitution was intended, in their view, to protect use of all property from interference, and the weight of judiciary opinion had consistently upheld this interpretation. Although the Sherman Anti-Trust Act of 1890 was the second real assertion of police power to regulate business (the Interstate Commerce Act of 1887 was the first), it was difficult to enforce against business, and, ironically, the legislation was used mainly against unions when they went out on strike.

In the early twentieth century, the judiciary gradually allowed legislatures and Congress to exercise police powers more often as the abuses of absolute power by the owners of capital became a greater threat to society. Gradually, the courts allowed the Sherman Act and the Interstate Commerce Act to be enforced.

Some elements of organized labor, particularly in the State of Washington, had become politically involved. Both the State Federation of Labor and the Seattle Central Labor Council joined with many middle-class groups to make the city and state better places in which to live.

The General Strike of 1919 represented a temporary loss of SCLC control by the Duncanites, who had dominated the council for years. After regaining the upper hand, the Duncanites became politically involved once again, but more directly, by actually forming their own party—the Democratic Party in the state was practically defunct, and the Republican Party usually was dominated by its most reactionary elements. Duncanism was not radical in this sense; it represented a dissatisfaction with the two major parties because they had become indistinguishable one from the other. As such, dissent found expression in a third party movement which only sought to make the existing social and economic system more bearable.

At this time, left-wing radicalism—inspired by the Russian Revolution and the expectation that capitalism would collapse—decimated the Socialist Party and the Industrial Workers of the World. Miniscule Communist off-shoots sprung forth, each preoccupied with its own peculiar doctrinal squabble or organizational dilemma. Substantially all of these Socialist Party and IWW remnants eschewed "parliamentarism," and preferred that the AFL disappear. All of the above comments are to remind the reader that the Seattle labor movement was, despite its eccentricity, a very "American" phenomenon.

That it became susceptible to suspicions of being radical, or even Bolsheviki, is a testimony to the pervasiveness of a mass hysteria that was whipped up against dissidents during World War I, and especially after the Russian Revolution. Open-shop advocates seized the chance to destroy organized labor—unless they, themselves did the organizing, as was the case with the Loyal Legion of Loggers and Lumbermen.[4]

Nevertheless, undaunted, the SCLC turned toward the upcoming city election of March 1920. It put up James Duncan for mayor, and endorsed incumbents: Hesketh, Lane, and Erickson, and six others. The King County Triple Alliance endorsed the SCLC ticket to the dismay of the three councilmanic incumbents, who promptly boycotted a Duncan-for-mayor meeting in order to steer clear of the Alliance. The Washington State Triple Alliance, which was dominated by the State Federation of Labor, refused to support its King County affiliate.

Other mayoral candidates were the incumbent Fitzgerald and Hugh Caldwell. The *Times* set the election's tone by practically ignoring Duncan while attacking the Alliance as a "Red ring" seeking "minority rule" and bringing "foreign materialism" to Seattle along with "class rule." The Duncan-Triple Alliance group was referred to as the "Who-Knows-Where-Ticket," reminding readers of Anna Louise Strong's trumpeting of the General Strike.

The *Times* hoped to divert supporters of Caldwell to its candidate, Councilman, C. B. Fitzgerald, in order to beat the popular Duncan. Caldwell, however, refused to run an anti-union campaign, although he was unsympathetic to unions. With the conservative forces split, Duncan ran just 2,000 votes behind Caldwell and ahead of Fitzgerald in the primaries. While the *Star* remained neutral, the *Times* and *P-I* joined in support of Caldwell, assuring Duncan's defeat by 17,000 votes, but not without him picking up 7,000 more votes than he did in the primaries. The *Times*, characteristically, rumored that Duncan wanted to establish a "Soviet form of government" and that he would "nationalize" women—and Duncan a church-going, prohibitionist, family man! Nevertheless, this show of strength lent encouragement to the third party movement, then underway. (July found Duncan chairing the convention of the National Labor Party in Chicago, at which the party name was changed to the "Farmer-Labor Party.")

On April 14, 1920, the Central Labor Council voted to affiliate with the National Labor Party, thereby splitting the state Alliance and Labor Federation simultaneously. This party was modeled on the British Labor Party and it planned to enter a full slate of candidates in the general election.

The Council also chose to support the state Triple Alliance, despite its unwillingness to help Duncan in the mayoral race; he was too radical for the farmers and the railway union leaders. Differences were buried temporarily, however, as they headed toward the fall election. Consequently, the four "producers" organizations: the Non-Partisan League, Triple Alliance, the Railwaymen's Political Club, and the Committee of 48 (a liberal rump of the Democratic Party) agreed to hold their state conventions simultaneously in Yakima in July. The purpose was to agree on a joint platform, candidates, and to decide whether or not to enter the Republican or Democratic party primaries, or to form an independent party.

The Non-Partisan League was strongest in eastern Washington; the Alliance was really the State Federation of Labor by now, and its strength lay in the western part of the state; the Railwaymen were strongest in eastern Washington; and the Committee of 48 tried to appeal to the liberal Democrats who had become discouraged with the policies of Wilson and Lister. (The Committee of Forty-eight included among its members City Councilman Lane, Viola Crahan of the Federation of Women's Clubs, and Port of Seattle Counsel C. J. France.)

The four groups had no trouble agreeing on a platform. Whether to run in the Republican primary or launch a third party was the sticky issue. Since the NPL and Railwaymen were nonpartisan, it was in the Alliance meeting that the issue was hotly debated. Short, of the state federation, argued for entering the Republican primary (the Democratic Party was written off), while the Socialists and labor radicals fought for a third party. The latter group won out, and Short accepted the verdict—to the dismay of Gompers and the national AFL leadership.

Following this outcome in the Alliance meeting, a compromise was worked out with the other non-partisan groups. The latter chose to enter the Republican primaries in eastern Washington, and the Alliance would enter a third party in western Washington. It voted to join the national Farmer-Labor Party. Then the King County Non-Partisan League rejected the action of the state body and voted to support the Farmer-Labor Party; five other county NPL bodies followed this lead. Their gubernatorial candidate was former Seattle Port Commissioner, Robert Bridges. He, already, had been barnstorming the state to promote the Farmer-

Labor Party, and had rejected the invitation from the NPL and Railwaymen to run as their gubernatorial candidate in the Republican primary, coupled with grange leader, Elihu Bowles as lieutenant-governor.

The new party drew heavily on disenchanted Democratic Party members, leaving the party in complete control of the conservatives, and without significant popular support. The Farmer-Labor Party ran Bowles for lieutenant-governor, Duncan for Congress in the First District, and C. J. France for Senate. Interest focused on the gubernatorial race because it provided the best chance for FLP success. As expected, the FLP was attacked for being dissident in general; but unexpectedly, the race issue was raised, and it colored the entire campaign.

Anti-Japanese feelings were running high in Washington in 1920. Following California's lead, Washington farmers agitated for an anti-alien land law aimed at Japanese residents. An initiative to that effect had just failed narrowly to qualify for the 1920 ballot. Democratic candidate, W. W. Black, in desperation, attacked Bridges for having leased some of his land to two Japanese farmers. Bridges, consistent with the "Equality" plank in the party's platform, defended his leasing on that ground and spoke out against exclusion legislation. This lost him considerable farmer support; and probably significant working class support, given the traditional bias against "cheap Oriental labor."

When the Farmer-Labor Party presidential candidate came to town and revealed his organization's advocacy of stricter immigration laws, Bridges' cause was further undermined. That he managed to garner 121,371 votes against Governor Hart's 210,662 seems incredible (Black received only 66,079). Even France, practically unknown in the state, received 99,309 votes (30,000 more than well-known Democrat George Cotterill). These strong showings at the polls attested to the relative strength of the new party, and to its hopes for the future.[5]

24

Municipal Ownership II

City Light and the Skagit

In August of 1918 City Light received permission from the Federal Trade Commission's Capital Issues Sub-Committee to issue a bond to pay for initial work on the Skagit River Gorge dam site. In preparation for the work, J. D. Ross immediately ordered a survey, but had to call it off once it began to snow. Ross believed that power from the Skagit would be forthcoming quickly enough to support area war production, but hostilities ended within three months. With the war over, City Light's obligations to the Capital Issues Sub-Committee, in particular those requiring the tie-in with the private company's lines, were ended.

City Light's power was generated at two locations: the Cedar River Dam and the Lake Union steam plant, which drew also on the reservoir at Volunteer Park. The Cedar River Dam had produced 10,000 kilowatts since December 1918 despite its seepage problems. With the addition of two boilers, the steam plant was able to produce 22,000 kilowatts; but this power was generated by expensive oil. However, Ross now believed seepage at the dam could never be eliminated; therefore, he expected to abandon the location for the site of the old wooden structure upstream. Councilman Erickson, however, opposed Ross in this matter. To get

Erickson's support for the Skagit, Ross would have to concede to Erickson on the sealing issue.[1]

Erickson's opposition to Ross's Skagit plans stemmed only in part from their differences over the sealing of the Cedar River Dam. They had locked horns previously over rates: as early as 1911 Erickson pressed for charges lower than those advocated by Ross; and Erickson, in his capacity as chair of the Council's Utilities Committee, interjected that group's concerns into administrative detail, as well as the making of policy.

For his part, Ross preferred long-range hydroelectric power development of the Skagit for Seattle, and he would push for other public power developments to serve rural customers and municipalities, as well. In time, he entertained the idea of constructing interties—a strategy that private power companies employed during the 1920s. With these strategic goals in view, Ross recommended the cessation of the Cedar River sealing operation and the construction of a 8,500 foot-long tunnel under Cedar Lake (to be used during the three years while the Skagit project was moving ahead). Ross believed the tunnel could triple the facility's capacity, and that construction costs would be paid back by savings in fuel costs of the Lake Union steam plant. The vulnerability of City Light's power source was dramatically demonstrated during a fuel shortage in June 1920, when Seattle had to contract with the ship *Devolante* for use of its oil.[2]

Erickson proved lukewarm to the entire Skagit project, having advocated in 1917 the purchase of a Stillaguamish River site as a cheaper power source. In his opposition to the Skagit project he got the City Council to back him in March 1919 when they denied funds to City Engineer, A. H. Dimock, for test drilling at Ruby Creek. Dimock was testing for bedrock to find the best location for a dam, and had had only limited success on Gorge Creek. Erickson insisted on a strict interpretation of the ordinance specifying only Gorge Creek and got a majority to join him. Donald Barnes reported to Stone and Webster on March 1, "...the outlook for the project is dubious." On March 11, he rejoiced ". . . a number of the councilmen [are] hampering and delaying the engineering department as much as possible." It seemed only a question of time before PSP&L could take it over.[3]

Dimock and Ross wanted only a crib dam at the Gorge site, and a masonry dam at Ruby. Paving the way for these projects in early May, Councilman Fitzgerald introduced and secured passage of two ordinances that allowed test drilling on the Ruby and Diablo creeks. Soon, these investigations revealed 200 feet of bedrock. Dimock and Ross were comforted by this discovery because it meant that the Gorge dam could be built less expensively and quicker as an earth-filled structure, and then permanent dams could be constructed upstream.

In September, the council approved $420,000 for preliminary work; this action was taken without debate, though Erickson and Lane voted against the authorization. Now, the Chamber of Commerce and the *Times* urged an investigation to learn the feasibility of the entire project, a stance they would take throughout the period. A frequent theme was the *Times*'s charge that City Light was selling power below cost and of operating at a perpetual loss. The Municipal League came to City Light's defense, along with the *Union Record* and the *P-I*, after William Randolph Hearst took it over; the latter touted the need for increased power to attract industry.

Between June and September Ross and Dimock persuaded the Council to appropriate $1.25 million for enlarging the Lake Union steam plant—the essential element in Ross' strategy of keeping up with and cultivating demand while the Skagit project was moving along its rough road to completion. (The steam plant supplied 46.9 percent of the electricity in the City's system in 1919.)

City Light weathered 1920 without accomplishing much by way of increasing its power generating capacity; but at year's end the City Council authorized the sale of $2,005,000 of utility bonds. One million dollars was for the Skagit project, and the rest was earmarked for extensions to existing plant—Ross agreed to continue with the sealing operation to gain Erickson's support. The utility seemed ready to move ahead.[4]

The Street Railway System

Before the street railway agreement between the City and Stone and Webster could be implemented the State Supreme Court had to approve the contract. Approval was registered on March 4, 1919. This action set the stage for takeover by the city on April 1. A. W. Leonard, president of the Puget Sound Traction, Light, and Power Company promised to deliver on that date 500 street cars, 210 miles of track, real estate, and 3,000 employees; but the company would cling to the power substations that were required to supply power to the trolleys. In the absence of an inventory that should have been compiled at the time of agreement in September 1918 Leonard's listing had to suffice.

Three issues faced City Utilities Superintendent Thomas Murphine: funds to upgrade the system, heading off a threatened strike for higher wages, and competition among jitney drivers.

Murphine requested $750,000 for embarking on about thirty projects. But most of the extensions and improvements citizens had pleaded for had to be postponed. However, the granting of free transfers between lines was forthcoming immediately, to everyone's relief.

The strike that had been threatened in August, before the contract was signed, and that had been postponed, was now threatened again if wage increases were not granted. Murphine, with City Council approval, established a wage scale providing $4.25 per day for the first six months of employment, $4.50 for the next six months, and $4.75 thereafter; this was an improvement over the traction company's hourly rates of forty-six, forty-eight, and fifty cents.

This scale left union members unhappy. Instead, they pressed for an eight-hour day and time and a half for overtime. The City Council acceded to this demand on May 19. But by mid-June the union requested $6.00 per day for trainmen. Negotiations continued into August, with agreement on a scale of $4.75, $5.00, and $5.25 per eight-hour day. Demonstrated here was evidence of a political force among civil service employees—especially strong when firemen and policemen were added—that would carry critical weight in the fight over the city manager and charter revision issues in the mid-1920s, and would short circuit Bertha Landes's mayorship.

Net revenues showed a modest rise during the first few months of operation in 1920, enough in Murphine's opinion to postpone a fare increase; but this promising start was not sustained. So, when Ole Hanson resigned on August 27 his mayoral successor, C. B. Fitzgerald, concentrated on jitney competition that had plagued the traction company and Colonel Blethen. Although the number of jitneys had been reduced from about 550 prior to the 1915 bonding requirement, to about 185, many operators made a practice of racing ahead of the trolleys and picking up waiting passengers. He wanted these vehicles restricted to serving as feeder lines, but the City Council would not agree to such regulation. Loss of revenue from this source and the wage increases resulted in a net loss of $517,173 for the first nine months of operation.

Hugh Caldwell had been Corporate Counsel at the time the purchase had been negotiated; but he resigned to take a commission in the Army. Now, he chose to run in the mayoral race of March 1920, promising to conduct an investigation of the street railway negotiations, fully expecting to find evidence of fraud and bribery.

If these suspicions were found to be valid, it was hoped that the contract could be voided or that the City could be indemnified. Upon his election to office, he fired Murphine, and he asked the Council to regulate jitneys. When the council passed a jitney ordinance that routed them out of competition, jitney drivers got the ordinance shelved in mid-June. A year later the jitneys would finally be ousted for good.

As to the investigation, Caldwell appointed the law firm of Tucker and Hyland to undertake it. They hired the Burns detective agency to do the sleuthing, and Cyrus Whipple to evaluate the properties. Neither investigation turned up anything new. Moreover, Murphine's replacement, Carl Reeves, could find no reports or inventories of the transferred properties; Caldwell was convinced that the records were never transferred. Whipple concluded that the value did not exceed $7,843,000. The Grand Jury, however, did find evidence that the Emergency Fleet Corporation representatives had manipulated the sale in the following telegram sent to the EFC office, September 9, 1918:

> Our efforts to get consent of City Council to increase in fare failed because of strong pro municipal ownership feeling on part of City Council and people and because of antagonism to local company. Taylor and I [Mr. Appel] therefore sold street railway lines to City for fifteen million dollars.

For the cloud that hung over the street railway purchase, the role of Walter Meier, as indicated in chapter 18, should not be overlooked. He had been assistant to Corporate Counsel Caldwell, and succeeded to the latter's position when Caldwell joined the Army. He disclaimed during the investigation that he had ever been involved in the transaction, that he had merely handled the papers of the deal after Caldwell's departure. However, it is significant that he subsequently joined the Company to joust on its behalf with City Light's J. D. Ross during the 1920s. Note also should be taken of ex-Mayor Hanson's departure to California where began his lucrative promotion of a real estate venture at San Clemente, his health fully recovered apparently. He was soon to be joined by his old friend Tom Murphine.[1]

The stage was now set for the dramatic contest over the next two decades between PSP&L and City Light, each with its traditional allies, interweaving with politics at city, county, state, and federal levels. While Ross focused on the Skagit project and alliance with other public ownership forces, the company and its counterparts and allies sought obstruction of that project and the public ownership forces represented primarily by the Grange.

Ross wanted to take over the company's city plant. The company, in turn, wanted to take over the City's plant. Its tactical gambit was to link the street railway's bonded debt with that acquisition. Events that highlight these attempts are: defeat of the Municipal League's City Manager proposition in 1925-1926, and the substitution of a freeholder's charter revision; an agreement between Mayor Bertha Landes and A. W. Leonard that did link the street railway and the city's electric plant; the firing of Ross by Mayor Frank Edwards; and the injection of the Grange District Power initiative into the overall picture. This would all be partially resolved by Mayor Arthur B. Langlie's adroit separation of the street railway's debt and rehabilitation from the city's attempts to acquire company property in Seattle and the company's parallel resistance to the Grange forces in acquiring its electrical holdings elsewhere in western Washington.

Concluding Comments

In large part, the wartime years and those of the early post-World War I period set the tone for Seattle throughout the 1920s and the Hoover years of the Great Depression. During these subsequent decades, Seattle's old problems were dramatically resurrected and upscaled: mass, chronic unemployment, which only made acutely inadequate the existing relief programs still covered by the antiquated poor laws; widespreading social and political protest; and conflict over the roles to be played by state and federal governments when attempting to deal with these and other problems generated by the system's failure.

Organized labor, once a political force in Seattle, became politically neutered by the end of 1920 by the local open-shop movement; this was the city's contribution to the nationwide "American Plan." Internal fights in the Central Labor Council extended the effects of the open shop as the CLC continued to "clean house"—something the Chamber of Commerce had been urging since the time of the General Strike of 1919. In the course of these events, the Teamsters developed into the city's most vital union. This organization adapted to the transportation revolution made possible by new technology, the internal combustion engine. The Teamsters not only took control of the Central Labor Council, but they accumulated their own political power, which would not be fully demonstrated until the mid-1930s. At that time, Teamsters were able to appeal to business leaders, offering their organization as a counterweight to the freshly politicized labor movement born of the early New Deal legislation.

While prohibition enforcement remained an issue throughout the 1920s, primarily it would color the decade, fading and shining ephemerally, just as vice, the gambling rackets, and moral reforms —as issues—had done earlier. The municipal ownership movement of the city's first two decades came to dominate city politics throughout the 1920s. Municipal ownership, in the century's first two decades, more than any other issue, had bound together those groups advocating reform. It endured long after the "moral issues" themselves—which had so often ignited the individual political campaigns—had subsided and were forgotten.

We have witnessed a setting of the stage, on which the issue of municipal ownership played itself out: the city's bonded indebtedness to Stone and Webster for purchase of the company's defunct street railway would be used by its Puget Sound Power and Light Company subsidiary as a tactic for acquiring Seattle's own electrical properties. City Light's Skagit project would become the main battle site. However, statewide consolidation of private power company control of all available hydroelectric power sites was countered by City Light's alliances with the State Grange and other municipal power utilities (mainly the one in Tacoma). This public ownership alliance would lead to voter approval of the Grange's District Power Initiative in 1930. The following year would see Mayor Frank Edwards recalled for firing City Light's J. D. Ross in what a majority of voters viewed as a measure of PSP&L's baleful political influence.

As the 1930s drew to a close, so too, would one long phase of the public ownership battle. At that time, Mayor Arthur B. Langlie skillfully exploited the willingness of Stone and Webster to settle their struggle with the city for about half the bonded debt. In addition, he took full advantage of the federal government's willingness to contribute funds to refinance and rehabilitate the ramshackle street railway system.

Throughout the contest with Puget Sound Power and Light, the Municipal League would prove to be a City Light stalwart. As it had from its inception in 1910, the league defended the Skagit project time and again against the incessant attacks mounted by the Chamber of Commerce and the *Times*. Notably, the *P-I* would join the *Star* in supporting public ownership once Hearst took over the *P-I* in 1921. As to the fate of the Municipal League's city manager plan in 1914, it met with Ross's determined opposition and defeat when reintroduced in 1925. Ross saw the hand of the "Power Trust" looming in the mist of city-manager rhetoric.

During World War I Seattle witnessed the disintegration of the coalition of middle-class businessmen and professionals, who looked to the Municipal League for leadership; to the Central Labor Council as representative of organized labor; to the Federation of Women's Clubs for providing political and moral expression of the desires of many women's organizations; to the Ministerial Federation for providing moral leadership according to the social gospel; and to the North End Federation (of community clubs) as the most ardent neighborhood proponent of municipal ownership. The period of the coalition's greatest effectiveness was from 1909 through 1916. During that time women exercised their right to vote, first by helping to recall Mayor Hiram Gill in 1911; they were also critical in the enactment of most of the reform measures enacted during the period. Finally, the Central Labor Council joined in support of all reform legislation that was passed during the era. But the coalition's most stunning victory might well have been the referendum defeat in 1916 of the reactionary legislation passed by the 1915 Washington Legislature.

Cracks began to appear in the coalition as early as 1914, when Seattle's open shop movement took on fresh life. At that time, the Employers' Association assumed almost tyrannical control of employer negotiations with organized labor. The prolonged and bitter teamsters' strike of 1913-1914, paralleled by a number of maritime strikes and the laundry workers' strike, caused an uneasiness among allies in the business and professional community. When the Central Labor Council declared its opposition to war measures in 1917, most of its middle-class support vanished, emphasized by the outright desertion of the Municipal League in favor of all-out war measures on the home front.

Although Seattle became a closed shop city during World War I, the patriotic hysteria generated by a legalized vigilantism that drew on businessmen and professionals for leadership, targeted all forms of dissent as being subversive. Labor unions fell under suspicion, and aliens and radicals were periodically rounded up in police and immigration office sweeps. However, notice should be taken of widespread public sympathy before the General Strike for the ordinary shipyard workers, combined, as it was, with public hostility to EFC's Piez in his drive to break the power of the Metal Trades Council and punish the city for trying to maintain its relatively high wage scale in the face of competition from foreign shipyards. The General Strike, of course, finally alienated middle-class support for unions in general, considering them even "un-American."

Culturally, before the war, Seattle made great strides. The

theater business flourished during the war as it provided a recreational alternative to the outlawed saloon. The symphony expanded in size and in program quality, although it was forced to cut back on its adult programs while expanding its children's component. The Ladies' Musical Club vigorously promoted classical music with its sponsorship of outstanding artists. The Cornish School bounded along despite its loss of students during the postwar recession as spunky Nellie Cornish inspired her tiny handful of art patrons to bolster her efforts to benefit their own children, their social class, and to provide an ambient environment wherein the city would spawn its own distinctive character. That she improvised a remarkable program during the "prosperous" 1920s without broader private funding beyond her intimate circle of wealthy benefactors is its own testimony.

Seattle's Public Schools had become a national model during the century's first two decades. Wartime hysteria, compounded by superpatriotism and intolerance of dissent cut into Seattle School Superintendent Frank Cooper's programs as he had to fight off the School Board's interference in matters of curriculum management. In addition, just as he had to contend with efforts to intrude military preparedness into the city's schools during World War I, his last fight was over such an issue in 1922. And just as the school system faced up to the issue of compulsory attendance through age sixteen, a Chamber of Commerce-led tax revolt in 1921 threatened financial stability. Ultimately, economy won out over quality and innovation. Socially sensitive programs for which Cooper had fought were also eliminated or scaled downward.

City beautification ended as a movement when the Bogue Plan for comprehensive development was rejected in the election of March 1912. The program for expanding parks and playgrounds was curtailed; nonetheless, improvements were made to existing facilities, along with the extension of supervised recreation. However, testifying to the city's preference for material things over cultural and civic amenities in the 1920s, Seattle's parks, playgrounds, and boulevards continued to suffer neglect until the 1930s when injections of federal money salvaged them. Finally, after a prolonged and bitter fight against the U.S. Forest Service and its industry allies, conservation leaders realized their dream of an Olympic National Park in 1938—critically aided by a sympathetic federal administration.

The period (1900-1940) covered by this volume and the second is essentially of a piece. The forces set in motion by the Yukon gold rush and the transcontinental railroad connection played against a backdrop unchanged in basic character. Represented was a city coming of age during the first two decades. The city then marked time until the Great Depression. Some of the turbulence of the earlier decades then revived as people, despairing during the worst years of the Depression, bounced back politically, forcing the federal government to assume an active function in resuscitating the economic system.

World War II decisively altered the city's economy, its demography, its political relations with federal and state governments, its relations with other Puget Sound counties, and with eastern Washington as that region was transformed by the Columbia River Basin development. Seattle, like other major cities in the West, became fully integrated with the rest of the nation during the second war and its aftermath. The stage was now set against a different backdrop.

Endnotes

Chapter 1

An Overview, 1900-1920

[no notes]

Chapter 2

Seattle's Political Economy, 1900-1910

Seattle and the Twentieth Century [and] James J. Hill and the Great Northern

1. This section is based mainly on two books and the manuscripts of two of the main participants. The books are: Robert C. Nesbit, *"He Built Seattle": A Biography of Judge Thomas Burke,* (Seattle: University of Washington Press, 1961) chapters 8 and 11 relating to Burke's ties to the Great Northern and James J. Hill; and Alan Hynding, *The Public Life Of Eugene Semple: Promoter And Politician Of The Pacific Northwest* (Seattle: University of Washington Press, 1973), chapters 9 and 10, relating to the Harbor Line Commission and the Lake Washington Canal. These two volumes are in turn based on the papers of each of these two figures in the Manuscript Collection of the University of Washington Libraries.{Manuscript Collection of the University of Washington Libraries is henceforth abbreviated: MSS,UW.} Roger Sales's *Seattle Past to Present* (Seattle: University of Washington Press, 1976), chapter 3 is good for conveying a general impression of the local setting. As a general reference Clarence B. Bagley's *History of Seattle* (Chicago: J. Clark, 1916), is indispensable, particularly for its biographical sketches and for data to

which he had ready access either from his personal contacts and memory or handy to him, but some of which since has been lost to posterity in its original form. The "History of the Lake Washington Canal" in *Washington Historical Quarterly* (Volume 25, April and July 1934) by Neil H. Purvis is excellent. A recent study by Robert E. Ficken, using the Army Engineers Records updates Purvis; see Ficken, "Seattle's 'Ditch': The Corps of Engineers and the Lake Washington Ship Canal," *Pacific Northwest Quarterly*, 77:1, (January 1986): pp. 11-20. {*Pacific Northwest Quarterly* is henceforth abbreviated *PNQ.*} Of particular value as a reference source is Mary McWilliams, *Seattle Water Department History 1854-1954, Operational Data and Memoranda,* (Seattle: n.p., 1973), pp. 53-100. See the "Eastern Car Shipments" series in the Port Blakely Mill Company, *Records*, MSS,UW.

Four unpublished studies are of special value: Keith A. Murray's 1946 dissertation, "The Republican Party and The Progressive Era" is particularly instructive on the political interests and influence of the railroads; Robert Saltvig's "The Progressive Movement in Washington" (Unpublished Ph.D.Dissertation, University of Washington, 1964) extends the scope of Murray's study and uses fresh archival sources in the Manuscript Collection; see his pp. 29-30, 36-39, 73-75, and 85-87 in particular, for the subject covered here; a third is Victoria Livingston, "Erastus Brainerd: The Bankruptcy of Brilliance" (Unpublished Master's Thesis, University of Washington, 1967), particularly pp. 22-24 and 39-44. Saltvig's study is the best single source for the period as a whole, needing very little updating from recent additions to the holdings in the University of Washington's Archives and Manuscript Collection if it were to be published. On the city's economy see Alexander Norbert MacDonald, "Seattle's Economic Development, 1880-1910" (Unpublished Ph.D. Dissertation, University of Washington, 1959). See also MacDonald's *Distant Neighbors: A Comparative History of Seattle and Vancouver* (Lincoln: University of Nebraska Press, 1984).

Of general value for presenting the national and regional setting are: Thomas C. Cochran and William Miller, *The Age Of Enterprise: A Social History of Industrial America* (New York: Harper Torchbooks, 1961), and Robert H. Wiebe, *Businessmen and Reform: A Study of the Progressive Movement.* (Chicago: Quadrangle Books, 1968) Murray Morgan's, *The Mill on the Boot: The Story of the St. Paul and Tacoma Lumber Company* (Seattle: University of Washington Press, 1982) provides background on the entry of the Northern Pacific into the state's lumber business, pp. 52-54 (the lumber company's records are also in the Manuscript Collection). Thomas R. Cox, *Mills and Markets: A History of the Pacific Coast Lumber Industry to 1900* (Seattle: University of Washington Press, 1974), chapter 9 is excellent for background.

Reginald H. Thomson and Civic Development

1. Thomson to Beaton 9 July 1914, Reginald H. Thomson Letterbooks, MSS, UW.

2. *Argus*, 25 August, 17 November 1900. Earlier, in the 31 March 1900 issue, Chadwick observed that not until the NP offered to build a

depot did the GN counter with a promise for one of its own. After the furor died down the GN neither said nor did anything more. When the NP applied for an easement over the GN's tracks to get to its docks GN opposed it. *Ibid.*, 2 June 1900. The depot issue would not go away: When Hill gained temporary control over the NP Chadwick commented that once again the GN and NP are "to construct a Union Depot," [and all he wants in return] is a hundred thousand dollars worth of King Street . . . The six streets south of King have already been vacated in order to permit Mr. Hill to erect his depot." Chadwick further accused Hill of building nothing but his own storage sheds and renting the condemned land to others. He pointed to Hill's record of broken promises. *Ibid.*, 3 May 1902. See also 31 May, 11 October, and 15 November 1902, and 23 May 1903 issues on the depot controversy.

3. *Argus*, 10 February 1900.

Thomas Burke, Spokesman for James J. Hill

1. Nesbit, *ibid.*, pp. 159-160; 215-219; but his entire chapter 8, "The Great Northern" portrays the general fusion of politics and economics in the city. When a monument to Hill was proposed for inclusion with the 1909 exposition on the University of Washington campus Chadwick saltily reminded readers about the original GN franchise: "[Members of] the city council secured options on property and made themselves wealthy"; *Argus*, 13 March 1909. The urge toward railroad monopolies did not die easily: that very year the NP was given an exclusive franchise by the City Council to run its tracks over the city's streets around Lake Union, thereby giving it control over traffic along the canal; only the mayor's veto prevented this from happening. *Ibid.*, 18 December 1909.

Fight for the Waterfront

1. Nesbit, *ibid.* chapter 8.

Reshaping the Waterfront

1. In addition to Hynding and Nesbit in general this exchange of letters between Burke and Stevens is instructive about the Hill tactics; see Thomas Burke Papers, File 6-21, MSS,UW.

Chapter 3
The Economy, 1900-1914

An Overview

1. See endnote 1 under Manufacturing 1899-1909.

Manufacturing 1899-1909

1. Of special value is the unpublished 1959 dissertation by Alexander Norbert MacDonald, "Seattle's Economic Development, 1880-1910." Clarence Bagley's history fills in useful economic data. The only source for data on imports and exports on a commodity and trading partner

basis is the Port Warden's annual reports. The most complete run is in the Seattle Public Library; a substantial series is also in the City Archives; and a partial one in the University of Washington Libraries. The series runs through 1932, and continues on a monthly basis without annual cumulations through 1938, at which time it ceases. Minutebooks of the Seattle Chamber of Commerce and of the Commercial Club (in the Seattle Public Library) provide useful but spotty economic data.

Railway And Marine News (*RMN*) provides a continuous flow of information and editorial opinion from 1904 on; but it is frustratingly weak on rail shipments in and out of the area—no such data source has yet been turned up here or in St. Paul, where the railroad records are located. Pamphlets, usually published annually by the Seattle Chamber of Commerce, often contain statistics not otherwise obtainable, but none carry serial cumulations. Of particular value are its: *Seattle, The Puget Sound Country and Western Washington . . . 1901; Seattle: A Great Shipping and Commercial Center* (15 July 1913); and *Seattle: An Industrial City* (1916). An excellent introduction to the history of the Seattle waterfront is provided by Hamilton Higday in the first (1914) Port of Seattle *Yearbook* (pp. 41-101). On the silk trade Haru Matsukata Reichauer, *Samurai And Silk: A Japanese and American Heritage* (Cambridge: Harvard University Press, 1986) pp. 209 ff., 228 are pertinent.

With respect to manufacturing the above sources are used, but the United States *Census of Manufacturing* is the only source providing a high degree of serial continuity; however its changes of categories, lack of distinctions within general categories, and discontinuities between one census and another make it a frustrating source to use, as the text makes apparent. Chamber of Commerce Minutebooks, 1898-1901 yield some good data.

The Port in Operation

1. *RMN*, 1:5, 1 December 1904 and 3:3, 1 November 1905.

2. Besides MacDonald, *ibid.*, and the federal census, see Roger Sales, *ibid.*, pp. 50-55. Bagley, *ibid.*, volume II, pp. 606 ff. describes the Moran Brothers operation.

Chapter 4
City Politics, 1900-1904

1. See Morgan, *Skid Road*, pp. 129-131; *Argus.* 10 and 17 February 1900. Before the Republican Party nominated Humes, Chadwick had been critical of him. But once nominated, Chadwick inflated Humes's qualifications somewhat piously in the hope that the candidate would live up to the businesslike and judicial standards that Chadwick believed the office required.

2. See Bagley, *ibid.*, volume I, pp. 194-195; Morgan, *ibid.*, pp. 178-179; Nesbit, *ibid.*, pp. 231 and 239-40; and *Argus*, 17 February 1900.

3. *Argus*, 3 March 1900. Chadwick learned that Colonel Blethen became so infuriated with a telephone operator after the defeat of his candidate that he actually destroyed the telephone. 10 March 1900.

4. *Argus,* 24 and 31 March; 19 May; 2 and 9 June; 7, 14, and 28 July; 11 August; and 1 September 1900.

5. *Argus,* 1, 8, 15, 22 September; and 20 October 1900. Chadwick urged a "united move by the wholesale interests . . . to center the tenderloin districts at some point where it will not interfere with legitimate business. . . ." 3 November 1900.

6. *Argus,* 10 and 24 November and 1 December 1900; Morgan, *ibid.,* pp. 131-132.

7. *Argus,* 23 March; 6 April; 25 May; 1 and 22 June 1901; Morgan, *ibid.,* pp. 132-135.

8. Morgan, *ibid.,* pp. 134-142 has a colorful account. The author is inclined to accept Chadwick's verdict that it was murder; see *Argus,* 29 June; 6 and 13 July; and 23 November 1901.

9. Hendrick, "The Recall in Seattle," *McClure's Magazine* 37 (October 1911), 647-663.

10. *Argus,* 27 July; 3 and 10 August 1901; 22 February; 1 and 8 March 1902. See also 3 May 1902 concerning Preston's candidacy, the *Times's* endorsement, and the role played by the Northern Pacific and Great Northern railroads.

11. *Argus,* 25 April; 13 and 20 June; 1 and 8 August; 5 September; and 10 October 1903; 9 January and 9 July 1904.

12. *Argus,* 12 and 26 March; 2 and 16 April 1904.

Chapter 5
Early Municipal Ownership Movement

Public Power Forces Coalesce

1. For the political setting see Saltvig, *ibid.,* pp. 39-45, 88-103; also, chapter below, "City Politics, 1904-1910." This section is based on the following: For specific utilities see Mary McWilliams, *Seattle Water Department. . . ,* pp. 53-68; Wesley A. Dick, *The Genesis of Seattle City Light,* (Unpublished Master's Thesis, University of Washington, 1965), pp. 1-81; Leslie Blanchard, *The Street Railway Era in Seattle: A Chronicle of Six Decades* (Forty Fort, Pennsylvania: Harold E. Cox, 1968); Harry Purdy, "Development And Cost Of Municipal Operation Of Seattle Street Railways" (Unpublished Master's Thesis, University of Washington, 1928). On the role of R. H. Thomson and regrading see Sales, *ibid.,* pp. 68-78; Arthur H. Dimock, "Preparing the Groundwork for a City: The Regrading of Seattle, Washington," Paper No. 1669 of American Society of Civil Engineers, *Transactions;* and V. V. Tarbill, "Mountain-Moving in Seattle," *Harvard Business Review,* July 1930, pp. 482-89; Denzil C. Cline, *Street Car Men of Seattle: a Sociological Study* (Unpublished Master's Thesis, University of Washington, 1926),pp. 20-23. The *Argus* sources are: 18 January 1902 on the Seattle Electric Company railway franchise; 12 August 1905 concerning J. A. Moore's attempt to establish a competing line; 26 August 1905 concerning the SEC's exclusive franchise on the Westlake route; 27 May 1905 concerning the delays encountered in arranging for the sale of the surplus power of the city's generating plant; and 5 August 1905 concerning the *Times* and *P-I* collaboration in trying to eliminate the municipal plant from competition.

The Electrical Industry Presses for State Regulation

1. On the strategy of the NELA see: Douglas D. Anderson, *Regulatory Politics and Electrical Utilities: A Case Study in Political Economy* (Boston: Auburn House, 1981), chapters 1 and 2. The Thomson letter is in the Thomson Papers, Letterbook, 6 July 1908. Thomson worked closely with James J. Hill's nephew, Samuel Hill, who was president of the Washington Good Roads Association, and was head of the Seattle Gas and Electric Company. This association and his felt camaraderie with the Empire Builder himself probably contributed to Thomson's misplaced confidence in Farrell.

Seattle: Microcosm in the Macrocosm

1. *Argus*, 9 and 16 March; 4 May 1901; 1, 8, 15, 22 February; 8 and 22 March 1902. In general see Saltvig, *ibid.*, pp. 88-104; Dick, *ibid.*, esp. pp. 47-51.

2. *Argus*, 9, 23 and 30 August; 27 December 1902; 28 February; 21 March; and 12 September 1903.

3. *Argus*, 5 March and 15 October 1904; 5 August 1905; 2 June 1906. In August the SEC was allowed a $1,000,000 reduction in its evaluation; for this the City Council was accused by the Grand Jury of having been corrupted by the SEC. See *Argus*, 30 Aug; 27 September 1902; 4 April 1903.

4. Puget Sound Power and Light Company (Hereafter cited as PSP&L) Records, Diary, 28 July 1904, and 25 June 1904, Box 166, MSS,UW.

5. PSP&L, *ibid.*, Monthly Reports, October 1906 through May 1907, Box 164.

6. Dick, *ibid.*, pp. 76-81, 90.

Chapter 6
Industrial Relations

Early Labor Activism

1. At the national level see Wiebe, *Businessmen And Reform. . . ,* regarding the National Association of Manufacturers. For trade associations in Seattle see Margaret Jane Thompson, "Development and Comparison of Industrial Relations in Seattle" (Unpublished Master's Thesis, University of Washington, 1929). For Citizens' Alliances in general see Philip Taft, *The A.F.of L. in the Time of Gompers* (New York: Octagon Books, 1970), chapter 16. On the National Civic Federation, citizen alliances, and the National Association of Manufacturers, see also David Montgomery, *The Fall of the House of Labor* (New York: Cambridge University Press, 1989), chapter 6. On the state labor movement, the Socialist Party, and the Seattle Central Labor Council see Jonathan Dembo, "A History of the Washington State Labor Movement, 1885-1935 (Unpublished Ph.D. Dissertation, University of Washington, 1978), esp. pp. 30-

74. Dembo has statistical tables on membership, employment/unemployment, and ethnic characteristics. On socialism see Barbara Winslow, "The Decline of Socialism in Washington, 1910-1925" (Unpublished Master's Thesis, University of Washington, 1969). For a general perspective see Carlos A. Schwantes's *Radical Heritage: Labor, Socialism, and Reform in Washington and British Columbia, 1885-1917* (Seattle: University of Washington Press, 1979), chapters 6 and 9 and pp. 171-78. The Blackman quotation is from Seattle Chamber of Commerce, *Semi-Centennial Celebration . . . 1903*, pp. 48-49. The Chamber's moderation at this time is reflected in its Minutes, 21 August 1901.

2. PSP&L, Records, Diary, 14 April 1904, Box 166. Denzil Cline, who relied heavily upon former PSTP&L employees for his thesis on the street car men, reported the following: When the SEC announced a wage cut in 1903 the men (who were working ten and one-half hour days, seven days a week, with time off if requested in advance, all for twenty cents an hour) formed a union and went on an unsuccessful eight-day strike. The company bought off some of the union officers, which prompted the secretary to return the local's charter to the international office because the union had ceased to exist. The SEC then decided to introduce a graduated scale that allowed an increase of one-cent an hour "every two or three years." In 1907 the company raised the hourly rate to twenty-two cents, then to twenty-five cents when it had trouble hiring. *Ibid.*,pp. 26-34.

3. PSP&L, *ibid.* 15 April and 5 May 1904.

4. Dembo, *ibid.*, pp. 59 ff.

Labor Legislation: A Common Ground

1. This entire section is derived from Joseph F. Tripp, "Progressive Labor Laws in Washington State," 1900-1925 (Unpublished Ph. D. Dissertation, University of Washington, 1973) chapters 2 and 3. See also his "Toward an Efficient and Moral Society: Washington State Minimum Wage Law, 1913-1925," *PNQ* 67:3 (July 1976), pp. 97-112. For the role of women's clubs in support of child labor legislation, minimum hours for women, and associated legislation see the Washington State Federation of Women's Clubs, Records, Minutes and "History," MSS, UW.

Chapter 7
Framework of Life in the City

Introduction

1. Two of the best sources conveying the social ambience of the city at the turn of the century are Murray Morgan, *Skid Road*, chapters 3 and 4, and Roger Sales, *Seattle, Past to Present*, chapter 3. The *Argus* conveys a special flavor in its weekly accounts and commentary on the Seattle scene. Editor Harry Chadwick serialized as targets for his caustic and irreverent commentary: Alden J. Blethen, John L. Wilson, James J. Hill, Rev. Mark A. Matthews and occasionally other clerics bent on moral reform, Reginald H. Thomson, and George F. Cotterill. Those issues from which quota-

tions are made in this introduction are: 26 October 1901 regarding Moore; 22 December 1900 on theaters; and 28 July 1900 on Alki.

Seattle's Population

1. The general sources from which this account is derived are: Janice L. Reiff, "Urbanization and the Social Structure: Seattle, Washington, 1852-1910" (Unpublished Ph.D. Dissertation, University of Washington, 1981), which is supplemented by two standard works: Calvin F. Schmid, *Social Trends in Seattle*, which brings the account down to 1940; and Schmid and Wayne W. McVey, Jr., *Growth and Distribution of Minority Races in Seattle, Washington*, which brings the account down to 1962. An early study by Andrew W. Lind, *A Study of Mobility of Population in Seattle* (University of Washington Studies in the Social Sciences, Volume 3, Number 1, Seattle, 1925) is useful. Roger Sales, *ibid.*,pp. 53-63, is helpful. See also the Chamber of Commerce Minutes for June 1905.

Chinese in the City

1. For accounts of the anti-Chinese movement, including the anti-Chinese riots in Seattle see the following: Calvin F. Schmid, *Social Trends in Seattle*, pp. 143-147, which reprints an account of the Seattle riot and background by George Kinnear, one of the members of the Home Guard protecting the Chinese; and Robert E. Wynne, *Reaction to The Chinese in The Pacific Northwest and British Columbia, 1850-1910* (New York: Arno Press, 1978). For population statistics see Schmid, *op. cit.*; and Schmid and Wayne W. McVey, Jr., *Growth and Distribution of Minority Races in Seattle, Washington*, pp. 18-21.

2. Lew G. Kay, "Seattle Chinese", *The Coast*, December 1909, p. 315. Kay later became a trustee and treasurer of the China Club, of which Thomas Burke was president: see Thomas Burke Papers, File 3-33. On Pekin Restaurant, see *Argus*, 16:46 (18 December, 1909), p. 64.

3. *Times*, 1 July 1929. See also Chin Gee Hee letters to Burke in the Thomas Burke Papers, File 33-1. His railroad was the Sun Ning Railway, which was to become a link with a French road through Indo-China, on to Burma and India.

4. Rose Hum Lee, *The Chinese in the United States of America* (Hong Kong: Hong Kong University Press/Oxford University Press, 1960), pp. 35-37, and p. 59 for quotation. Roger Daniels, *Asian America: Chinese and Japanese in the United States Since 1850* (Seattle: University of Washington Press, 1988), p. 77.

5. Seattle-specific data is fragmentary, a matter that is true for most Chinese communities; however, both Lee and Daniels believe that the general holds true for the particular metropolitan areas because Chinese tended to congregate there, and their economic, social, and cultural organization was common one to the other. See Lee, *ibid.* for associations and the Six Companies, pp. 144-152; tongs, pp. 161-173; quotation is from p. 161; Daniels, *ibid.*, pp. 81-91.

6. Quoted in Daniels, *ibid.*, p. 23.

7. Daniels, *ibid.*, p. 68-72. My table is derived from Daniels' on p. 69. See also Lee, *ibid.*, pp. 42-44 for sex ratios.

Seattle's Japanese Community

1. Of most general value are: Kazuo Ito, *Issei; A History of Japanese Immigrants in North America* (Seattle: Japanese Community Service, 1973); Yuzo Murayama, "The Economic History of Japanese Immigration to the Pacific Northwest, 1890-1920" (Unpublished Ph.D. Dissertation, University of Washington, 1982); Shotaro Frank Miyamoto, *Social Solidarity Among the Japanese in Seattle* (Seattle: University of Washington Publications in the Social Sciences, Volume 11, Number 2, Seattle, 1939), and Schmid and McVey, noted above. An excellent occupational census is the 4 June 1917 report of the Seattle Ministerial Federation's Committee on Orientals. For the origins of anti-Japanese prejudice see Carey McWilliams *Prejudice Japanese-Americans: Symbol of Racial Intolerance* (Boston: Little, Brown and Company, 1944) and Roger Daniels, *The Politics of Prejudice: The Anti-Japanese Movement in California and the Struggle for Japanese Exclusion* (New York: Atheneum, 1972).

2. Ito, *ibid.*, and Miyamoto, *ibid.*

3. Murayama, *ibid.*, pp. 145, 189, 198, 199-200.

4. Murayama, *ibid.*, pp. 184-186.

5. Miyamoto, pp. 64-65; chapter 3.

6. Seattle Ministerial Federation, *ibid.*

7. See below, chapters on the 1916 longshoremen's strike, and the General Strike.

8. *Town Crier*, 4 July 1914, p. 9.

9. *Argus*, 21 April 1900; 7 November 1903; 3 April 1909; 9 September and 16 December 1911.

Seattle's Jewish Community

1. The general sources from which the following account is derived are: Albert Adatto, "Sephardim and the Seattle Sephardic Community" (Unpublished Master's Thesis, University of Washington, 1939); Lori Etta Cohn, "Residential Patterns of the Jewish Community of The Seattle Area, 1910-1980" (Unpublished Master's Thesis, 1982). A useful brief survey is by Howard Droker in the *Newsletter* of the Washington State Jewish Historical Society, 3:1, November 1982. On Settlement House, see Jean Devine, *From Settlement House to Neighborhood House*, 1906-1976 (Seattle: Neighborhood House, 1976). See also Bagley, *ibid.*, II, p. 499. A biography of Rabbi Samuel Koch by Julia N. Eulenberg, "Samuel Koch: Seattle's Social Justice Rabbi" (Unpublished Master's Thesis, University of Washington, 1984) is helpful. The date of the quotation from the *Argus* is 17 April 1909. For a comparison with the New York Jewish population, describing the impact of the migration of the eastern European Jews upon the established German Jews, see Ronald Sanders, *The Downtown Jews: Portraits of an Immigrant Generation* (New York: New American Library, 1976). See also, Irving Howe, *World of Our Fathers* (New York: Harcourt Brace and Johanovich, 1976).

Seattle's Italians

1. Nellie Roe, "Italian Immigrants in Seattle" (Unpublished Master's Thesis, University of Washington, 1915); and Schmid, *ibid.*, pp. 117, 119, 123.

Seattle's Black Community

1. Besides Schmid, *ibid.*, pp. 132, 137-141 and Schmid and McVey see *The Republican*, January 1896 (published in Seattle by Horace R. Cayton) for a useful survey; S. Leonard Bell "Seattle's First Black Journalist" (*Post-Intelligencer*, "Northwest Today," (1 September 1968), and his "Horace Cayton, Jr.: Man Without a Race" (*ibid.*, 27 October 1968); Richard S. Hobbs, "Horace Cayton—Seattle's Black Pioneer Publisher" (*Seattle Times*, "Magazine," 26 February 1978); Horace R. Cayton, *Long Old Road: An Autobiography* (University of Washington Press, Seattle, 1963) by a son of the publisher. An excellent social history is Esther Hall Mumford's *Seattle's Black Victorians, 1852-1901* (Ananse Press, Seattle, 1980). On strikebreaking as a major factor in Black migration to the state see Richard C. Berner, "Labor History: Sources and Perspectives," *PNQ* 60:1 (January 1969), pp.31-33; and his "Preserving Ethnic History," *Puget Soundings*, June 1977, pp. 24-26; and Robert A. Campbell, "Blacks and the Coal Mines of Western Washington, 1886-1896," *PNQ*, 73:4 (October 1982), pp. 146-155. On William Grose [Gross], see Donald Duncan, "Driftwood Diary," *Times*, 31 December 1967. For Blacks on the waterfront see Joseph Sylvester Jackson, "The Colored Marine Employees Benevolent Association" (Unpublished Master's Thesis, University of Washington, 1939), pp. 5-17.

Pike Place Market and Ethnicity

1. See the Pike Place Public Market Scrapbooks in the Special Collections in the University of Washington Libraries: articles by Lucille McDonald in the *Times*, 19 January 1964, and other clippings. On rivalry between commission merchants and local farmers see *Seattle Sun*, 3 February 1913.

Education in the City

1. This section on the public school system is derived almost wholly from Bryce E. Nelson, "Good Schools: the Development Of Public Schooling In Seattle, 1901-1922" (Unpublished Ph. D. Dissertation, University of Washington, 1981, published by the University of Washington Press in 1988)—and his "Frank B. Cooper: Seattle's Progressive School Superintendent, 1901-22," *PNQ*, 74:4, (October 1983), pp. 167-177. Some general reference has also been made to the School Board *Minutes* in the Seattle Public School Archives.

The University of Washington

1. This account is drawn mainly from: Georgia Ann Kumor, Thomas Franklin Kane and the University of Washington, 1902-1913 (Unpublished Master's Thesis, University of Washington, 1981), chapters 2

and 3; her "A Question of Leadership. . . ." *PNQ*, 77:1, (January 1986), pp. 2-10; Thomas C. McClintock, "James Allen Smith and the Progressive Movement: A Study in Intellectual History" (Unpublished Ph. D. Dissertation, University of Washington, 1959), pp. 157-60, 393, 395-406, 409-11, 412-14, 436-47, 445-68; and Charles M. Gates, *The First Century at the University of Washington*, 1861-1961 (Seattle: University of Washington Press, 1961), chapters 7, 9, 10. The PTA source is from the Parents-Teachers Association Minutes, 1912, Box 2, Accession 342, MSS,UW.

Popular Entertainment: Theater Life

1. This section is derived almost entirely from Eugene C. Elliott, *A History of Variety-vaudeville in Seattle from the Beginning to 1914* (Seattle: University of Washington Press, 1944), pp. 27-65; and from Murray Morgan, *Skid Road*, Chapter 3.

Popular Entertainment: Music and Art

1. The best published account of the LMC is Karen Blair, "The Seattle Ladies Musical Club, 1890-1930" in Thomas G. Edwards and Carlos A. Schwantes, editors, *Experiences in the Promised Land: Essays in Pacific Northwest History* (Seattle: University of Washington Press, 1986), pp. 124-38. The LMC's Scrapbooks at the Museum of History and Industry are indispensable, though disappointingly sketchy.

2. See Esther W. Campbell, *Bagpipes in the Woodwind Section: A History of the Seattle Symphony Orchestra and its Women's Association* (Seattle: Seattle Symphony Women's Association, 1978)

3. The most authoritative published source is *Miss Aunt Nellie: The Autobiography of Nellie C. Cornish*, edited by Ellen V. Browne and Edward N. Beck (Seattle: University of Washington Press, 1964). Indispensable are the Cornish School Scrapbooks, MSS, UW.

4. Seattle Art Museum Records, Seattle Fine Arts Society subgroup, MSS,UW.

Outdoor Recreation: The Beginning of Organized Mountaineering and The Conservation Movement

1. This section is derived from "Thirty Years in Retrospect: The First Decade in Mountaineer Annals," by L. A. Nelson; and "The Second Ten Years. . . ," by Joseph T. Hazard in *The Mountaineer*, 30:1, (15 December 1937), pp. 9-16.

2. Ben W. Twight, *Organizational Values and Political Power: the Forest Service Versus the Olympic National Park* (University Park, Pennsylvania: Pennsylvania State University Press, 1983), ch.3.

Beautifying the City . . . For Eternity?

1. Two general sources give a broad perspective: Padraic Burke, "City Beautiful Movement in Seattle" (Unpublished Master's Thesis, University of Washington, 1973), and Seattle Park Department *Annual Report*, 1916-1917 for an historical account. Burke's account of the Bogue

plan and its failure to get voter approval in March 1912 is superseded by his *History of the Port of Seattle*. For specific citation see Seattle Board of Park Commissioners, Report, 1892. On architecture three recommended sources are: the Washington Office of Archaeology and Historic Preservation, *Built in Washington: 12,000 Years of Pacific Northwest Archaeological Sites and Historic Buildings* (Pullman: Washington State University Press, 1989); Lila Gault, *The House Next Door: Seattle's Neighborhood Architecture* (Seattle: Pacific Search Press, 1981) and Sally B. Woodbridge and Roger Montgomery, *A Guide to Architecture in Washington State* (Seattle: University of Washington Press, Seattle, 1980), pp. 19-22. On Cotterill see Bagley, *ibid.*, Volume 3, pp. 25-30.

2. Donald Sherwood's unpublished "Description and History of Seattle's Parks" is the best single source on park history; it is in the Special Collections Division of the University of Washington Libraries. Bagley, *ibid.*, Volume I chapter 15 is a good general source. Roger Sales, *ibid.*, pp. 79-84 provides a general perspective. On the race tracks and associated vices see *Argus*, 12 August 1911 and 12 September 1908. On a bill to close down the Meadows see *Argus*, 13 March 1909.

3. *Argus*, 29 May 1909.

4. A copy of the Olmsted plan is in the John J. McGilvra Papers, File 9-27, MSS,UW. The most recent account of the Olmsted plan is Norman J. Johnston, "The Olmsted Brothers and the Alaska-Yukon-Pacific Exposition: 'Eternal Loveliness'," *PNQ*, 75:2 (April 1984), pp. 50-61. See also Sales. *Ibid.*, pp. 81-86.

5. Seattle Park Board, *Annual Report*, 1909, 1912.

Chapter 8
City Politics, 1904-1910
Mayoral Administrations of Ballinger, Moore, Miller, and Gill

1. Saltvig, *ibid.*, p. 87 for the quotation; pp. 73-75, 85-87, and chapter 4, "The City For The People," in general. For general background see also Keith A. Murray, "Republican Party Politics. . . ," pp. 50-118, and for Farrell and the Washington Political Bureau, pp. 58-66. The general content of this chapter is derived mainly from Saltvig and Murray, supplemented from other sources as indicated. Helpful, also as a general source is Mansel G. Blackford, "Sources of Support for Reform Candidates and Issues in Seattle Politics 1902-1916" (Unpublished Master's Thesis, University of Washington, 1967), Chapters 1-4; and his "Reform Politics in Seattle During the Progressive Era, 1902-1916," *PNQ* 59:4 (October 1968), pp. 177-185.

The *Argus* covered these events in some detail. In 1904 Chadwick claimed the railroad interests in King County were looking for a candidate to run against McBride, and found Mead, whose Whatcom County constituents needed a railroad. Then Farrell, who was a Democrat with a dominating influence in the Republican Party, put up ex-Senator, George

Turner of Spokane, as the Democratic candidate. Turner was accorded credit for being a "known railroad tool." In the general election Sam Hill was a major contributor to the Mead campaign (James Hill supported Parker for president because of Roosevelt's role in breaking up the NP-GN merger). *Argus*, 19 March; 14 May; 22 October; 5 and 12 November 1904. In the city itself the GN continued efforts to block entry of other railroads into the city, first the Union Pacific, then the Chicago, Milwaukee, and St. Paul. In this match the GN had to contend with Farrell, who had resigned as president of the Great Northern Steamship Company to join forces with the Harriman lines. Chadwick cautioned the City Council about granting $5 million "worth of streets and alleys" to the UP, reminding that body that the road was coming to Seattle because it was in its interest to do so. Chadwick also saw Thomson's hand in trying to get an ordinance passed that was unfair to the "Milwaukee"; Thomson was accused of having given Hill earlier, "everything in sight." *Argus*, 20 July; 23 December 1905; 21 July; 17 February; 10 March; 5 May; 1 September 1906. On Mead and the railroads subsequently see *Argus*, 14 March; 20 and 27 June 1908.

2. Saltvig, pp. 42-45 and 88-96.

3. Dembo, *ibid.*, pp. 52-53; *Argus*, 3 March, 10 March, and 24 March 1906.

4. Saltvig, pp. 96-102; *Argus*, 24 February, 3 March, and 10 March 1906.

5. *Argus*, 12 and 26 May 1906; 16 September 1905; 16 June 1906. Chadwick also suggested on 4 August 1906 that Thomson's opposition to a municipal street railway only showed his alliance with the Seattle Electric Company.

6. Saltvig, pp. 102-106.

7. Saltvig, pp. 105-106; *Argus*, 2/1, 2/8, 15 February, 22 February, 29 February 1908.

8. PSP&L, Records, "Outward Correspondence," 1909.

9. *Argus*, 21 March; 2 May; 4 and 18 July; 29 August; 5 September; and 5 December 1908; 13 February and 15 May 1909. Chadwick noted that because the City limited the number of saloon licenses a premium has been placed on them, with the result that the possessors sell them as though they, not the City, owned them, May 22, 1909. A late 1909 Supreme Court ruling forced Miller to also close "every bar and buffet connected with social clubs," thereby causing these customers as well as the "clubless" to suffer. 12 November 1909. Also, *Argus*, 4 December 1909, on the *Times*.

The 1910 City Election

1. Saltvig, pp. 106-107. For the Freeman quotation see *P-I*, 7 February 1910; *Argus*, 18 December 1909.

2. See *P-I* of this time for general election coverage.

3. Burton Hendrick, *ibid.* The Gill quotation is in the *P-I*, 6 February 1910.

1911: Reform Forces Coalesce

1. *Cf.*, Saltvig, *ibid.*, pp. 106-15, 148-51, 170-79; Blackford, "Sources. . . ," chapter 4; Lee F. Pendergrass, "Urban Reform and Voluntary Association: A Case Study of the Seattle Municipal League" (Unpublished Ph. D. Dissertation, University of Washington, 1972), pp. 38-39, and his "The Formation of a Municipal Reform Movement: The Municipal League of Seattle," *PNQ* 66:1 (January 1975), pp. 13-25. Rising expectations for commerce once the Panama Canal was completed was a running theme in the media of the period. See also Claudius O. Johnson, "The Adoption of the Initiative and Referendum in Washington," *PNQ* 35:4 (October 1944), pp. 291-303.

2. For the relation of the PWL to the Municipal League see Pendergrass, *ibid.*, chapter 2.; Blackford, "Sources . . . ," chapter 5, which is also the source for the quotation (p. 46).

3. Pendergrass, *ibid.*, chapter 2.

4. Morgan, *ibid.*, pp. 170-171.

5. *Argus*, 4 February 1911.

6. Morgan, *Skid Road*, 166-82; Hendrick, *ibid.*; Blackford, "Sources . . . ," chapter 4; Pendergrass, *ibid.*, pp. 30-38. The most thoroughgoing account of Matthews's role in the recall is found in Dale Soden, "Mark Allison Matthews: Seattle's Southern Preacher" (Unpublished Ph. D. Dissertation, University of Washington, 1980), pp. 218-21; and his "Mark Allison Matthews: Seattle's Minister Rediscovered," *PNQ* 74:2(April 1983), pp. 50-58. Soden accounts for Matthews's shift from being a politically active Social Gospel minister to one pre-occupied with combatting forces identified with tolerance and social amelioration of the urban environment— spiced with xenophobia and his view of Americanism.

7. Dick, *ibid.*, chapter 8 on the significance of Arms's appointment. P. C. Spowart, who later joined City Light, recalled (when he was still with PSTP&L) a telephone conversation between the company's chief engineer and Gill in which the former recommended Arms for the position, and once on the job, "stopped the Department from making extensions, particularly into the Ballard area." Copy in Frank Fitts, Papers, Box 8, MSS, UW.

8. PSP&L, Records, Outward correspondence, 8 February 1911, Box 150.

9. *Literary Digest*, 23 March 1912, p. 577, and the general sources cited above.

10. The *Argus* defended Wappenstein, reminding people that he had run such a clean town as Mayor Moore's chief that "crooks gave this city a wide berth . . . ."; furthermore, that when Gill declared for an open town and told Wappy to abide by those broad terms the new chief did so: "If Wappenstein is guilty of any crime he is guilty of receiving some of the proceeds of a system . . . which [was] inaugurated by those above him. He simply took some of the profits of those engaged in vice. . . ." It was the white slave linkage that was effectively used against him. Sarcastically, Chadwick concluded: "Had Wappenstein been a cheap crook like Gid Tupper he would never have been compelled to stand trial." 28 December 1912.

Chapter 9
The City in Transition
Dilling's Administration

1. PSP&L, Records, Outward correspondence, 22 February 1911, Box 150.
2. PSP&L, *ibid.*, 16 Feb; 8 March 1911, Box 150; 2 October 1911, Box 145; 27 September 1911, Box 145; 10 May 1911, Box 150.
3. PSP&L, *ibid.*, 12 July and 28 June 1911; 9 and 23 August 1911, Box 151.
4. For Erickson's claque PSP&L, *ibid.*, 1 June 1911, Box 151, and 24 May 1911, Box 150. Continuation of the Erickson-Ross rivalry is covered in Volume 2 of this history. For Dilling's tour see PSP&L, *ibid.*, 25 August 1911, Box 164; for competition see: 12 July; 10 October; 9 December 1911, Box 150.
5. *Argus*, 5 August 1911.
6. Saltvig, *ibid.*, pp. 184-186; *Argus*, 10 February 1912.

Legislation: More Common Ground Found

1. For the general political setting see Saltvig, *ibid.*, pp. 170-79, and Dembo, *ibid.*, chapter 3, esp., pp. 84-93 on the workmen's compensation bill. The most comprehensive coverage is found in Tripp, *ibid.*, chapters 2, 3, and Tripp, "Toward. . . ." *PNQ, ibid.* See also Robert E. Ficken, *Lumber and Politics: The Career of Mark E. Reed* (Seattle: University of Washington Press, 1979), pp. 81-82, 86-87. Corresponding to Reed's political temper in matters of labor legislation was that of the *Argus*: Chadwick congratulated Governor Hay for his role in getting both the passage of the workmen's compensation bill and a full-crew on railroads law, to protect "life and limb." *Argus*, 12 October 1912. Chadwick had supported passage of other labor/social legislation in the past as well.
2. *Cf.* John A. Rademaker, "The Ecological Position of the Japanese Farmers in the State of Washington" (Unpublished Ph. D. Dissertation, University of Washington, 1939), pp. 21-28, and Miyamoto, *ibid.*, pp. 87-94.

City Beautiful, the Waterfront, and the "Interests"

1. For the most recent account, in which records of the Army Engineers Seattle District Office were used, see Robert E. Ficken, "Seattle's Ditch. . . ," in *PNQ* 77:1 (January, 1986). Also Gordon B. Dodds, *ibid.*, chapter 6, esp. pp. 130-42 for a general account. See also Padraic Burke, "City Beautiful Movement. . . ," For Thomson quotation see R. H. Thomson, Papers, Letterbook, 20 July 1907. For the role of the American Institute of Architects (AIA), Seattle Chapter see its Minutes for: 28 January 1909; 5 January 3 February 1910; 29 and 31 August, and 26 September 1911. AIA. Seattle Chapter, Records, MSS, UW.
2. *RMN*, 7:1, January 15, 1911, pp. 5-7; PSP&L, Records, Chamber to PSTP&L, 8 July 1911, and outgoing letter of 8 November 1911, Box 153; *RMN*, 9:1, January 15, 1911, p. 8.

3. Besides Ficken and Dodds as noted above; see Thomson to Piles, 8 February 1910 on payoff, Thomson, Papers. For other Thomson commentary see Thomson to Piles 1 April 1910. Chittenden's letters to Brainerd are in the Erastus Brainerd, Papers, 15 February and 29 March 1910, MSS,UW.

4. Thomson to Piles, 23 February 1910; Thomson to Humphries, 23 April 1910, Thomson, Papers.

5. See Ficken and Dodds as noted above.

The City Gets a Center . . . and More

1. See Nesbit, *ibid.*, pp. 227-37.

2. Nesbit, *ibid.*, pp. 241-43, and Chamber of Commerce, *ibid.*, October 1901.

3. Tarbill, *ibid.*

4. William H. Wilson, "How Seattle Lost the Bogue Plan," *PNQ* 75:4 (October 1984),pp. 171-80; J. M. Neil, "Paris or New York? The Shaping of Downtown Seattle, 1903-14," *PNQ* 75:1 (January 1984), pp. 22-33; AIA, *ibid.*, January 1910.

5. Wilson, *ibid.*

6. This section on the university's downtown tract is derived from Neal O. Hines, *Denny's Knoll: A History of the Metropolitan Tract of the University of Washington* (Seattle: University of Washington Press, 1980), chapter 4.

Epilogue

1. Hines, *ibid.*, chapters 5 and 6 are the basis for this epilogue. The quotations are from pp. 114 and 147 respectively.

The Port of Seattle versus Private Interests

1. *Town Crier*, 3 September 1910, p. 15; 3 December 1910, pp. 9,10.

2. Padraic Burke, *Port of Seattle* . . . pp. 25-29. A. L. Kempster reported to Stone and Webster the opening of industrial sites "south of Seattle," resulting in the moving of some "well capitalized concerns from other towns," PSP&L, *ibid.*, 15 May 1912, Box 122. Goaded by the legislation the railroad companies and a majority of the waterfront property owners formed the Seattle Harbor Improvement Association; see *RMN*, 9:2, 1 February 1911, pp. 8 and 21.

3. AIA, *ibid.*, 26 September 1911. For the role of the AIA in general see its Minutes for: 28 January 1909; 5 January and 2 March 1910; 29, 31 August; and 26 September 1911.

4. Virgil Bogue, *Plan of Seattle* (Seattle: Lowman and Hanford, 1911), 2 volumes, is the basic document. See Sale, *ibid.*, pp. 95-105 for a general account of the Bogue plan. For the most recent account see William H. Wilson, *ibid.*; Burke, *ibid.*, chapter 5 gives a comprehensive account of the Harbor Island controversy.

5. Burke, *op. cit.*; Dodd, Chittenden, pp. 186-91; see the Times and *P-I*, 27 January 1912.

6. Burke, *op. cit.*; Dodd, *op. cit.*; *Town Crier*, 10 February 1912.
7. Thomson to Burke, 7 February 1912, Thomson, Papers.
8. *Town Crier*, 24 February 1912; Times, 15 February 1912; Burke, *op. cit.*
9. *Municipal News* (hereafter cited as *Muni News*), 24 February and 2 March 1912.
10. The author conducted the survey to see how much attention was given the Bogue plan in the furor over Harbor Island since that had not been done before. Given their neglect of and/or hostility to the plan its defeat is not surprising. Chadwick's epitaph was published as early as the February 10 issue of The *Argus*: "The co-called civic center plan is also lost in the shuffle . . . The Bogue plans will keep."
11. The newspapers are the source for the election results. On Chittenden's plans see Star, 7 March 1912, and Burke, *ibid.*, pp. 41-48.

Epilogue

1. Burke, *op. cit.*; Dodd, *op. cit.* See Seattle Port Commission, Records, File 2-7, MSS, UW for Bridges statement.
2. A. L. Kempster reported to Stone and Webster that the *P-I*, *RMN*, and the *Pacific Fisherman* had switched support, while the *Times* held out for Harbor Island; PSP&L, Records, Outward correspondence, 20 June 1913, Box 122. Burke, *ibid.*, p. 39; Wilson, *ibid.*; *Sun*, 26 March and 23 April 1913.
3. See J. M. Neil, "Paris or New York? The Shaping of Downtown Seattle," *PNQ* 75:1 (January 1984), pp. 22-33. For Gould attitude see AIA, *ibid.*, 10 April 1912.

Thomson Reflects on the Cost of it All

1. Thomson, Papers, *ibid.*, 21 November 1913.

Chapter 10
Politics and Labor: The 1912-1914 Interlude

Mayor Cotterill Meets the Colonel Head-On

1. The three most extensive accounts of the Potlatch riot are those of Murray Morgan in chapter 4 of *Skid Road*, which includes background on Alden Blethen, and on the riot itself on pp. 182-90; Roger Sales, *ibid.*, pp. 109-12; and Harvey O'Connor, *Revolution in Seattle: A Memoir* (New York: Monthly Review Press, 1964), pp. 21-28. O'Connor relies heavily on Wells's autobiography and on a personal interview with Wells. Newspaper sources are obvious in the text, and are not cited specifically.
2. For background on the Harbor Island episode see "Port of Seattle vs. Private Interests," above. See also: Burke, *ibid.*, pp. 34-40; G. Dodds, *ibid.*, pp. 188-189; Robert Saltvig, *ibid.*, chapter 7.
3. On the nationwide program of the National Electric Light Association see Douglas Anderson, *Regulatory Politics. . .* , chapters 1 and 2.
4. Wells, [Autobiography], "I Wanted To Work," pp. 138-179.

5. Wells, *ibid.*; Morgan, *ibid.*, p. 180.

6. Wells, *ibid.*

7. Wells, *ibid.*

8. There is no agreement on how the fight began; consequently, I have blended a plausible scenario which depends mainly on Morgan's account, p. 184.

9. *Sun*, 19 July 1913.

10. *Times*, 19 July 1913.

11. *Sun, ibid.*

Industrial Relations: a Case in Point

1. *Cf.*, Wiebe, *ibid.*, in general; Cochran and Miller, *ibid.*, chapters 7-14; Taft, *ibid.*, chapters 6, 7, 10-16, 18. Montgomery, *ibid.*, chapter 6. For labor policies of the railroads, in their efforts to thwart unionization, see W. Thomas White, "A History of Railroad Workers in the Pacific Northwest, 1893-1934" (Unpublished Ph.D. Dissertation, University of Washington, 1981), and his "Railroad Labor Protest, 1894-1917," *PNQ* 75:1 (January 1984), pp. 13-21.

2. PSP&L, Records, Outward correspondence, 25 June; 8, 26 September 1904, Box 166. For tactics in general see Denzel C. Cline, *ibid.*

3. PSP&L, *ibid.*, 25 May 1909, Box 150; Employers' Association subgroup, undated report, 1914, on IBEW, Local 77; and Kempster to J. B. Middleton, 11 June 1913, Box 147.

4. PSP&L, *ibid.*, undated report, above; report of Agent Number 6, 15 January 1915, Box 147.

5. PSP&L, *ibid.*, Box 147. After the strike the strikebreakers were laid off. The Company, however, signed a closed shop agreement with the Bricklayers. See also 1 and 8 May; 10 July; 23 and 30 October 1912, Box 122.

6. PSP&L, *ibid.*: regarding the PCUA see PCUA subgroup, Box 147; it was organized 2 September 1913. Re EA and the Reid-McNulty factions see EA subgroup 31 March and 6 May 1913.; and Kempster to Kerrigan 6 June 1914, Box 147; for inter-company agreement see 6 May 1913, in PCUA subgroup, Box 147.

7. PSP&L, *ibid.*, PCUA subgroup, B.C. Electric Railway Co., to Kempster, 22 May 1913, and Grambs to Kempster, 12 May 1913, Box 147.

8. PSP&L, *ibid.*, PCUA subgroup, Kerrigan to Grambs, 19 January 1914, Box 147.

9. PSP&L, *ibid.*, PCUA subgroup, "Confidential Reports" signed by Kerrigan, 4 and 9, February 1914, Box 147.

10. PSP&L, *ibid.*, Kempster to A. W. Leonard, 8 October 1914; and EA subgroup, 30 December 1914 and 5 January 1915. On 22 September 1915 the EA announced formation of its Employers Free Labor Bureau.

Labor Movement vs. Employers' Association

1. PSP&L, Records. *ibid.*, 15 May 1912.

2. In general see Dembo, *ibid.*, chapter 3; Saltvig, *ibid.*, pp. 403-26.

On Teamsters' strike see Thompson, *ibid*, pp. 34-35; Carl G. Westine, "The Seattle Teamsters" (Unpublished Master's Thesis, University of Washington, 1937), p. 12. Teamsters' early history is given in *Union Record* (hereafter cited as *UR*), 24 January 1914. The best source for continuous coverage of the year-long strike and of other labor disputes of the period is the *UR*. The *Town Crier* (hereafter cited as *TC*), gives the Employers' Association historical view in its 9:12 (March 1914), pp. 5-6 issue—"The Truth About the Teamsters' Strike," in which San Francisco is portrayed as a closed shop town under teamster domination. The *TC* issue of 9:3 (17 January 1914), pp. 13-14, covers Rev. Matthews' views. On Cudihee see Blackford, *ibid.*, p. 80. On Ballard dispute and the 17 months-long Renton strike see *Sun*, 7 and 12 April 1913 respectively. The Grambs-Cotterill episode is well reported in the *Sun*, *P-I*, and *UR*; the *Sun* reported on 11 December that: "Following recent warlike declarations of the employers' association for an open shop, the CLC Wednesday decided to concentrate its fight against the association. . . ."

3. *UR*, 17 and 24 January 1914.

4. PSP&L, Records, Employers' Association subgroup, [January 1914].

5. *UR*, 7 March 1914; *TC*, 17 January 1914.

6. *UR*, 24 and 31 January; 11 and 25 April; 9 May 1914; Blackford, *ibid.*, pp. 82-89.

7. *UR*, 12 April 1913; 10 and 24 January and 23 May 1914; Chamber of Commerce, Minutes, 3 February 1914.

8. *UR*, 9 and 30, May; 6 June; 1 August 1914. Too Late to be included in the text, but excellent for its detailed coverage of women in the Seattle work force is Maurine Weiner Greenwald, "Working-Class Feminism and the Family Wage Ideal: the Seattle Debate on Married Women's Right to Work, 1914-1920", *Journal of American History*, 76:1 (June 1989), pp. 118-149. The female component in the work force expanded from 4,774 in 1900 to 33,114 by 1920; married women, 881 in 1900 and 9,203 in 1920.

9. *TC*, 15 August 1914; *UR*, 15 August and 16 October 1914.

10. *UR*, 21 March 1914; 28 August; 11 September; 2 and 23 October 1915. While the Chamber of Commerce declined to contribute financially to the Employers' Association campaign it did declare ". . . every effort possible should be made to maintain [the open shop] and the Chamber of Commerce pledges to use its influence towards that end." C of C Minutes, 3 February 1914. On the Mutual Laundry see *UR*, 16 and 23 October and 18 December 1915. The *UR* of 31 July 1915 shows a facsimile copy of the Skinner letter.

11. *UR*, 1, 8, 15, 26, May; 3 July 1915. As a footnote to this episode, the Italians established the Italian Laborers' Union, Local 361 of the AFL. But note the ethnic separation required, which lends support to Jonathan Dembo's thesis distinguishing between "new" and "old" immigrant groups.

The Legislature and the City, 1913

1. In general, see: Saltvig, *ibid.*, chapter 8; Pendergrass, *ibid.*, chapter

3; Dembo, *ibid.*, pp. 111-115; Blackford, *ibid.*, pp. 72-77; *Seattle Sun*, 3 and 25 February, 1913. Kempster reported the Home Rulers' defeat was "most notable" achievement of the legislature. Lister "showed his complete mastery of the situation." 19 March 1913, PSP&L Records, Box 122.

2. Louise Beck, *Seattle Mail and Herald* 8:6 (17 December 1904), 20-21; Washington State Federation of Women's Clubs, Records, Minutes, and "History," Box 1, MSS,UW. The *Seattle Sun* noted on 12 March that, of the 58,995 registered voters in Seattle, 20,376 were women, and that of the 41,752 who voted in the March 4 election, 12,317 were women. The *Seattle Sun* noted in its February 14 issue that the Municipal League refused to endorse any of the three women candidates for City Council on the grounds that women were not yet sufficiently experienced to hold public office, to which the president of the Seattle Federation of Women's Clubs agreed, but over the protest of the North End Progressive Club.

3. *Town Crier*, 4 and 18 January 1913.

4. *Seattle Sun*, 3 February; 17 and 19 March 1913.

5. *Seattle Sun*, 4, 11, 15, and 17 February; 11 and 12 March 1913.

City Politics and Municipal Ownership

1. Kempster's weekly and monthly reports to Stone and Webster were the main source for the above economic information. See also *Seattle Sun*, 4 December 1913 for Chittenden's report.

Chapter 11
The Economy, 1914-1920

An Overview

1. In general see Dembo, *ibid.*, pp. 111-15; 124, 127,141; and pp. 154-200 for the political impact of the labor shortage generated by the war, and the resulting growth of labor militancy, accompanied by repression of civil liberties. Port of Seattle, *Yearbook*, 1918; *RMN*, 16, Number 6, June 1918, p. 32; PSP&L, Records, Weekly letter 27 April, 18 May; 12 June; 3 and 12 August 1918, Box 122.

2. PSP&L, Records, Weekly letter, 20 March; 6, 10, and 13 April; and 8 June 1918; Business Conditions letter, 12 October, 11 and 23 November 1918. United States, *Census of Manufactures*, 1920.

3. All of the above shipping statistics are from the Port Warden, *Annual Reports*.

4. PSP&L, Records, 31 January and 21 April 1917; 4 May 1918. While lumber and the coal trade were still depressed in early 1915 food products were picking up, providing the general impetus for the economic improvement of 1914 over conditions in 1913. PSP&L, *ibid.*, 5 January 1915, Box 122. *RMN* provides a running commentary on the economy for the period; see esp., 13 Number 1, January, p. 21; Number 4, April, p. 32; and Number 7, July 1915, p. 29 for the impact of the opening of the Panama Canal on railroad shipments; and 13, 11 November 1915, p. 20, and 15 Number 4 April 1917, p. 7 for the impact when the canal closed for repairs in November 1915.

The Dark Side of the Economy: Unemployment

1. For general coverage see Pendergrass, *ibid.*, pp. 63-66 and Saltvig, *ibid.*, pp. 420-22. In the winter of 1913-1914 Mayor Cotterill had promoted the use of the former Providence Hospital building. Reportedly about 500 "hoboes" were accommodated under the leadership of Jeff Davis, "king of the hoboes" and head of the Itinerant Workers Union. It was called "Hotel de Gink." *Sun*, 24 December 1913, p. 6. See also *Sun*, 25 February 1913. In late October the SCLC passed a resolution urging the AFL to declare unemployment to be the most important problem facing the working class. *UR*, 30 October 1915.

2. *Sun*, 17 and 19 December 1913; *UR*, 14 November 1914. For Gill's remarks see *UR*, 12 June 1915.

3. *Muni News*, 13 March and 3 April 1915. The *Muni News* gives a history of the Hotel Liberty in its *News*, 10 April 1915. The League boasted of the huge success of the free employment office. On employment agencies see Tripp, *Progressive Labor Laws.* . . . pp. 115-127. Between 1910 and 1914 there were annually about 20,000 more men employed in October than in January.

4. *UR*, 28 November 1914.

5. Chamber of Commerce, Minutes, 11 September 1914.

6. *UR*, 28 November 1914. The hotel was providing for about 600 single men. An Unemployed League was formed (as would occur again in 1931 with longer range effects).

Chapter 12
City Politics, 1914-1915

The Setting

1. In general see Saltvig, *ibid.*, pp. 186-92; Austin Griffiths, Papers, Scrapbook, Box 21.

2. Pamphlet, "Police Bill No. 30451 . . ."; drafts of letters to *P-I*, August 21 to 9 November 1912 in Griffiths, Papers, File 19-11. After his loss to Gill in the 1914 election Gill appointed Griffiths Police Chief and supported without a whimper the many reforms instituted by Griffiths, Griffiths Papers, File 20-3, MSS,UW.

3. PSP&L, Records, Weekly reports, 7, 14, January 4, and 26 February 1914, Box 122. In Box 147 is a carbon copy of a report by Martin Flyzik, president of the UMW, District 10, in which Flyzik contends the strikes were really lockouts because the owners closed down the mines once they learned the miners were organized.

4. See Dembo, *ibid.*, pp. 113-23; Saltvig, *ibid.*, pp. 416-22; Pendergrass, *ibid.*, pp. 58-65; and Blackford, *ibid.*, pp. 83-86.

5. *UR*, 1 November 1913.

6. PSP&L, Records, Weekly reports, 21 January; 22 and 29 April; 27 May; 10 and 17 June; 21 July; 26 August; and 9 and 30 September; and 30 December 1914, Box 122.

7. *UR*, 30 May 1914.

8. *TC,* 16 May 1914, p. 6.
9. Kumor, *ibid.,* chapter 6.
10. *TC,* 16 May and 18 July 1914.

City Politics, 1914

1. See Blackford, *ibid.,* pp. 82-92; Saltvig, *ibid.,* p. 203 for quotation, and pp. 190-202; Pendergrass, *ibid.,* pp. 60-62; Dembo, *ibid.,* pp. 116-18. The Central Labor Council thanked Griffiths for his opposition to the charter revision. Charter Revision Committee members Blaine, Kellogg, Bolton, and Doyle, along with civic leaders Rev. Matthews, former mayor John Miller, James Haight, and Cotterill wound up opposing, after supporting the idea earlier; see Griffiths Papers, File 7-22. As to Griffiths' defeat by Gill the *Argus's* Harry Chadwick told his friend, Griffiths, that he was obligated to Gill, but that Griffiths lost a bulk of votes ". . . because of the active part which the churches took in your campaign."; File 7-20 in Griffiths, Papers. On Matthews and the charter revision see Soden, *ibid.,* pp. 226-27.

2. *TC,* 6 June 1914, p. 10; *Muni News,* 2 May 1914.

Seattle Endorses Prohibition

1. "Prohibition in the City." This section is derived from Norman H. Clark, *The Dry Years: Prohibition and Social Change in Washington* (Seattle: University of Washington Press, 1965), chapter 8. Also, Clark, "The 'Hell-Soaked Institution' and the Washington Prohibition Initiative of 1914," *PNQ* 56:1 (January 1965) pp. 1-16. The executive committee of the Citizens' Anti-Prohibition Association reads like a Chamber of Commerce roster: Thomas Burke, J. D. Lowman, J. F. Douglas, Henry Broderick, and Charles E. Horton. In its "Open Letter" it argued that the liquor trade was a primary source of tax revenues, and it should therefore be continued; in Thomson, Papers, Scrapbook, Number 1, 1 October 1914. On Matthews' role see Soden, *ibid.,* pp. 228-30.

Municipal Ownership

1. Dick, *Genesis* . . . in chapters 10 and 11 gives the most comprehensive account to both the Cedar Dam "fiasco" and the search for other sites. Councilman Griffiths reported to the council on 5 May 1912 that the Board of Engineers (Joseph Jacobs, E. H. Baldwin, and Glover Perin) had checked on the potential seepage problem, and concluded the chosen site ". . . is the best on the river, the design is oversafe, and the foundation will stand all the load put upon it." Griffiths urged "further thorough investigations." Griffiths, Papers, File 20-3.

2. *Muni News,* and the *Sun,* 24 January 1914; *Muni News,* 31 January 1914. A. L. Kempster commented to the Boston Office on the League, judging it to be "radical in tendency," and it had been an element in that it "aspires to . . . the promulgation of new theories." PS&PL Records, Box 122. The course of these issues can be followed in the scrapbooks of the Seattle Lighting Department, MSS,UW. The clippings are carefully identified and provide an excellent organized alternative to gleaning information from newspapers on microfilm.

3. Seattle Lighting Department, Scrapbooks.

Port of Seattle

1. *RMN*, 13:1 (January 1915), p 21; and 13:4 (April 1915), p. 32.

2. *RMN*, 13:9 (September 1915, p. 33; 14:2 (February 1916); 15:1 (January 1917); and 15:2 (February 1917) for Seattle's relative positions. See also, Burke, *Port of Seattle* . . . , pp. 50-53. *San Francisco Examiner* 22 November 1917, p. 1, has a feature article pointing to Seattle's ascendancy to fourth place in the United States and its foreign commerce exceeding San Francisco's by $90 million in the fiscal year 1916-1917. San Francisco returned to hegemonic status in 1921.

3. Burke, *op. cit.*

4. On the belt-line controversy see, Burke, *ibid.*, pp. 60-62.

5. On the *Minnesota* and *Dakota* see *RMN* 13:5 (May 1915), p. 27 and 15:3 (March 1917), p. 27. On the effect of the Panama Canal slides see *RMN* 13:11 (November 1915), p. 20. San Francisco's loss of the Pacific Mail Line in 1915, as a result of the passage of the Seamen's Act redounded to Seattle's advantage; the entire issue of *RMN* 13:9 (September 1915) was devoted to the consequences of the legislation. Because of World War I, the act's provisions were not, however, enforced. On Waterhouse, see *RMN* 13:10 (October 1915), pp. 21-22. *RMN* 15:4 (April 1917): "each of the great railroad systems reaching Puget Sound [was] established through cargo arrangements with the Orient and Vladivostock . . . ," p. 7.

The University and the City

1. This section is derived from the following: Kumor, *ibid.*, chapter 6; Jack Van de Wetering, "The Appointment of Henry Suzzallo: The University of Washington Gets a President," *PNQ* 50:3 (July 1959), pp. 99-107; Gates, *ibid.*, pp. 138-45; Donald T. Williams, Jr., "The Remarkable Dr. Henry Suzzallo: A Biography" (Unpublished manuscript, n.d.), pp. 95-106. A copy is in the University of Washington Archives.

The Legislature and the City, 1915

1. For the general setting see Saltvig, *ibid.*, pp. 392-93 and 400-02; Dembo, *ibid.*, pp. 124-27. On Centralia strike see *UR*, 13 March 1915. On Public Service Commission see PSP&L, Records, *ibid.*, 6 and 13 January 1915, Box 122. Kempster volunteered that the aim was to bring the municipals under control of the commission. Kerr of the *RMN* looked favorably upon the bill introduced by King County senators to abolish the existing port commission. *RMN*, 13:3 (March 1915), p. 31.

2. PSP&L, Records, *ibid.*, 13 January and 24 March 1915, Box 122.

3. PSP&L, Records, *ibid.*, 21 April, 5 and 12 May 1915, Box 122.

4. PSP&L, Records, *ibid.*, 10 March 1915, Box 122.

5. PSP&L, Records, *ibid.*, Employers' Association subgroup, 25 February 1915, Box 17.

6. *UR*, 27 March 1915.

7. On Ladies Garment Workers see *UR*, 26 December 1914, 2 and 23 January 1915. On laundry workers see *UR*, 30 January and 13 February 1915. On lecture series see *UR*, 13 March 1915.

8. Tripp, *Progressive Labor Legislation.* . . . pp. 127-143 in general, and pp. 135-140 for 1915 first aid amendment.

9. *UR*, 6, 13, and 27 March and 3 April 1915. The SCLC organized a mass protest against Stone and Webster for refusing to negotiate with the union. Kempster reported to headquarters that attempts to organize had been made over the past few months without success; that the *Star* has been "rabid in its utterances"; and "The mob surged down the street intent on stampeding the men . . . [but the] effect on the employees has seemed to be of a most gratifying nature." PSP&L, Records, *ibid.*, 2 April 1915, Box 122.

10. *UR*, 20 March, 3 April, and 14 August 1915.

Chapter 13
1916: Improvement . . . for a Time

News Briefs:

1. Clark, *Dry Years.* . . . p. 134. For general setting see Dembo, *ibid.*, pp. 125-36.

2. *UR*, 15 and 22 January and 20 May 1916.

Dry Law Takes Effect

1. This section is derived from Clark, *ibid.*, pp. 134-40.

Industrial Relations Intensify

1. *UR*, 11 and 18 December 1915, 29 January, 19 February 1, and 8 April, 10 and 24 June 1916.

2. *UR*, 12 February; 25 March; 15, 22, and 29 April; 6 and 13 May; 3, 10, and 17 June; 9 and 30 September; 14 and 28 October; and 2 December 1916.

3. The most comprehensive account of the 1916 longshoremen's strike is in George Michael Jones, "Longshoremen's Unionism on Puget Sound: A Seattle-Tacoma Comparison" (Unpublished Master's Thesis, University of Washington, 1957), pp. 55-61. Jones also gives the general historical background and accounts of earlier and later strikes through 1956. In March 1915 the employers reduced wages by twenty-five to thirty-five percent without giving prior notice to the longshoremen, telling the men that if they did not like it there were plenty of unemployed who would take their place. Negotiations dragged on through the summer, with the ILA threatening to strike as the intermittent lockouts continued. See *UR*, 20 March, 3 April, 14 and 28 August 1915. For the 1916 strike see *UR*, 24 June; 1, 8, 15, 22, and 29 July; 5, 12, 19, and 26 August; 23 and 30 September 7, 14, and 21 October; 4 November; 30 December

1916. For Municipal League role see *Muni News*, 1 July; 12 and 26 August; 23 September; and 7 October 1916; *RMN* 15:2 (February 1917), p. 13.
   4. Joseph S. Jackson, "The Colored Marine Employees Benevolent Association of the Pacific. . . ," p. 90.

The Everett Massacre and Seattle Labor

   1. For general accounts (from which mine is derived) see Norman H. Clark, *Mill Town: A Social History of Everett . . . to . . . the Everett Massacre* (Seattle: University of Washington Press, 1970), pp. 168-227; Harvey O'Connor, *ibid.*, pp. 29-57; Lowell S. Hawley and Ralph B. Potts, *Counsel for the Damned: A Biography of George Francis Vanderveer* (Philadelphia: J. B. Lippincott, 1953), pp. 187-209; Robert L. Tyler, *Rebels of The Woods: The I.W.W. in the Pacific Northwest* (Eugene: University of Oregon, 1967), chapter 3; and Melvyn Dubofsky, *We Shall Be All: A History of the Industrial Workers of the World* (Chicago: Quadrangle Books, 1969), pp. 339-43. The *UR* gave a weekly account of the aftermath and the trial.

Also on the Labor Front

   1. On the teamsters see the *UR*, 15 January; 11 March; 29 April; 6 May; 24 June; and 19 August 1916. On theaters see *UR* 22 January 1916; on Mutual Laundry see *UR*, 22 April; 2 and 16 December 1916.

The City vs. the Legislature's Referred Acts of 1915

   1. In general see Saltvig, *ibid.*, pp. 399-401 and 428-34; and Dembo, *ibid.*, pp. 126-29 and 134-36; Tripp, *Progressive Labor Legislation. . . .* pp. 113-115, 135-140, and 154-58 for both enactment of the anti-picketing law and its rejection in 1916. But the courts continued to uphold rulings against picketing; the St. Germain ruling in May 1917 confirmed past court decisions (pp. 159-62). Also *UR* issues of September and October 1915. On Employers' Association see *UR*, 26 January 18 and 25 March and 8 April 1916. On PSTP&L see *UR*, 17 June 1916. Judge D.F. Wright, of Thurston County, ruled that the courts could not assume jurisdiction over the initiative petitions until after they had been voted upon; but he was overruled, 5 to 4, by the Supreme Court in July, which ruled that the court can interfere with legislation in process. *UR*, 1 April and 22 July 1916.
   2. *UR*, 16 September 1916.
   3. *Muni News*, 28 October and 4 November 1916.
   4. *Times*, 14 October 1916.
   5. See Saltvig, *ibid.*, p. 401 for voting results.

The University, City, and State

   1. This section is derived mainly from Donald T. Williams, Jr., *ibid.*, chapter 7, supplemented by Charles M. Gates, *ibid.*, pp. 141-56, and Thomas McClintock, "J. Allen Smith. . . ," pp. 426-45. For a discussion of the

controversy between the University of Washington and the State College of Washington in Pullman, see George A. Frykman, *Creating the People's University: Washington State University, 1890-1990* (Pullman: Washington State University Press, 1990).

Chapter 14
War Preparedness and War in the Schools

1. This section is derived mainly from Bryce Nelson, "Good Schools . . . ," chapter 7; supplemented by Stephanie F. Ogle, "Anna Louise Strong: Progressive and Propagandist" (Unpublished Ph.D. Dissertation, University of Washington, 1981), pp. 128-42; Sarah Ellen Sharbach, "Louise Olivereau and the Seattle Radical Community 1917-1923" (Unpublished Master's Thesis, University of Washington, 1986), chapter 3, esp., pp. 55-57; and Tracy B. Strong and Helene Keyssar, *Right in Her Soul: The Life of Anna Louise Strong* (New York: Random House, 1983), pp. 66-69. The general setting as well as specific cases (Wells, Strong, and Olivereau) is found in Albert F. Gunns, "Civil Liberties and Crisis: The Status of Civil Liberties in the Pacific Northwest, 1917-1940" (Unpublished Ph.D. Dissertation, University of Washington, 1971), pp. 11-19. The role of the Minute Men is detailed in Nelson, *ibid*, pp. 236-41; and the school board career of Strong on pp. 242-44.

In the *Legislative Federationist*, February 1918, Strong was defended by the editor on ground that the ballot made no provision for a response from her, and that the charges were for acts done before passage of the draft act.

Chapter 15
Industrial Relations and the War

The Growth of Patriotic Fervor

1. In general see Tripp, *ibid*., chapter 5; Saltvig, *ibid*., chapter 14; Dembo, *ibid*., p. 121 and 136-186; Albert Gunns, *ibid*., chapter 1. Kempster's commentary is in PSP&L, Records, *ibid*., 17 January 1917, Box 122.

2. Kempster, *op. cit.*, 28 May; 2, 16, 23 June; 18 July; 11 August 1917.

Tensions Accumulate

1. *Muni News*, 6 January 1917; *UR*, 13 January; 17 February; 3 and 10 March 1917; *Muni News*, 2 and 23 June 1917.

2. *UR*, 20 January 1917.

3. *UR*, 30 December 1916; 17 March; 16 and 30 June; and 14 July 1917.

4. Dembo, *ibid*. pp.135-38; *UR*, 19 May.

War on the Home Front

1. *UR*, 7, 14, and 21 April 1917.

2. *UR*, 7 April 1917.

3. *Muni News*, 7 April, 7 July, and 29 December 1917.

4. *UR*, 14, 21, and 28 April 1917.

5. *UR*, 5 and 12 May 1917.

The Trainmen's Strike

1. Cline, *ibid.*, pp. 36-45; Blanchard, *ibid.*, pp. 87-88; *Muni News*, 21 July 1917; Kempster reports to Boston, 17 March; 12 May; 23 and 30 June; 21 and 28 July; 9, 15, 23, and 29 September; 6, 13, 20 October; 3, 10, and 17 November 1917, PSP&L Records, Box 122. Kempster, himself, was deputized by Sheriff John Stringer; and when he was acting in 1920 for the New Orleans Public Service Corporation in quelling a strike there, his reputation was that of "the street car boss of the great Northwest." Kempster, Papers, MSS, UW. See also *UR*, 13 January; 7, 21, and 28 July; 4, 11, and 25 August 1917; 5 January 1918.

2. See *UR* for the entire period from July through December 1917.

The Great Lumber Strike of 1917

1. This monumental strike has been extensively written about. The most comprehensive study is by Harold M. Hyman, *Soldiers and Spruce: Origins of the Loyal Legion of Loggers and Lumbermen* (Los Angeles: Institute of Industrial Relations, University of California, 1963). Other works covering the strike from which my account is derived, are: Robert L. Tyler, *Rebels. . . .* chapter 4; Dubofsky, *We Shall Be All*, pp. 361-65; O'Connor, *Revolution. . . .* chapter 3; Saltvig, *ibid.*, pp. 436-41; and Dembo, *ibid.*, pp. 156-69; Robert E. Ficken, *The Forested Land: A History of Lumbering in Western Washington* (Seattle: University of Washington Press, 1987), pp. 140-149. For the Ames quotation see Ames to Herman Chapin, 3 April 1918, Edwin G. Ames, Papers, File 17-50 MSS,UW.

The Edwin G. Ames, Papers, provide his views on developments: Writing to J. H. Weston in Mississippi, he reported on August 31 that the backbone of the strike had been broken, and that 5,000 workers will be discharged from the Camp Lewis construction, and will drift into the cities and lumber mills, relieving the labor shortage, File 16-23; and responding to Shipping Board chairman, Edward Hurley on September 19 about the 8-hour day issue, "Regional eight hour day is impossible and will wreck the industry unless all competitive territory are operated on same basis . . . lumbermen on this Coast will work for eight hour day national in character," File 16-30. Everett Griggs of the St. Paul and Tacoma Lumber Company also wrote Hurley, "The eight hour day in the lumber industry adopted regionally is suicidal," File 16-31. As to the troublemakers, it was the "transients," not the "old-timers," according to Ames, File 16-19. Papers of Disque that Harold Hyman used are also in the Manuscript Collection of the UW.

Chapter 16
The University and the War

1. This section is derived mainly from Donald T. Williams, Jr. *ibid.*, chapter 7, supplemented by Charles M. Gates, *The First Century. . .* , pp. 153-56; and Thomas McClintock, "J. Allen Smith. . . ," pp. 426-45.

Chapter 17
City Headed for Crisis

The Beginning of the Crisis

1. In general, see Dembo, *ibid.*, pp. 177-93; Gunns, *ibid.*, chapter 1; and O'Connor, *ibid.*, chapter 4.

2. *Times*, 24 and 26 December 1917; *UR*, 29 December 1917. O'Connor, *ibid.*, 103-04.

3. *Times*, 11 and 12 December; 4 and 9 January 1918. Harry Chadwick viewed the city's placement on the off-limits list as the turning point for Gill. In his opinion the citizens had not realized until then how wide-open Seattle had become. *Argus*, 23 February 1918.

4. In the election Harry Chadwick accused both Hanson and the "Socialist Brown" of trying "to hang the stone of socialism around the neck of . . . Bradford." He believed Bradford would give everyone a "square deal." *Argus*, 2 March 1918. On the shipyards see: Seattle Lighting Department, Scrapbooks for the period. See also "Outward Correspondence" 5 and 26 January; 11 February; 18 March; 3 August (Charles Schwab of the Shipping Board threatened to withhold future shipbuilding contracts unless Seattle solved the housing problem, 9 September 1918), PSP&L Records, Box 122.

5. Mary Joan O'Connell, "The Seattle Union Record, 1918-128: A Pioneer Labor Daily" (Unpublished Master's Thesis, University of Washington, 1964), pp. 43-44; O'Connor, *ibid.*, pp. 95-96; *UR*, for all of January 1918.

6. *UR*, 8, 15, 22, and 29 December 1917; 5 January; 2, 9, and 16 February; 16 March; and 25 May 1918.

7. Jones, *ibid.*, pp. 61-64; Jackson, *"ibid.,"* for background; Richard B. Peterson, "A Rational Employment System for the West Coast Longshoremen's Industry," *University of Washington Business Review*, 26:3 (Spring 1967), pp. 50-56; *UR*, 19 January; 13 and 20 April; 21 and 28 September; 5 October; 9 November; 14 and 21 December 1918.

8. Gunns, *ibid.*, pp. 20-30 esp. for Minute Men and American Protective League; Dembo, *ibid.*, pp. 183-88; *Times*, 25 November 1917 reported that the IWW office had been raided and records seized; that a round-up would probably follow, and that this was the first raid since September 5 if one of three weeks earlier were not counted—when records were seized from occupants in the Alaskan Hotel; also *Times*, 9 February and 2 March 1918.

9. Gunns, *ibid.*, pp. 7-13; O'Connor, *ibid.*, pp. 84-89; Dembo, *ibid.*, pp. 188-93; *UR*, 16 and 23 Feb; 13 April; and 3 August 1918; Wells, [*Autobiography*], pp. 188-203.

The Erosion of Civil Liberties

1. In general, see Saltvig, *ibid.*, chapter 13; Gunns, *ibid.*, chapter 1, and for quotation see p. 26; Dembo, *ibid.*, pp. 177-82; O'Connor, *ibid.*, chapter 4; Sharbach, *ibid.*, chapter 3. On *Star*, see Sale, *ibid.*, pp. 117-23.

2. Gunns, *ibid.*, pp. 24-25.

3. Gunns, *ibid.*, pp. 15-19; O'Connor, *ibid.*, pp. 85-89; Sharbach, op.cit.

4. Jan C. Dawson, "A Social Gospel Portrait: The Life of Sydney Dix Strong, 1860-1938" (Unpublished Master's Thesis, University of Washington, 1972), pp. 56-62; Pendergrass, *ibid.*, pp. 74-76; *Muni News*, 13 October 1917.

5. For the League in general during the war, see Pendergrass, *ibid.*, pp. 73-86.

Federalized Vigilantism

1. The most recent study of the APL is Joan M. Jensen, *The Price of Vigilance* (Chicago: Rand McNally, 1968); see pp. 17-31, 125-29, and 154-55 for Seattle and the state. Also Gunns, *ibid.*, pp. 25-32. A contemporary account by a defender of the APL is Emerson Hough, *The Web: The Authorized History of the American Protective League* (Chicago: Reilley and Lee, 1919). On the Minute Men in the Seattle public schools see Nelson, *op. cit.* See also American Protective League, Minute Men Division, Seattle, Records, MSS, UW, for constitution, by-laws, membership applications, reports, and correspondence. A report in these records lists a total of 6954 cases for King County. of this total 2127 cases had been "turned in by Government for investigation"; 4827 had been "turned in by precinct"; 2329 were "turned over to Government for action"; 2498 had been "Closed by us without reference to the Government"; and 428 "arrests made, or caused by us." Of these cases 915 were listed as "pro-German radicals"; 828 as "Liberty Bond and Red Cross slackers"; 633 as IWWs; 508 as draft evaders; 322 as "disloyal citizens"; and 228 as "alleged spies or German agents."

On 26 February 1918, Henry M. White, Commissioner of Immigration, commended W. A. Blackwood, Secretary of the Minute Men, for their help in "apprehending I.W.W.'s now held by this service for deportation . . . [W]e have arrested on deportation proceedings about two hundred I.W.W.'s," most of whom he attributed to Minute Men efforts.

Chapter 18
Municipal Ownership I

City Light Acquires the Skagit Site

1. See Dick, "Genesis. . ." pp.145-58; and William O. Sparks, "J. D. Ross and Seattle City Light 1917-1932" (Unpublished Master's Thesis, University of Washington, 1964), chapter I. Sparks is mistaken about the relationship of the Municipal League to City Light, equating as he does, its position with that of the Chamber of Commerce. The League was a consistent supporter of City Light, like a rock throughout the 1920s, falling under Ross's suspicions only when the League pushed for its pet project, the city manager form of municipal government, which Ross viewed as a device of the power trust to undermine his authority. PSP&L Records are filled with information on City Light's search for sites, the company's steady loss of residential customers, and loss of a growing number of commercial and industrial customers - see Kempster's weekly reports from 1913 on.

2. See Sparks, *ibid.*, pp. 24-32 especially, and pp. 17-24 for general background.

3. On the role of the Capital Issues Sub-committee of the Federal Trade Commision see Sparks, *ibid.*, pp. 42-57. See also the U.S. Federal Trade Commission, Capital Issues Sub-Committee, Records, Boxes 6 and 7, MSS,UW.

City Gets a Street Railway. . . Bargain or Not

1. For general background see Blanchard, *ibid.*, pp. 93-96. An excellent recapitulation is to be found in a letter from William H. McGrath to Frank McLaughlin (Leonard's successor), 24 November 1931. In its *News* of 17 March 1917 the Municipal League, in referring to the company's system as a "tramp" also claimed it was trying to put the jitneys out of business instead of improving its service to meet the competition, concluding that the company was only trying to protect its capital. To impress the Shipping Board, the City Council had funded an elevated system along the waterfront to facilitate the delivery of shipyard workers to their jobs. Kempster's weekly reports to Boston are a running source of information on developments. Kempster, reporting, July 20, on the Shipping Board's Charles Schwab's visit to the city: "He patted us on the back, said we were doing fine, but ended up by giving some very pointed advice relative to the labor situation." PSP&L, Records, Box 122.

2. *Times*, 22 October 1918; Erickson to Cotterill, 4 November 1918, File 3-45; and Hogsdon to Cotterill, n.d., File 4-28, Cotterill, Papers, MSS,UW. George Hogsdon was a Representative in the state legislature from Seattle. *Argus*, 26 October 1918.

3. *P-I*, 7, 8, and 9 September 1918; *Star*, 2 November 1918.

"Congratulations"

1. Henry Bradlee (of the New York office of Stone and Webster) to Pratt, 1 October 1918, PSP&L, Records, Box 146.

2. Catlett news note in *National Municipal Review*, Volume 8, pp. 194-95 and 329-30.

An Epilogue

1. Earl V. Minich, Affidavit, [21 November 1923], Homer T. Bone, Papers, University of Puget Sound Library; copy lent by Terry Slatten, biographer of Bone.

Chapter 19

Shipbuilding and the U. S. Shipping board

1. For general background, see Friedheim, *ibid.*, chapter 2; Dembo, *ibid.*, pp. 169-75; O'Connor, *ibid.*, 125-27. Kempster's reports provide a running account of the economy, and of the reaction of the business community to the stresses introduced by the war, PSP&L, Records, Box 122. Indicating the full expectation of the business community that shipbuilding in the city would continue indefinitely after the war is a statement signed by Charles H. Bebb, president of the Seattle chapter of the American Institute of Architects, in which he explained that the influx of the 20,000 or so mechanics should be considered a permanent addition to the population and the Chamber should plan for appropriate housing: "No room for doubt that Puget Sound if not now will be the location of the greatest shipbuilding industry that the world has ever seen." Copy in Edwin G. Ames, Papers, File 17-20. The *Star* reported the Chamber's More Homes Bureau to be advertising a demand for more than 5,000 houses at a minimum; "millions of dollars in contracts depend upon it."; 3 September 1918. As to the Skinner and Eddy yards Kenneth Kerr of the *RMN* attacked the "easy going" David Rodgers for his personnel practices, and he congratulated the Shipping Board's going after S&E for paying exceptional wages. Kerr called Skinner an "amateur builder." He claimed these high wages were demoralizing all the yards on the Coast; and further added his disapproval of the company's refusal to accept lumber from any but those operating on an eight-hour day basis. *RMN*, 15, Number 10G (October 1917), pp. 9 and 26.

Chapter 20
Shipyard Strike to General Strike

1. The following account is derived from: Friedheim, *ibid.*, chapters 3 and 4; O'Connor, *ibid.*, pp. 108-29; Sale, *ibid.*, pp. 126-35; Dembo, *ibid.*, pp. 194-214. For special reference to Anna Louise Strong's role: Ogle, *ibid.*, pp. 160-65; and Strong and Keyssar, *ibid.*, pp. 74-77. Hulet Wells's [Autobiography] is also used as noted, pp. 209-216. Nancy Rockafeller "In Gauze We Trust: Public Health and Spanish Influenza on the Home Front, 1918-1919," *PNQ* 77:3 (July 1986), pp. 104-113. William Breen portrays a struggle for control of the "shipbuilding labor market in Seattle" as an example of an experiment with "centralized government control." The four contesting parties were the Department of Labor, the EFC, the city's labor movement, and the city's shipyard management. See his "Administrative Politics and Labor Policy in the First World War: The U. S. Employment Service and the Seattle Labor Market Experiment," *Business History Review* 61 (Winter 1987), pp. 582-605. Newspaper citations are identified in the text, and are not repeated in the Notes. Whenever a source is used that has not been published in any of the above publications it is specifically cited.

2. Short to Gompers, 29 November 1918, Washington State Federation of Labor, Records, Box 41, MSS, UW. Hereafter cited WSFL, Records.

3. Chamber of Commerce, Minutes, 30 January 1919.

4. *Ibid.*, 22 January 1919.

5. Robert Friedheim, Collection, Todd to C. W. Wiley 11 February 1919, MSS,UW.

6. Short to Morrison, 3 February 1919, WSFL, Records.

Chapter 21
The General Strike

1. The following account is derived from: Friedheim, *ibid.*, chapters 5 and 6; O'Connor, *ibid.*, chapter 6; Dembo, *ibid.*, chapter 5; Sale, *op. cit.*; Anna Louise Strong for the General Strike Committee, *The Seattle General Strike* (Seattle: Union Record Publishing Co., n.d.); O'Connell, *ibid.*, pp. 66-80; and Wells, *op. cit.* For Anna Louise Strong's role see Ogle, *ibid.*, pp. 164-75. An article by William MacDonald, "The Seattle Strike and After-wards," in *Nation*, v. 108, pp. 469-70 gives a national perspective. The King County Central Labor Council (hereafter abbreviated KCCLC), Records, Minutes for the period are useful, but frustratingly limited for detail; MSS, UW. Newspaper sources are adequately noted in the text and are not repeated in the Notes.

2. Friedheim, *ibid.*, pp. 110-12; and Ogle, *ibid.*, 167-68.

3. A copy of the transcript of People of Illinois vs. Lloyd, et al., is in the Friedheim, Collection, MSS, UW.

4. *Illinois vs. Lloyd*, Friedheim Collection.

Chapter 22
The Strike's Aftermath

Civil Liberties

1. The *UR* published the *Town Crier* editorial in full with commentary in its 15 September 1919 issue. General background, from which much of the section is derived, is provided in: Gunns, *ibid.*, chapter 2, in which the course of the anti-syndicalism law is traced; Friedheim, *ibid.*, chapter 7, esp. pp. 151-53 and 169-76; O'Connor, *ibid.*, pp. 151-56 and 159-69; O'Connell, *ibid.*, pp. 80-84. Sarah Sharbach, *ibid.*, pp. 78-85, records the many raids and arrests made on open charges from December 1918 on.

2. *Cf.*, *Star* report on the first day of the strike noting the deportation from Seattle of 42 "aliens" who had been gathered from various parts of the Northwest; *UR*, 10 February 1919, reporting a police raid of Socialist headquarters and arrest of 3 men for circulating its organ, the *International Weekly*.

3. KCCLC, Records, Minutes, 12 March and 11 June 1919; *UR*, 27 May and 3 June 1919.

4. *UR*, 25 April; 3 and 31 May; and 5 June 1919.

5. Report of Agent Number 106, 3 May 1919 in Broussais Beck, Papers; MSS, UW. This agent and others to be noted later, were employed by the Associated Industries of Seattle. Beck was manager of the Bon Marche. Hereafter cited as "Report of Agent Number 106." Robert Friedheim cited these papers as "Papers on Industrial Espionage," but they were in possession of Beck.

6. Report of Agent Number 106, 5 July 1919; *UR*, 19 March 1919.

7. Keith A. Murray, "The Charles Niederhauser Case: Patriotism in

the Seattle Schools," *PNQ*, 74:1 (January 1983), pp. 11-17; Nelson, *ibid.*, pp. 264-89 in general, and pp. 269-72 on the Niederhauser case, and pp. 273-74 on the Robinson-Beard text; *UR* 8 and 11 March 1919.
  8. Gunns, *ibid.*, pp. 42-46; Tripp, *Progressive Labor Laws.* . . ., pp.143-48; Ficken, *Lumber And Politics* . . . , pp. 39-40.

Dissent Within Labor

  1. This section is derived mainly from Dembo, *ibid.*, pp. 223-43; Friedheim, *ibid.*, 152-59; O'Connor, *ibid.*, pp. 156-58; O'Connell, *ibid.*, pp. 80-98; Thompson, *ibid.*, pp. 63-65; supplemented by specific sources as cited in context. Philip Taft's *AFL* places the Seattle Central Labor Council in the larger picture in pp. 455-57.
  2. KCCLC, Records, Minutes, 26 February and 9 April 1919; *UR*, 23 April 1919.
  3. According to the UR's Earl Shimmons in his 1923 unpublished history of the *UR*, the conservative locals withdrew support from the SCLC, leaving the radicals in control, the IWW filling "the galleries at the Labor Temple every Wednesday night to scoff at the [SCLC] . . . The *Union Record* pursued a moderate course in comparison . . . [and its] circulation finally surpassed that of its] chief rival [the *Star*]." Shimmons was the Tacoma Correspondent for the *UR*; hence his knowledge of the Blethen-Saunders arrangements. Harry (E. B.) Ault, Papers, "Shimmons . . . ," pp. 18-20, File 7-9a; MSS, UW.
  Agent Number 106 reported on 3, 5, and 7 May 1919 that the crafts are "cutting their own throats" because work is "getting scarce"; that Local 104 of the Boilermakers is "about to split up," to the benefit of the IWW; that there is much resentment directed at the AFL internationals for obstructing the locals; and that Short attacked the *UR* for "withholding federation news" causing a bitter fight with Frank Turco and drawing Duncan into combat with Short for defaming him in a circular letter. Minutes of 5 March record a 90 minute debate followed the introduction of a resolution by the produce Workers barring "Reds"; it was "overwhelmingly" defeated on grounds that it would appear that the council would seem to be following the order of the Chamber of Commerce to clean house.
  On the Federated Union, Agent Number 106 reported, May 9, it was an industrial type, and it was being promoted because its leaders accused the SCLC of being "too busy with politics to look after its unions." See also KCCLC, *ibid.*, 14 and 21 May; and 4 June 1919.
  4. KCCLC, Records, Minutes, 9 April; 11 June; 6 and 13 August 1919; Agent Number 106, Reports, 18 May and 1 July 1919.

Resurgence of the Open Shop Movement

  1. For the general, local setting, see Dembo, *ibid.*, pp. 221-25; Friedheim, *ibid.*, pp. 159-65; O'Connell, *ibid.*, pp. 135-36; O'Connor, *ibid.*, pp. 158-59; De Shazo, *ibid.*, pp. 74-84; Thompson, *ibid.*, pp. 69-71. For the national setting, see Irving Bernstein, *The Lean Years.* . . . pp. 155-57 and

165-69; and Taft, *ibid.*, pp. 401-03. For the specific instances cited see KCCLC, *ibid.*, Minutes, 12 and 19 February and 24 September 1919; *UR*, 2 March 1919; Agent Number 106 Report of 7 May 1919 in Beck Papers.

2. KCCLC, *ibid.*, 9 April and 7 May 1919; *UR*, 15, 17, 18, 19, 22, and 23 April; 1, 9, and 16 May 1919; and Agent Number 106, Reports of 7 and 8 May 1919, Broussais Beck Papers.

3. *UR*, 18 and 29 October 1919; Agent Number 106 Reports of 7, 14, 18, and 24 May 1919.

4. *UR*, 7, 29, and 30 May; 15 and 30 Sept.; 1,2, and 15 October 1919; KCCLC, *ibid.*, 1 and 28 October 1919; Agent Number 181 Report of 10 March 1919 in the Roy Kinnear, Papers, MSS, UW.

5. *UR*, 15 September 1919.

6. Short to Morrison, 23 October 1919, WSFL, Records, Box 41; *UR*, 21 October 1919.

Centralia Massacre

1. Shimmons "History. . . ." in Ault, Papers, *ibid.*; Agent Number 106 daily reports to Beck from 12 November to 8 December 1919, Broussais Beck Papers, MSS, UW.

2. Short to Morrison 8 October and Short to Gompers, 14 November 1919, WSFL, Records, Box 41; KCCLC, *ibid.*, 13 November 1919.

3. J. P. Mundy to Frank P. Walsh, 16 December 1919 in Ault, Papers, File 1-54.

Chapter 23
Labor Movement Turns To Politics

1. This section is mainly derived from the following: Dembo, *ibid.*, chapter 6; Robert L. Cole, "The Democratic Party in Washington State, 1919-1933: Barometer of Social Change" (Unpublished Ph.D. Dissertation, University of Washington, 1972), pp. 27-44; Hamilton Cravens, "A History of the Washington Farmer-Labor Party, 1918-1924 (Unpublished Master's Thesis, University of Washington, 1962); Cravens, "The Emergence of the Farmer-Labor Party in Washington Politics, 1919-20," *PNQ* 57:4, (October 1966) pp. 148-57; O'Connell, *ibid.*, pp. 139-65; and Carlos A. Schwantes, "Farmer-Labor Insurgency in Washington State: William Bouck, the Grange, and the Western Progressive Farmers," *PNQ* 76:1 (January 1985), pp. 2-11; and Tripp, *Progressive Labor Laws . . .*, pp. 226-39. On the American Plan at the national level see Taft, *ibid.*, pp. 401-02. On the "Red Scare," nationwide, see Robert K. Murray, *Red Scare: A Study in National Hysteria*, 1918-1920 (Minneapolis: University of Minnesota Press, 1955).

2. O'Connell, *ibid.*, pp. 139-41.

3. Chamber of Commerce, Minutes, 19 October 1920.

4. For general background on the left-wing splits see Theodore Draper, *The Roots of American Communism* (New York: Viking, 1957), chapters 9-13.

5. See references in endnote 1.

Chapter 24
Municipal Ownership II

City Light and the Skagit

1. For general background see Sparks, *ibid.*, pp. 58-62.

2. Seattle Lighting Department Scrapbooks, clippings dated 2 July 1919 and 6 January 1920.

3. *Op. cit.*, clipping dated 13 June 1920.

4. *Times, Star,* and *P-I*, 4 and 22 March 1919; Business Conditions Letter, 21 February 1 and 11 March 1919, PSP&L, Records, Box 122; Lighting Department scrapbooks for the period offer continuing coverage.

The Street Railway

1. Blanchard, *ibid.* Lighting Department Scrapbooks, clippings re Caldwell investigation: *P-I*, 21 and 26 May 1920; *Times*, 27 May 1920.

Concluding Comments

[no notes]

Appendix I—Economic Characteristics

**TABLE 1—Comparison of Imports and Exports,
1903 and 1914 (in thousands of dollars)**

Trading area/nation	1903		1914	
	Imports	Exports	Imports	Exports
Foreign				
Orient (Japan & China)	$10,672	$8,948	$32,018	$6,016
British Columbia	1,110	1,590	3,615	4,625
England	1,128	646	596	3,677
Ireland				931
Germany	678		322	
Norway			141	
Italy			150	
France			78	
Sweden			79	
Holland			77	
Switzerland			44	
Belgium			167	
South America	25	81	186	641
Australia		566	405	103
Siberia	15	71		152
India			1,265	
Straits Settlements			897	131
Approx. total values	$13,600	$12,000	$40,000	$16,000

Table 1 (cont.)

Trading area/nation	1903		1914	
	Imports	Exports	Imports	Exports
Domestic				
Coastwise (1903 combines				
Alaska and California	$16,212	$21,531		
Pacific Coast (Calif.)			$15,330	$13,903
Alaska			14,056	18,489
Local (Mosquito Fleet)	7,033	10,165	13,193	9,746
New York		461	3,576	3,454
Philippines		614	1,422	1,171
Hawaii		14	281	1,986
Fishing Banks			1,317	
Approx. total values	$23,000	$33,000	$49,000	$49,000

TABLE 2—Major Commodities Traded with Each Trading Partner/Area 1903 (in thousands of dollars)

Imports, 1903

Coastwise:	merchandise	$14,115
	salmon	2,084
Local:	merchandise	7,033
Foreign		
Germany	cement	$663
Orient	silk	9,258
	tea	650
England	steel billets	182
	iron bars	177
	pig iron	132
	rails	351

Exports, 1903

Coastwise:	merchandise	$18,279
	cannery supplies	1,327
	coal	1,391
	livestock	300
	lumber	167
Local:	merchandise	10,165
New York:	salmon	461
Hawaii:	lumber & shingles	14
Philippines:	hay	218
	oats	163
	lumber	51
	beer	36
	flour	33

Table 2 (cont.)

Exports, 1903

Orient:	flour	$3,158
	cotton	1,860
	sheeting	1,286
	cigarettes/tobacco	661
	machinery	227
British Columbia:	merchandise	735
	smoked meat	138
	salmon	145
	sheep	138
Australia:	flour	437
	wheat	82
England:	salmon	516
	wheat	129
Siberia:	flour	34
South America:	lumber	32
	salmon	25
	flour	17

TABLE 3—Major Commodities Traded with Each Trading Partner/Area 1914 (in thousands of dollars)

Imports, 1914

Pacific Coast:	merchandise	$11,500
	sugar	2,600
	canned goods	633
Alaska:	salmon	7,831
	gold dust	3,133
	merchandise	2,759
	halibut	318
Local:	merchandise	12,446
	logs	747
Fishing Banks:	halibut & cod	1,317
New York:	merchandise	3,576
Philippines:	hemp	1,335
Hawaii:	pineapple	196
Orient:	silk	21,000
	tea	3,500
	merchandise	1,800
	camphor	903
	braid	890
	hemp	673
British Columbia:	merchandise	2,229
	copper blisters	621
	paper	276
	coal	206

Table 3 (cont.)

Imports, 1914

England:	steel wire	275
	merchandise	155
Germany:	merchandise	154
	creosote	96
	toys	30
France:	liquors	$33
Sweden:	merchandise	43
	iron & steel	31
Norway:	sardines	64
	merchandise	51
Italy:	olive oil	77
	cheese	51
Switzerland:	cheese	32
Belgium:	iron and steel	66
	creosote	63
Holland:	creosote	65
South America:	coffee	137
Australia:	meats	165
	butter	160
Straits:	tin	751
	rubber	126
India:	jute	1,186

Exports, 1914

Pacific Coast:	merchandise	$9,300
	canned goods	1,500
	flour	1,400
	salmon	505
Alaska:	merchandise	10,500
	hardware	1,215
	machinery	1,000
	merchandise	9,746
Local:	salmon	2,900
New York	merchandise	373
	shingles	101
	flour	334
Philippines:	salmon	259
	merchandise	240
	merchandise	791
Hawaii:	flour	190
	beer	112
Orient:	cotton	2,200
	flour	1,900
	wheat	586
	merchandise	550

Table 3 (cont.)

	Exports, 1914	
British Columbia:		
	merchandise	$2,654
	machinery	257
	meats	174
	coal	145
	autos	133
Ireland:	books	125
England:	wheat	921
	salmon	2,200
	wheat	655
	barley	433
Germany:	lumber	108
South America:	merchandise	27
	flour	201
	barley	127
	lumber	124
Australia:	wheat	44
Siberia:	lumber	96
	flour	63
Straits:	machinery	63
	box shooks	63
	salmon	52

CHART 1—Foreign and Domestic Water-Borne Commerce, Seattle, 1900 to 1939

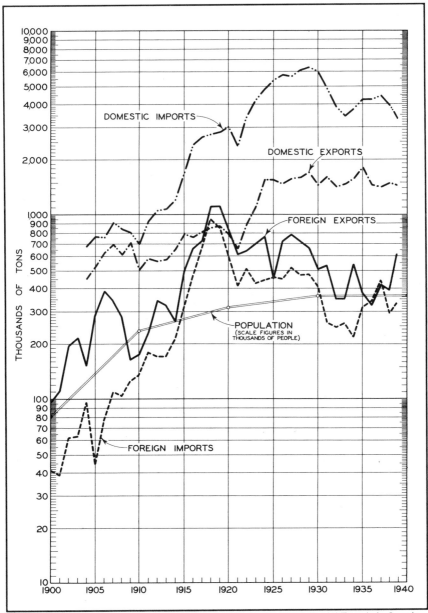

From Calvin Schmid, *Social Trends in Seattle*

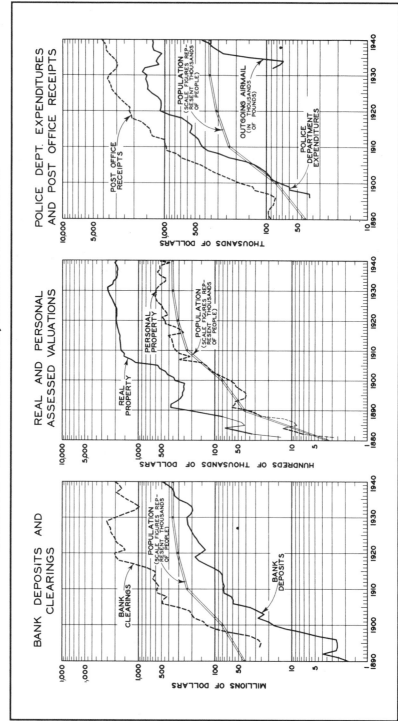

CHART 2—Indices of Growth, Seattle: 1880 to 1940

From Calvin Schmid, *Social Trends in Seattle*

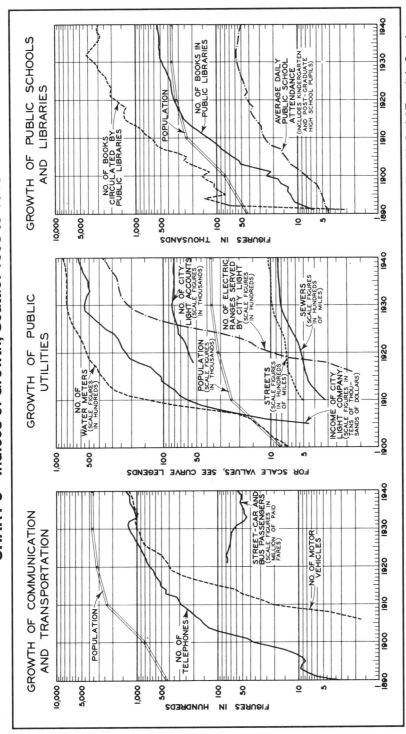

CHART 3—Indices of Growth, Seattle: 1890 to 1940

From Calvin Schmid, *Social Trends in Seattle*

CHART 4—Intra-City Transportation, Seattle, 1890 to 1941

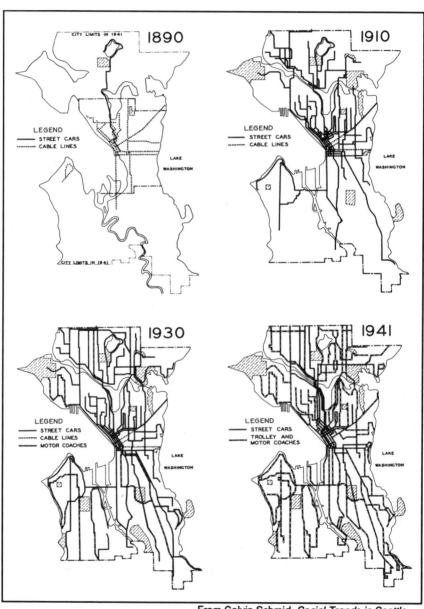

From Calvin Schmid, *Social Trends in Seattle*

Appendix II

CHART 1—Population Density, Seattle, 1900

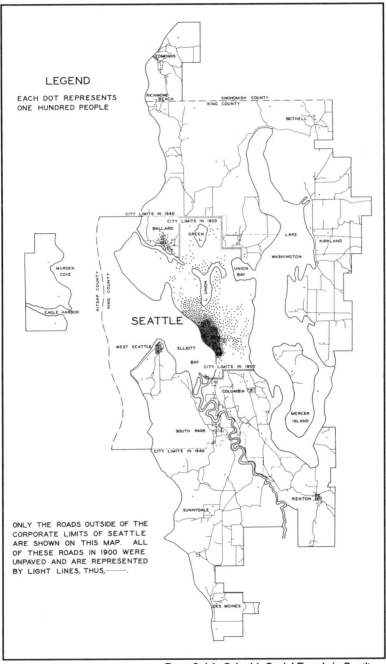

LEGEND

EACH DOT REPRESENTS
ONE HUNDRED PEOPLE

ONLY THE ROADS OUTSIDE OF THE
CORPORATE LIMITS OF SEATTLE
ARE SHOWN ON THIS MAP.   ALL
OF THESE ROADS IN 1900 WERE
UNPAVED AND ARE REPRESENTED
BY LIGHT LINES, THUS,————.

From Calvin Schmid, *Social Trends in Seatlte*

CHART 2—Population Density, Seattle, 1910

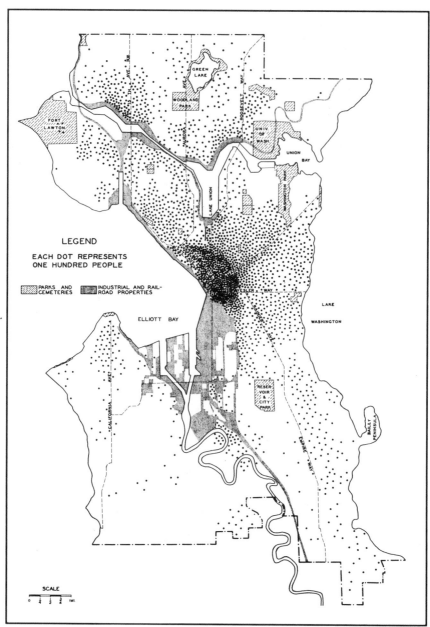

From Calvin Schmid, *Social Trends in Seattle*

CHART 3—Foreign-Born Population, Seattle, 1890 to 1940

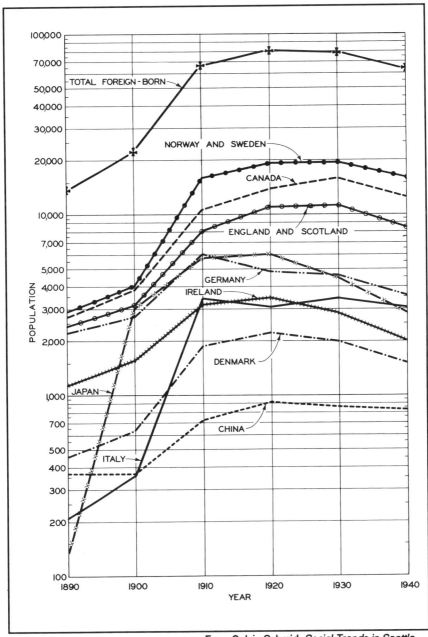

From Calvin Schmid, *Social Trends in Seattle*

CHART 4—Age of Dwelling Units, Seattle, 1940; Proportion Built in 1899 or Earlier

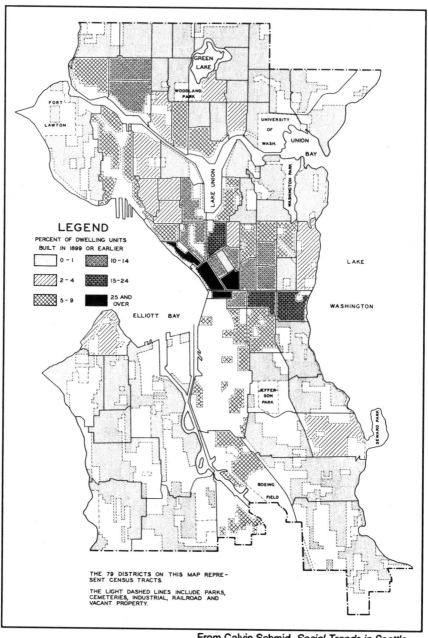

From Calvin Schmid, *Social Trends in Seattle*

Bibliography

Archival Sources

Museum of History and Industry, Seattle

Ladies Musical Club. Records

Seattle City Comptroller's Office

City Archives. Comptroller's Records

Seattle Public Libraries

Seattle Chamber of Commerce. Minute Books
Seattle Commercial Club. Minute Books

Seattle Public Schools Archives

University of Puget Sound

Homer T. Bone. Papers (for E.V. Minich Affidavit)

University of Washington Libraries
Manuscript Collection

American Institute of Architects. Seattle Chapter Records
American Protective League. Minute Men Division, Seattle
Edwin G. Ames. Papers
Harry E.P. Ault. Papers
Broussais Beck. Papers
Erastus Brainerd. Papers
Thomas Burke. Papers

Hiram M. Chittenden. Papers
Cornish School. Records and Scrapbooks
George F. Cotterill. Papers
Brice P. Disque. Papers
Frank Fitts. Papers
Robert L. Friedheim. Collection relating to Seattle General Strike
Austin E. Griffiths. Papers
Arthur L. Kempster. Papers
Roy Kinnear. Papers
King County Central Labor Council. Records. (includes those of Se-
    attle Central Labor Council)
John J. McGilvra. Papers
Mark A. Matthews. Papers and Scrapbooks
Parents-Teachers Association, Seattle. Records
Puget Sound Power and Light Company. Records
Seattle Art Museum. Records
Seattle Port Commission. Records ("Robert Bridges Papers")
Seattle Lighting Department. Records and Scrapbooks
Eugene Semple. Papers
Anna Louise Strong. Papers
Sydney Dix Strong. Papers
Reginald H. Thomson. Papers and Scrapbooks
United States Federal Trade Commission. Capital Issues Subcommit-
    tee. Records
Washington State Federation of Labor. Records
Washington State Federation of Women's Clubs. Records
Hulet Wells. Papers
Donald T. Williams, Jr., "The Remarkable Dr. Henry Suzzallo: A Biog-
    raphy," (Unpublished manuscript, University of Washington Li-
    braries. University Archives.)

University of Washington Libraries
Special Collections Division

Pike Place Public Market. Scrapbooks
Donald Sherwood, "Description and History of Seattle Parks". (Un-
    published manuscript)

Newspapers

The Argus
Railway and Marine News
Seattle Municipal News
Seattle Post-Intelligencer
Seattle Star
Seattle Sun
Seattle Times
Seattle Union Record
The Town Crier

Books and Government Documents

Anderson, Douglas D. *Regulatory Politics and Electric Utilities: A Case Study in Political Economy*. Boston: Auburn House, 1981.

Bagley, Clarence B. *The History of Seattle from its Earliest Settlement to the Present Time*. 3 volumes. Chicago: S. J. Clarke, 1916.

Bernstein, Irving. *The Lean Years: A History of the American Worker, 1920-1933*. Baltimore: Penguin Books, 1966.

Blanchard, Leslie. *The Street Railway Era in Seattle: A Chronicle of Six Decades*. Forty Fort, Pennsylvania: Harold E. Cox, 1968.

Bogue, Virgil. *Plan of Seattle*. 2 volumes, Seattle: Lowman and Hanford, 1911.

Browne, Ellen V. and Edward N. Beck, editors. *Miss Aunt Nellie: The Autobiography of Nellie C. Cornish*. Seattle: University of Washington Press, 1964.

Burke, Padraic. *The History of the Port of Seattle*. Seattle: Port of Seattle, 1976.

Campbell, Esther W. *Bagpipes in the Woodwind Section: A History of the Seattle Symphony Orchestra and its Women's Association*. Seattle: Seattle Symphony Women's Association, 1978.

Cayton, Horace R. *Long Old Road: An Autobiography*. Seattle: University of Washington Press, 1964.

Clark, Norman H. *The Dry Years: Prohibition and Social Change in Washington*. Seattle: University of Washington Press, 1965.

_____. *Mill Town: A Social History of Everett, Washington, from its Earliest Beginnings . . . to the Everett Massacre*. Seattle: University of Washington Press, 1970.

Cobb, John N. *The Pacific Salmon Fisheries*. Bureau of Fisheries Document Number 902. Washington, D. C.: U. S. Superintendent of Documents, 1921.

Cochran, Thomas C. and William Miller. *The Age of Enterprise: A Social History of Industrial America*. New York: Harper Torchbooks, 1961.

Daniels, Roger. *Asian America: Chinese and Japanese in the United States Since 1850*. (Seattle: University of Washington Press, 1988)

_____.*The Politics of Prejudice: The Anti-Japanese Movement in California and the Struggle for Japanese Exclusion*. New York: Atheneum, 1972.

Dembo, Jonathan. *Unions and Politics in Washington State, 1885-1935*. Modern American History Series. New York: Garland Publishing Company, 1983.

Devine, Jean. *From Settlement House to Neighborhood House, 1906-1976*. Seattle: Neighborhood House, 1976.

Dodds, Gordon B. *Hiram Martin Chittenden: His Public Career*. Lexington: University of Kentucky Press, 1973.

Draper, Theodore. *The Roots of American Communism*. New York: Viking Press, 1957.

Dubofsky, Melvin. *We Shall Be All: A History of the Industrial Workers of the World*. Chicago: Quadrangle Books, 1969.

Edwards, Thomas G. and Carlos A. Schwantes, editors. *Experiences in the Promised Land: Essays in Pacific Northwest History.* Seattle: University of Washington Press, 1986.

Elliott, Eugene C. *A History of Variety-Vaudeville in Seattle from the Beginning to 1914.* Seattle: University of Washington Press, 1944.

Ficken, Robert E. *The Forested Land: A History of Lumbering in Western Washington.* Seattle: University of Washington Press, 1987.

_____.*Lumber and Politics: The Career of Mark E. Reed.* Seattle: University of Washington Press, 1979.

Friedheim, Robert L. *The Seattle General Strike.* Seattle: University of Washington Press, 1964.

Frykman, George A. *Creating the People's University: Washington State University, 1890-1990.* Pullman, Washington State University Press, 1990.

Gates, Charles M. *The First Century at the University of Washington, 1861-1961.* Seattle: University of Washington Press, 1961.

Gault, Lila. *The House Next Door: Seattle's Neighborhood Architecture.* Seattle: Pacific Search Press, 1981.

Gunns, Albert F. *Civil Liberties in Crisis: The Pacific Northwest, 1917-1940.* New York: Garland Publishing Company, 1983.

Hawley, Lowell S., and Ralph B. Potts. *Counsel for the Damned: A Biography of George Francis Vanderveer.* Philadelphia: J. B. Lippencott, 1953.

Hines, Neal O. *Denny's Knoll: A History of the Metropolitan Tract of the University of Washington.* Seattle: University of Washington Press, 1980.

Hough, Emerson. *The Web: The Authorized History of the American Protective League.* Chicago: Reilley and Lee, 1919.

Hyman, Harold M. *Soldiers and Spruce: Origins of the Loyal Legion of Loggers and Lumbermen.* Los Angeles: Institute of Industrial Relations, University of California, 1963.

Hynding, Alan. *The Public Life of Eugene Semple: Promoter and Politician of the Pacific Northwest.* Seattle: University of Washington Press, 1973.

Ito, Kazuo. *Issei: A History of Japanese Immigrants in North America.* Seattle: Japanese Community Service, 1973.

Jensen, Joan M. *The Price of Vigilance.* Chicago: Rand McNally, 1968.

Lee, Rose Hum. *The Chinese in the United States of America.* Hong Kong: Hong Kong University Press/ Oxford University Press, 1960.

Lind, Andrew W. *A Study of Mobility of Population in Seattle.* University of Washington Publications in the Social Sciences, volume 3 number 1. Seattle: University of Washington Press, 1925.

MacDonald, Norbert. *Distant Neighbors: A Comparative History of Seattle and Vancouver.* Lincoln: University of Nebraska Press, 1984.

McWilliams, Carey. *PREJUDICE Japanese-Americans: Symbol of Racial Intolerance.* Boston: Little, Brown and Company, 1944.

McWilliams, Mary. *Seattle Water Department History, 1854-1954: Operational Data and Memoranda.* Seattle: Water Department, 1955.

Miyamoto, Shotaro Frank. *Social Solidarity Among the Japanese in Se-*

attle. University of Washington Studies in the Social Sciences, volume 11 number 2. Seattle: University of Washington Press, 1939.

Montgomery, David. *The Fall of the House of Labor: the Workplace, the State, and American Labor Activism,* 1865-1925. Cambridge: University, paperback edition, 1989.

Morgan, Murray. *Mill on the Boot: The Story of the St. Paul and Tacoma Lumber Company.* Seattle: University of Washington Press, 1982.

_____. *Skid Road: An Informal Portrait of Seattle.* New York: Ballantine Books, 1960.

Mumford, Esther Hall. *Seattle's Black Victorians, 1852-1901.* Seattle: Ananse Press, 1980.

Murray, Robert K. *Red Scare: A Study in National Hysteria, 1918-1920.* Minneapolis: University of Minnesota Press, 1955.

Nesbit, Robert C. *"He Built Seattle": A Biography of Judge Thomas Burke.* Seattle: University of Washington Press, 1961.

O'Connor, Harvey. *Revolution in Seattle: A Memoir.* New York: Monthly Review Press, 1964.

Port of Seattle. *Yearbook.* Seattle: Port of Seattle, 1914.

Redford, Grant H., editor. *That Man Thomson.* Seattle: University of Washington Press, 1950.

Reichauer, Haru Matsukata. *Samurai and Silk: A Japanese and American Heritage.* Cambridge: Harvard University Press, 1986.

Robinson, Marilyn Druck. *Washington State Statistical Abstract.* Seattle: University of Washington Press, 1952.

Sales, Roger. *Seattle: Past to Present.* Seattle: University of Washington Press, 1976.

Schmid, Calvin F. *Social Trends in Seattle.* University of Washington Studies in the Social Sciences, volume 14. Seattle: University of Washington Press, 1944.

_____., and Wayne W. McVey, Jr. *Growth and Distribution of Minority Races in Seattle, Washington.* Seattle: Seattle Public Schools, 1964.

_____., and Stanton E. Schmid. *Growth of Cities and Towns: State of Washington.* Olympia: Washington State Planning and Community Affairs Agency, 1969.

Schwantes, Carlos A. *Radical Heritage: Labor, Socialism, and Reform in Washington and British Columbia, 1885-1917.* Seattle: University of Washington Press, 1979.

Seattle Chamber of Commerce. *Seattle: A Great Shipping and Commercial Center.* Seattle Chamber of Commerce, 1913.

_____. *Seattle, the Puget Sound Country and Western Washington . . . 1901.* Seattle: Chamber of Commerce, 1901.

_____. *Semi-Centennial Celebration. . .* Seattle: Chamber of Commerce, 1903.

_____. *Seattle: An Industrial City.* Seattle: Chamber of Commerce, 1916.

_____. *Profitism, Slackism, and You.* Seattle: Chamber of Commerce, 1920.

Seattle Park Department. *Annual Report[s]*. Seattle: Seattle Park Department, 1892-1920.

Seattle Port Warden. *Annual Report[s]*. Seattle: Seattle Port Warden, 1895-1920.

Seattle Times. *Seattle and the Orient*. Seattle: The Times Publishing Company, 1900.

Strong, Anna Louise. *The Seattle General Strike*. Seattle: Seattle Union Record Publishing Company [1919].

Strong, Tracy B., and Helene Keyssar. *Right in Her Soul: The Life of Anna Louise Strong*. New York: Random House: 1983.

Taft, Philip. *The AFL in the Time of Gompers*. New York: Harper and Row, 1957.

Twight, Ben W. *Organizational Values and Political Power: The Forest Service Versus the Olympic National Park*. University Park, Pennsylvania: Pennsylvania State University Press, 1983.

Tyler, Robert L. *Rebels in the Woods: The I.W.W. in the Pacific Northwest*. Eugene: University of Oregon Press, 1967.

United States Census Bureau. *United States Census*. Washington, D.C.: Government Printing Office, 1900, 1910, 1920.

Washington State Federation of Labor. *Proceedings*. Seattle: Washington State Federation of Labor, 1911-1925.

Wiebe, Robert H. *Businessmen and Reform: A Study of the Progressive Movement*. Chicago: Quadrangle Books, 1968.

Woodbridge, Sally B. and Roger Montgomery. *A Guide to Architecture in Washington State: An Environmental Perspective*. Seattle: University of Washington Press, 1980.

Articles

Beck, Louise C. "What Women are Doing for Seattle." *Seattle Mail and Herald*, 8:6 (17 December 1904): pp 20-21.

Bell, S. Leonard. "Seattle's First Black Journalist" *Seattle Post-Intelligencer*, September 1968.

_____. "Horace Cayton, Jr. Man without a Race." *Seattle Post-Intelligencer*, October 1968.

Berner, Richard C. "Labor History: Sources and Perspectives." *PNQ*, 60:1 (January 1969): pp. 31-33.

_____. "Preserving Ethnic History." *Puget Soundings* (June 1977): pp. 24-26.

Blackford, Mansel G. "Reform Politics in Seattle During the Progressive Era, 1902-1916." *PNQ*, 59:4 (October 1968): pp. 177-185.

Blackman, William. "[Labor Unions,]" in Seattle Chamber of Commerce. *Semi-Centennial Celebration of the Founding of Seattle*. Seattle: Chamber of Commerce, 1903, pp. 48-49.

Blair, Karen. "The Seattle Ladies Musical Club, 1890-1930, in Thomas G. Edwards and Carlos A. Schwantes. *Experiences in the Promised Land: Essays in Pacific Northwest History*. Seattle: University of Washington Press, 1986

Breen, William. "Administrative Politics and Labor Policy in the First World War: the U.S. Employment Service and the Seattle Labor Market Experiment." *Business History Review*, 61(Winter,1987) pp. 582-605.

Burke, Padraic. "Struggle for Public Ownership: Early History of the Port of Seattle." *PNQ*, 68:3 (April 1977): pp. 60-71.

Byler, Charles. "Austin E. Griffiths: Seattle Progressive Reformer." *PNQ*, 76:1 (January 1985): pp. 22-32.

Campbell, Robert A. "Blacks in the Coal Mines of Western Washington, 1886-1896." *PNQ*, 73:4 (October 1982): pp. 146-155.

Clark, Norman H. "The 'Hell-Soaked Institution' and the Washington Prohibition Initiative of 1914." *PNQ,*56:1 (January 1965): pp. 1-16.

Cravens, Hamilton. "The Emergence of the Farmer-Labor Party in Washington Politics, 1919-20." *PNQ*, 57:4 (October 1968): pp. 148-157.

Dimock, Arthur H. "Preparing the Groundwork for a City: The Regrading of Seattle, Washington." Paper Number 1669, American Society of Civil Engineers. *Transactions*: 1928.

Douglas, Paul. "Seattle Municipal Railway System." *Journal of Political Economy*, 29 (June 1921): pp. 455-477.

Duncan, Donald. "Driftwood Diary." *Seattle Times*, December 31, 1967.

Ficken, Robert E. "Seattle's 'Ditch': The Corps of Engineers and the Lake Washington Ship Canal." *PNQ*, 77:1 (January 1986): pp. 11-20.

Friedheim, Robert L., and Robin Friedheim. "The Seattle Labor Movement, 1919-1920." *PNQ*, 55:4 (October 1964): pp. 146-169.

Frykman, George A. " The Alaska-Yukon-Pacific Exposition, 1909." *PNQ*, 53:3 (July 1962): pp. 89-99.

Greenwald, Maurine Weiner. "Working-Class Feminism and the Family Wage Ideal: The Seattle Debate on Married Women's Right to Work, 1914-1920." *Journal of American History* 76:1 (June 1989): pp. 118-149.

Hazard, Joseph T. "The Second Ten Years . . . ." *The Mountaineer*, 30:1 (December 1937): pp. 13-16.

Hendrick, Burton J. The Recall in Seattle." *McClure's Magazine*, 37 (October 1911): pp. 647-663.

Higday, Hamilton. [History of the Port of Seattle.] in: *Port of Seattle Yearbook*. Seattle: Port of Seattle, 1914: pp. 41-101.

Hobbs, Richard S. "Horace Cayton—Seattle's Black Pioneer Publisher." *Seattle Times*, 26 February 1978.

Johnson, Claudius O. "The Adoption of the Initiative and Referendum in Washington." *PNQ*, 34:4 (October 1944): pp. 291-303.

Johnson, Warren B. "Muckraking in the Northwest: Joe Smith and Seattle Reform." *Pacific Historical Review*, 40 (November 1971): pp. 478-500.

Johnston, Norman J. "The Olmsted Brothers and the Alaska-Yukon-Pacific Exposition: 'Eternal Loveliness.'" *PNQ*, 75:2 (April 1984): pp. 50-61.

Kumor. Georgia Ann. "A Question of Leadership: Thomas Franklin

Kane and the University of Washington, 1902-1913." *PNQ*, 77:1 (January 1986): pp. 2-10.

Larson, T. A. "The Woman Suffrage Movement in Washington." *PNQ*, 67:2 (April 1976): pp. 49-62.

MacDonald, William. "The Seattle Strike and Afterwards." *The Nation*, 108:2804 (29 March 1919): pp. 469-470.

Marple, Elliott. "The Movement for Public Ownership in Washington." *Journal of Land and Public Utility Economics*, 2 (February 1931): pp. 61-66.

McClintock, Thomas C. "J. Allen Smith, a Pacific Northwest Progressive." *PNQ*, 53:2 (April 1962): pp. 49-59.

Murray Keith A. "The Charles Niederhauser Case: Patriotism in the Seattle Schools." *PNQ*, 74:1 (January 1983): pp. 11-17.

Neil, J. M. "The Shaping of Downtown Seattle, 1903-1914." *PNQ*, 75:1 (January 1984): pp. 22-33.

Nelson, Bryce E. "Frank B. Cooper: Seattle's Progressive School Superintendent, 1901-1922." *PNQ*, 74:4 (October 1983): pp. 167-177.

Nelson, L. A. "Thirty Years in Retrospect: The First Decade in Mountaineer Annals." *The Mountaineer*, 30:1 (December 1937): pp. 9-12.

Pendergrass, Lee F. "The Formation of a Municipal Reform Movement: The Municipal League of Seattle." *PNQ*, 66:1 (January 1975): pp. 13-25.

Peterson, Richard B. "A Rational Employment System for the West Coast Longshore Industry." *University of Washington Business Review*, 26:3 (Spring 1967): 50-56.

Purvis, Neil H. "History of the Lake Washington Canal." *Washington Historical Quarterly*, 25:2 (April 1934): pp 114-127; 25:3 ((July 1934): pp. 210-213.

Rockafeller, Nancy. "'In Gauze We Trust': Public Health and Spanish Influenza on the Home Front, 1918-1919." *PNQ*, 77:3 (July 1986): pp. 2-11.

Schwantes, Carlos A. "Farmer-Labor Insurgency in Washington State: William Bouck, the Grange, and the Western Progressive Farmers." *PNQ*, 76:1 (January 1985): pp. 2-11.

Soden, Dale. "Mark Allison Matthews: Seattle's Minister Rediscovered." *PNQ*, 74:2 (April 1983): pp. 50-58.

Tarbill, Von V. "Mountain-Moving in Seattle." *Harvard Business Review* (July 1930): pp. 482-489.

Tripp, Joseph F. "Toward an Efficient and Moral Society: Washington State Minimum Wage Law, 1913-1925." *PNQ*, 67:3 (July 1976): pp. 97-112.

Van de Wetering, Jack. "The Appointment of Henry Suzzallo: The University of Washington Gets a President." *PNQ*, 50:3 (July 1959): pp. 99-107.

White, W. Thomas. "Railroad Labor Protests, 1894-1917: From Community to Class in the Pacific Northwest." *PNQ*, 75:1 (January 1984): pp. 13-21.

Wilson, William H. "How Seattle Lost the Bogue Plan: Politics Versus Design." *PNQ*, 75:4 (October 1984): pp. 171-180.

Theses and Dissertations

Blackford, Mansel G. "Sources of Support for Reform Candidates and Issues in Seattle Politics, 1902-1916." Unpublished Master's Thesis, University of Washington, 1967.

Burke, Padraic. "The City Beautiful Movement in Seattle." Unpublished Master's Thesis, University of Washington, 1973.

Bushue, Paul B. "Dr. Hermon Titus and Socialism in Washington State, 1900-1909." Unpublished Master's Thesis, University of Washington, 1967.

Cline, Denzel C. "The Street Car Men of Seattle: A Sociological Study." Unpublished Master's Thesis, University of Washington, 1926.

Cole, Robert L. "The Democratic Party in Washington State, 1919-1933: Barometer of Social Change." Unpublished Ph.D. Dissertation, University of Washington, 1972.

Cravens, Hamilton. "A History of the Washington Farmer-Labor Party, 1918-1924." Unpublished Master's Thesis, University of Washington, 1962.

Dawson, Jan C. "A Social Gospel Portrait: The Life of Sydney Dix Strong, 1860-1938. Unpublished Master's Thesis, University of Washington, 1972.

De Shazo, Melvin. "Radical Tendencies in the Seattle Labor Movement as Reflected in the Proceedings of its Central Body." Unpublished Master's Thesis, University of Washington, 1925.

Dembo, Jonathan. "A History of the Washington State Labor Movement, 1885-1935." Unpublished Ph.D. Dissertation, University of Washington, 1978. (See entry above for its published version.)

Dick Wesley A. "The Genesis of Seattle City Light." Unpublished Master's Thesis, University of Washington, 1965.

Doig, Ivan. "John J. McGilvra: The Life and Times of an American Frontiersman, 1827-1903." Unpublished Ph.D. Dissertation, University of Washington, 1969.

Gramm, Warren S. "Employer Association Development in Seattle and Vicinity." Unpublished Master's Thesis, University of Washington, 1948.

Gunns, Albert F. "Civil Liberties and Crisis: The Status of Civil Liberties in the Pacific Northwest, 1917-1940." Unpublished Ph.D. Dissertation, University of Washington, 1971. (See entry above for its published version.)

Hall, Margaret A. "A History of Women Faculty at the University of Washington, 1896-1970." Unpublished Ph.D. Dissertation, University of Washington, 1984.

_____. "Henry Suzzallo and the Washington State Council of Defense." Unpublished Master's Thesis, University of Washington, 1975.

Hoffland, Laura F. "Seattle as a Metropolis: the Integration of the Puget Sound Region through the Dominance of Seattle." Unpublished Master's Thesis, University of Washington, 1933

Jackson, Joseph Sylvester. "The Colored Marine Employees Benevolent Association of the Pacific, 1921-1934." Unpublished Master's Thesis, University of Washington, 1939.

Jones, George Michael. "Longshore Unionism on Puget Sound: Seattle-Tacoma Comparison." Unpublished Master's Thesis, University of Washington, 1957.

Kimmons, Neil C. "The Historical Development of Seattle as a Metropolitan Area." Unpublished Master's Thesis, University of Washington, 1942.

Kumor, Georgia Ann. "Thomas Franklin Kane and the University of Washington, 1902-1913." Unpublished Master's Thesis, University of Washington, 1981.

Lechner, Anna Bell. "The Seattle Municipal Street Railway." Unpublished Master's Thesis, University of Washington, 1936.

Livingston, Victoria H. "Erastus Brainerd: The Bankruptcy of Brilliance." Unpublished Master's Thesis, University of Washington, 1967.

MacDonald, Alexander Norbert. "Seattle's Economic Development, 1880-1910." Unpublished Ph.D. Dissertation, University of Washington, 1959.

McClintock, Thomas C. "J. Allen Smith and the Progressive Movement: A Study in Intellectual History." Unpublished Ph.D. Dissertation, University of Washington, 1959.

Miller, Virginia. "The Development of Leisure Time Activities in Seattle, 1851-1910." Unpublished Master's Thesis, University of Washington, 1972.

Moe, Ole K. "An Analytical Study of the Foreign Trade Through the Port of Seattle." Unpublished Master's Thesis, University of Washington, 1932.

Murayama, Yuzo. "The Economic History of Japanese Immigration to the Pacific Northwest: 1890-1920." Unpublished Ph.D. Dissertation, University of Washington, 1982.

Murray, Keith A. "Republican Party Politics in Washington During the Progressive Era." Unpublished Ph.D. Dissertation, University of Washington, 1946.

Nelson, Bryce E. "Good Schools: The Development of Public Schooling in Seattle, 1901-1922. Unpublished Ph.D. Dissertation, University of Washington, 1981.

Nishinori, John I. "Japanese Farms in Washington." Unpublished Master's Thesis, University of Washington, 1926.

O'Connell, Mary Joan. "The Seattle Union Record, 1918-1928: A Pioneer Labor Daily. Unpublished Master's Thesis, University of Washington, 1964.

Ogle, Stephanie Francine. "Anna Louise Strong: Progressive and Propagandist." Unpublished Ph.D. Dissertation, University of Washington, 1981.

Pendergrass, Lee Forrest. "Urban Reform and Voluntary Association: A Case Study of the Seattle Municipal League." Unpublished Ph.D. Dissertation, University of Washington, 1972.

Pullen, Douglas R. "The Administration of Washington State Governor Louis F. Hart, 1919-1925." Unpublished Ph.D. Dissertation, University of Washington, 1974.

Purdy, Harry. "Development and Cost of Municipal Operation of the Seattle Street Railways." Unpublished Master's Thesis, University of Washington, 1928.

Rademaker, John A. "The Ecological Position of the Japanese Farmers in the State of Washington." Unpublished Ph.D. Dissertation, University of Washington, 1939.

Reiff, Janice L. "Urbanization and the Social Structure: Seattle, Washington, 1852-1910." Unpublished Ph.D. Dissertation, University of Washington, 1981.

Roe, Nellie. "Italian Immigrants in Seattle." Unpublished Master's Thesis, University of Washington, 1915.

Saltvig, Robert D. "The Progressive Movement in Washington." Unpublished Ph.D. Dissertation, University of Washington, 1966.

Sharbach, Sarah Ellen. "Louise Olivereau and the Seattle Radical Community, 1917-1923." Unpublished Master's Thesis, University of Washington, 1986.

Soden, Dale E. "Mark Allison Matthews: Seattle's Southern Preacher." Unpublished Ph.D. Dissertation, University of Washington, 1980.

Sparks, William O. "J. D. Ross and Seattle City Light, 1917-1932." Unpublished Master's Thesis, University of Washington, 1964.

Tattersall, James N. "The Economic Development of the Pacific Northwest to 1920." Unpublished Ph.D. Dissertation, University of Washington, 1960.

Thompson, Margaret Jane. "Development and Comparison of Industrial Relationships in Seattle." Unpublished Master's Thesis, University of Washington, 1929.

Tripp, Joseph F. "Progressive Labor Laws in Washington, 1900-1925." Unpublished Ph.D. Dissertation, University of Washington, 1973.

Westine, Carl G. "The Seattle Teamsters." Unpublished Master's Thesis, University of Washington, 1937.

White, William Thomas. "A History of Railroad Workers in the Pacific Northwest." Unpublished Ph.D. Dissertation, University of Washington, 1981.

Winslow, Barbara. "The Decline of Socialism in Washington, 1910-1925." Unpublished Master's Thesis, University of Washington,

Wynne, Robert E. "Reaction to the Chinese in the Pacific Northwest and British Columbia: 1850-1910." Unpublished Ph.D. Dissertation, University of Washington, 1964.

Index

Y